# THE LAW OF STATE AID IN THE EUROPEAN UNION

# The Law of State Aid in the European Union

*Edited by*

ANDREA BIONDI, PIET EECKHOUT
and
JAMES FLYNN

OXFORD
UNIVERSITY PRESS

# OXFORD
UNIVERSITY PRESS

Great Clarendon Street, Oxford OX2 6DP

Oxford University Press is a department of the University of Oxford.
It furthers the University's objective of excellence in research, scholarship,
and education by publishing worldwide in

Oxford New York

Auckland Bangkok Buenos Aires Cape Town Chennai
Dar es Salaam Delhi Hong Kong Istanbul Karachi Kolkata
Kuala Lumpur Madrid Melbourne Mexico City Mumbai Nairobi
São Paulo Shanghai Taipei Tokyo Toronto

Oxford is a registered trade mark of Oxford University Press
in the UK and in certain other countries

Published in the United States
by Oxford University Press Inc., New York

British Library Cataloguing in Publication Data

Data available

Library of Congress Cataloging in Publication Data

Data available

ISBN 0-19-926532-1

1 3 5 7 9 10 8 6 4 2

Typeset by Kolam Information Services Pvt. Ltd, Pondicherry, India
Printed in Great Britain
on acid-free paper by
T.J. International Ltd, Padstow, Cornwall

# Contents

# Introduction

## I

In Europe the provision of subsidies and other forms of aid by the State or through State resources still forms an accepted part, indeed often a central part, of economic policy, even in those countries most attached to the model of the free market.

It is not difficult to see its appeal, since State aid may serve a variety of purposes, ranging from the concern to shore up failing industries and to prevent further unemployment and knock-on failures, to the desire to encourage new industry at the forefront of technological innovation.

Yet the very existence of State aid, a temptation stronger than ever when times are hard, poses obvious problems for the single market for which the European Union is striving. On the one hand, the very realization of the single market, the dismantling of barriers to trade and the increase in competition may all intensify the pressures to grant aid. On the other hand, such aid makes ever less sense. One Member State's subsidy is all too obviously another Member State's unemployment. At worst, competitive subsidies or counter-measures cancel each other out, to the economic cost of all parties, and with no resulting benefit.

Within the European Community, therefore, State aid—still running at huge levels (on recent estimates, approaching 100 billion euro a year)—must be regulated, if it is to be regulated at all, essentially at the supranational level of the Community itself.

## II

The EC law of State aid raises issues of the greatest social, economic, and political importance, as well as a great variety of difficult and fascinating legal problems.

Yet the subject of State aid law has been remarkably neglected, especially if comparison is made with other aspects of EC competition law, of which State aid law forms a constituent part. There have, of course, been some excellent treatises. But this book breaks new ground in a way in which a treatise cannot; a collective work of this kind can provide a level of specialist expertise and a depth of analysis of different topics which a text book could hardly equal. That is what this book achieves: the contributions, all of them by carefully selected specialists, deal in depth with the analysis of specific and fundamental problems in a way which would not be possible in a general treatise.

### III

Mention must first be made of the sources of the law: the Treaty provisions, the case-law of the European Courts (Court of Justice and Court of First Instance, but reference should also be made to the decisions of national courts), and the practice of the European Commission.

In the EC Treaty the provisions on State aid form Section 2 of the chapter entitled 'Rules on competition'. Section 1, 'Rules applying to undertakings', contain the provisions more familiar to most practitioners, including Articles 81 and 82. Section 2, 'Aids granted by States' (Articles 87–89), completes the chapter. Section 1 covers of course anti-competitive agreements between undertakings and abuse of a dominant position. One of the recurring themes in State aid, which the reader of this book will observe, is the opportunity for comparison and contrast between the rules applying to undertakings and the provisions on State aid, both having the common goal, in the overall scheme of the Treaty, of ensuring that competition in the internal market is not distorted (Article 3(g)).

The provisions on State aid themselves are drafted with the elegance and lucidity characteristic of the original text of the EEC Treaty, and have required almost no amendment in nearly half a century.

Their effect can be set out in a very brief format. Article 87(1) contains the basic prohibition. It applies to 'any aid granted by a Member State or through State resources in any form whatsoever which distorts or threatens to distort competition by favouring certain undertakings or the production of certain goods'. Unless otherwise provided in the Treaty, such aid shall, in so far as it affects trade between Member States, be incompatible with the common market.

Article 87(2) lists certain forms of aid which are to be deemed to be compatible with the common market. Article 87(3) lists certain forms of aid which *may* be considered to be compatible with the common market.

Article 88 sets out the procedure whereby the Commission keeps under review all existing aid, and examines proposals by Member States to grant or alter aid. It contains the key provision, in the last sentence of Article 88(3), that Member States shall not put their proposed measures into effect until the Commission has taken a final decision.

Article 89 empowers the Council to make regulations for the application of Articles 87 and 88. Under Article 89 the Council adopted in 1999, for the first time, a major piece of legislation laying down detailed rules for the application of Article 87. The regulation (Council Regulation No 659/1999)[1] contains certain definitions and a series of chapters on procedural issues.

---

[1] OJ 1999, L 83, p. 1.

## IV

This book offers a panoramic survey of the rich variety of issues arising. In this introduction, which seeks merely to set the scene and to provide a brief overview, reference can be made only to a few of the issues.

When considering them, it may be useful to have in mind a schematic classification of the main subjects falling within the overall compass of this book.

A threefold classification might be suggested, on the following lines, although it corresponds only approximately with the classification followed in this book.

1. First, there is the concept of State aid itself, which despite the lucid definition in Article 87(1) is by no means straightforward. These conceptual issues include the relationship between the State aid provisions and other provisions governing the internal market, with boundaries which are not always clear-cut.

   Once the existence of aid is established, issues of the compatibility of the aid with the common market will arise in determining whether the aid is prohibited.

2. The second area focuses on the object and purpose of the aid: this focus provides a basis for classifying different types of aid, each of which may raise different issues or require different approaches.

   A number of purposes may be distinguished. First, should be mentioned State aid for investment purposes. Of particular importance here are general aid schemes, regional aid, and aid for small and medium-sized enterprises (SMEs).

   Then there are the types of aid designed for other purposes. Most significant are those with what are intriguingly described as 'horizontal objectives'; these include aid for employment; aid for training; innovation, research and development; environmental protection; and public health.

   Next, within this general classification of the subject matter of the aid, there is State aid for particular industries—traditional industrial sectors such as coal and steel, shipbuilding and textiles, and more recent manifestations such as public sector broadcasting.

3. The third and final area concerns supervision and enforcement: supervision of State aid by the European Commission; judicial review of Commission decisions; and judicial enforcement of State aid law, both in the European Courts and in the national Courts.

## V

To mention only a few of the issues, there is first a range of remarkably difficult definitional problems: what counts as State aid? Should the main focus of scrutiny be on the purpose of the measure, or on its effects? What is involved in the notion of the use of State resources? What are the implications of the requirement that the measure should be specific rather than general, and where is the border-line between aid and the whole range of State support for social and economic policies, or social and economic legislation which has differential effects on different sectors of the economy? How in particular is the requirement of specificity to be applied to fiscal measures? What are the appropriate criteria for a normal return on public investment, and what is the correct application of the crucial 'private investor' test?

Legal certainty is of exceptional importance in this field, since both Member States and economic operators need to know whether and when aid is granted, especially in view of the serious procedural consequences of failure to notify a proposed new aid. Yet, despite an abundant case-law, legal certainty remains in some areas a chimera, and there are even suggestions of the existence of a 'rule of reason' which, although it may accord with common sense, fits badly with the requirement of legal certainty.

Further analysis of the concept of aid, and its demarcation from other economic interventions, may prove valuable in establishing more firm parameters. In general the Treaty seeks to leave open the extent and scope of the role of the State in the economy. To that end EC law upholds the principle of neutrality with regard to the system of property ownership (a principle reflected in Article 295 of the Treaty) and the principle of equal treatment between public and private undertakings. In the context of State aid those principles find their expression in the 'private investor test', applied to distinguish public investment from State aid. But again the private investor test is less straightforward than it appears, and the demarcation between investment and aid is not an easy one.

## VI

After the definitional issues, important and interesting questions arise of the relationship between the substantive rules and the policy underlying the law on State aid and other values and policies. Issues treated in different parts of the book (and it is neither possible nor desirable, in these introductory remarks, to be wholly systematic) include the relationship between aid and other aspects of the internal market; between the rules on aid and the competition rules applying to undertakings; and between State aid and general taxation. How does State aid law interact with the protection of the environment? And how does the law on State aid apply in different sectors—in education; in public service broadcasting; in transport?

To take an example from the environment—now recognized as one of the highest priorities among Union policies. At first sight, aid for the protection of the environment may seem one of the more legitimate objectives of State aid. Yet there is an immediate potential contradiction with a fundamental principle of environmental policy—the 'polluter pays' principle, enshrined in Article 174(2) of the Treaty; and the Treaty provides no guidance for resolving the conflict.

Or aid for public service broadcasting, where the Treaty provisions contain a similar kind of antinomy: the Amsterdam Protocol (Protocol on the system of public broadcasting in the Member States) provides that the Treaty shall be without prejudice to:

the competence of Member States to provide for the funding of public service broadcasting insofar as such funding is granted to broadcasting organisations for the fulfilment of the public service remit as conferred, defined and organised by each Member State, and insofar as such funding does not affect trading conditions and competition in the Community to an extent which would be contrary to the common interest, while the realisation of the remit of that public service shall be taken into account.

Thus the public financing of public service broadcasting is taken outside the State aid provisions of the Treaty, but the exemption is subject to an open-ended and undefined condition that competition is not affected to an extent which would be contrary to the common interest. Inevitably perhaps the conflict is not resolved by the Commission's communication on 'the application of State aid rules to public service broadcasting'.[2]

## VII

Issues such as these lead naturally to the great debate on the relationship between the State aid provisions and the special regime reserved by the Treaty to services of general economic interest. Article 86(2) of the Treaty provides:

Undertakings entrusted with the operation of services of general economic interest or having the character of a revenue-producing monopoly shall be subject to the rules contained in this Treaty, in particular to the rules on competition, insofar as the application of such rules does not obstruct the performance, in law or in fact, of the particular tasks assigned to them. The development of trade must not be affected to such an extent as would be contrary to the interests of the Community.

Several contributions to this book rightly emphasize the great importance of this issue, which has attracted the attention of the Governments of the Member States at the highest level.

Since the Treaty of Amsterdam, services of general economic interest have been given an even higher profile in the Treaty, a special regime for such services being provided for by one of the opening articles of the Treaty—Article 16, contained in Part One, 'Principles'. That article goes so far as to spell out 'the place occupied by services of general economic interest in the shared values of the Union as well as their role in promoting social and territorial cohesion'. It accordingly requires both the Community and Member States to ensure that

---

[2] Communication of 15 November 2001, OJ 2001, C 320, p. 4.

such services operate on the basis of principles and conditions which enable them to fulfil their missions.

How then is the funding of public services to be reconciled, as Article 16 also envisages, with the Treaty provisions on State aid? Two alternative approaches can be found in the case-law of the Court.

Broadly, under the first approach, State funding granted to an undertaking for the performance of services of general interest in principle constitute State aid but may be justified under Article 86 if the conditions of that derogation are fulfilled and, in particular, if the funding complies with the principle of proportionality.

Under the second approach however such funding amounts to State aid only to the extent that the economic advantage which it confers exceeds the appropriate remuneration for the services provided or the costs of providing the services.

Clarification of the issue is now awaited in the pending judgment of the Court of Justice in *Altmark*. One of the contributors to this book suggests that the significance of this line of case-law in relation to arguments about the decentralization of State aid law is immense, and that the outcome will have huge implications for the other strands of political and legal development that have been emerging on the proper relationship between EC and national responsibilities in relation to the delivery of public services.

## VIII

One of the special features of State aid law is the difficulty of finding analogues in other systems, of a kind which might provide guidance or at least the possibility of comparison and contrast. In this respect State aid law seems increasingly to diverge from its sister subject, the competition rules applying to undertakings, where comparisons between the EC rules and other systems of competition law seem increasingly relevant and helpful.

The latter form of comparison is best exemplified by comparison between EC competition law and US anti-trust. In the early years of EC competition law, it is true, such comparison seemed less appropriate because EC law then had a very specific function of helping to dismantle barriers to trade between Member States and contributing to the realisation of the single market. That function could indeed be used to explain significant differences between EC and US law—for example, the stricter scrutiny of vertical restraints. However, with the increasing realisation of the internal market the EC and US models are becoming more similar. Increasingly, parallels can be found between the systems. Where there are differences—as recently in relation to merger control—the differences are criticized, and attempts are made at the policy level to reduce them.

Increasingly, too, there is convergence between the EC competition rules and the rules applied at the national level in the Member States. Most of these now have rules directly modelled on the EC rules, in some cases after very radical reform of systems which—as in the UK—were very different. A number of forces have been at work in achieving this convergence. First, there is the practical convenience of a similar regime operating at national and Community level. Second, there is, perhaps, a recognition, in some instances, of the greater merit and relative simplicity of the Community scheme – and it must be acknowledged that the previous UK regime, in particular, was widely regarded as both peculiarly arcane and strikingly ineffective. Third, there is a tendency to accept the need to harmonise the law as a matter of legal obligation.

The position is very different in relation to State aid law. No real comparison can be drawn with the US, where there has never been anything approaching an 'aid regime', despite the recurring disputes about US subsidies to airlines. It is almost equally difficult to make comparisons between EC law and the laws of the Member States—in contrast to the similarities with rules applying to undertakings.

This book contains nonetheless chapters of great interest for comparative purposes. First, there is the discussion of the State aid regime of the EEA which is closely modelled on the EC regime, but which has a different focus related to the special character and objectives of the EEA itself. Secondly, there is the analysis of the State aid regimes of the candidate countries, with reference in particular to by far the largest economy, that of Poland. Thirdly, there is the illuminating exposition of the international aspect of the subject of State aid law and policy, namely the regulation of subsidies in the WTO.

Comparisons between the EC and the WTO are generally helpful whether they disclose similarities or differences: similarities may suggest a common underlying economic logic, while differences often reflect, in an illuminating way, systemic differences between an advanced form of economic and political integration and a scheme still essentially multilateralist albeit with a rapidly advancing tendency towards compulsory judicial settlement.

In the WTO the main focus is naturally on export subsidies, although 'domestic' subsidies may also be in issue, and countervailing duties may be imposed in response to both. Countervailing duties are of course excluded within the EC, and the reach of State aid law (provided always that there is an effect on trade between Member States—a condition relatively easy, and increasingly easy, to satisfy) is far greater. Yet parallels can still be found.

Here the comparison is by no means straightforward, and therefore all the more significant: in some respects EC control, both in substance and in procedure, is more developed, yet in other respects the WTO system goes further.

## IX

Rights without remedies, laws without enforcement, are but words.

In few areas, perhaps, is this so true as in the case of State aid. This book therefore rightly contains several chapters devoted to remedies and enforcement.

I confess to having a particular interest in this subject, which I have had to address in a number of cases. Of great practical importance, as I see it, are two aspects in particular. There is first the scope of the Commission's power, and indeed in certain circumstances its obligation, to require a Member State to recover aid which it has paid unlawfully.

Secondly, there is the scope of the power, and obligation, of national courts to order recovery. Most obviously, Member States may be required to use their courts to recover aid which it transpires that they have granted unlawfully. Here difficult issues may arise where defences based on principles of national law are invoked by beneficiaries of the unlawful aid.

Remedies in the way of orders for recovery may also be available to competitors of the beneficiaries, or indeed to others, for example, enabling those who have paid parafiscal charges, levied to finance an unlawful aid, to recover them from the State. National courts may also be able, under certain conditions, to provide other remedies, such as an award of damages against the State to compensate claimants for loss suffered by reason of the grant of such aid.

The Court held long ago that a breach of the obligation of Member States to notify a proposed aid is sufficient, not only to affect the validity of measures giving effect to the aid, but also to impose on national courts an obligation to draw 'all necessary inferences' as regards, inter alia, the recovery of aid and possible interim measures.[3]

Nonetheless, the experience of national courts, as described and discussed by several contributors to this book, shows that there are difficulties of many kinds in using the national courts for the enforcement of the State aid rules. In part the difficulties arise from the lack of understanding, and lack of transparency, of the system itself—features which the book itself will help to improve. But the effectiveness of the system will continue, it seems, to depend to a great extent on action by the European Commission. The scope for decentralization, 'modernization', and private enforcement will not be as great as for Articles 81 and 82 of the Treaty.

X

In conclusion, this brief survey will have demonstrated the great wealth of issues illuminated by this book.

F. G. Jacobs<br>
*Advocate General at the European Court of Justice, Luxembourg*

---

[3] Case C-354/90 *FNCE* [1991] ECR I-5505, paragraph 12 of the judgment.

# Stop Press: The Altmark *Judgment*

Since this book went to press, the European Court of Justice gave judgment in the *Altmark* case,[1] settling many of the questions concerning the application of the EC State aid rules to compensation granted to undertakings entrusted with the operation of services of general economic interest.[2]

The Court held that such compensation did not confer an advantage on the undertaking concerned and therefore cannot be considered as a State aid within the meaning of the EC Treaty.

The Court began its judgment by reiterating that for a State measure to be classifiable as State aid, it must be capable of being regarded as an '*advantage*' conferred on the recipient undertaking which that undertaking would not have obtained under normal market conditions. There is no such 'advantage' where a State financial measure must be regarded as compensation for the services provided by the recipient undertakings in order to discharge public service obligations.

However, for such compensation not to represent an advantage, four conditions must be satisfied.

First, the recipient company must actually have public service obligations to discharge and those obligations must be clearly defined.

Secondly, the parameters on the basis of which the compensation is calculated must be established in advance in an objective and transparent manner.

Thirdly, the compensation cannot exceed what is necessary to cover all or part of the costs incurred in the discharge of the public service obligations, taking into account the relevant revenue and a reasonable profit.

Fourthly, when the company is not chosen in a public procurement procedure, the level of compensation must be determined by a comparison with an analysis of the costs that a typical company in the sector would incur (taking into account its revenues and a reasonable profit from discharging the obligations).

The solution provided by the Court may be considered as an attempt to find a reasonable compromise between the 'compensation approach' and the 'State aid approach'. In fact, although as a matter of form *Ferring* has been upheld, the Court went well beyond that judgment in an attempt to address the concerns expressed most notably by Advocate General Léger in his two Opinions in the same case but also by many commentators. Clearly (indeed, expressly) drawing inspiration from the Opinion of Advocate General Jacobs in GEMO,[3] the Court

---

[1] C-280/00, *Altmark*, judgment of 24 July 2003, not yet reported.

[2] For a full discussion of the *Altmark* case and the related issues see in this volume the contribution of Rizza. See also the contributions of Biondi and Eeckhout, Plender and Ross.

[3] Case C-126/01 *Ministre de l'Economie, des Finances et de l'Industrie v GEMO*, Opinion of 30 April 2002, nyr,

has subjected *Ferring* to a number of very stringent conditions aimed at ensuring that the 'compensation approach' may in reality be used only in very clear-cut cases. Cumulatively, the four conditions significantly restrict the Member States' power to organize their public services thus dispelling fears that the adoption of a compensation approach—which does not require notification—would result in a substantial number of measures in the area of public sector financing, escaping the Commission's control. Indeed, it is quite likely that the factual situation of *Ferring* itself might not pass the new tests.

The four conditions represent also a clear indication of what the Court thinks the best policy is: the allocation of public service obligations through open bid procedures. The fourth condition in particular makes this very plain: as the definition of what is a reasonable profit might be very difficult and uncertain, the safest bet for Member States is recourse to a public bid procedure. This approach should have the effect of increasing the efficiency of the public service providers as, in the future, recipients of public compensation must benchmark their performance against that of an efficient company.

The *Altmark* judgment is thus in many ways legislative in nature, imposing specific requirements on Member States and indicating possible solutions for the Community Institutions. There are certainly still several issues which will require further clarification. Most notably *Altmark* represented a chance for the Court to address the question of the relationship between Article 86(2) and State aid. That opportunity was not seized. In particular it is still not clear how to use Article 86(2) in those cases where the State support in favour of an undertaking entrusted with public service would not benefit from the *Altmark* test. *Altmark* also sheds no light on whether the Court considers that there is a limit to the scope of what can be characterized as a public service. Notwithstanding those (and other) remaining uncertainties, the judgment is a major step forward on the difficult road of construing a clear and workable definition of what constitutes aid.

Andrea Biondi, Piet Eeckhout, and James Flynn

# Tables of Cases

**Numerical**

**France**

**International**

*EFTA*

**United Kingdom**

# Tables of Legislation

*Commission and Council Decisions*

*Treaties*

### France

### Germany

### International

# Notes on Contributors

**Konstantinos Adamantopoulos** Partner, Hammonds, Brussels.

**Christian Ahlborn** Partner, Linklaters, London.

**Kelyn Bacon** Barrister, Brick Court Chambers, London.

**Claudia Berg** Associate, Linklaters, London.

**Andrea Biondi** Senior Lecturer and Co-Director, Centre of European Law, King's College London; Professor, College of Europe (Natolin); 2 Harcourt Building Chambers, London.

**Sandra Coppieters** Legal Adviser for 'Vlaamse Radio en Televisieomroep' (VRT), Belgium.

**Piet Eeckhout** Professor of European Law and Director, Centre of European Law, King's College London; Professor, College of Europe (Bruges).

**Gerry Facenna** Barrister, Monckton Chambers, London.

**James Flynn QC** Brick Court Chambers, London and Brussels; formerly a Legal Secretary at the European Court of Justice.

**Leo Flynn** Legal Service, European Commission, Brussels.

**Anna Fornalczyk** Professor of the Business University-National Louis University (WSB NLU), Nowy Sacz, Poland.

**Mark Friend** Partner, Allen & Overy, London.

**F. G. Jacobs** Advocate General at the European Court of Justice, Luxembourg.

**Sir Jeremy Lever KCMG, QC, MA,** Monckton Chambers, Gray's Inn, London; Dean, All Souls College, Oxford.

**Richard Plender QC** 20 Essex Street, London; former Director of the Centre of European Law, King's College London.

**Conor Quigley QC** Brick Court Chambers, London and Brussels.

**Maria Rehbinder** Head of Unit, European Commission, Brussels.

**Cesare Rizza** Associate, Cleary, Gottlieb, Steen, and Hamilton, Rome; formerly a Legal Secretary at the European Court of Justice.

**Malcolm Ross** Professor of European Law, University of Sussex.

**Luca Rubini** Legal Secretary, European Court of Justice, Luxembourg; PhD candidate, Kings College London.

**Michael Sánchez Rydelski** Legal and Executive Affairs Department, EFTA Surveillance Authority, Brussels.

**The Hon Mr Justice Silber** High Court Judge assigned to the Queen's Bench Division.

# GENERAL ISSUES

# 1

# Definition of Aid

## RICHARD PLENDER QC

## I. INTRODUCTION

Seldom have the rules of Community law governing State aids been invoked more frequently than at present. Seldom has the definition of a State aid presented more difficulties.

Even before the attack on the World Trade Center on 11 September 2001, it had been predicted[1] that State aid would be 'bound to increase as a result of Monetary Union as governments deal with structural adjustments required by the move to convergence and the single currency'. Since that event, demands have been made to the Commission for the authorization of State aid, not only to the European airlines[2] and to manufacturers of aero-engines[3] but also to the insurance and tourism industries.[4]

The frequency with which European undertakings have made public their demands for State aid has been matched by an increase in the pace of the Community institutions' activity. In the last twelve months alone, the Commission has made Regulations on training aid,[5] on the application of the *de minimis* principle to State aids,[6] and on the application of State aid rules to small and medium-sized enterprises;[7] it has published Guidelines on State Aid for Environmental Protection[8] and on State Aid to Fisheries and Aquaculture,[9] a Communication on State Aid and Risk Capital,[10] and a proposal for a Regulation on State Aid to the Coal

---

[1] S. Bishop, 'The European Commission's Policy Towards State Aid: A Role for Rigorous Competitive Analysis', [1997] 2 ECLR 84.

[2] See *Financial Times*, 13 October 2001, 'Airline Chiefs in Brussels Appeal for Aid'.

[3] See *Financial Times*, 19 October 2001, approval of long-term aid of £250m ($358m) from the UK Government to Rolls-Royce that will help the UK aerospace group to develop an engine range for the Airbus A380 'superjumbo'.

[4] See *The Investor's Chronicle*, 14 September 2001.

[5] Commission Regulation 68/2001 of 12 January 2001 on the application of Articles 87 and 88 of the EC Treaty to Training Aid, OJ 2001 L10/20.

[6] Regulation 69/2001 of 12 January 2001 on the application of Articles 87 and 88 of the EC Treaty to *De Minimis* Aid, OJ 2001 L10/30.

[7] Regulation 70/2001 of 12 January 2001 on the application of Articles 87 and 88 of the EC Treaty to State Aid to Small and Medium-Sized Enterprises, OJ 2001 L10/33.

[8] *Community Guidelines on State Aid for Environmental Protection*, OJ 2001 C37/3.

[9] *Community Guidelines on the Examination of State Aid to Fisheries and Aquaculture*, OJ 2001 C19/7.

[10] 23 May 2001, OJ 2001 C253/3.

Industry[11]; and has made some twenty-eight Decisions on individual aid schemes, including six in the United Kingdom.[12]

In the two European Courts, the volume of litigation devoted to State aids has increased in recent years, although in the case of the Court of First Instance, the rise in the number of State aid judgments from sixteen in 1998 to eighty in 2000 is to be explained in part by disposal of some joined cases with many parties.[13]

Just at the time when the pace of activity is increasing, several new aspects of the problem of defining a State aid have presented themselves.

Recent litigation has drawn attention to difficulties arising from the compendious nature of Article 87(1) of the EC Treaty.[14] That Article is commonly

---

[11] COM (2001) 423 final.

[12] Austria: Decision 669 of 25 April 2001 on the State aid in favour of Voest Alpine Stahl Linz GmbH, OJ 2001 L235/13; Belgium: Decision 198 of 15 November 2000 concerning State aid to Cockerill Sambre SA, OJ 2001 L71/23; Decision 698 of 18 July 2001 on the training aid to Sabena, OJ 2001 L249/21; Finland: Decision 60 of 9 January 2001 on aid for cereal seeds, OJ 2001 L21/17; Decision 61 of 9 January 2001 on aid for seeds, OJ 2001 L21/18; France: Decision 678 of 23 May 2001 authorizing aid to the coal industry, OJ 2001 L239/35; Decision 477 of 19 June 2001 on the granting of aid for the distillation of certain wine sector products, OJ 2001 L171/10; Germany: Decision 685 of 13 February 2001 on the State aid implemented for KataLeuna GmbH Catalysts, OJ 2001 L245/26; Decision 673 of 28 March 2001 on State aid for EFBE Verwaltungs GmbH & Co. Management KG, OJ 2001 L236/3; Decision 361 of 21 December 2000 on aid to the coal industry, OJ 2001 L127/55; Decision 695 of 8 May 2001 on State aid to Philipp Holzmann AG, OJ 2001 L248/46; Greece: Decision 88 of 21 April 1999 concerning aid to two fertilizer companies, OJ 2001 L30/45; Decision 259 of 31 January 2001 on State aid scheme for fruit and vegetable growers, OJ 2001 L93/48; Italy: Decision 323 of 29 November 2000 on State aid to five ECSC steel undertakings, OJ 2001 L113/8; Decision 466 of 21 December 2000 on State aid in favour of the steel companies Lucchini SpA and Siderpotenza SpA, OJ 2001 L163/24; Decision 70 on aid by the Region of Sicily for fisheries and maritime activities, OJ 2001 L62/18; Decision 489 of 28 February 2001 on State aid to Fiat Sata SpA at Melfi, OJ 2001 L177/76; Decision 818 of 20 June 2001 on aid towards an investment by RIVIT SpA (non-ECSC steel), OJ 2001 L234/14; Netherlands: Decision 371 of 21 December 2000 on the exemption from mineral levies under the manure law, OJ L130/42; Decision 517 of 13 February 2001 on the State aid for SCI-Systems, OJ 2001 L186/43; Decision 521 of 13 December 2000 on the aid scheme for six manure-processing companies, OJ 2001 L 189/13; Decision 522 of 7 February 2001 on State aid to China in the form of development assistance for the construction of a high-technology dredger, OJ 2001 L189/21; Spain: Decision 247 of 29 November 2000 on the aid scheme in favour of the shipping company Ferries Golfo de Vizcaya, OJ 2001 L89/28; Decision 605 of 26 July 2000 on the aid scheme for the purchase of commercial vehicles, OJ 2001 L212/34; Sweden: Decision 690 of 21 December 2000 on the reduced social contributions aid scheme, OJ 2001 L244/32; United Kingdom: Decision 114 of 15 November 2000 on the modernization, rationalization, and restructuring plan for the coal industry, OJ 2001 L43/27; Decision 398 of 17 January 2001 on State aid for Nissan Motor Manufacturing (UK), Ltd, OJ 2001 L140/65 Decision 406 of 13 February 2001 on the aid scheme 'Viridian Growth Fund', OJ 2001 L144/23; Decision 683 of 8 May 2001 authorizing the grant of aid to the coal industry, OJ 2001 L241/10; Decision 597 of 11 April 2001 authorizing the grant of aid to nine coal production units and to amend the restructuring plan for the coal industry, OJ L210/32; Decision 340 of 13 February 2001 authorizing the grant of aid to the coal industry, OJ 2001 L 122/23.

[13] The judicial statistics for the Court of Justice show an increase in the number of judgments relating to State aids from 6 in 1998 to 9 in 2000. Those for the Court of First Instance show an increase from 16 to 80 in the same period but the figure for 2000 includes 59 cases on State aids in Italy.

[14] 'Save as otherwise provided in this Treaty, any aid granted by a Member State or through State resources in any form whatsoever, which distorts or threatens to distort competition by favouring certain undertakings or goods shall, in so far as it affects trade between Member States, be incompatible with the common market'.

dissected into four or more component parts: there must be an 'aid'; it must be 'granted by a Member State or through State resources in any form whatsoever'; it must 'distort or threaten to distort competition by favouring certain undertakings or the production of certain goods'; and aid is incompatible with the common market 'in so far as it affects trade between Member States'.[15] It has, however, become increasingly apparent that these elements are interdependent. It is impossible to identify an 'aid', conceived as a benefit or advantage, without identifying the group in relation to which that advantage is enjoyed. To identify the group it is necessary to address the problem of specificity presented by the expressions 'certain undertakings' and 'certain goods'. In order to determine whether aid is granted by a Member State or through State resources it may be relevant, although not decisive, to enquire whether the relevant advantage was granted by the State itself or by a public or private body designated by it.[16] This question may prove inseparable from the identification of the 'advantage'.[17] The detection of a propensity to distort competition is closely connected to detection of an effect on intra-Community trade.

That, however, is by no the means the whole of the story. There has been a discernible trend in recent years to invoke the Community's rules on State aid in certain sectors in which the role of the State has traditionally been predominant, including public broadcasting, postal services, medicine, education, and taxation. The tendency to resort to the rules of State aid in these sectors may be attributable, on occasions, to the absence of the political agreement which would be necessary to regulate a perceived problem by legislation. If so, that would only underscore the necessity for an understanding of the precise boundaries of 'State aid'.

## II. Benefit or Advantage

The rules in the Community treaties governing State aids trace their origin to those of the General Agreement on Tariffs and Trade, where the material word is

---

[15] A. Evans, *EC Law of State Aids*, 1997; R. D'Sa, *European Community Law on State Aids*, 1998 and 'When is Aid Not State Aid? The Implications of the English Partnerships Decision for European Competition Law and Policy', 25 ELRev (2000) 139; C. Kepenne, *Guide des aides d'État en droit communautaire*, 1999; L. Hanscher, T. Ottervanger and P. Slot, *EC State Aids*, 2d ed., 1999; C. Bellamy and G. Child's *European Community Law of Competition*, 5th ed., 2001, Chapter 19; K. Bacon, 'State Aids and General Measures', 17 *Yearbook of European Law* (1997) 269; M. Ross, 'State Aids and National Courts: Definition and Other Problems: A Case of Premature Emancipation?', [2000] CMLR 401; and 'State Aids: Maturing into a Constitutional Problem', 15 *Yearbook of European Law* (1995) 79; S. Bishop, 'The European Commission's Policy Towards State Aid: A Role for Rigorous Competitive Analysis', [1997] 2 ECLR 84; and 'State Aids: Europe's Spreading Cancer', [1995] ECLR 331; B. Roger, 'State Aid: A Fully Level Playing Field', [1999] ECLR 251; T. Jestaeldt, T. Ottervanger, and J-P van Cutsem, *Application of EC State Aid Law by the Member State Courts*, 1999; P. Slotboom, 'State Aid in the Community: A Broad or Narrow Definition?' [1995] ELR 289.

[16] Joined Cases C-72/91 and C-73/91, *Sloman Neptun Schiffahrts AG v Seebetriebsrat Bodo Ziesemer der Sloman Neptun Schiffahrts AG*, [1993] ECR I-887, paragraph 19.

[17] As the Court found in Case C-189/91, *Kirshamer-Hack v Sidal*, [1993] ECR I-6185, paragraph 18.

'subsidy'.[18] When construing the expression 'subsidies or aids granted by States' as it appears in Article 4(c) of the Treaty establishing the European Coal and Steel Community ('ECSC Treaty') the Court of Justice drew attention to the origin of the expression and continued:

A subsidy is normally defined as a payment in cash or in kind made in support of an undertaking other than the payment by the purchaser or consumer for the goods or services which it produces. An aid is a very similar concept, which, however, places emphasis on its purpose and seems especially devised for a particular objective which cannot normally be achieved without outside help. The concept of aid is nevertheless wider than that of a subsidy because it embraces not only positive benefits, such as subsidies themselves, but also interventions which, in various forms, mitigate the charges which are normally included in the budget of an undertaking and which, without, therefore, being subsidies in the strict meaning of the word, are similar in character and have the same effect.[19]

## A. Identification of Aid by Reference to Effects

The final sentence in that passage, which emphasizes the breadth of the word 'aid', tends to be better known than the antecedent sentence, which concentrates on the State's 'purpose' or 'objective'. This reference to the State's aim demands some explanation, for by contrast with the provisions governing concentrations,[20] those governing State aids refer only to the effects of the measure and not to its object. Moreover in a well known series of judgments, beginning in 1974, the two European Courts have stated that Article 87(1) draws no distinction according to the causes or aims of aid but defines it in relation to its effects.[21]

---

[18] General Agreement on Tariffs and Trade, Geneva, 30 October 1947, Article 16: 'If any contracting party grants or maintains any subsidy, including any form of income or price support, which operates directly or indirectly to increase exports of any product from, or to reduce imports of any product into, its territory, it shall notify the Contracting Parties in writing of the extent and nature of the subsidization, of the estimated effect of the subsidization on the quantity of the affected product or products imported into or exported from its territory and of the circumstances making the subsidization necessary'.

[19] Case 30/59, *De Gezamenlijke Steenkolenmijnen in Limburg v High Authority*, [1961] ECR 1 at 19, reiterated in the context of the same Treaty in Case C-390/98, *Banks v British Coal and Secrtary of State*, 20 September 2001, paragraph 30. The passage was applied to aids under the EC Treaty in Case C-387/92, *Banco de Crédito Industrial SA, now Banco Exterior de España SA v Ayuntamiento de Valencia*, [1994] ECR I-877 at 907 paragraphs 12 and 13; Case C-295/97, *Industrie Aeronautiche e Meccaniche Rinaldo Piaggio SpA v International Factors Italia SpA and Others*, paragraph 34 and Case C-200/97, *Ecotrade Srl v Altiforni e Ferriere di Servola SpA*, [1998] ECR I-7907, paragraph 34. It is therefore well established that the grant of aid may take the form of a partial exoneration from the charges, in the form of taxation or social costs, which an undertaking would otherwise bear in consequence of national legislation, where the exoneration is not justified by the nature or scheme of the system: Case 173/73, *Commission v Italy*, [1974] ECR 709, paragraph 41; Case C-301/87, *France v Commission*, [1990] ECR I-307, paragraph 41; Case C-251/97, *France v Commission*, [1999] ECR I-6639, paragraph 36. Likewise the sale of public land at an undervalue may constitute the grant of aid: *Land Berlin/Daimler Benz*, OJ 1992 L283/43; Case T-15596R, *City of Mainz v Commission*, [1996] ECR II-1665.

[20] EC Treaty, Articles 81 and 82.

[21] Case 173/73, *Commission v Italy*, [1974] ECR 709, paragraph 27; Case 61/79, *Amministrazione Italiana delle Finanze Denkavit Italiana SpA*, [1980] ECR 1205, paragraph 31; Case 290/83, *Commission v France*, [1985] ECR 439, paragraph 20; Case 310/84, *Deufil v Commission*, [1987] ECR

In particular, a public measure which has the effect of conferring a selective advantage on an undertaking or sector is not relieved of its quality as an aid by reason of the fact that it was adopted for social purposes.[22] That is implied in the classic definition of 'aid' given by the Court of Justice in Case 61/79, *Amministrazione Italiana delle Finanze Denkavit Italiana SpA*.[23] In that case the Court stated that the word: 'refers to the decisions of the Member States by which the latter, in pursuit of their own economic and social objectives, give by unilateral and autonomous decisions, undertakings or other persons resources or procure for them advantages intended to encourage the attainment of the economic and social objectives sought'.

It would, however, carry semantic purity to the point of unreality if we were to deny that a Court may take any account of the purpose for which a national measure was adopted in determining whether it amounts to the conferral of a benefit or advantage. The point was made by Clarke LJ in *R v Customs and Excise Commissioners ex parte Lunn Poly and Bishopsgate*.[24] His conclusion in that case was that the maintenance of a differential rate of taxation, justified by the aim of countering tax avoidance, did not amount to 'aid'. In reaching that conclusion he noted that the case-law of the Court of Justice establishes that the social aim of a measure cannot shield it from the application of Article 87; but it does not 'go so far as to say that the aim or purpose of the measure is irrelevant'. His comment derives support from several judgments of the Court of Justice.

For instance, in Case C-6/97, *Italy v Commission*,[25] the Court, when finding that the introduction of a tax credit scheme for Italian road hauliers constituted an aid, stated that: 'the national legislation at issue in the contested decision was intended to reduce the tax burden on road hauliers operating for hire or reward . . . that legislation meets the condition that it should relate to specific undertakings, which is one of the defining features of State aid . . .'

901, paragraph 8; Case T-67/94, *Ladbroke Racing v Commission*, [1998] ECR II-1, paragraph 52; Case C-241/94 *France v Commission*, [1996] ECR I-4551, paragraph 20; Case T-106/95, *Fédération Française des Sociétés d'Assurances (FFSA) and Others v Commission*, [1997] ECR II 229, paragraph 195; Case C-480/98, *Spain v Commission (Magafesa)*, [2000] ECR I-8717, paragraph 16. In the words of Mr Advocate General Lenz in Case 44/93, *Namur-Les Assurances du Crédit v Office Nationale Ducroire*, [1994] ECR I-3929, paragraph 66: 'The concept of aid stands for the grant of certain unmarketlike advantages attributable to the State which are liable to improve the economic situation of the undertaking which benefits from the aid in comparison with that of other undertakings. In other words it covers the effects to which the State measure gives rise at the level of the undertaking or undertakings which benefit from the advantages.' See further J. Mégret, J-V. Louis, D. Vignes, and M. Waelbroeck, *Le droit des Communautés européennes*, 1972–, Vol. IV, p. 380 and H. Vonder Groeben, C-D. Ehlermann, J. Thiesing, and H. ron Boeckh, *Die Europäische Wirtschaftsgemeinschaft: Kommentar zum EWG Vertrag*, 1960–, p. 273.

[22] Case C-241/94, *France v Commission*, '*Kimberly Clark*', [1996] ECR I-4551, paragraph 21; Case C-75/97, *Belgium v Commission*, [1999] ECR I-3671, paragraph 25; Case C-251/97, *France v Commission*, [1999] ECR I-6639, paragraph 37.

[23] [1980] ECR 1205, paragraph 31.

[24] [1999] 1 CMLR 1357, paragraph 61.

[25] [1999] ECR I-2997, paragraph 17.

In Joined Cases C-72/91 and C-73/91, *Sloman Neptun Schiffahrts AG v See-betriebsrat Bodo Ziesemer der Sloman Neptun Schiffahrts AG*,[26] the Court held that the partial non-application of German employment legislation to foreign crews of vessels flying the German flag did not constitute a grant of aid to the owner. It reasoned: 'The system at issue does not seek, through its object and general structure, to create an advantage which would constitute an additional burden for the State or the above-mentioned bodies, but only to alter in favour of shipping undertakings the framework within which contractual relations are formed between those undertakings and their employees'.

In Case C-189/91, *Kirshamer-Hack v Sidal*,[27] the Court concluded that the exclusion of small businesses from a legal regime requiring payment of compensation in the event of socially unjustified dismissals did not amount to the grant of an aid to the businesses concerned, reasoning that it: 'derives solely from the legislature's intention to provide a specific legislative framework for working relationships between employers and employees and to avoid imposing on those businesses financial constraints which might hinder their development'.

The Commission was therefore correct in asserting, in a Notice published in 1995, that the objective of the body granting a benefit may to be taken into account when determining whether it amounts to an aid.[28] It may in particular be relevant when determining whether a certain undertaking or sector has in reality received an advantage in relation to others. For instance, where the aim pursued by the national authority is to rectify an imbalance between two classes of undertaking which would otherwise exist in consequence of national legislation, it must be proper to take account of that fact when determining whether the measure adopted for that purpose confers a benefit. In that limited sense, the aim may be material when assessing the effect. In a far wider sense, of course, the aim is to be taken into account by the Commission when exercising its powers of review to determine whether an aid is compatible with the common market.[29]

## B. The Market Investor Principle

The identification of a benefit or advantage constituting an aid presents particular difficulties when services are supplied by an entity subject to the control of the State to recipients who are alleged to have paid less than they are worth; or where an undertaking which has provided services to the State is alleged to have received a reward exceeding their value. The principle consistently applied to these circumstances by the Court of Justice in such cases is the

---

[26] [1993] ECR I-887, paragraph 21.

[27] [1993] ECR I-6185, paragraph 17.

[28] Notice on Cooperation between National Courts and the Commission in the State Aid Field, OJ 1995 C312/8, paragraph 7.

[29] That it may be taken into account for this purpose is well established. See Case T-189/97, *Comité d'Entreprise de la Société Française de la Production and Others v Commission*, [1998] ECR II-335, paragraph 40; Case T-14/96, *Bretagne Angleterre Irlande (BAI) v Commission*, [1999] ECR II-139, paragraph 40.

'market investor' test. The Court enquires whether the recipient has received an economic advantage which it would not have obtained under normal market conditions.[30] That test was expressed by Mr Advocate General Jacobs in the following words:

Although it is sometimes suggested that financial assistance granted by the State must, in order to qualify as State aid, be gratuitous, the better view is surely that State aid is granted whenever a Member State makes available to an undertaking funds which in the normal course of events would not be provided by a private investor applying ordinary commercial criteria and disregarding considerations of a social, political or philanthropic nature.[31]

The test can be applied both to the case of the recipient who pays an undervalue and to that of the overpaid provider of goods or services. Thus there was 'aid' where an undertaking subject to State control fixed the tariff for a source of energy at a level lower than that which it would otherwise have chosen, so as to confer preferential treatment on a category of energy users;[32] there was 'aid' when a local authority made advance payment for a block of transport vouchers to be used on a route operated by a ferry company;[33] and there was 'aid' (and not a 'special charge') when licences and leases were granted to British Coal and the State companies succeeding it without any consideration, whereas all the other operators obtained licences only on payment of royalties.[34]

The test may be applied, in particular, to the provision of public funds to undertakings, whether in the form or loans or capital injections. The Commission's *Notice on Cooperation between National Courts and the Commission in the State Aid Field*[35] states that investments from public funds constitute aids when they are made in circumstances in which a private investor would have withheld support.[36] In its judgment in Case T-296/97, *Alitalia v Commission*, the Court of First Instance stated:

the test based on the conduct of a private investor operating in normal market-economy conditions ensues from the principle that the public and private sectors are to be treated equally, pursuant to which capital placed directly or indirectly at the disposal of an undertaking by the State in circumstances which correspond to normal market conditions cannot be regarded as State aid.

A capital contribution from public funds must therefore be regarded as satisfying the private investor test and not constituting State aid if, *inter alia*, it was made at the same

---

[30] Case C-39/94, *Syndicat Français de l'Express International (SFEI) and Others v La Poste*, [1996] ECR I-3547, paragraph 60.
[31] Joined Cases C-278/92, C-279/92, and C-280/92, *Spain v Commission*, [1994] ECR I-4103 at 4112, paragraph 28.
[32] Joined Cases 67, 68, and 70/85, *Kwekerij Gebroders Van der Kooy BV and Others v Commission*, [1988] ECR 219, paragraph 28.
[33] Case T-14/96, *Bretagne Angleterre Irelande (BAI) v Commission*, [1999] ECR II-139, paragraph 40.
[34] Case C-390/98, *Banks v British Coal and Secrtary of State*, [2001] ECR I-6117, paragraph 42.
[35] Notice on Cooperation between National Courts and the Commission in the State Aid Field, OJ 1995 C312/8.
[36] OJ 1995 C312/8, paragraph 7.

time as a significant capital contribution on the part of a private investor made in comparable circumstances.[37]

Not only does the grant of loans at reduced rates of interest amount to an aid, where it enables the recipient to avoid costs which would normally have had to be met out of its own financial resources;[38] but so too does the provision of loans at market rates where it is apparent, from the size of the capital injection and the circumstances in which it is made, that a private investor would not have acted as the public authority did.[39] In the words of Mr Advocate General Slynn in Case 84/82, *Germany v Commission*: 'At the very least, assistance constitutes an aid if the recipient obtains a benefit which he would not have received in the normal course. A loan at a rate of interest below normal commercial rates is an obvious example. So, however, may be the provision of capital under normal market conditions but on a scale not normally available in the capital market'.[40]

The market investor test presents particular difficulties, however, when the State entrusts the provision of public services to an undertaking, particularly if it is a public one, for which the State must make appropriate payment. The problem is one of current controversy in the broadcasting sector.

## C. Public Broadcasting

Some sharp disagreements have been provoked in recent years by the increasing tendency of the Commission to scrutinize the support given by Member States to public broadcasters, for compatibility with the Treaty rules on State aids.[41]

It is possible to argue that where the benefit received by the broadcaster is no greater than the cost that it incurs in discharging a duty, imposed on it by the State, to provide a public service, there is no aid element at all. Some support for that view may be found in the Opinion of Mr Advocate General Fennelly in Case C-251/97, *France v Commission*, where he said:

The position becomes more complicated where public authorities engage to pay undertakings to provide goods or services or more intangible benefits, in the general public interest. Such benefits could include ... inclusion of a certain amount of public interest

---

[37] 12 December 2000, paragraphs 80–81 of the judgment. The Court here referred to Case C-303/88, *Italy v Commission*, [1991] ECR I-1433, paragraph 20 and Case T-358/94, *Air France v Commission*, [1996] ECR II-2109, paragraphs 70 and 148–149.

[38] Case C-301/87, *France v Commission*, [1990] ECR I-307, paragraph 41; see also *Cityflier Express v Commission*, [1998] ECR II-757, paragraph 88.

[39] Case C-234/84, *Belgium v Commission, 'Meura'*, [1986] ECR 2263, paragraph 14; Case 301/87, *France v Commission, 'Boussac-Saint-Frères'*, [1990] ECR I-307, paragraph 40; Case T-358/94, *Air France v Commission*, [1996] ECR II-2109, paragraph 105. See further I. Van Bael and J. Bellis, *Competition Law of the European Community*, 3rd ed., 1994, 830.

[40] [1984] ECR 1451 at 1501.

[41] See U. Bartosch: 'The Financing of Public Broadcasting and E.C. State Aid Law', [1999] ECLR 197; H. Simboeck, 'Public Service Broadcasts and State Aids', 4(5) *Communications Law* (1999) 187; V. Porter, 'Public Service Broadcasting in the European Union: State Aids, Competition Policy and Subsidiarity', 15(2) *Journal of Media Law and Practice* (1994) 38.

content in broadcasts. Depending on the precise circumstances in which the authorities 'purchase' such benefits at market prices, it is possible to argue that there is no aid element at all, or that there is aid which is, at least potentially, compatible with the common market.[42]

The argument that the Advocate General had in mind had been advanced to the Court of First Instance earlier in Case T-95/96, *Gestevisión Telecino v Commission*,[43] on the basis of a judgment of the *Conseil constitutionnel* rendered more than forty years ago.[44] Although the Advocate General's statement is correct in principle, it would be unusual for national authorities to purchase at market prices the provision of public service broadcasting by public tendering or other transparent manner. Where, by contrast, the State provides funding for a public broadcaster and requires the latter to discharge a remit in the public interest, it may well generate complaints from private competitors that they are they are denied the opportunity to compete for the right to provide similar services in return for a similar public reward.

In Case T-46/97, *Sociedade Independente de Comunicação SA v Commission*,[45] the Commission had made a Decision finding that that grants paid by the Portuguese State to the broadcaster RTP did not constitute aid because they were intended to offset the actual cost of meeting the public service obligations that RTP assumed. Annulling that Decision, the Court noted that the Commission had itself acknowledged, in the contested measure, that the grants paid to RTP had the result of giving that undertaking a 'financial advantage'. At paragraph 82 of the judgment the CFI stated: 'The fact that, according to the Decision, the grants were merely intended to offset the additional cost of the public service tasks assumed by RTP cannot prevent them from being classified as aid within the meaning of Article 92 [now 87] of the Treaty'.

It reasoned further that the fact that a financial advantage is granted to an undertaking by the public authorities in order to offset the cost of public service obligations which it is claimed to have assumed has no bearing on the classification of that measure as aid within the meaning of Article 88(1) of the Treaty. That fact may, however, be taken into account when considering whether the aid in question is compatible with the common market under Article 88(2) of the Treaty.[46]

That judgment is correct in principle. It is compatible with the rule whereby the characterization of a measure as aid is to be determined by reference to its effects; and it takes account of the fact that even the provision of no more funding than is required to offset the cost of providing a public service may

---

[42] [1999] ECR I-6639, paragraph 20.

[43] [1998] ECR II-3407.

[44] Decision 60–8DC of 11 August 1960, paragraph 9.

[45] 10 May 2000.

[46] Case T-106/95, *Fédération Française des Sociétés d'Assurances (FFSA) and Others v Commission*, [1997] ECR II 229, paragraphs 178 and 199, confirmed by the Order in Case C-174/97 P, *Fédération Française des Sociétés d'Assurances (FFSA) and Others v Commission*, [1998] ECR I-1303, paragraph 33.

entail the conferral of an advantage on the body entrusted with the performance of that task. The proper approach to this question, it is suggested, is to apply Article 86(2) of the EC Treaty, which shields undertakings entrusted with the performance of services of general economic interest from the effects of Article 87 of the EC Treaty, to the extent that the application of the latter would obstruct the performance of the tasks entrusted to them.

In the context of Article 86(2), the term 'economic interest' is not to be construed so narrowly as to exclude public services in the nature of broadcasting.[47] In Case 155/73, *Sacchi*,[48] Mr Advocate General Reischl emphasized the 'great cultural and educational significance' of television broadcasts and the Court of Justice, following his lead, dealt with the case on the premise that public broadcasters were undertakings entrusted with the operation of services of general economic interest. The Court of First Instance took a similar view on Case C-17/96, *Télévision Française 1 SA v Commission*.[49]

On this view, the grant of public monies, and the public provision of licence fees or other benefits to a broadcaster, constitute aid, and are subject to the rules in the Treaty governing notification to the Commission; but to the extent that it is required for the performance of the tasks entrusted to the recipient, it is not incompatible with the common market.[50]

This view is supported, not weakened, by Protocol No 32 to the Treaty of Amsterdam. This reads as follows:

The provisions of this Treaty shall be without prejudice to the competence of Member States to provide for the funding of public service broadcasting in so far as such funding is granted to broadcasting organizations for the fulfilment of the public service remit as conferred, defined or organized by each Member State, and that such funding does not affect trading conditions and competition in the Community to an extent that would be contrary to the common interest, bearing in mind what is required for the realization of the remit of that public service.

That wording confirms that in principle the provision of finance from public sources for public service broadcasting amounts to the grant of aid. The draftsmen have used language reminiscent of Article 87 of the EC Treaty, in affirming

---

[47] According to the Court of Justice, services are of general economic interest when they exhibit special characteristics as compared with the general economic interest of other economic activiities: Case C-266/96, *Corsica Ferries SA and Grupo Antichi Ormeggiatori del Porto di Genova Coop. Arl, Gruppo Ormaggiatori del Golfo di La Spezia Coop. Sarl, Ministero dei Transporti e della Navigazione*, [1998] ECR I-3949, paragraph 45. In Case 66/86, *Ahmed Saeed Flugreisen and Others v Zentrale zur Bekämpfung Unlauteren Wettbewerbs*, [1989] ECR 803, paragraphs 55–57, the Court of Justice omitted the word 'economic' when ruling that what is now Article 86(2) may be applied to air carriers required to perform services of general interest. In its Communication on *Services of General Interest in Europe*, OJ 1996 C281/3, paragraph 51, the Commission expressed the view that the term 'services of general economic interest' covered, among other matters, broadcasting.

[48] [1974] ECR 409; Opinion of Mr Advocate General Reischl at page 443; judgment of Court at paragraph 15.

[49] [1998] ECR II-3407.

[50] Although not listed among the matters set out in Article 87(2) of the EC Treaty.

that such financing must not affect trading conditions contrary to the common interest.[51] On the other hand, they have confirmed that it is for the Member States to define the public service broadcasting remit; and they have stated that the provision of funding to enable an undertaking to discharge of that remit is lawful, to the extent that it does not affect competition contrary to the common interest.[52]

## D. Infrastructure Aid

Difficulties of a different character arise from the proposition that the provision of capital at normal market rates may constitute 'aid' when it is made available by the State on a scale, or in circumstances, in which it could not be obtained under ordinary market conditions. It is characteristically the function of the State to make provision for precisely those services that would not be supplied by private investors. That is the case, for instance, with development aid.

According to the Commission, the provision by public authorities of infrastructure that is traditionally paid out of public funds does not normally constitute an aid; but it may do so if the works are carried out specifically in the interests of a certain undertaking or type of product.[53] The statement is so cautious as to yield only modest guidance. The reference to tradition appears to be misleading. The Treaty draws no distinction between projects traditionally undertaken by the State and those not traditionally undertaken by them. However, in stating that the conditions of Article 87 may be met if the condition of specificity is satisfied, the Commission implies that assistance for infrastructure is not *per se* removed from the scope of the Treaty's State aid rules. That is consistent with the Court's approach in Case C-225/91, *Mantra v Commission*[54] where it upheld a Decision of the Commission which had found that the infrastructure and training measures in question would not benefit the joint venture exclusively. The reasoning proceeds on the premise that there was 'aid' which, however, did not meet the condition of specificity.

Under a scheme applied in the United Kingdom, known as the 'Partnership Investment Programme' a statutory body, called English Partnerships,[55] provided funding to fill the gap between the estimated development cost of urban land and its developed value. The developer presented his proposal to English

---

[51] This is confirmed by the judgment of the Court of First Instance in Case T-95/96, *Gestevisión Telecino v Commission*, [1998] ECR II-3407, paragraphs 52, 82, 83, where it ruled that the Commission had failed to fulfil its obligations by omitting to adopt a Decision on the complaints made by the Applicants about the provision of public funds to public sector broadcasters in Spain.

[52] On this subject see *Kinderkanal and Phoenix* and *BBC News 24*, XXIXth Report on Competition Policy (1999) point 226.

[53] Commission Answer to Written Question, JO 1967, 2311.

[54] [1993] ECR I-3203, paragraph 29.

[55] Created pursuant to Part III of the Leasehold Reform, Housing and Urban Development Act 1993.

Partnerships and negotiated with the latter the sharing of risks and costs. *Ex hypothesi*, private investors would not develop the land independently because their investment would, under ordinary market conditions, result in a loss; but the Government considered that a partnership between a private undertaking and a public body was more cost-effective than development of the site by public enterprise alone for the reason, among others, that it spared the exchequer the cost of purchasing the site.[56]

In a Decision dated 22 December 1999[57] the Commission held that the whole of the 'gap funding', comprising the difference between the development cost and the developed value of the land and the profit made by the developer, constitute 'aid'. It terminated the implementation of the Partnership Investment Programme in its original form, without however disturbing schemes for which application for clearance had been made prior to the Commission's Decision; and it declared that a modified scheme was compatible with the common market. The principal modification required notification of any cases in which a private partner is active in certain sensitive sectors, including motor vehicles, shipbuilding, coal, and steel.

The Commission's reasoning, although consonant with traditional criteria, gives rise to extraordinary results. A scheme devised for the purpose of reducing the amount of public investment required for an infrastructure project is characterized as aid, whereas the direct investment of greater amounts of public money in development of the site by the State itself would not have been so characterized. Had the project not been notified, there would have applied the oft repeated *dictum* of the Court of Justice that the 'withdrawal of an unlawful aid by way of recovery is the logical consequence of finding that it is unlawful';[58] but in the case of the Partnership Investment Programme, the sum to be recovered would comprise a loss, save for the element attributable to the developer's return. In the case of that element, it falls within the sum characterized by the Commission as aid although it is assessed so as to produce precisely the amount that the developer would have received had he invested under ordinary market conditions. In view of these and other factors, Professor D'Sa makes a powerful case for the proposition that there should be a new framework, distinct from the regional aid and development guidelines, to address these issues.[59]

---

[56] R. D'Sa, 'When is Aid Not State Aid? The Implications of the English Partnerships Decision for European Competition Law and Policy', 25 *ELRev* (2000) 139.

[57] OJ 1999 C39/99.

[58] Case C-142/87, *Belgium v Commission, 'Tubemeuse'*, [1990] ECR I-959; Case C-354, *Fédération Nationale du Commerce Extérieur des Produits Alimentaires et Syndicat National des Négotiants et Transformateur de Saumon v French State*, [1991] ECR I-5505, paragraph 12; Case C-183/91, *Commission v Greece*, [1993] ECR I-3131, paragraph 16; Case C-39/94, *Syndicat Français de l'Express International (SFEI) and Others v La Poste*, [1996] ECR I-3547, paragraph 68; Case C-390/98, *Banks v British Coal and Secretary of State*, [2001] ECR I-6117, paragraph 74.

[59] R. D'Sa, 'When is Aid Not State Aid? The Implications of the English Partnerships Decision for European Competition Law and Policy', 25 *ELRev* (2000) 139 at 156.

## E. Education

According to Hanscher, Ottervanger, and Slot: 'Aid for vocational training and education ... is traditionally regarded as one of the Member State's responsibilities towards the labour force and normally does not fall within the criteria of Article 87'.[60]

As a description of traditional public attitudes in much of Europe, and of what is ordinarily the case with general schemes of public education available to all without discrimination, the statement is no doubt unexceptionable. It cannot, however, draw support from the judgment of the Court of Justice in Case 263/86, *Humbel v Belgian State*.[61] In that case the Court stated: 'The state in establishing and maintaining [a national education system] is not seeking to engage in gainful activity but is fulfilling its duties towards its own population in the social, cultural and educational fields. Secondly, the system in question is, as a general rule, funded from the public purse and not by pupils or their parents.'

The Court there had in mind the Treaty's rules relating to the freedom to supply services, not those on State aid. Had it considered the latter, it would have been bound to apply the principle that it is the effect and not the aim of the measure that determines whether it constitutes an aid.

The Commission put the matter acceptably in its *Communication concerning a Framework on Training Aid*, 1998. It stated: 'Being general measures, many training measures are not caught by [Article 87(1)] of the Treaty. Most training forms part of the tasks traditionally carried out by the State and by and large benefits people and workers everywhere'.[62]

As those words disclose, the reason why the provision of public funding for education commonly falls outside Article 87(1) is that it is general in application: the 'condition of specificity' is not met.

In several Member States, however, the private sector is increasingly engaged in the provision of educational services; and in all there is a mixture of public and private provision of vocational training.[63] In such cases, the selective conferral of an advantage on the public sector, or a part of it, may constitute an aid. The Commission itself has stated as much in a pair of Decisions, first with some timidity in 1985,[64] then with greater confidence in

---

[60] L. Hanscher, T. Ottervanger and P. Slot, *EC State Aids*, 2d ed., 1999; C. *Bellamy and G. Child's European Community Law of Competition*, 5th ed., 2001 by P.M. Roth, paragraph 3–037.

[61] [1988] ECR 5365, paragraphs 17 to 18.

[62] OJ 1998 C343/10 at paragraph 13.

[63] The point was made by the United Kingdom in Case C-109/92, *Stephen Max Wirth v Landeshauptstadt Hannover*, [1993] ECR I-6447, paragraphs 15–18. The Court apparently accepted the observation, stating that 'When courses are given in such establishments, they become services within the meaning of Article [50] of the Treaty. Their aim is to offer a service for remuneration.'

[64] Decision 85/233 of 16 April 1985 terminating the anti-subsidy proceeding concerning imports of soya meal originating in Brazil, OJ 1985 L106/9, paragraph 7.3: 'measures normally regarded as being in the public interest, for instance to improve a country's ... education ... do not have a distorting effect. For there to be distortion of competition, the advantages must be conferred selectively.'

1991.[65] Indeed, in its Decision of 11th May 1999[66] the Commission held that where Italian law made provision for fixed-term training and work experience contracts for unemployed persons of up to 29 (later 32) years of age, this entailed a grant of State aid, since the employers received a partial exoneration from social security contributions otherwise due in respect of their employees. That was so even though the relevant programmes conferred a specific qualification; they were usually drawn up by consortia of firms or trade associations; and they were approved by the employment office, which checked whether at the end of the training period the employee had actually received the training required.

Likewise in the case of assistance for training provided to Eli Lilley Ltd. the Commission took the view that it amounted to State aid requiring approval, notwithstanding the fact that it prepared participants for transferable qualifications that were nationally recognized.[67]

The conclusion to be drawn is that the grant by a Member State or through State resources of selective assistance to an undertaking engaged in competition with others in the provision of educational and vocational services is to be characterized as aid. The same is true of the selective grant of public resources to promote projects of cultural significance, such as literature in the national language.[68] The statement of this conclusion does not, however, solve the problem. Many of the services characteristically supplied by the State in the field of education face private competition. That is true of primary and secondary schooling, of tertiary education in its various forms, and of the dissemination of educational material through printing and mass media.

In order to determine whether Article 87(1) of the EC Treaty avails the private educational institution, dissatisfied with the disadvantage that it faces in relation to its publicly funded competitor, it is necessary to focus on the condition of specificity. The reason why a private school cannot complain that the funding of public schools constitutes 'aid' is, in most cases, that the rules governing the funding of public schools are general. The private school does not accept the obligations, in respect of admission, curriculum, and otherwise, that apply to the public sector. When, on the other hand, a public institution publishes and sells educational materials, the support that it receives from public funds may well constitute 'aid' which distorts or threatens to distort competition by favouring certain undertakings or the production of certain goods.

---

[65] Decision 91/390 of 26 March 1991 on aid granted by the French Government to the undertaking Saint-Gobain (Eurofloat) at Salaise-sur-Sanne (Glass sector), OJ 1991 L215/11: 'where specific training is involved, falling outside the general system of education and training and corresponding to the particular needs of a particular undertaking sector or region, any contribution by the public authorities to the costs of such training may constitute aid within the meaning of Article [87(1)] of the Treaty'.

[66] Decision 2000/128 of 11 May 1999 concerning aid granted by Italy to provide employment and training, OJ 2000 L42/1.

[67] Case N-452/98, reported in *European Community Competition Policy*, 1999, point 251.

[68] On this point see Case T-49/93, *Société Internationale de Diffusion et d'Édition (SIDE) v Commission*, [1995] ECR II-2501 and Case C-332/98, *French Republic v Commission, 'Coopérative d'Exportation du Livre Français'*, [2000] ECR I-4833.

## III. Granted by the State or through State resources

The draftsmen use demonstrably broad language in stipulating, as a condition of its capture by Article 87(2), that aid must be 'granted by a Member State or through State resources in any form whatsoever'. A grant of aid plainly meets this condition when it takes the form of a sum of money granted by the central or local authorities of the State[69] or revenue, including taxation and social contributions, foregone by the State's authorities.[70]

It is equally obvious that assistance is granted by a Member State or through State resources when it originates in the State but is administered by the intermediary of an independent body. As the Court of Justice has stated, on several occasions, Article 87 'covers all aid granted by a Member State or through State resources and there is no necessity to draw any distinction according to whether the aid is granted directly by the State or by public or private bodies established or appointed to administer the aid'.[71]

### A. Transfer of State Resources

There is, however, some basis on the wording of Article 87(1), and in the case-law of the Court of Justice, for the proposition that aid may be granted 'by a Member State or through State resources' although it entails no transfer of resources from the State, even in the form of revenue foregone. Use of the word 'or' in the opening paragraph of Article 87 might be taken to imply that aid may be granted by the State even though it is not granted through State resources; and it is possible to identify several cases in which the Court of Justice has detected aid without either a grant of money from the State or the foregoing of revenue.

In Joined Cases 67, 68, and 70/85, *Kwekerij Gebroders Van der Kooy BV and Others v Commission*[72] the Court of Justice upheld the Commission's view that aid was granted 'by a Member State or through State resources' when Gasunie, a company in which the Netherlands Government owned 50 per cent of the capital, fixed the tariff for a source of energy at a level lower than that which it would otherwise charge. The Court placed reliance on the fact that the State,

[69] Case 301/87, *France v Commission, 'Boussac-Saint-Frères'*, [1990] ECR I-307; Case C-17/99, *French Republic v Commission*, 22 March 2001; Case C-332/98, *French Republic v Commission, 'Coopérative d'Exportation du Livre Français'*, [2000] ECR I-4833; Case C-156/98, *Germany v Commission, 'New Lander'*, [2000] ECR I-6857.

[70] Case C-387/92, *Banco de Crédito Industrial, now Banco Exterior de España v Ayuntamiento de Valencia*, [1994] ECR I-877; Case C-251/97, *France v Commission*, [1999] ECR I-6639; Case T-106/95, *Fédération Française des Sociétés d'Assurances (FFSA) and Others v Commission*, [1997] ECR II 229; C-6/97, *Italy v Commission*, [1999] ECR I-2951.

[71] Case 290/83, *Commission v France, 'Poor Farmers'*, [1985] ECR 439, paragraph 14; Case 57/86, *Greece v Commission*, [1988] ECR 2855, paragraph 12; Joined Cases C-72/91 and C-73/91, *Sloman Neptun Schiffahrts AG v Seebetriebsrat Bodo Ziesemer der Sloman Neptun Schiffahrts AG*, [1993] ECR I-887.

[72] [1988] ECR 219, paragraph 28.

or the entity on which it exerted an influence, forewent the profit which it could normally realize.

It is suggested by Miss Bacon[73] that the burden on State resources was not the decisive feature in the case. Rather, she suggests, the crucial factor was the involvement of the State in the decision-making process. She claims to find support for her view in Case C-56/93, *Belgium v Commission*[74] in which it concluded that on the facts of that case 'the question whether the profits were ultimately realized by the Groningen Association rather than by Gasunie is not pivotal'. Miss Bacon's conclusion is that the Court is willing to regard as State aid an advantage to an undertaking granted at the expense of an entity on which it exerts a dominant influence.[75] Her view is shared by Slotboom, who contends that no transfer of resoirces is required in the event of State aid.[76]

It is thought, however, that this attempt to diminish the significance of a transfer of resources from the State to the beneficiary is against the weight of the authorities. In the first case in which the Community's rules on State aid were invoked in relation to the public fixing of prices, Mr Advocate General Capotorti reasoned as follows: 'It is clear that for a measure which has the effect of favouring certain undertakings to constitute an aid, it must entail a financial burden for the State. This follows from the actual wording of Article [87(1)] in which reference is made to "any aid granted by a Member State or through State resources".[77] [...] It is thus necessary that the State should grant certain undertakings, selected individually or by categories, an advantage entailing a burden on the public finances in the form either of expenditure or of reduced income'.[78]

The Court followed his Opinion. In Joined Cases C-72 and C-73/91, *Sloman Neptun Schiffahrts AG v Seebetriebsrat Bodo Ziesemer der Sloman Neptun Schiffahrts AG*[79] rejected the contention that German provisions exonerating shipowners from certain charges fell within Article 87(1). The Court proceeded on the premise that the exoneration was capable of constituting 'aid' but concluded that it was not to be viewed as being granted through State resources.

Likewise, in Case C-189/91, *Petra Kirsammer-Hack v Nurhan Sidal*[80] the Court rejected the contention that the statutory exclusion of certain small businesses from the system of protection against unfair dismissal amounted to

---

[73] K. Bacon, 'State Aids and General Measures', 17 *Yearbook of European Law* (1997) 269 at 285.
[74] [1996] ECR I-723, paragraphs 18–20.
[75] Miss Bacon does not refer in this context to Case 290/83, *Commission v France*, [1985] ECR 439, paragraph 14, where the Court stated that 'aid need not necessarily be financed from State resources to be classified as State aid'. It appears, however, from the context, and particularly from the reference to Case 78/76, *Steinike and Weinlig v Germany*, [1977] ECR 595, that the Court had in mind the indirect transfer of State resources through a public body under State control. That is the view of the editors of C. Bellamy and G. *Child's European Community Law of Competition*, 5th ed., 2001 by P.M. Roth, paragraph 19–013.
[76] P. Slotboom, 'State Aid in the Community: A Broad or Narrow Definition?' [1995] ELR 289.
[77] Case 82/77, *Openbaar Ministerie v Van Tiggele*, [1978] ECR 25, paragraph 25.
[78] Ibid., page 52 paragraph 8.
[79] [1993] ECR I-887, paragraph 21.
[80] [1993] ECR I-6185, paragraph 16.

a form of State aid in favour of such businesses. There was no 'direct or indirect transfer of State resources'. The Court reiterated the same language in Joined Cases C-52, C-53, and C-54/97, *Epifanio Viscido, Mauro Scandella, Massimiliano Terragnolo and Others v Ente Poste Italiane*[81] where it reasoned that:

non-application of generally applicable legislation concerning fixed-term employment contracts to a single undertaking does not involve any direct or indirect transfer of State resources to that undertaking.

It follows that a provision of the kind at issue in the main proceedings does not constitute a means of directly or indirectly granting an advantage through State resources.[82]

More recently[83] the Court of Justice concluded that an obligation imposed on private electricity supply undertakings to purchase electricity produced from renewable electricity sources at fixed minimum prices did not involve any direct or indirect transfer of State resources to undertakings which produce that type of electricity. Therefore the allocation of the financial burden arising from that obligation for those private electricity supply undertakings between them and other private undertakings could not constitute a transfer of State resources or State aid.

These cases were so clear that it was not necessary for the Commission, or for the Court of First Instance, to define the criteria by which acts of bodies constitutionally independent of the State are attributable to the latter, for the purposes of Article 87(1) of the Treaty. There is, however, some indication of the appropriate test in the Opinion of Mr Advocate General Van Gerven in Case C-305/89, *Italian Republic v Commission*,[84] when he concurred with the Commission's conclusion that IRI had not acted 'autonomously and independently of the Italian Government'.[85] What is crucial is not to determine whether any message from the State

---

[81] [1998] ECR I-2629, paragraphs 14–15.

[82] More recently, in his Opinion dated 8 May 2001 in Case C-53/00, *Ferring SA v Agence Centrale des Organismes de Sécurité Sociale*, paragraphs 43 to 45, Mr Advocate General Tizzano proceeded on the *premise* that it is necessary to identify a transfer of State resources: '*Sur ce point aussi, le cas d'espèce laisse quelque peu perplexe. Comme on l'a vu, en effet, la loi du 19 décembre 1997 n'a prévu aucun transfert directe de fonds en faveur des grossistes répartiteurs, mais à institué une taxe (à la charge des laboratoires pharmaceutiques) destineé à apporter des nouvelles ressources à l'État. Il y aurait donc lieu d'exclure que l'avantage conféré aux grossistes répartiteurs soit financé au moyen de ressources publiques. Comme Ferring et la Commission, nous ne pensons cependant pas que cette conclusion soit correcte. Comme nous l'avons déjà observé plus haut . . . , la non-imposition de la taxe litigieuse équivaut à accorder un dégrèvement fiscal aux grossistes répartiteurs, lesquels ont en substance été exonérés du paiement de la taxe instituée par la loi du 19 décembre 1997 pour financer la Caisse nationale d'assurance maladie. Cela signifie que les autorités françaises ont en pratique renoncé à percevoir des recettes fiscales au bénéfice des grossistes répartiteurs et leur ont ainsi accordé un avantage économique évident. Il y a donc lieu d'en déduire que cette avantage a été accordeé au moyen des ressources d'État.*'

[83] Case C-379/98, *PreussenElektra SG and Schleswag AG in the presence of Windpark Reussenköge III GmbH and Land Schleswig-Holstein*, [2001] ECR I-2099 paragraphs 59 and 60.

[84] [1991] ECR I-1603 at 1621

[85] Miss Bacon pleads that the proper test is to determine whether the grant is 'government-mandated' rather than 'encouraged': 'State Aids and General Measures', 17 *Yearbook of European Law* (1997) 269 at 282. This appears to be the corollary drawn from her proposition that it is

was sufficiently imperative but whether the body granting the aid was subject to the State's control or, on the other hand, autonomous and independent.

## IV. THE CONDITION OF SPECIFICITY

In the words of Article 87(1) of the EC Treaty, an aid is *inter alia* a measure granted in favour of 'certain undertakings or the production of certain goods'. The Court of Justice has therefore stated repeatedly that one of the essential and defining features of a State aid is the 'condition of specificity': in order to amount to aid, the measure must confer assistance or advantage to specific undertakings.[86] 'According to established case-law, it is necessary to determine whether the [measures in question] ... entail advantages accruing exclusively to certain undertakings or certain sectors and do not therefore fulfil the condition of specificity which constitutes one of the characteristics of the concept of State aid namely the selective character of the measures in question'.[87]

That condition is, of course, satisfied when the beneficiary of the assistance is a certain undertaking, singled out by name[88] or all undertakings in 'a given sector of the economy of a Member State', such as textiles.[89] That is so even though the assistance may have been granted pursuant to national conjunctural policy.[90] The last point follows from the proposition that Article 87(1) draws no distinction according to the causes or aims of aid but defines it in relation to its effects.[91]

It may also be regarded as evident that a measure which essentially confers a benefit on a particular undertaking or sector is not deprived of its quality as 'aid' by reason of the fact that it may have incidental effects on others, such as downstream users of the product on which the advantage is conferred. This appears from the judgment in Case C-169/84, *Société Cdf Chimie Azote et*

sufficient for the aid to be attributable to the State, although involving no transfer of State resources. The difficulties that would be involved in distinguishing between the encouragement and the mandating of aid are sufficiently obvious to cast further doubt on the theory that no transfer of State resources is required.

[86] C-200/97, *Ecotrade v Altiforni e Ferriere di Servola SpA (AFS)*, [1998] ECR I-7907, paragraph 40; Case C-6/97, *Italy v Commission*, [1999] ECR I-2951, paragraph 17.

[87] Case C-75/97, *Belgium v Commission*, [1999] ECR I-3671, paragraph 26.

[88] Case 301/87, *France v Commission*, 'Boussac-Saint-Frères', [1990] ECR I-307.

[89] Case 173/73 *Commission v Italy*, [1974] ECR 709, paragraph 17.

[90] Case 310/84, *Deufil v Commission*, [1987] ECR 901, paragraph 8.

[91] See also Case 248/84, *Germany v Commission*, [1987] ECR 4013 paragraph 18 (aid in the labour market regions of Borken-Bocholt and Siegen in accordance with the guidelines for the granting of investment aid for the improvement of the regional economic structure of the Land North Rhine-Westphalia); Case C-75/97, *Belgium v Commission*, [1999] ECR I-3671, paragraph 6 ('The Belgian legislature defined the economic sectors concerned ... Consequently, the undertakings receiving increased reductions are undertakings operating in sectors such as the extraction of non-energy materials, the chemical industry, the metal-processing industry, the precision instrument industry, the optical instrument industry and other processing industries'); Case 57/86, *Hellenic Republic v Commission*, [1988] ECR 2855 (interest rate on export credits whose effect is to afford export undertakings an economic advantage by reducing the costs incurred by them in respect of sales on the markets in other Member States).

*Fertilisants SA and Société Chimique de la Grande Paroisse SA v Commission*: 'The fact that an undertaking which is not in the ammonia manufacturing industry is charged tariff F does not undermine the finding that it is to that industrial sector that the tariff is essentially intended to apply'.[92]

In a recent case before the Court of First Instance[93] the applicants challenged a Commission Decision holding that the Spanish Government had failed to fulfil its obligations by adopting, without first informing the Commission, the *Plan Renove Industrial* ('PRI'). The latter provided for subsidies towards the purchase of industrial vehicles for natural persons, small and medium-sized enterprises, regional public bodies, and bodies providing local public services. The applicants contended that the PRI was insufficiently selective to amount to State aid because it did not define in advance the specific recipients but set out objective criteria pursuant to which the subsidies might be granted to those who were able to meet them. Rejecting that submission, the Court stated:

information provided by the Kingdom of Spain during the course of the administrative procedure—and which the applicant has not challenged before the Court—confirms that the sole beneficiaries of the PRI were legal persons falling within the 'category of regional public bodies and bodies providing local public services' . . . and 'natural persons or SMEs, covered by the definition laid down in the Community guidelines on State aid for SMEs and the Commission Recommendation of 3 April 1996 concerning the definition of small and medium sized enterprises, engaged in transport for hire-and-reward but also own account transport operations' . . .

It follows from all of the foregoing that the PRI was intended to, and did in fact, benefit, among users of commercial vehicles, only natural persons, SMEs, local and regional public bodies and bodies providing local public services. Other users of vehicles of that type, namely large undertakings, were not eligible under the PRI even when, like the beneficiaries of the PRI, they acquired a new commercial vehicle in place of a used vehicle for the purposes of their transport businesses.

It will not escape attention that in the two last-mentioned cases the Court referred to the State's intention when reaching, or confirming, its conclusion that the aid was sufficiently selective. In both cases, however, it was able to detect the selectivity on the basis of the express terms of the measure authorizing of the grant. More difficult questions arise when the State confers a discretionary power to authorize or grant aid and that power is exercised in favour of specified recipients or sectors.

## A. Exercise of Discretion

The problem was presented in the litigation arising in 1994 from the financial participation of the *Fonds National de l'Emploi* ('FNE') in the implementation

---

[92] [1990] ECR I-3083, paragraph 22.
[93] Case T-55/99, *Confederación Española de Transporte de Mercancías v Commission*, [2000] ECR II-3207, paragraphs 39–48.

of a social plan by the company Kimberly Clark Sopalin.[94] It was contended on behalf of the French Republic that the FNE enjoyed a degree of latitude in the exercise of its functions, which enabled it to determine the circumstances under which it would grant assistance, the beneficiaries, and the amount of assistance to be provided. The Court concluded that in these circumstances, by virtue of its aim and general scheme, the system under which the FNE contributes to measures accompanying social plans is liable to place certain undertakings in a more favourable situation than others and thus to meet the conditions for characterization as aid. In that case it was not the general scheme that satisfied the condition of specificity but its application in individual cases. In the words of Mr Advocate General Jacobs: 'It is clear that FNE's discretion enables it to benefit 'certain' undertakings by agreeing or refusing to enter into agreements, by modifying the level of its contribution or by dispensing the undertaking from its financial participation'.[95]

The issue arose again two years later, in Case C-256/97, *Déménagements-Manutention Transport SA*.[96] The question referred for preliminary ruling in that case was whether measures in the form of payment facilities, granted by the Belgian *Office Nationale de Sécurité Sociale* ('ONSS') amount to aid when they enable a commercial company to retain over a period of at least eight years a proportion of the sums collected from staff and to use them in support of its commercial activities, and the undertaking is unable to obtain the funding under normal market conditions. Mr Advocate General Jacobs took the provisional view that the condition of specificity was satisfied: 'It appears that in the present case the ONSS enjoys a discretionary power to accord facilities for later payment to whichever undertakings and, to a certain extent, on what terms it sees fit: on the assumption that this is correct, therefore, the measures in question cannot be considered as having a general character'. The Court expressed the same conclusion, taking care to articulate what was implicit in the Advocate General's Opinion: it was the function of the national court to determine whether the ONSS enjoyed sufficient discretionary powers to satisfy the condition of specificity.[97]

Likewise in Case C-387/92, *Banco de Crédito Industrial, now Banco Exterior de España v Ayuntamiento de Valencia*,[98] an exemption from taxation granted by Spanish law to public credit institutions was held to be a form of State aid.

---

[94] Case C-241/94 *France v Commission*, [1996] ECR I-4551, paragraphs 23 and 24.
[95] [1996] ECR I-4551, page 4561 paragraph 38.
[96] [1999] ECR I-3913.
[97] The Court stated at paragraphs 27 and 28 of the judgment: '... general measures which do not favour only certain undertakings or the production of only certain goods do not fall within that provision. By contrast, where the body granting financial assistance enjoys a degree of latitude which enables it to choose the beneficiaries or the conditions under which the financial assistance is provided, that assistance cannot be considered to be general in nature. It is for the national court in the main proceedings to determine whether ONSS's power to grant payment facilities is discretionary or not and, if it is not, to establish whether the payment facilities granted by the ONSS are general in nature or whether they favour certain undertakings.' Cf Advocate General's Opinion at paragraph 40.
[98] [1994] ECR I-877.

There was a specific exemption from general taxation in favour of specified institutions.

In its seminal judgment in C-200/97, *Ecotrade v Altiforni e Ferriere di Servola SpA (AFS)*, the Court held that there was a State aid where the Italian Minister of the Interior exonerated a company from the ordinary rules of insolvency in force in that State, his decision being influenced by the Government's aim of preserving the economic activity of the undertaking in the public interest. The condition of specificity, 'which constitutes one of the characteristics of State aid' was satisfied in view of the fact that the Minister exercised a power of discretion in the matter; and did so in favour of a particular category of undertakings, to which the legislation applied.[99]

The sequel was Case C-295/97, *Industrie Aeronautiche e Meccaniche Rinaldo Piaggio SpA v International Factors Italia SpA and Others*,[100] in which the Court of Justice, considering the same legislation as was in issue in *Ecotrade*, observed that it was intended to apply selectively for the benefit of large industrial undertakings in difficulties which owe particularly large debts to certain, mainly public, classes of creditors. It was highly probable that the State or public bodies would be among the principal creditors of the undertaking in question. Moreover, the exercise of the minister's discretion was conditioned by concern to maintain the undertaking's economic activity in the light of national industrial policy considerations. 'In those circumstances, having regard to the class of undertakings covered by the legislation in issue and the scope of the discretion enjoyed by the minister when authorising, in particular, an insolvent undertaking under special administration to continue trading, that legislation meets the condition that it should relate to a specific undertaking, which is one of the defining features of State aid'.

In *Ecotrade* the Court, adopting the reasoning of Mr Advocate General Fenelly, applied the same standard to the identification of aid under Article 4(c) of the ECSC Treaty as to Article 87(1) of the EC Treaty. That was so even though Article 4(c) does not refer to aids liable to distort competition 'by favouring certain undertakings or the production of certain goods'. The Advocate General was surely right to say that:

The essential distinction between general measures and selective aids is made in Article 67(3) of the ECSC Treaty, and should also, in my view, be applied, in the case of

---

[99] 'Furthermore, even if the decisions of the Minister for Industry to place the undertaking in difficulties under special administration and to permit it to continue trading are taken with regard, as far as possible, to the interests of the creditors and, in particular, to the prospects of increasing the undertaking's assets, they are also influenced, as the Italian Government itself has acknowledged in its pleadings and at the hearing, by the concern to maintain the undertaking's economic activity in the light of national industrial policy considerations. In those circumstances, having regard to the class of undertakings covered by the legislation in issue and the scope of the discretion enjoyed by the minister when authorising, in particular, an insolvent undertaking under special administration to continue trading, that legislation meets the condition that it should relate to a specific undertaking, which is one of the defining features of State aid': [1998] ECR I-7907, paragraphs 39–40.

[100] [1999] ECR I-3735.

Article 4(c). The alternative would imply a generalised review of all State regulation in such fields, by reference to the yardstick, not of the normally applicable rules in that State (for these themselves would be the subject-matter of the examination) but, presumably, of the regulations in the other Member States.[101]

It is not necessary to look far to explain the omission from the ECSC Treaty of a reference to 'certain undertakings or the production of certain goods'. The subject-matter of the Treaty itself was a certain sector or sectors; at the time of its conclusion production in those sectors was highly concentrated within the several Member States.

## B. Autonomy and Independence

Where assistance is granted to an undertaking from a financial or other institution over which the State has a certain degree of influence, it may be necessary to determine whether the extent of the State's influence is sufficient to characterize the benefit as an aid granted by the Member State, or through its resources.

The issue arose in the case of the injections made to Alfa Romeo by the Italian public holding companies IRI and Finmeccanica. In a robust Opinion, Mr Advocate General Van Gerven concluded that the activities of those bodies were attributable to the Italian State: 'It is sufficient to point out that the capital of IRI and Finmeccanica is completely controlled by the Italian public authorities; that all the members of the management bodies of IRI and Finmeccanica are appointed by the Italian Government; and finally that IRI and Finmeccanica operate within the framework of directives issued by an interministerial committee'.[102]

The Court of First Instance was equally firm in the case of a capital injection of some FF 20 billion to Air France.[103] It was contended on behalf of the French Republic that the Commission had given a broad interpretation to the phrase 'by a Member State or through State resources', proceeding on the erroneous premise that mere State influence on an economic actor is sufficient to bring a body within Article 87(1) of the Treaty, even if the sums that it invests do not come from public sources. On that basis, the French Republic complained, the Commission had attributed to the State a decision made by the *Caisse des Dépôts et de Consignations-Participations* ('*CDC-P*'), a wholly owned subsidiary of a public body established by statute called the *Caisse des Dépôts et de Consignations* ('the *Caisse*'). Rejecting that contention the Court reasoned as follows:

Even though the subscription to the securities in question was formally carried out by the *CDC-P*, a limited company governed by private law, the applicant has expressly accepted

---

[101] Paragraph 25 of the Opinion.
[102] Case C-305/89, *Italian Republic v Commission*, [1991] ECR I-1603 at 1621.
[103] Case T-358/94, *Compagnie Nationale Air France v Commission*, [1996] ECR II-2109, paragraphs 43 and 57–59.

that this 'investment' was carried out at the decisive instigation of the majority share-holder [the *Caisse*] and with the funds which the *Caisse* placed at its disposal'. It follows that, on any view, the subscription in question is attributable to the *Caisse*. Consequently the applicant's argument that the *CDC-P* is independent is irrelevant.

The *Caisse* was established by the Finance Law of 1816 as an '*établissment spécial*' placed 'under the supervision and guarantee of the legislature'. Its tasks—including the administration of public and private funds composed of compulsory deposits—are governed by statutory and regulatory rules and its Director is appointed by the President of the Republic, the appointment of other directors being a matter for the government.

These factors are sufficient for it to be held that the *Caisse* belongs to the public sector. Although it is subject only to the 'legislature', the legislative power is one of the powers of the State, and thus conduct of the legislature is necessarily imputable to the State.

Nevertheless, the law on this point continues to be clouded by the troublesome decision of the Court of Appeal in *R v Attorney General, ex parte ICI*.[104] In that case the question was 'whether the postulated acceptance by the Revenue, contrary to the provisions of the statute, of an undervalue for the purposes of assessment of Petroleum Revenue Tax, constitutes an aid'. Lord Oliver of Aylmerton there came to the conclusion that if the Commissioners had by error accepted an undervalue, thereby favouring BP in relation to ICI, this would not amount to State aid. He reasoned as follows:

In considering... whether the misapplication of the provisions of the Act was made in good faith and without the intention of granting an aid, the learned judge accepted that it was the effect rather than the intent which is of primary importance. He concluded however: 'When the provisions of Articles [87 and 88] are looked at as a whole, the misapplication of a fiscal provision by Revenue Officials does not appear to be what the language is seeking to deal with. It is an inapt application of State legislation which if properly applied should not give rise to an aid.' The learned judge went on to find that the Commission's task would be impossible if it had to investigate whether fiscal legislation which should not constitute an aid was being administered in such a manner as inadvertently to give rise to an aid. He concluded 'Even if the Revenue were to benefit the oil companies by adopting a wrong valuation, this would not be a matter which could be remedied by reliance upon Article [88(3)] because no aid would be involved. On the footing that the learned judge was confining himself to the inadvertent adoption of a wrong valuation, I for my part, entirely agree with his analysis...'

On the contrary, there appears to be no good reason for distinguishing between the exercise of discretion consistently with national law and the exercise of discretion inconsistently with it, when determining whether this gave rise to an aid favouring certain undertakings or the production of certain goods.[105] Acceptance by the revenue authorities of an undervalue of a taxable item may very well constitute conferral of an advantage in favour the person who would

---

[104] [1987] 1 CMLR 72, *per* Lord Oliver at page 103, paragraphs 93 and 97–100.
[105] See to this effect K.P.E.Lasok, 'State Aids and Remedies under the EEC Treaty', [1986] ECLR 53; T. Sharpe, 'The Role of National Courts in Relation to Community Law of State Aids' in *State Aid: Community Law and Policy*, Band 4, Schriftenreihe der Europäische Rechtsakadamie Trier, 1993 at 93.

otherwise be taxed. In this respect the aim of the official exercising a statutory power of assessment cannot be material.[106] Moreover the difficulties that Lord Oliver claimed to detect in acceptance of the opposite point of view are overstated, bearing in mind, in particular, that Article 87(1) of the EC Treaty does not produce direct effects.[107]

## C. Taxation

In 1992 the Commission published a report of a committee, known by the name of its chairman as the Ruding Committee, proposing action to be taken with a view to harmonization of company taxation in the Community. Although that report received a qualified welcome in the Economic and Social Committee[108] and was commended to the Council by Resolution of the Commission,[109] it proved impossible to attain consensus on the proposals among the Member States, let alone unanimity.[110] Following publication by the Council early in 1998 of a series of Conclusions on harmful tax competition, including a Code of Conduct,[111] the Commission devoted resources to the application to business taxation of the Community's rules on State aid. Late in the same year it published its *Notice on the Application of the State Aid Rules to Measures Relating to Direct Business Taxation.* (At the same time it perseveres in presenting to the Council ambitious proposals for tax coordination by new instruments.[112])

The application of the State aid rules to taxation presents particular difficulties since schemes of taxation tend to be expressed generally while producing effects unequally on taxpayers according to their circumstances. When the income or turnover of companies is subjected to progressive rates of taxation, it might be contended that those who are subjected to lower rates, as a proportion of the whole taxable revenue or turnover, are 'certain undertakings' more favourably treated than others. When duty is charged on a specified product, such as petroleum, it might be contended that producers or users of competing fuels are 'certain undertakings' aided by exoneration from the burden borne by others. The Court of Justice appears to have had this obvious difficulty in

[106] This appears to have been the view taken by the Court of Justice in Case C-480/98, C-480/98, *Spain v Commission (Magafesa)*, [2000] ECR I-8717, paragraph 20 where the Spanish authorities neglected, by inadvertence or otherwise, to secure recovery of the substantial debts owed by the Magafesa company, permitting the latter to continue to trade.

[107] Case 6/64, *Costa v ENEL*, [1964] ECR 585; Case 77/72, *Capolongo v Maya*, [1973] ECR 611; Case 120/73, *Lorenz v Germany*, [1973] ECR 1471; Case 78/76, *Steinike and Weinlig v Germany*, [1977] ECR 595.

[108] OJ 1993 C19/65. See further OJ 1994 C397/53.

[109] OJ 1994 C128/92. See further OJ 1997 C182/59.

[110] See L. Bovenberg, S. Conssen, F.J.G.M. Vanistendael, and J.W.B. Westerbergen, *Harmonisation of Company Taxation in the European Community: Some Comments on the Ruding Committee Report*, 1992.

[111] OJ 1998 C2/1.

[112] See most recently Communication from the Commission to the Council, the European Parliament, and the Economic and Social Committee on Tax Policy in the European Union, OJ 2001 C284/6 (10 October 2001).

mind when, in an early decision, it held that the partial reduction of social charges pertaining to family allowances devolving on employers in the textile sector is a measure intended partially to exempt undertakings of a particular industrial sector from the financial charges arising from the normal application of the general social security system 'without there being any justification for this exemption on the basis of the nature or general scheme of the system'.[113] The clear implication is that differences which arise between those liable to pay a tax or social charge do not amount to aid in favour of those more leniently treated when they are justified on the basis of the nature or general scheme.[114]

The Commission's *Notice on the Application of the State Aid Rules to Measures Relating to Direct Business Taxation* therefore states that:

The main criterion in applying Article [87](1) to a tax measure is...that the measure provides in favour of certain undertakings in a Member State an exception to the application of the tax system. The common system applicable should thus be determined. It must then be examined whether the exception to the system or differentiations within that system are justified 'by the nature or general scheme' of the tax system, that is to say, whether they derive directly from the basic or guiding principles of the tax system in the Member State concerned. If this is the case, then State aid is not involved.[115]

That form of words, frequently restated by the Court,[116] or paraphrased by references to differences which are 'inherent in the system'[117] or arise from its 'logic',[118] postpones the difficulty, but does not resolve it. Which differences between taxpayers are to be tolerated on the ground that they are justified by the nature of the scheme?

In Joined Cases C-72 and C-73/91, *Sloman Neptun Schiffahrts AG v Seebetriebsrat Bodo Ziesemer der Sloman Neptun Schiffahrts AG* the Court of Justice held that the differences between shipping undertakings employing foreign seafarers, on one hand, and other shipping undertakings, on the other, were 'inherent in the system and not a means of granting a particular advantage to the undertakings concerned'.[119] The reasoning is so astringent that it is difficult to

---

[113] Case 173/73 *Commission v Italy*, [1974] ECR 709, paragraph 15. Mr Advocate General Warner, at page 727, distinguished between a general reform of the social security system in a Member State, with the incidental effect of reducing the rate of employers' contributions, which might not be a State aid, and the particular measure in question, which was confined to the textile sector, in view of the particular difficulties confronting it, and 'was, and was intended to be, an aid'.

[114] See P. Farmer and R. Lyal, *EC Tax Law*, 1994, 328–330. For a further illustration of recent litigation on State aid in respect of taxation see Case C-204/97, *Portuguese Republic* supported by *Kingdom of Spain v Commission* supported by *French Republic*, [2001] ECR I-3175 (French aid to producers of liqueur wines and *eau de vie*).

[115] OJ 1998 C384/3.

[116] Opinion of Mr Advocate General Cosmas in Case C-353/95 P, *Tiercé Ladbroke SA v Commission*, [1997] ECR I-7007, paragraph 19; Case C-75/97, *Belgium v Commission*, [1999] ECR I-3671, paragraph 33; Opinion of Mr Advocate General Fenelly in Case C-251/97, *France v Commission*, [1999] ECR I-6639, paragraph 25.

[117] Joined Cases C-72/91 and C-73/91, *Sloman Neptun Schiffahrts AG v Seebetriebsrat Bodo Ziesemer der Sloman Neptun Schiffahrts AG*, [1993] ECR I-887, paragraph 21.

[118] Case C-353/95 P, *Tiercé Ladbroke SA v Commission*, [1997] ECR I-7007, paragraph 35.

[119] [1993] ECR I-887, paragraph 21.

detect the *ratio decidendi*. The Court acknowledged that it was influenced by the object of the German legislature and by the fact that the potential loss of tax revenue, to which the Commission drew attention, were incidental effects of a scheme designed for different purposes: to establish a framework for collective bargaining on behalf of German nationals and residents. Since, however, the characterization of a measure as aid must depends on its effects, we must look further for a correct appreciation of the decision. Assistance is to be found in the Opinion of Mr Advocate General Darmon, who acknowledges candidly the difficulty presented by the facts of the case, citing Conor Quigley's comment that: 'The dividing line between general aids and general measures of economic policy may be rather obscure'.[120]

He concluded nevertheless: 'The only fundamental precondition for the application of Article [87(1)] is that the measure should *constitute a derogation*, by virtue of its actual nature, from the scheme of the general system in which it is set'.[121]

By adding to the word 'derogation' the phrase 'by virtue of its actual nature' the Advocate General must be taken to have directed attention to the consistency of the contested measure with the scheme and general system in which it is set, irrespective of the manner in which the legislation is cast. An amendment to a scheme of taxation, qualifying its application in a certain respect, does not constitute a derogation so long as it is consistent with the scheme.

That approach would be consonant with the Court's judgment in Case C-353/95 P, *Tiercé Ladbroke SA v Commission*.[122] It there held that no State aid was entailed by French tax legislation which treated bets on French races differently from bets on Belgian races. Although bets on horse races abroad were subject to the statutory and fiscal retentions in force in the country where the races were organized, this did not amount to the conferral of a specific advantage on organizers of Belgian races: it was justified for reasons relating to the logic of the totalizator system.

It is also consistent with the judgment of the Court of Appeal in *R v Customs and Excise Commissioners ex parte Lunn Poly and Bishopsgate*.[123] In that case Lord Woolf MR was able to deal briefly with the contention, advanced on behalf of the Commissioners, that the imposition of a higher rate of insurance premium tax on insurance provided by suppliers of certain travel services than on insurance provided by others did not constitute State aid because the higher rate was applied to the generality of taxpayers. The aid given to those paying tax at the lower rate was precisely a derogation from the general scheme. Those whose

---

[120] C. Quigley, 'The Notion of a State Aid in the EEC', 13 *ELRev* (1988) 243 at 245, cited in Opinion of Mr Advocate General Darmon, [1993] ECR I-887, paragraph 50.

[121] Opinion of Mr Advocate General Darmon, [1993] ECR I-887, paragraph 50, emphasis in original.

[122] Case C-353/95 P, *Tiercé Ladbroke SA v Commission*, [1997] ECR I-7007, paragraph 35. See Opinion of Mr Advocate General Cosmas at paragraph 36. The Court itself applied this reasoning in Case C-480/98, *Spain v Commission (Magafesa)*, [2000] ECR I-8717, paragraph 18.

[123] [1999] 1 CMLR 1357, *per* Lord Woolf MR, paragraph 36.

products were subjected to tax at the lower rate were specifically identified. The aid was both specific and selective.[124]

Some extraordinary consequences may enure from the practice of identifying a selective advantage by reference to a derogation from a general scheme. This is illustrated by a Decision of the Commission on the rate of corporation tax in Ireland.[125] With effect from the beginning of 1981 Ireland introduced an effective rate of corporation tax of 10 per cent for the manufacturing sector. This replaced the 'export sales relief' scheme whereby manufacturing companies had been granted relief from corporation tax on profits earned from export sales. The superseded scheme certainly satisfied the condition of specificity: it constituted a derogation from the ordinary rules relating to corporation taxes, in favour of exporters of manufactured goods. The Commission considered at the time that the new system entailed no State aid: it applied without discrimination to all manufacturers subject to corporation tax. Following the entry into force of the Code of Conduct published early in 1998 the Commission examined afresh the law introduced at the beginning of 1981 and concluded that it constituted State aid. That was so because the rate of corporation tax applied to the manufacturing sector was lower than the rate applied to other sectors, notably services. According to the Commission, the distinction between manufacturing and other sectors had been drawn: 'without any justification for this on the basis of the nature or general scheme of the Irish tax system. The reason for the lower rate is rather the attraction of mobile investment in the manufacturing sector to Ireland through the reduction of the sector's costs of production.'

The Commission was apparently correct in stating that in Ireland there is a single 'scheme' of company taxation, under which the manufacturing sector is treated more favourably than others by being subjected to a tax at a lower rate. It is perfectly possible to imagine circumstances, however, in which there might be two entirely separate schemes of taxation, one applied to the service sector and another to the manufacturing sector. If they are sufficiently diverse to defy characterization as a single scheme formally divided into two parts, there would be no scope for concluding that, to the extent that one scheme bears less heavily on those subject to it than another, it confers a form of State aid.

In *R v Commissioners of Customs and Excise ex parte Professional Contractors' Group and Others*,[126] the Court of Appeal was seised of the question whether there is a selective advantage, amounting to aid, when the legislation of a Member State is amended so as to insert anti-avoidance provisions with the stated aim of ensuring 'that people working in what is, in effect, disguised employment

---

[124] The Special Commissioners followed the same reasoning in *Gil Insurance Limited and Others v Commissioners of Customs and Excise*, LON/98/9005–9010, 27 July 2001, paragraphs 204–210, notwithstanding the fact that, in an unusually lengthy Order, they decided to refer to the Court of Justice for preliminary ruling a series of questions on Council Directive 77/388 of 17 May 1977, OJ 1977 L 145/1 on turnover taxes, 'the Sixth Directive', and on Article 87(1) of the EC Treaty.

[125] Decision E/2/98, OJ 1998 C395/19.

[126] [2002] 1 CMLR 46 CA.

will, in practice, pay the same tax and national insurance as someone employed directly'.[127] Under the contested legislation[128] a worker is treated as having received Schedule E income, in any tax year, where he performs services for a client in pursuance of arrangements involving an intermediary in which he has a material interest, or receives a payment directly from the intermediary which is not subject to tax under Schedule E and that payment can reasonably be taken to represent remuneration for services provided to the client, and the circumstances are such that if the services had been provided under a contract directly between the client and the worker, the latter would be regarded for income tax purposes as an employee of the client. At first instance Burton J held that the condition of specificity was not satisfied. The contested legislation applied indiscriminately to workers in all sectors of the economy. Although, like most fiscal legislation, its effects were perceived more in some sectors than others, this was not sufficient to enable him to detect an advantage conferred on 'certain undertakings or the production of certain goods'.[129]

His reasoning is not merely consistent but identical with that of the Commission in its Decision of 17 May 2000 on the amendment of the Danish Statute on Tax Deducted At Source.[130] The purpose was to offer highly paid foreign experts, employed for a limited period in a Danish business or research organization, taxation at a gross fixed rate. Reversing its earlier reasoning on the unamended Scheme, the Commission decided that it did not confer State aid:

The Act itself is not seen as benefiting certain businesses or certain activities, since it applies to experts in all areas and its area of application is not restricted to regions or sectors. The application is assessed on the basis of objectives and non-discriminating criteria without tax authorities being given discriminating powers.

The information from the Danish authorities shows that the scheme is used in more than 150 sectors, by small and medium-sized businesses and by large businesses in the private and public sectors. The reason for the concentration in the office equipment, software and fuel sectors is that salaries are especially high in these sectors... schemes aimed at the high-paid will have considerably greater effect in sectors with high salaries but this still does not constitute State aid.

In the context of this litigation, a 'derogation' from a 'general scheme' may prove elusive. The contested legislation is, and is not, a derogation from such a scheme. It departs from the general principle, previously followed, of treating receipts of companies and individuals separately for the purposes of Schedule E; but does so for the declared purpose of realizing the aim of treating on a basis of equality, under Schedule E, those who are in employment (or would be so but for the interposition of an intermediary, in which they have a sufficient interest, between

---

[127] IR 35 Press Release, Core Bundle 2, p. 533.
[128] The contested legislation is section 60 of and schedule 12 to the Finance Act 2000; sections 75 and 76 of the Welfare Reform and Pensions Act 1999; and the Social Security Contributions (Intermediaries) Regulations 2000.
[129] [2001] EWHC Admin 236.
[130] SG (2000) D/103729.

them and the person for whom they provide services). It may prove necessary for the Court to ask whether the contested legislation has, in the Commission's words, 'any justification...on the basis of the nature or general scheme of the...tax system'.[131]

## V. Propensity to affect trade between Member States

A propensity to affect trade between Member States is not, properly speaking, an aspect of the definition of State aid in Article 87(1) of the EC Treaty. Rather it is the standard by reference to which the compatibility of aid with the common market is to be assessed.[132] Nevertheless it is so closely associated with the part of the definition related to liability to distort competition that the two are commonly considered together.[133]

### A. The Propensity to Affect Trade

Whereas Articles 81 and 82 of the EC Treaty use the expression 'may affect trade between Member States', Article 87 states that aid is incompatible with the common market 'in so far as it affects trade between [those] Member States'. The difference in wording provokes the question whether the same test is to be applied in Article 87 as in Articles 81 and 82, for the purpose of gauging the extent of a propensity to affect trade.

Plainly it is unnecessary to demonstrate an actual effect on intra-Community trade as the foundation of the Commission's power to determine whether it is compatible with the common market. That must be so not only because such incompatibility is semantically separate from the definition of 'aid' but also for practical reasons, to which the Court of First Instance drew attention in the *Alzetta* case.[134] The Commission is not required to demonstrate a real effect on

---

[131] See further M. Quaghebeur, 'A Bridge over Muddled Waters: Coherence in the Case Law of the Court of Justice of the European Communities relating to Discrimination against Non-Resident Tax-payers', [1995–6] *EC Tax Review* 109 and P. Farmer, 'EC Law and Direct Taxation: Some Thoughts on Recent Issues', [1995–6] *EC Tax Review* 101.

[132] A. Götz, 'Subventionsrecht' in M. Dauses, ed., *Handbuch des EG Wirtschaftsrecht*, 1996, para. 29.

[133] C. Bellamy and G. Child's *European Community Law of Competition*, 5th ed., 2001 by P.M. Roth, paragraphs 19–019–19–021. In the words of the Court of First Instance: 'the conditions under which trade between Member States is effected and competition is distorted are as a general rule inextricably linked': Joined Cases T-298, T-312, T-313, T-315, and T-600 to T-607/97, T-1 to T-6/98 and T-23/98, *Mauro Alzetta, and Others supported by Italian Republic v Commission*, 15 June 2000, paragraph 81; 'in matters relating to State aid, the two conditions for the application of Article [87](1) of the Treaty, namely that trade between Member States must be affected and competition distorted, are as a general rule inextricably linked': Case T-288/97, *Regione Autonoma Friuli-Venezia v Commission*, 4 April 2001, paragraph 41.

[134] Joined Cases T-298, T-312, T-313, T-315, and T-600 to T-607/97, T-1 to T-6/98 and T-23/98, *Mauro Alzetta and Others supported by Italian Republic v Commission*, 15 June 2000, paragraphs 76–79.

trade when exercising its power to review existing aid under Article 88(1) and (2) of the Treaty.[135] It could not therefore be required to demonstrate such an effect in the event of a new grant of unnotified aid, for otherwise there would be an advantage conferred on Member States which grant aid in breach of the obligation to notify, to the detriment of those which do notify aid at the planning stage.[136]

What is required is that there should be a propensity to affect trade between Member States. This denotes not a hypothetical conjecture but a foreseeable prospect. In Case C-142/87, *Belgium v Commission, 'Tubemeuse'*,[137] the Court of Justice reasoned that it was 'reasonably foreseeable' that the recipient would redirect its activities towards the internal Community market, so that the grant of aid would affect intra-Community trade. Similarly, in Joined Cases T-447/93 to T-449/93, *Associazone Italiana Tecnico Economica del Cemento and Others v Commission*, as there was no trade between Member States at the time when the aid was disbursed, the Court of First Instance held that the Commission was required, at the time of this payment, to consider 'the foreseeable effects of the aid on competition and intra-Community trade'.[138]

Where there is over-capacity in the particular sector where the aid is granted, a propensity to affect intra-Community trade will often be foreseeable, since the probable effect of the grant is to increase or maintain the market share of the recipient, thereby reducing the chances for undertakings established in other Member States to their products to the market in that Member State.[139] Against this, of course, it may be appropriate to take account of the low level of aid granted; but this raises a particular question of comparison between Article 87(1) of the EC Treaty, on one hand, and Articles 81 and 82 on the other.

## B. Relationship with EC Rules on Agreements, Concerted Practices, and Dominant Positions

It is perhaps the intimacy of the connection between effects on trade and distortion of competition which has provoked debate on the question whether there should be inferred into Article 87 of the EC Treaty a qualification excluding aid granted in very small amounts from the definition, as is done in the case of Articles 81 and 82. Mr Advocate General Capotorti rejected the submission that such a qualification was to be inferred in Case 730/79, *Philip Morris Holland*

---

[135] Case C-387/92, *Banco de Crédito Industrial, now Banco Exterior de España v Ayuntamiento de Valencia*, [1994] ECR I-877, paragraphs 15 and 20.

[136] Case C-301/87, *France v Commission, 'Boussac-Saint-Frères'*, [1990] ECR I-307, paragraphs 32 and 33, and Case T-214/95, *Vlaams Gewest v Commission*, [1998] ECR II-717, paragraph 67.

[137] [1990] ECR I-959 paragraphs 35 to 40.

[138] [1995] ECR II-1971, paragraphs 139 and 141.

[139] Case 102/87, *France v Commission*, [1988] ECR 4067, paragraph 19; Case 303/88, *Italy v Commission*, [1991] ECR I-1433, paragraph 27; and Case C-75/97, *Belgium v Commission*, [1999] ECR I-3671, paragraphs 47–49.

*BV v Commission.*[140] The matter came to the Court of Justice in that case by way of an application made by Philip Morris for the annulment of a Commission Decision requiring the Netherlands to refrain from implementing a proposal to provide aid of some 2.4 million EUA to assist it in transferring production from Eindhoven to Bergen-op-Zoom. The Applicant contended that in assessing an effect on trade between Member States, under the Treaty's rules relating to State aids, the Commission should adopt the same standard as is applied in the rules relating to agreements, decisions, concerted practices, and abuses of dominant positions. It should assess the relevant product market and geographical market to assess how far the aid in question affects relations between competitors. Since it had failed to do so, its Decision should be annulled.

That submission was plausible. The common aim of the 'rules applying to undertakings' and the rules relating to 'aids granted by States' is to eliminate measures which may distort competition and affect trade between Member States.[141] Moreover, the sum to be supplied from public resources in the case amounted to only 3.8 per cent of the capital to be invested: it is far from certain that this had a decisive effect on the recipient's decision to relocate its business. However, neither the Advocate General nor the Court considered that these considerations brought the subsidy outside the scope of what is now Article 87(1). In the most frequently quoted passage of his Opinion, Mr Capotorti stated that: 'It is permissible . . . to start from the presumption that any public aid granted to an undertaking distorts competition—or threatens to do so where the aid is only proposed and not yet granted—unless exceptional circumstances exist (for example the total absence in the common market of products which are identical to or may be substituted for those manufactured by the recipient of the aid)'.[142]

The Court expressed a similar view: when State financial aid strengthens the position of an undertaking compared with others engaged in intra-Community trade, the latter must be regarded as affected by that aid.[143] On this point both

---

[140] [1980] ECR 2671 at 2693. See J. Flynn, Case note, 6 *Eur. L. Rev.* (1981) 208. See further J. Flynn, 'State Aid and Self-Help', 8 *EL Rev.* (1983) 297–312; D.R. Gilmour, 'Enforcement of Community Law by the Commission in the Context of State Aids: The Relationship between Articles 93 and 169 and the Choice of Remedies', 18 *CML Rev.* (1981) 63–77; D. Muffat-Jeandet, 'Contrôle de la Commission des Communautés Européennes sur les aides individuelles autorisés par les états', 19 *Rev. trim. dr. eur.* (1983) 1–37; H.G. Rahn, 'Zum Recht des Ausfundrerstattungen', 26 *Recht der Internationalen Wirtschaft* (1980) 563–569.

[141] Case C-387/92, *Banco de Crédito Industrial SA, now Banco Exterior de España SA v Ayuntamiento de Valencia*, [1994] ECR I-877 at 907 paragraphs 12 and 13.

[142] Case 730/79, *Philip Morris Holland BV v Commission*, [1980] ECR 2671 at 2698. In making that statement the Advocate General acknowledged the precedent set by Mr Advocate General Warner in Case 173/73, *Italy v Commission*, [1974] ECR 709 at 728: 'Once it is clear that the natural consequence of the grant of an aid to industry in a Member State must be to increase that industry's competitiveness *vis-à-vis* its competitors in other Member States, the inference can, in my opinion, properly be drawn that the aid does (or would if introduced) distort competition . . .' Sir Jean-Pierre Warner did not, however, state that there is a presumption that the natural consequence of the grant of an aid to industry must be to increase its competitiveness.

[143] Case 730/79, *Philip Morris Holland BV v Commission*, [1980] ECR 2671 at 2688.

the Opinion and the judgment are expressed with some subtlety. Neither asserted that it is unnecessary for the Commission to assess the effects of State aid on competition, on the premise that such effects are invariably produced.[144] Rather, they took the view that the point of departure is the presumption that public aid distorts competition.

That decision has some importance for the procedure to be followed by the Commission when assessing the compatibility of State aids with the Treaty. Since it must set out in its Decisions the reasons on which they are based, so as to enable the persons concerned to defend their rights,[145] the Commission cannot characterize a form of public intervention as 'aid . . . which distorts or threatens to distort competition' unless it identifies the considerations which led it to conclude that this was the case.[146]

In Case C-142/87, *Belgium v Commission*,[147] the Government contended that as Tubemeuse exported 90 per cent of its production, particularly to the Soviet Union, the aid granted to that undertaking could not distort competition. The Court upheld the Decision, reasoning that in view of the interdependence between the markets on which Community undertakings operate, aid might distort competition, even if the recipient exports most of its production. In view of this fact together with a recession in the industry (which made access to export markets particularly important for the Community's tube-makers generally) the Court concluded that 'the Commission's assessment, made in the contested measure, that the aid granted to Tubemeuse was likely to affect the competitive position of other Community undertakings in the sector concerned and, therefore, to affect trade and distort competition within the meaning of Article [87](1) is adequately reasoned and does not appear to be erroneous'.

Similar reasoning led to a similar result in Case 102/87, *France v Commission*,[148] where the arguments advanced by the applicant government were the mirror image of those advanced in Case C-142/87, *Belgium v Commission*. The

---

[144] This was the construction placed on the judgment by the Commission's *XI Report on Competition Policy* (1981) at page 176.

[145] Article 253 of the EC Treaty and Case 24/62, *Germany v Commission*, [1963] ECR 63 at 69.

[146] 'Even if in certain cases the very circumstances in which the aid is granted are sufficient to show that the aid is capable of affecting trade between Member States and of distorting or threatening to distort competition, the Commission must at least set out those circumstances in the statement of reasons for its decision': Joined Cases 296 and 318/82, *Netherlands and Leeuwarder Papierwarenfabriek v Commission*, [1985] ECR 809 at 824, paragraph 24. The assessment of such circumstances is, of course, distinct from the exercise conducted by the Commission when reviewing aid pursuant to Article 87(3): 'the principle of compensatory justification'. In Case T-106/95, *Fédération Française des Socétés d'Assurances (FFSA) and Others v Commission*, [1997] ECR II 229, paragraph 100, the Court of First Instance, referring to what is now Article 87(3) of the EC Treaty, stated that 'since the present case involves an assessment of complex economic facts, the discretion exercised in evaluating additional public service costs is all the more wide'. Even in the case of Article 87(3), however, the Commission's power is more accurately described as one of appraisal than as one of 'discretion', which is defined by the Oxford English Dictionary as: 'the power to decide within the limits allowed by positive rules of law'.

[147] [1990] ECR I-959 at 1015, paragraph 40.

[148] [1988] ECR 4067 at 4087 paragraph 19.

Government contended that its aid to a brewery did not threaten to distort competition since the recipient did not export its products. The Court concluded:

However, aid to an undertaking may be such as to affect trade between the Member States and distort competition where that undertaking competes with products coming from other Member States, even if it does not itself export its products. Such a situation may exist even if there is no over-capacity in the sector at issue. Where a Member State grants aid to an undertaking, domestic production may for that reason be maintained or increased with the result that, in circumstances such as those found to exist by the Commission, undertakings established in other Member States have less chance of exporting their products to the market in that Member State. Such aid is therefore likely to affect trade between Member States and distort competition.

## C. Absence of Judicial Principle of '*De Minimis*'

Since the presumption that aid is liable to distort competition is not irrefutable, it is of some importance to know whether there applies to State aids the principle *de minimis non curat lex*, in much the same form as it applies to the rules applying to undertakings.[149] There was, at least prior to the Regulation on *de minimis* aid, some basis for the view that it does so. Writing in a personal capacity, a senior Commission official responsible for State aid matters suggested that the application of a *de minimis* rule to State aids is justified by the principle of subsidiarity.[150] The Commission itself stated that: 'below a certain level, aid cannot affect trade between Member States and does not therefore distort competition at Community level'.[151]

In Case 248/84, *Germany v Commission*,[152] the Court annulled a Decision by which the Commission had prohibited the grant of certain regional aid. It stated:

In the case of an aid programme the Commission may confine itself to examining the characteristics of the programme in question in order to determine whether, by reason of the high amounts or percentages of aid, the nature of the investments for which aid is granted or other terms of the programme, it gives an appreciable advantage to recipients in relation to their competitors and is likely to benefit in particular undertakings engaged in trade between Member States.'

Those words, and particularly the reference to 'an appreciable advantage', led one respected commentator to conclude that the Court has sanctioned the application of the *de minimis* principle to State aid cases.[153]

---

[149] Case 5/69, *Völk v Établissements Verwaeke*, [1969] ECR 295; C. Bellamy and G. Child, *Common Market Law of Competition*, 4th ed, 2–105 *et seq*.

[150] EC Treaty, Article 3b; A. Petersen, 'State Aids and European Union: State Aid in the Light of Trade, Competition, Industrial and Cohesion Policies', in I. Harden, *State Aid: Commentary, Law and Policy*, 1993, 20 at 22.

[151] *XXII Report on Competition Policy*, 1993, 79.

[152] [1987] ECR 4013 at 4041 paragraph 18.

[153] R. Barents, 'Recente ontwikkelingen in de rechtspraak over steunmaatregelen', [1988] *Sociaal Economische Wetgeving* 352 at 356.

However, the Court has not done so: at least, not in the manner in which it applies that principle to the rules applicable to undertakings. In Case 248/84, *Germany v Commission*, the Court was concerned with a regional aid programme. To such programmes there applies the presumption that they are liable to distort competition by favouring undertakings or the production of certain goods.[154] It would be possible to rebut the presumption by showing that a particular programme or grant did not give any appreciable advantage to recipients in relation to their competitors; and before making a Decision the Commission must enquire whether the presumption is rebutted. When determining whether the aid distorts or threatens to distort competition, on the other hand, the focus of the Commission's enquiry is not upon the market share of the recipient. Rather, it is to ask whether it is foreseeable that the recipient will gain a real advantage in relation to its competitors, as opposed to one that is merely theoretical.

There is no suggestion in the Court's language that the turnover or market share of the recipients is decisive, as it might be if the same test were to be applied to State aid as to agreements and concerted practices. In 1988 the Commission found aid to be liable to distort competition where the recipient's exports to other Member States amounted to only 0.03 per cent of the Community's trade.[155] Recently the Court of First Instance has stated: 'even aid of a relatively small amount is liable to affect trade between Member States where, as here, there is strong competition in the sector in which the recipient operates'.[156]

The *Guidelines on Aid to Small and Medium-Sized Enterprises*[157] do indeed indicate that save in certain specified sectors the Commission will not normally object to the grant of aid to undertakings whose turnover and work-force fall below certain limits. Those *Guidelines* find their true basis, however, in Article 87(3) of the Treaty,[158] which creates derogations from Article 87(1) particularly in the case of 'aid to facilitate the development of certain economic activities or of certain economic areas, where such aid does not adversely affect trading conditions to an extent contrary to the common interest'. They confirm, therefore, that such aid falls within Article 87(1) as aid which 'distorts or threatens to distort competition' where it has a perceptible effect on intra-Community trade.

There are reasons of principle, as well as practical ones, for rejecting the view that aid of limited intensity falls outside the prohibition contained in Article 87(1) of the Treaty. In the words of Andrew Evans:[159]

Whereas it is in the nature of a market with a competitive structure that conduct of undertakings with a limited effect on this structure is tolerable, the same may be less true

---

[154] See the Opinion of Mr Advocate General Darmon, esp. at p. 4028, where he cited Case 730/79, *Philip Morris Holland BV v Commission*, [1980] ECR 2671, 2693.

[155] Decision 88/174, OJ 1988 L79/29.

[156] Case T-214/95, *Vlaams Gewest v Commission*, [1998] ECR II-717, paragraph 49.

[157] Regulation 70/2001 of 12 January 2001 on the application of Articles 87 and 88 of the EC Treaty to State Aid to Small and Medium-sized Enterprises, OJ 2001 L10/33.

[158] Point 3.3.

[159] *EC Law of State Aid*, 1997, 100.

of State action. For example, in [Case 259/85, *France v Commission*[160]] the Court noted that profit margins in the sector concerned were always very narrow. Hence, the Commission did not exceed the limits of its discretion in taking the view that even relatively little aid would adversely affect trading conditions to an extent contrary to the common interest.

The view that grants of aid are in principle liable to affect trade between Member States even when they are minor, when viewed in their economic context, derives explicit support from the Opinion of Mr Advocate General Lenz in Case 102/87, *France v Commission*,[161] where he referred to the exceptions set out in what are now Article 87(2) and Article 87(3) of the EC Treaty, then continued: 'In the light of those extensive exceptions contained in the aforementioned provisions, it cannot be assumed that there should be further unwritten exceptions to the prohibition of aid. Therefore the argument that minor hindrances to competition and intra-Community trade should be allowed within the framework of Article 92 of the EEC Treaty cannot be upheld.'

That view, it is submitted, is correct. The Court of Justice appears to have confirmed the point, or at any rate lent support to it, in a brief passage in a judgment dated 9 October 2001.[162] It there said: 'the classification of aid corresponds to an objective situation which is continuing and which does not depend on the assessment made at the stage of the initiation of the procedure under Article 88(2) EC'.

This is not to suggest that the intensity of the aid, or the size of the recipient, is necessarily immaterial when determining whether aid is liable to distort competition or may affect trade between Member States. As a matter of legal analysis, however, the size and intensity of the aid are not decisive. The Commission may disallow small grants of aid provided that it explains, in an appropriate case, why it has concluded that the conditions set out in Article 87(1) are satisfied.[163]

## D. Regulation 69/2001 on *De Minimis* Aid

Acknowledgment of that principle fails to resolve the practical problem arising from the overburdening of the Commission with notification of relatively small grants of State aid. From 1992 the Commission announced that aid not amounting to € 50,000 need not be notified in the case of small and medium-sized enterprises;[164] and by its *Notice on the* De Minimis *Rule for State Aid*,[165] published in 1996, it declared that it was no longer necessary for enterprises of

[160] [1987] ECR 4393 at 4419.
[161] [1988] ECR 4067 at 4079.
[162] Case C-400/99, *Italian Republic v Commission*, 9 October 2001, paragraph 58.
[163] The author has expressed elsewhere the views set out in the preceding section of this article. See 'The *Philip Morris*' case in Retrospect, in *Divenire Sociale e Adeguamento del Diritto: Studi in onore di Francesco Capotorti*, 1999, Vol. II, 319 at 321–326.
[164] *Community Guidelines on State Aid for Small and Medium-Sized Enterprises*, OJ 1992 C213/2, point 3.2.
[165] OJ 1996 C68/9.

any size to notify grants of aid amounting to less that € 100,000 over a three-year period, save in the case of 'export aid'.

The source of the Commission's authority to adopt these administratively convenient rules is not easy to locate. The most indulgent view to be taken on that question is, perhaps, that the basis is to be found not on an appreciation of effects on trade between Member States but on propensity to distort competition. Aid falling below the ceiling set in the *Notice* is incapable of distorting competition by favouring certain undertakings or the production of certain goods.

The uncertainties arising from the Commission's decision to relieve itself of overwork by issuance of *Guidelines* and a *Notice* have now been resolved by the Council. On 7 May 1998 that institution made a Regulation[166] authorizing the Commission to set out in a Regulation of its own the threshold under which aid measures are deemed not to meet the criteria of Article 87(1) and therefore do not require to be notified. In that Regulation the Commission declares that: 'It can be established that aid not exceeding a ceiling of €100,000 over any period of three years does not affect trade between Member States and/or does not distort or threaten to distort competition and therefore does not fall under Article 87(1) of the Treaty'.[167]

The period of three years has a mobile character so that for each new grant of *de mininis* aid, the total amount of *de mininis* aid granted during the previous three years needs to be determined. The Regulation does not apply to undertakings in the transport, agriculture, fishery, or ECSC sectors, or to export-related activities or aid contingent on the use of domestic rather than imported goods.

## VI. Conclusion

Recent litigation has drawn attention to a several significant difficulties in the definition of State aid. It has done so at a time when the term is likely to call for more frequent and varied application and when national courts are expected to take an increasing part in the application of the Community's State aid rules, pursuant to Regulation 659/99.[168]

The breadth of the language used in Articles 87 and 88 may be contrasted with the detailed expressions now used in the developed form of the Agreement on which this part of the EC Treaty was based. For example, in place of the cryptic terms 'certain undertakings or the production of certain goods', which form the

---

[166] Council Regulation 994/98 of 7 May 1998 on the Application of Articles 92 and 93 [now 87 and 88] of the Treaty establishing the European Community to Certain Categories of Horizontal State Aid, OJ 1998 L142/1, Article 2.

[167] Commission Regulation 69/2001 of 12 January 2001, OJ 2001 L10/30, fifth paragraph of the Preamble.

[168] Council Regulation 659/99 of 12 March 1999 laying down detailed rules for the application of Article 88 EC, OJ 1999 L83/1.

basis for the principle of selectivity in Community law, Article 2 of the Agreement on Subsidies and Countervailing Measures, forming part of the Uruguay Road, sets out a coherent series of rules by reference to which the selectiveness of a subsidy is to be determined.[169]

In the *Sloman Neptune* case[170] and in *Viscido and Others v Ente Poste Italiane*[171] the Court of Justice had to confront some of the more fundamental issues involved in the ascertainment of the proper scope of 'State aid'. In the second of those cases Mr Advocate General Jacobs, after referring to the first of them and to an article in the *Industrial Law Journal*,[172] asked why it is that Article 87(1) does not cover all labour and other social measures which, by virtue of being selective in their impact, might distort competition and thereby have an equivalent effect to State aid. He responded to his question as follows: 'The answer is perhaps essentially a pragmatic one: to investigate all such regimes would entail an inquiry on the basis of the Treaty alone into the entire social and economic life of a Member State'.[173] His response is one of disarming candour; but it is not, and does not purport to be, a touchstone for the identification of a State aid.

In the absence of precision in the founding Treaty comparable with that now available in the instruments of the World Trade Organization, those whose duty it is to construe Article 87(1) of the EC Treaty have no alternative but to apply what Bishop terms 'rigorous competitive analysis'[174] tempered by the common sense which has led the two European Courts, time and again, to refer to the objective of the contested measure, while maintaining the principle that it is to be characterized by its effects.

---

[169] The Article begins as follows: 'For the purpose of this Agreement, a subsidy shall be deemed to exist if: (a)(1)there is a financial contribution by a government or any public body within the territory of a Member (referred to in this Agreement as 'government'), i.e. where: (i) a government practice involves a direct transfer of funds (e.g. grants, loans, and equity infusion), potential direct transfers of funds or liabilities (e.g. loan guarantees); (ii) government revenue that is otherwise due is foregone or not collected (e.g. fiscal incentives such as tax credits); (iii) a government provides goods or services other than general infrastructure, or purchases goods; (iv) a government makes payments to a funding mechanism, or entrusts or directs a private body to carry out one or more of the type of functions illustrated in (i) to (iii) above which would normally be vested in the government and the practice, in no real sense, differs from practices normally followed by governments; (a) (2) there is any form of income or price support in the sense of Article XVI of GATT 1994; and (b) a benefit is thereby conferred.'

[170] Joined Cases C-72 and C-73/91, *Sloman Neptun Schiffahrts AG v Seebetriebsrat Bodo Ziesemer der Sloman Neptun Schiffahrts AG,* [1993] ECR I-887.

[171] Joined Cases C-52, C-53, and C-54/97, *Epifanio Viscido, Mauro Scandella, Massimiliano Terragnolo and Others v Ente Poste Italiane,* [1998] ECR I-2629.

[172] P. Davies, 'Market Integration and Social Policy in the Court of Justice', [1995] *Ind. LJ* 49.

[173] Joined Cases C-52, C-53, and C-54/97, *Epifanio Viscido, Mauro Scandella, Massimiliano Terragnolo and Others v Ente Poste Italiane,* [1998] ECR I-2629 at 2635, paragraph 16.

[174] S. Bishop, 'The European Commission's Policy Towards State Aid: A Role for Rigorous Competitive Analysis', [1997] 2 *ECLR* 84.

# 2

# Can State Aid Control Learn from Antitrust? The Need for a Greater Role for Competition Analysis under the State Aid Rules

CHRISTIAN AHLBORN and CLAUDIA BERG[1]

Over the last two decades, state aid control has lost its role as the 'ugly duckling' of competition policy. The success of state aid control as a competition policy instrument is reflected both in the increasing number of negative decisions taken by the Commission, which more than doubled over the last decade, and in the extended application to state measures such as state guarantees and taxation. Guidelines and notices have helped to clarify the rules and to limit the political influence in state aid control (although politics clearly still plays an important role).

Despite its success, state aid control has remained analytically distinct from other areas of competition policy. Cross-fertilization (which can be observed, for example, between control of dominance and merger control) does not seem to include state aid control: despite similar substantive standards, state aid control and control of restrictive agreements, for example, have developed distinct analytical frameworks.

One key distinguishing factor between state aid cases on one hand and antitrust and merger control on the other is the role of competition analysis and the extent to which competition analysis is based on an economic assessment of market characteristics.

This chapter describes the development of competition analysis under Article 81 from the early period of legal formalism to the more effects-based approach post-*Delimitis*, highlights the impact of the changes in analysis, and contrasts the development under Article 81 with the current position under state aid rules. The comparison reveals striking similarities between the early approach under Article 81 and the current policy under the state aid provision and suggests that a greater role of an effects-based competition analysis may remedy some of the failings of state aid policy.

[1] The authors would like to thank their colleagues Carin Dahlquist, Jennie Tonnby, and Armin Trafkowski for their help with this chapter.

## I. Competition policy twins: Articles 81 and 87 compared

In order to assess the role of competition analysis in the context of state aid control and its impact on the scope of the policy, it is helpful, as a preliminary step, to look at the development of competition analysis in relation to EC antitrust, to assess how the increasing role of an effects-based analysis has affected the scope of antitrust, and to contrast the antitrust position with that under state aid control. Such a comparison will indicate how an effects-based analysis could also be applied in the area of state aid control and how such an approach would impact on the scope of state aid control. Of the various antitrust instruments, the control of restrictive arrangements under Article 81 is particularly suited as a comparator to state aid control under Article 87 due to the obvious similarities between the two provisions.

First, Articles 81 and 87 share the same substantive structure: both contain a general prohibition. Article 81 prohibits restrictive agreements between independent undertakings, while Article 87 prohibits distortive aid which is financed by Member States or through state resources. Both prohibitions are subject to a number of exemptions which are based on efficiency or public policy considerations. Second, Articles 81 and 87 use similar jurisdictional conditions (namely, an effect on trade between Member States) and substantive tests (i.e. a distortion or restriction of competition). The fact that the jurisdictional and substantive tests are worded slightly differently[2] should not distract from the overall similarities of the two provisions. Finally, both controls have, up to now,[3] relied on *ex ante* pre-notification as an enforcement mechanism.

### A. The Development of Competition Analysis under Article 81

#### 1. Early legal formalism

The early phase of enforcement under Article 81 was characterized by a high degree of legal formalism. The Commission took the position that any restriction of economic freedom between parties to an agreement (such as an exclusive purchase obligation restricting the buyer's freedom to turn to other suppliers) amounted to a restriction of competition within the meaning of Article 81.[4] While German competition law had applied the concept of restriction of eco-

---

[2] Article 81 prohibits '... *all agreements*... *which may affect trade between Member States and which have as their object or effect the prevention, restriction or distortion of competition within the common market*', whereas Article 87 provides that aid '*which distorts or threatens to distort competition by favouring certain undertakings or the production of certain goods shall, insofar as it affects trade between Member States, be incompatible with the common market*'.

[3] On 27 November 2002 the Commission published the final text of its reform of Regulation 17/62 which governed the application and enforcement of Article 81. The reform abolishes the requirement that agreements must be notified in order to obtain an individual exemption, and gives direct effect to Article 81(3).

[4] This position reflected the strong German influence on EC competition policy during that period, in particular of the ordo-liberalism of the Freiburg School: Hawk [1985] 32 *CMLRev* 973, 978; Whish, Competition Law, 4th ed, 18.

nomic freedom to horizontal agreements, EC competition law extended its application also to vertical arrangements. This was in part due to the fact that the Commission and the Court regarded competition law as an instrument for market integration, which at times led to a critical approach towards certain vertical restrictions not merited on pure competition grounds.[5]

The focus on the restriction of economic freedom as the primary analytical tool during the early years of EC competition law had two unfortunate side effects. First, the concept of restriction of freedom was a poor proxy for restrictions of competition and it was vastly over-inclusive: it covered many agreements which did not have a negative impact on competition, not only arrangements which, due to the parties' lack of market power, were incapable of affecting output or prices in the market, but also arrangements which were pro-competitive rather than anti-competitive; for example, selective distribution agreements which facilitated market entry and increased efficiency in distribution. Second, it favoured a formalistic approach: agreements fell within the scope of the general prohibition of Article 81 if they contained certain types of clauses. Not surprisingly, market definition did not play a significant role, nor was it necessary to take a closer look at the market characteristics. There was no meaningful economic analysis to take into account the particular effects of an agreement on competition in the relevant market. Barry Hawk described these failings as a vicious circle of vast over-inclusion, analysis by pigeon-holing, and legal uncertainty.[6]

The Commission's form-based approach brought within the scope of Article 81 a large number of pro-competitive agreements as well as agreements without any effect on competition; it was left to the analysis under Article 81(3) to distinguish between agreements which had a positive and those which had a negative impact on consumer welfare.

At the same time, the Commission did not have a workable intellectual framework to determine the effect of an agreement on consumer welfare and, as a result, turned to an analysis by pigeon-holing, i.e. the application of special rules to different formal legal categories: '*one set of rules applies to exclusive distribution, another to selective distribution, another to franchising, and a chaotic array of considerations apply to distribution arrangements that are not neatly pigeon-holed. Paradoxically, these rules have become enshrined by the very block exemptions that were issued to relieve the harsher aspects of the Commission's rigid application of Article [81(1)].*'[7]

Ultimately, the legal formalism of the Commission led to considerable legal uncertainty and distortion of business practices. Parties to agreements without

---

[5] One of the earliest examples is Joined Cases 56 and 58/64 *Consten and Grundig v Commission* [1966] ECR 299 where the Court held that an exclusive distribution agreement infringed Article 81(1) because it conferred absolute territorial protection.

[6] Barry E Hawk: System Failure: Vertical Restraints and EC Competition Law, *CML Review* 32: 973–989, 1985.

[7] Ibid, at 984.

any detrimental effect on consumer welfare in terms of prices or output had to balance the risk of unenforceability of their agreements against tailoring their arrangements in such a way as to fit into the formalistic categories foreseen by the Commission's exemptions. The Commission's early approach equated to imposing contractual straitjackets upon the parties which were sometimes unnecessary and sometimes thoroughly harmful to effective competition.

## 2. Move towards an economic effects-based analysis

Relatively early on, the Court of Justice took steps to mitigate the Commission's legal formalism. In *Voelk v Vervaecke*[8] it held: '*an agreement falls outside the prohibition in Article [81] when it has only an insignificant effect on the market, taking into account the weak position which the persons concerned have on the market in question*'.[9]

In this case, a German producer of washing machines granted an exclusive distributorship to Vervaecke in Belgium and Luxembourg and guaranteed it absolute territorial protection against parallel imports. It turned out that Voelk's share of the production of washing machines in Germany amounted to less than 1 per cent.

*Voelk v Vervaecke* imposed on the Commission at least a rudimentary effects-based competition analysis. The Commission had to define the relevant market in which the agreement had an impact and to assess some basic market characteristics (in particular, the market shares of the parties to the agreement). Nevertheless, the Commission's analysis under Article 81 remained predominantly form-based, i.e. it continued to focus on the type of agreement (or clause within the agreement) rather than its effect on prices or output.

In light of the deficiencies of legal formalism, the Court continued to push a reluctant Commission towards a more effects-based competition analysis. A major step was the *Delimitis* judgment, which concerned an exclusive purchasing agreement between a brewery and a licensee of a public house. The Court pointed out the imperfect relationship between a restraint of freedom and a restriction of competition and concluded: '*in the present case, it is necessary to analyse the effect of a beer supply agreement, taken together with other contracts of the same type, on the opportunities of the national competitors or those from other Member States to gain access to the market for beer consumption or to increase their market share and, accordingly, the effect on the range of products to the consumer*'.[10]

The shift in the *Delimitis* judgment away from the proxy of restriction of freedom towards a direct assessment of restriction of competition has had a number of important policy implications. It has significantly narrowed the scope of Article 81 and, in particular, has reduced the number of false positives, i.e. the number of pro-competitive agreements held to contravene Article 81(1). By

---

[8] Case 5/69 *Voelk v Vervaecke* [1969] ECR 295.			[9] Ibid, at 302.
[10] Case C-234/89 *Delimitis (Stergios) v Henninger Brau AG* [1991] ECR-I 935, 984.

moving from the formalistic assessment of the nature of the agreement to its effect, there has been far greater emphasis on the issue of market definition and the analysis of market characteristics, such as concentration, barriers to entry, and nature of the products. Most importantly, it has imposed a greater need for more clarity about the meaning of competition (for example, whether it is process-related or outcome-related) as well as the ultimate purpose of competition policy (e.g. open access to market, enhancement of consumer welfare, etc.) and has turned the concept of 'restriction of competition' into an independent element of the analysis.

## B. The Role of Competition Analysis under State Aid Control

The issue of competition analysis in the context of state aid control was first considered in *Philip Morris Holland B.V. v Commission*[11] where the applicant had claimed that, due to *Voelk v Vervaecke*, the Commission was under a duty to carry out an appreciability analysis as under Article 81. The Court, rejecting the applicant's position, held that: '*[w]hen State financial aid strengthens the position of an undertaking compared with other undertakings competing in intra-Community trade, the latter must be regarded as affected by that aid*'.

In *Leeuwarder v Commission*[12] the Court made it clear that the Commission could not merely rely on the presumption that a particular aid distorted competition and affected inter-state trade; it had to provide sufficient reasoning for its finding. According to the Court, this required a description of the relevant market, of the position of the beneficiary to the aid, of the characteristics of the aid, and of the pattern of trade between Member States. As subsequent case law has made clear, this requirement of sufficient reasoning does not, however, require any detailed competition analysis. The Commission's analysis is generally confined to establishing that a particular measure reduces the cost which a company generally has to bear; an example is the decision[13] underlying the judgment in the case of *French Republic v Commission*[14] where the Commission held that the pecuniary assistance intended to restore the beneficiary's financial position reduced the costs which it would normally have incurred to an extent which placed it at an advantage over its competitors.

At times, the Commission also relies on certain additional factors, such as over-capacity or intense competition in the market:

*The Commission also states that there is a world-wide crisis, recession and increased competition in the seamless tubes sector marked by substantial surplus capacity in the producer countries; this is accentuated by the import restrictions imposed by the United States and by the new production capacity in the developing and state-trading countries.*

---

[11] Case C-73/79 *Philip Morris Holland B.V. v Commission* [1980] ECR 2671, 2688.
[12] Case C-296/82, 318/82 *Leeuwarder Papierwarenfabriek B.V. v Commission* [1985] ECR 809.
[13] Commission Decision 87/585/EEC of 15 July 1987 OJ [1987] L352, 42.
[14] Case C-301/87 *French Republic v Commission* [1990] ECR I-307.

*Any advantage to an undertaking in this sector is therefore likely to improve its competitive position in regard to other undertakings.*[15]

In other cases, however, the absence of these additional factors has not affected the outcome of the analysis. In *French Republic v Commission*[16] the French government pointed out that the Commission had neither found over-capacity nor mentioned sales by the beneficiary into other Member States. The Court held that: '*aid to an undertaking may be such as to affect trade between the Member States and distort competition where that undertaking competes with products coming from other Member States, even if it does not itself export its products. Such a situation may exist even if there is no over-capacity in the sector at issue.*'

It strongly suggests that in order to establish a distortion of competition it is generally sufficient that a measure somehow improves the relative market position of the recipient, for example by reducing his cost, given that a gratuitous benefit made available on a selective basis (almost) inevitably leads to an improvement of the recipient's relative market position. As a result, the distortion of competition is not an independent criterion of the analysis and there is no need for an effects-based competition analysis involving an assessment of the market characteristics. Contrary to Article 81, the Court does not require the Commission to establish that the measure had an appreciable effect on competition.

In *Regione Autonoma Friuli-Venezia Giulia v Commission* before the CFI, the applicant claimed that the aid was *de minimis*. According to the applicant, the beneficiaries, the road hauliers from the Venezia Giulia region, held only a marginal share of the market, so the effect of the aid in question was insignificant. The CFI rejected the applicant's arguments.

[I]t is settled case law that even aid of a relatively small amount is liable to affect trade between Member States where there is strong competition in the sector in which the recipient operates...[17]
... Moreover, because of the structure of the market, a feature of which is the presence of a large number of small-scale undertakings in the road haulage sector, even relatively modest aid is liable to strengthen the position of the recipient undertakings as compared with its competitors in intra-Community trade.[18]

Apart from the absence of a *de minimis* threshold, there are strong similarities between the analysis under Article 87 and the approach under Article 81 pre-*Delimitis*, in particular the limited (to non-existent) role of competition analysis. In the same way as agreements containing certain restrictions were deemed to amount to a restriction of competition during the early years of Article 81, a gratuitous benefit made available on a selective basis, improving a beneficiary's

---

[15] Case C-142/87 *Belgium v Commission* [1990] ECR I-959, I-1014.
[16] Case 102/87 *French Republic v Commission* [1988] ECR 4067, 4087.
[17] Case T-288/97 *Regione Autonoma Friuli-Venezia Giulia v Commission* [2001] ECR II-1169, para 44.
[18] Ibid, at para 46.

*relative* market position is equally deemed to restrict competition. In both cases the need for an effects-based analysis is removed.

Not surprisingly, state aid control suffers from the same policy failures which Barry Hawk highlighted in relation to Article 81, namely over-inclusion, legal uncertainty, and analysis by pigeon-holing.

The net of state aid control has been cast increasingly wide. In particular, the criterion of specificity has been expanded to the point where almost any state measure which imposes a burden on state resources arguably falls within the state aid rules. In relation to many of these state measures it is questionable whether the Commission should second-guess the actions of national governments under the state aid rules (ranging from the misapplication of a discretion by the tax authorities to labour and other social measures). As under the early Article 81 regime, however, state aid control currently does not provide any consistent method to distinguish the problematic state aid cases from the unproblematic ones.

The tendency towards over-inclusion and the absence of a workable intellectual framework have led to considerable legal uncertainty. Case law is riddled with inconsistency: a reduction of employers' contributions to promote the employment of women has been held to amount to state aid on the basis that industries with a higher proportion of women benefited more than other industries,[19] while a reduction of the employers' social security contributions for firms which introduced shorter working hours was regarded as a general measure,[20] despite the fact that the introduction of shorter working hours is clearly possible to a greater extent in some industries than others. State aid cases have been decided on the basis of the purpose and intention of a specific measure. Advocate General Jacobs even went so far as to suggest pragmatism as a decision criterion.[21]

Finally, state aid control has developed the analysis by pigeon-holing to an even greater extent than the early phase of Article 81. State aid control is divided into a grid by different 'horizontal' types of aid, such as regional aid, environmental aid, research and development aid, and 'vertical' (i.e. sectoral) types of aid, such as aid for textiles and synthetic fibres, shipbuilding, etc. Each type of aid is subject to its own particular rules and thresholds.

## C. An Article 81-type Analysis as Panacea for State Aid?

The previous subsections have shown that state aid control is currently characterized by legal formalism and the limited role of competition analysis, and suffers from deficiencies (over-inclusion, analysis by pigeon-holing, legal

---

[19] Case 203/82 *Commission v Italy* [1983] ECR 2525.

[20] Commission Decision N232/2001 of 3 July 2001.

[21] 'Advocate General Jacobs [was] asked why it is that Article 87(1) does not cover all labour and other social measures which by virtue of being selective in that impact might distort competition and thereby have an equivalent effect to State aid. He responded to this question as follows: "The answer is perhaps essentially a pragmatic one: to investigate all such regimes would entail an inquiry on the basis of the Treaty alone into the entire social and economic life of a Member State".' See contribution by Plender, above.

uncertainty) similar to the Commission's control of restrictive agreements pre-*Delimitis*. Furthermore, the development of competition analysis under Article 81 showed that increasing the role of competition analysis can remedy at least some of the system's deficiencies.

This indicates that a greater role for competition analysis may help to address certain policy failures in state aid control in the same way as it did in Article 81. It cannot be concluded, however, that exactly the same type of competition analysis as under Article 81 should be used for state aid control. While it seems clear from their wording and position in the structure of the EC Treaty (Title VI and context with Article 3 g) that both Article 81 and Article 87 seek to protect competition, a comparison of the competition issues which arise under the two policies shows that a carbon copy Article 81-type analysis would be inappropriate for state aid control.

*The concept of competition in the context of Article 81 and Article 87*

Article 81 is concerned with the question of whether a particular horizontal or vertical agreement is likely to lead to a market outcome which is harmful from a consumer welfare perspective. In other words, restriction of competition is defined in terms of higher prices, reduced output, lower quality, or reduced innovation. Antitrust analysis under Article 81 therefore focuses on the issue of market power, i.e. the ability to raise prices or reduce output. Agreements between parties which do not have any market power are unlikely to raise competition concerns. This, in turn, has an impact on how markets are defined. Market definition under Article 81 serves as a framework for the assessment of the power to raise prices. The relevant question for the purpose of market definition is therefore whether a hypothetical monopolist supplier of a particular set of products can increase prices by a small but significant amount.[22]

Article 87 is, to some extent, the mirror image of the concerns in respect of restrictive agreements: Article 87 is not concerned with harmful market outcomes, i.e. state aid is not likely to lead to an increase in prices or a restriction of output. On the contrary, if anything, state aid will help companies keep their prices down. The concern is rather that, as a result of the aid, the beneficiary may be able to expand its position relative to his competitors even if his competitors are equally or more efficient. The impact of state aid on consumer welfare is more indirect than that of restrictive agreements under Article 81 as it occurs at the input stage of the production chain rather than at the output stage in the form of for example higher prices. State aid helps inefficient undertakings to survive or expand at the expense of more efficient competitors. This, in turn, leads to productive inefficiency: goods and services are no longer produced at the lowest cost possible. From an economic point of view, society's wealth is wasted. As John Fingleton pointed out, '*this could occur either because the aid reduces the*

---

[22] The 'SSNIP' (Small but Significant Non-transitory Increase in Price) test is set out in paragraph 17 of the Commission Notice on the definition of relevant market for the purposes of Community competition law, 97/C 372/03.

*marginal costs of the [beneficiary] or because it reduces its fixed costs and enables it to continue in the market*.[23] The question, therefore, is: for a given set of outputs, does the state measure negatively affect the use of inputs? Two consequences flow from this difference.

First, the transmission mechanism for the distortion of competition is different for Article 81 and Article 87. Contrary to Article 81, market power is not a prerequisite for a restriction of competition. Second, the way in which markets are defined for the purpose of restrictive agreements and state aid is different. As mentioned above, market definition under Article 81 serves as a framework for the assessment of market power. The ability to raise prices depends on demand-side substitutability away from the product (which alternative products would customers turn to in the event of a price increase?) and supply-side substitutability towards the product (which suppliers would start producing the product in question in the event of a price increase?)

Market definition in the context of state aid control, meanwhile, serves as a framework for the assessment of the impact of state aid. According to John Fingleton: *'The purpose of the market definition here is to identify any competitors that might be negatively affected by [the beneficiary's] increase in output which we may consider to be equivalent to a price reduction'*.[24]

The impact of the aid, in turn, depends on demand-side substitutability towards the products of the beneficiary in the event of a price rise and supply-side substitutability away from the beneficiary's product. The state aid market definition would then provide a framework for a proper economic effects-based analysis. This would ultimately provide answers to the question of harm of a particular state measure in the context of particular market conditions (such as over-capacity in the market, barriers to exit and low profit margins).

## II. Competition Analysis and the Scope of State Aid Control

### A. Towards an Effects-based State Aid Analysis

The starting point of an effects-based state aid analysis is the development of 'distortion of competition' as an independent analytical concept (in much the same way as it became an independent concept under Article 81). This current definition of distortion, namely an improvement of the market position of the beneficiary as a result of the aid, is inappropriate for this purpose. It follows automatically once the other criteria are satisfied and therefore has no life of its own.[25]

---

[23] John Fingleton, Frances Ruane, Vivienne Ryan, A Study of Market Definition in Practice in State Aid Cases in the EU, 14 December 1998.

[24] Ibid.

[25] For example, Commission Decision 87/585/EEC *Boussac* of 15 July 1987: 'The aid in issue in the present case distorts competition because it calculably improved the recipient's financial position [...], thereby giving him a competitive advantage over other manufacturers who have completed or intend to complete similar actions at their own expense'.

Arguably, the standard of improvement of the beneficiary's relative market position is a necessary condition for a 'distortion of competition', as a measure which does not alter the relative market position of the beneficiary cannot distort competition. It is doubtful, however, whether it is also a sufficient condition: not every measure which affects the relative position of competitors in the market should be seen as a 'distortion of competition' in that market. Looking at the purpose of state aid control may help to clarify this point.

## B. The Purpose of State Aid Control

We stated above that state aid control is currently concerned with the potential negative impact which an aid measure may have on competitors to the beneficiary. As with other areas of competition policy, however, the ultimate aim is the protection of competition, not the protection of competitors. This means that state aid control should not necessarily be concerned with any harm to competitors, but only harm to competitors which are at least as efficient. Such understanding of the purpose of state aid dovetails with the underlying rationale of competition policy: effective competition is said to be conducive to productive efficiency, i.e. goods and services are produced at the lowest cost possible. Therefore, state aid raises competition concerns where it allows inefficient undertakings to survive artificially in a competitive market to the detriment of more efficient competitors.

The predatory pricing rules under Article 82 may serve as an example of this point. Under the predatory pricing rule developed in *AKZO*[26] (to which there are one or two infamous exceptions[27]) prices are generally not regarded as predatory as long as they exceed average total cost. The *AKZO* rule does not prevent harm to competitors: a dominant firm which lowers its prices to its average total cost may well harm some of its competitors. The rule is, however, designed to protect equally efficient competitors. Equally efficient competitors will always be able to match a price which equals average total cost and hence cannot be driven out of the market.

The focus on harm to equally efficient competitors is an important qualification for state aid control. The current benchmark of distortion of competition, namely the impact on the relative market position, takes as the reference point the status quo prior to the aid measure in question and assumes that the status quo reflects a level playing field. This assumption is particularly questionable where competing firms operate in different regulatory environments (for example, if they are subject to different tax jurisdictions) and a particular measure (for example, a sectoral tax reduction) applies equally to all firms within the same regulatory environment.

---

[26] Case C-62/86 *AKZO v Commission* [1991] ECR I-3359.
[27] See for example *CEWAL*, OJ 1993 L20/1.

The following sections focus more closely on the three remaining elements of state aid: namely specificity, state resources, and gratuitous benefit (excluding effect on inter-state trade) and assess how a more economic, effects-based analysis impacts on their scope.

## C. The Scope of Specificity

Article 87 states that for a measure to be state aid, it has to be granted in favour of *'certain undertakings or the production of certain goods'*. This specificity criterion is intended to distinguish general measures of economic policy (such as the lowering of interest rates) from more targeted state interventions which are subject to competition policy scrutiny.

### 1. An ever-expanding universe

Over the years, the scope of the specificity condition has increased significantly to catch a range of measures which previously would have been regarded as general. Initially, the Commission concluded specificity on the basis of the express terms of the measure, in particular, where the beneficiary of the aid was one undertaking singled out by name.[28] Where a measure was worded in general terms, and therefore potentially all undertakings were eligible for the aid, the Commission held that specificity was satisfied where it conferred discretionary power upon the national authority to grant benefits to certain undertakings.[29]

The Commission extended the concept of specificity significantly when it included measures which had the effect of benefiting undertakings or sectors to a different degree. A prime example is the case *of Italian Social Security Contributions*,[30] which we discussed above. In this case, as mentioned earlier, the Commission decided to treat as aid the partial taking over by the state of employers' contributions involving a greater reduction in those contributions to the sickness insurance scheme for female employees than for male employees. The effect of this scheme was to favour certain Italian industries employing large numbers of female employees, namely the textile, footwear, and leather industries. The Commission concluded that the scheme amounted to state aid in favour of these industries.

Since Advocate General Darmon's opinion in *Sloman Neptun*, a key factor in determining the specificity criterion (in certain cases) has been whether a state measure *'constitutes a derogation, by virtue of its actual nature, from the scheme of the general system in which it is set'*.[31] Advocate General Darmon was well

---

[28] Commission Decision *Boussac-Saint Frères*, 87/585/EEC of 15 July 1987.

[29] See for example Case C-241/94 *France v Commission* (*'Kimberly-Clark'*) [1996] ECR I-4551, I-4576.

[30] Commission Decision 80/932/EEC of 15 September 1980 concerning the partial take-over by the State of employers' contributions to sickness insurance schemes in Italy.

[31] Opinion of Advocate General Darmon of 17 March 1992 in Joined Cases C-72/91 and C-73/91 *Sloman Neptun*, para 50.

aware of the legal uncertainty involved in the hazy concept of derogation. He attempted to make it more clear by emphasizing that '*a measure constitutes a derogation where it does not apply to all the undertakings or all the sectors of industry which, in view of the nature of the scheme, would be capable of benefiting from it*'.[32] The inherent difficulty of this approach lies obviously in defining what constitutes a general rule and a derogation.

The inherently hazy distinction between 'general rule' and 'exception' was further blurred by the Commission in the *Irish Corporation Tax* case.[33] In 1980 Ireland introduced a dual rate of corporation tax: 10 per cent for the manufacturing sectors and 45 per cent for other sectors of the economy. At the time of the introduction of the system, the Commission had taken the view that it did not satisfy the specificity condition as the measure applied to all manufacturers without discrimination. In 1990 the Irish government decided to continue the 10 per cent corporation tax until 2010. The Commission re-examined the tax measure and, this time, came to the opposite conclusion. It held that the measure imposed a lower rate of tax on manufacturing companies than those in other sectors without any justification for this on the basis of the nature or general scheme of the Irish tax system.

While the Commission presented the tax rate for the manufacturing industry as a favourable exemption to the general tax rate for the other sectors, the tax rate for the non-manufacturing sectors could also be viewed as being an unfavourable exception to the general tax provisions for the manufacturing industry. Specificity has consequently become synonymous with unjustified discrimination. Basically, this often means that where the state measure does not apply across the board to all undertakings in every sector and in every region of a Member State, it is at present likely to be held specific.

The Commission took a very similar line in its notice on the application of state aid rules to measures relating to direct business taxation.[34] This notice draws on earlier case law regarding specificity and makes the following distinctions between general tax measures and specific tax measures. First, a tax measure provides an advantage in favour of certain undertakings if it constitutes an exception to the application of the general tax system; second, it is clear from the wording of the EC Treaty that a tax measure under which the main effect is to promote one or more sectors of activity constitutes aid. Third, a tax measure may be specific where it confers discretionary power upon the tax authorities, in particular where exercise of discretionary power goes beyond the simple management of tax revenue by referral to objective criteria (see Commission Decision *Kimberly-Clark*[35]). However, as far as administrative rulings merely contain

---

[32] Opinion of Advocate General Darmon of 17 March 1992 in Joined Cases C-72/91 and C-73/91 *Sloman Neptun*, para 58.

[33] Commission Decision E/2/98 *Ireland* of 18 December 1998.

[34] OJ 1998 C 384/3, Commission notice on the application of the State aid rules to measures relating to direct business taxation.

[35] Commission Decision SG(94)D/8907 of 27 June 1994.

an interpretation of general rules, they do not give rise to a presumption of aid. Finally, the derogation may be justified by the *'nature or general scheme'* of the system. Despite its selective character, a tax measure does not constitute state aid where its *'economic rationale makes it necessary to the functioning and effectiveness of the tax system'*, or where it is *'inherent in the logic of the tax system'*.[36] Also, some exceptions may be justified by objective differences between taxpayers.

## 2. The problem of non-discrimination

The expansive interpretation of specificity has turned state aid control into a broad rule against unjustified discrimination through state measures, which is at the heart of many of the problems of state aid control.

First, the application of specificity in its widest interpretation barely leaves any scope for general measures. As M.J. Sussman has put it, *'no government benefit is used by every citizen, all accrue to specific sectors. For example, paved roads are mainly used only by vehicle drivers ... '*[37] Given that most state measures apply unevenly across sectors or firms (along the lines of *Commission v Italy*[38]) state aid control has been transformed into a control mechanism for any state measure which happens to impact negatively on state resources.

Second, there is no clear guidance as to the criteria which determine whether any discrimination is justified. Not surprisingly, in light of the limited resources available to the Commission, the definition of specificity (and the enforcement of the state aid rules) has followed a random path: contrast, for example, *Commission v Italy*,[39] discussed above, where there was a reduction in contributions to the sickness insurance scheme for female employees, with a case regarding Belgian legislation,[40] which provided for a reduction of employers' social security contributions for firms which introduced shorter working hours. Both measures clearly have an unequal impact across sectors: in the *Commission v Italy*[41] case, the measure was held to be specific on the basis that it favoured certain Italian industries employing large numbers of female employees; the measure in the Belgian case, on the other hand, was regarded as a general measure as it applied automatically to all firms in Belgium, and all workers whether in the private or public sector. The distinction is hard to justify.

Third, there is no link between the concept of unjustified discrimination and distortion of competition. In other words, it is hard to reconcile this wide definition with an effects-based competition policy.

Having opened Pandora's box by turning specificity into a form of discrimination, the concept of justification becomes central to the definition of state aid. It requires criteria which enable the Commission to distinguish unjustified

---

[36] Ibid.
[37] Countervailing Duties and the Specificity Test: an Alternative Approach to the Definition of Bounty or Grant, Law and Policy in International Business, 1986, vol. 18, p. 475.
[38] Case 203/82, *Commission v Italy* [1983] ECR 2525.
[39] Ibid.
[40] Commission Decision N232/2001 *Belgique* of 3 July 2001.
[41] N 38 above.

measures, such as the *Irish Corporation Tax* case[42] (where the Irish government was aiming at mobile investors) from justified measures, such as the *Sloman Neptun* case, where the ECJ held that '*the system at issue does not seek, through its object and general structure, to create an advantage which would constitute an additional burden for the state, but only to alter in favour of shipping undertakings the framework within which contractual relations are formed between those undertakings and their employees*'.[43] This entails the risk of the Commission making value judgements about national policies where it should exclusively be concerned with the anti-competitive effects of a measure.

Finally, losing the concept of 'justification' for the definition of state aid blurs the distinction between the assessment of a measure as aid under Article 87(1) and the applicability of an exemption under Article 87(3), as it is not clear what distinguishes justifications at the definition stage from justifications at the exemption stage.

### 3. The solution of causality

A first step towards an effects-based approach would be the requirement of a causal link between discrimination and the impact on competition. This contrasts with the current position where a measure which unduly discriminates and simultaneously affects competition (even if the effects on competition are not the result of the discrimination) satisfies the specificity condition.

The earlier *Commission v Italy*[44] case may help to illustrate the point: according to the Commission and the Court, a measure reducing the employers' contributions to the sickness insurance scheme for female employees favoured Italian industries employing large numbers of female employees to the detriment of Italian industries that did not. The impact on competition, however, occurred largely between the favoured Italian industries and their foreign counterparts. An impact on competition would only be a direct consequence of the discrimination to the extent that industries with a large percentage of female employees were in competition with industries with a smaller percentage of female employees. (See Table 2.1.)

Contrast this case with the German *Landesbanken* case[45] where the discrimination between *Landesbanken* and other banks in terms of state guarantees was the cause of competition concerns. (See Table 2.2.)

The causality requirement would narrow the scope of state aid, moving away from a general policy of discrimination, de-emphasizing the criterion of justification. It would provide a consistent approach for the narrowing in scope, reducing the current inconsistencies.

[42] Commission Decision E/2/98 *Ireland* of 18 December 1998.
[43] Joined Cases C-72/91 and 73/91 *Firma Sloman Neptun Schiffahrts AG v Seebetriebsrat Bodo Ziesemer der Sloman Neptun Schiffahrts AG* [1993] ECR-I 887, I-934.
[44] N 38 above.
[45] Commission press release IP/01/665 of 8 May 2001 '*Commission requests Germany to bring state guarantees for public banks into line with EC law*'.

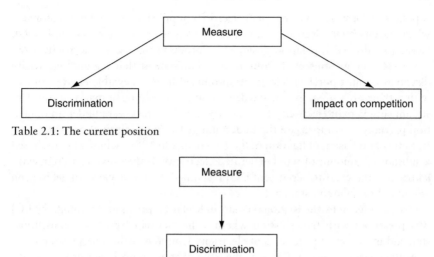

Table 2.1: The current position

Table 2.2: The solution of causality

## D. The Scope of State Resources

Article 87(1) applies only to aid *'granted by a Member State'* or *'through state resources'*. It is clear from case law that the concept of 'state' embraces regional or local authorities and other public bodies set up by the state.[46] Moreover, the criterion covers revenue forgone as a result of exemptions from taxation and other compulsory levies.[47]

### 1. The problem of private funds under state control

In the past, a particular controversy has arisen as to whether (and to what extent) the concept of state resources should cover measures which are financed through resources of private undertakings in circumstances where the state exercises control over the private resources.

This issue arose in the recent case of *PreussenElektra*.[48] PreussenElektra was a large electricity producer in Germany, which supplied electricity to municipal utility companies, large industrial undertakings, and regional electricity

---

[46] Case C-5/89 *BUG-Alutechnik* [1990] ECR I-3437; Case 177/78 *Pigs and Bacon Commission v McCarren* [1979] ECR 2161.

[47] Bellamy & Child, European Community Law of Competition (Fifth Edition), 19–015; Rose M. D'Sa, European Community Law on State Aid, 3–22.

[48] Case C-379/98 *PreussenElektra v Schleswag* [2001] ECR I-2099.

suppliers. Schleswag was a regional electricity supplier servicing final customers, which purchased its electricity almost exclusively from PreussenElektra. In 1990 Germany adopted legislation designed to promote the use of electricity from renewable energy sources. It contained a requirement that regional electricity distributors must purchase electricity produced from renewable energy sources within their area of supply at fixed minimum prices (above market rate). Upstream suppliers of electricity from conventional sources were under an obligation partially to compensate the undertakings for the additional costs resulting from this purchasing obligation of 'green' energy. In 1998, Schleswag purchased a substantial amount of wind-generated electricity. It then invoiced PreussenElektra for these costs. PreussenElektra claimed that the German legislation amounted to unlawful state aid.

Upon a referral by the Regional Court in Kiel for a preliminary ruling, the ECJ was presented with the question whether the German legislation constituted state aid in favour of producers of electricity from renewable energy sources.

At the heart of this question was the issue of state control over private funds, i.e. whether, as a result of the state interference, PreussenElektra's funds should be regarded as state resources within the meaning of Article 87(1) of the EC Treaty (see Tables 2.3 and 2.4).

PreussenElektra claimed that the mechanism established by German law amounted to state aid. Their claim was based on two arguments. First, they argued that financing through state resources should not be a constituting

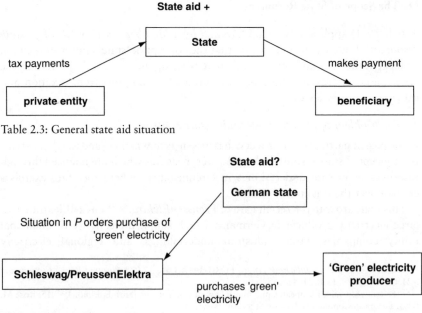

Table 2.3: General state aid situation

Table 2.4: State aid?

element of state aid; it should be sufficient that the measure was the result of action by a Member State regardless of whether the aid was privately or publicly funded. In the alternative, they argued that the German legislation had the effect of converting private resources into public resources. They likened the system established by the German legislation to a parafiscal charge: the legislation had '*effects analogous to the ones produced by taxation in that it withdraws resources from the private sphere and commits them to a public interest objective*'.[49]

## 2. State resources as a constituting element

Advocate General Jacobs (followed by the Court) expressly rejected the more extensive interpretation of Article 87(1) that any measure by a Member State, irrespective of its funding, be it public or private, was capable of being state aid. In contrast to positions previously taken by the Commission as well as by several Advocates General[50], Jacobs took the view that financing through state resources was a necessary element of the concept of state aid. He argued, among others, that a more narrow reading of Article 87(1) was more natural and raised fewer consequential problems. Specifically, it provided more legal certainty since a broader interpretation of the concept of state resources would bring more legislation within the scope of the state aid rules and would then have to be assessed in light of the notoriously difficult selectivity criterion. He also ran the systematic argument that if the state aid rules were to cover systematically measures financed from private resources, one would expect to find in Article 87 rules dealing with their procedural rights and obligations.

With his strict interpretation, Advocate General Jacobs followed the earlier Court cases of *van Tiggele*[51] and *Sloman Neptun*.[52]

---

[49] Ibid., Opinion Jacobs AG, para 163.

[50] For example, in Case 57/86 *Greece v Commission* [1988] ECR 2855, 2867, Advocate General Slynn clearly stated that '*it is enough to satisfy Article [87(1)] that aid is paid at the State's behest or by order of a body empowered to that effect by the State, as is the Bank of Greece, even if it is not financed directly through state resources*'. In Joined Cases 213/81 to 215/81 *Norddeutsches Vieh-und Fleischkontor, Norddeutsches Vieh-und Fleischkontor v Balm* [1982] ECR 3583, Advocate General VerLoren van Themaat mentioned, as a possible example of state aid financed from private resources, the reduced rates which Member States might require private electricity companies to grant to certain undertakings.

[51] Case 82/77 *Openbaar Ministerie v Van Tiggele* [1978] ECR 25, 41. *Van Tiggele* concerned a measure fixing a minimum retail price for gin. The ECJ held that such a measure could not constitute state aid since the advantages which public intervention entailed for the distributors were '*not granted directly or indirectly through state resources*' given that the gin was paid for by private consumers.

[52] N 43 above. In the case of *Sloman Neptun*, German law enabled certain German-registered shipping undertakings to subject seafarers, who were nationals of non-EU Member States, to rates of pay and working conditions less favourable than those applicable to German nationals. The Court confirmed the formula enshrined in *van Tiggele* and emphasized that '*advantages granted from resources other than those of the State do not fall within the scope of the provisions in question*'. On that basis, it concluded that the German registration did not lead to the creation of an advantage which was granted through state resources. The only possible burden for the state was a potential loss in tax resources. This, however, was '*inherent in the system and not a means of granting a particular advantage to the undertakings concerned*'.

### 3. Control and the definition of state resources

Having stated that financing though state resources was a necessary condition of Article 87, Advocate General Jacobs also rejected the view that PreussenElektra's funds had been converted into state resources as a result of the mandatory mechanism established by German law. He based his rejection on the grounds that PreussenElektra's funds never were and never would be at the disposal of the German government (unlike, for example, in the case of parafiscal charges). In his view, these funds never left the private sphere and therefore could not be regarded as state resources. This is a rather formalistic approach which fails to address the underlying competition concerns raised by state-controlled private funds, which are redirected onto a private beneficiary.

In *PreussenElektra* the state determines simultaneously where to take funds and how to allocate them while in general state aid cases this decision is taken sequentially. The central question is whether this is a valid distinction to treat the latter as state aid but not the former, in other words whether, by virtue of the purpose of state aid law, directly allocated funds as in *PreussenElektra* should be caught by Article 87(1). If this is so, the appropriate legal 'box', i.e. whether the scope of Article 87(1) should be expanded to include private funds under State control, or whether such funds are converted into state resources, seems less meaningful.

The claim that where private funds are under the direct control of the state, they should be caught by the state aid rules (because they should be regarded as state resources) deserves further consideration.

As mentioned earlier, it is clear from the wording of Article 87(1) and a systematic interpretation of the EC Treaty (Article 3(g) and the position of Article 87(1) in Title VI) that the state aid rules are designed to protect competition. The specific competition risk of state aid is that the aid helps inefficient high-cost companies to 'compete' with their more efficient low-cost competitors. Goods and services will not be produced at the lowest cost possible. This loss in productive efficiency is detrimental to society's wealth, usually not directly as consumers do not pay a higher price but indirectly through the taxpayer who funds inefficient high-cost production for the subsidized goods. As a result, competition is distorted.

A state measure which confers a specific advantage on certain undertakings does not become less anti-competitive when it is financed through private, rather than public, resources. On the contrary, the distortion may even be greater where the cost of the measure is borne by competitors of the aided undertakings and not by the general public. In this situation, the state not only helps inefficient undertakings (i.e. those unable to produce electricity at a competitive rate) but, by virtue of its public powers, forces their more efficient competition (e.g. PreussenElektra) to finance these inefficiencies from their budget. In fact, this is a potentially very serious distortion of competition which should not, *a priori*, escape the Commission's regulatory control.

The current approach to the concept of state resources, however, invites Member States to circumvent the application of the state aid rules. Instead of distributing the money themselves, they can devise schemes (e.g. in the telecommunications sector) for compulsory direct payments from one individual to another, which thus conveniently avoid state aid control by the Commission.

The introduction of an effects-based competition analysis into state aid control can help avoid attempts to elude the grasp of Article 87, because it is concerned not with legal form of a funding but with underlying economic substance. In the same way in which one analyses whether companies are private or public by looking at underlying economic reality rather than legal form,[53] one should also have to look at the underlying economic reality in respect of the scope of the concept of state resources. The economic essence of private funds lies in the ability of the owner to determine how to deal with these assets, i.e. the ability to control these funds.

The fact that a private owner's control may be restricted to some extent does not *per se* alter the private nature of the funds. A prime example is the case of *van Tiggele*:[54] where a public authority fixes the minimum retail price for a product, the decision whether or not to buy the product (and thus to confer an economic advantage on the retailer) lies entirely with the consumer. He is in control of his funds. The state's control relates merely to the question of how much the consumer would have to spend on, in this case, gin. This is insufficient control to convert private funds into public funds.

Where, however, as in the case of *PreussenElektra*, private control is completely removed and replaced with state control, the underlying funds are no longer private because the 'owner' has lost control. In *PreussenElektra*, clearly, the German state controlled the funds of both regional electricity distributors such as Schleswag and upstream electricity suppliers such as PreussenElektra. These companies were under a statutory obligation to make payments to certain other undertakings: in the case of Schleswag, to the producers of electricity from renewable sources and, in the case of PreussenElektra, to Schleswag as compensation. The German state had the power to decide whether or not to make the payment, to whom the money should go, and how much should be given to the beneficiary. Therefore, the funds in issue came from state resources and the German legislation did constitute state aid to the benefit of producers of 'green' energy.

The underlying logic of an effects-based analysis was in fact applied by the ECJ in the recent case of *Stardust Marine*.[55] In this case the ECJ annulled a Commission decision that capital injections made by two subsidiaries of the bank Crédit Lyonnais to the French pleasure boat chartering firm, Stardust Marine, amounted to state aid. Contrary to the Commission's position, the ECJ held that the mere fact that Crédit Lyonnais and its subsidiaries were owned and controlled by the French state was not in itself sufficient to turn their funds into state resources.

[53] Case C-188/89 *Foster v British Gas* [1990] ECR I-3313.    [54] N 51 above.
[55] Case C-482/99 *France v Commission (Stardust Marine)* [2002] ECR-I 4397.

Additionally, it was necessary to determine whether the specific measure conferring funds to a beneficiary was imputable to the French state.

Conversely, in a scenario such as *PreussenElektra*,[56] the mere fact that funds are formally owned by a private undertaking must not be sufficient to exclude these funds from the scope of state aid control. It ought also be necessary to determine whether or not the decision to confer these funds to a beneficiary was indeed taken by the private undertaking or rather by the state, by forcing the private company to enter into certain contracts or make payments. In the first case, the funds do not constitute state resources. In the second, however (i.e. where this decision is taken by public authorities) private funds do constitute state resources within the meaning of state aid control.

## E. The Scope of Aid ('Gratuitous Benefit')

The European Courts have defined the concept of aid as '*a direct or indirect economic advantage on the beneficiary, which it would not have obtained in the ordinary course of business*',[57] i.e. a 'gratuitous benefit'. Examples are straightforward subsidies, such as the payment of DM 145 million by the government of the German Land of Saxony to Volkswagen,[58] or transactions at under-value, such as loans at a rate of interest below normal commercial rates[59] or sales of goods at a reduced price.[60]

Article 87(1) provides that aid can be awarded 'in any form whatsoever'. In light of this wording, it is not surprising that the concept of 'aid' is the one area of state aid law where an effects-based competition analysis already plays a key role. In the early 1960s the Court adopted an effects-based approach to bring 'negative benefits' within the concept of aid: '*The concept of an aid encompasses not only positive benefits [...] but also interventions which [...] mitigate the charges which are normally included in the budget of an undertaking and which, without therefore being subsidies in the strict sense of the word, are of the same character and have the same effect*'(emphasis added).[61] Examples of the mitigation of charges include certain tax exemptions, reduction in social security contributions, and reduction in customs duties.

The definition of aid measures by reference to their effects also means that the aim of the state in granting the aid is in principle not relevant.[62] It is therefore no defence for a Member State to claim that the measure in question pursues economic or financial objectives or other policy objectives such as the promotion

---

[56] N 48 above.
[57] Case 61/79 *Amministrazione delle Finanze dello Stato v Denkavit Italiana Srl* [1980] ECR 1205, 1228.
[58] Commission Press Release, DN: IP/01/1016, 18 July 2001.
[59] Case T-16/96 *Cityflyer Express Ltd. v Commission* [1998] ECR II-757.
[60] Case 40/75 *Produits Bertrand v Commission* [1976] ECR 1.
[61] Case 30/59 *Steenkolenmijnen v High Authority* [1961] ECR 19; Case C-39/94, *SFEI v LaPoste and Others* [1996] ECR I-3547, I-3595.
[62] N 57 above.

of investment, the struggle against unemployment, or the protection of the environment.[63] Having said that, the motivation of the state may become relevant when assessing whether aid is justified under Article 87(2) or (3).

## 1. *The controversy surrounding the public service obligation*

The concept of a public service obligation involves '*obligations which the undertaking in question, if it were considering its own commercial interests, would not assume or would not assume to the same extent or under the same conditions*'.[64] An example is the delivery of letters in remote areas of the national territory. In relation to public service obligations, the state has the choice either to carry out the activity itself or to outsource it to a private company and provide a form of compensation. In the latter event, the issue of state aid arises.

The question of whether (and to what extent) state compensation for the performance of public service obligation under Article 87(1) (or in the language of Article 86(2), services of general economic interest) can be regarded as a 'gratuitous advantage' has led to inconsistent answers by the Court of Justice.[65] Two lines of cases have been developed by the Court which cannot be reconciled.

The compensation approach (from *ADBHU* to *Ferring*). One line of cases is what may be called the compensation approach, according to which state funding for services of general interest amounts to state aid only if, and to the extent that, the compensation provided by the Member State exceeds adequate remuneration for the services provided by the undertaking.

Initially, the Court followed the compensation approach. The *ADBHU* case[66] involved the granting of indemnities not exceeding the actual yearly costs to waste oil disposal undertakings as compensation for the obligations imposed on them to collect and dispose of waste oil. The Court held that the indemnities did not constitute state aid as they were appropriate consideration for the waste disposal services.

Whilst the Court did not adapt this approach in subsequent cases, it recently reverted to the compensation approach in its decision in *Ferring*.[67] French law required wholesale distributors of medicinal products to keep a permanent stock sufficient to ensure their ability to provide a month's supply to the pharmacies in their distribution area. The distributors also had to guarantee delivery of all medicines within twenty-four hours of receiving the relevant order. The French government subsequently introduced a tax measure requiring pharmaceutical laboratories to pay a contribution of 2.5 per cent of their pre-tax turnover derived from wholesale sales of medicinal products to pharmacies in France.

---

[63] See, for example, in respect of promotion of investment, Joined Cases T-346, T-347/99 and T-348/99 *Basque Regions v Commission* [2002] ECR, para 54.

[64] Council Regulation (EEC) No 1191/69 of 26 June 1969 on action by Member States concerning the obligations inherent in the concept of a public service in transport by rail, road, and inland waterway, Article 2(1).

[65] See also the contribution by Rizza, below.

[66] Case 240/83 *Procureur de la République v ADBHU* [1985] ECR 531, 550.

[67] Case C-53/00 *Ferring SA v ACOSS* [2001] ECR I-9067.

The contribution was not levied on sales of medicinal products by wholesale distributors in order to restore the competitive balance between wholesale distributors and pharmaceutical laboratories which had been regarded as distorted by the wholesale distributors' aforementioned duty of public service. Ferring, a pharmaceutical laboratory subject to the tax on direct sales, sought reimbursement of the sums paid on the grounds that restricting the tax to sales by pharmaceutical laboratories amounted to the grant of (unlawful) state aid to wholesale distributors. The French Social Security Court asked the ECJ by way of a preliminary ruling whether the tax on direct sales constituted state aid within the meaning of Article 87(1).

The Court concluded that where the (tax) advantages merely offset the costs of providing a public service they did not need to be assessed under Article 86(2), implying that they might not amount to state aid at all. The Court also seemed to mean that if the (tax) advantages had exceeded the additional costs of providing the public service, there would have been state aid which must be assessed under Article 86(2).

The formal approach (from *Banco Exterior de España* to *Altmark Trans*). The second line of cases follows a more formal approach. Under the formal approach, any state compensation granted to an undertaking for the performance of a public service obligation is viewed as aid. This aid may, in certain circumstances, be justified under Article 86(2), particularly if the funding complies with the principle of proportionality. The formal approach was followed by the ECJ in *Banco Exterior de España*[68] and later by Advocate General Léger in the pending *Altmark Trans* case.[69]

In *Banco Exterior de España* the Court held that a Spanish tax exemption for public banks constituted existing state aid and that as long as the Commission had not found the aid to be incompatible with the common market, it was not necessary to examine whether and to what extent the aid in question was capable of falling outside the prohibition of Article [87 EC] by virtue of Article [86(2) EC]. Under the compensation approach the Court would have had to examine first whether public service obligations of Spanish public banks precluded the exemption from being state aid.

In the case of *Altmark Trans*,[70] a German provision required a licence to be obtained for the purpose of transporting passengers by regular service vehicles. The granting of the licence was dependent on the applicant's financial status and reliability. The competent local German authority issued a licence to the company, Altmark Trans, for the operation of a regional bus line, and rejected an application by the competing bus operator, NVGA. NVGA lodged an appeal

---

[68] Case C-387/92 *Banco Exterior de España* [1994] ECR I-877.
[69] Case C-280/00 *Altmark Trans GmbH and Regierungspraesidium Magdeburg v Nahverkehrsgesellschaft Altmark GmbH, interested party: Oberbundesanwalt beim Bundesverwaltungsgericht* (currently pending before the European Court of Justice), Advocate General Léger delivered Opinions on 19 March 2002 and on 14 January 2003.
[70] Ibid.

against the decision, claiming that the award of the licence was unlawful since Altmark Trans could not survive financially without receiving public subsidies which, in NVGA's view, were incompatible with European state aid rules.

The German Federal Administrative Court referred the question whether state subsidies granted to offset the cost of public service obligations (here imposed on an undertaking operating a passenger transport service) constituted state aid under Article 87(1) to the Court of Justice. In his Opinion of 19 March 2002, Advocate General Léger expressly invited the Court of Justice to revise its recent *Ferring*[71] judgment. In his second Opinion in the same case[72] he confirmed that this remained his approach.

He presented two main arguments in support of this view. First, in his view the effects-based approach would deprive Article 86(2) of any role in the control of state aid cases on the basis that (a) where state support offset the costs of a public service obligation, Article 87(1) would not apply; and (b) where state support exceeded the costs of a public service obligation, it could not be justified under Article 86(2) as the aid would be disproportionate. Second, the compensation approach would remove the control of the public financing of public services carried out by private undertakings from the Commission.

## 2. Effects-based analysis

In *GEMO*, Advocate General Jacobs, whilst calling for a compromise between the formal and compensation approach, *de facto* rejected the formal approach in favour of a modified approach.[73] He suggested that where the financing measure is clearly intended as a *quid pro quo* for a clearly defined public service obligation, there is no aid. For this to apply there must be a clear and manifest link between the state financing measure and the clearly defined public service obligation. He referred to public services contracts awarded after a public procurement procedure as the clearest example: one contract defines the obligations of the undertaking entrusted with the operation of a public service and the remuneration it will receive in return. The public procurement process ensures that the undertaking is merely adequately compensated, including a reasonable profit margin, for the extra costs it incurs as a result of operating an unprofitable service.

The compensation approach as presented by Advocate General Jacobs in his opinion in *GEMO* is in line with an effects-based analysis: a cost-reflective compensation (i.e. where compensation covers no more than incremental costs) for a clearly defined public service suggests that the recipients of the compensation does not receive a 'gratuitous' advantage, i.e. does not receive an economic advantage over his competitors. In other words, the company in question should be largely in the same position as if it had not provided the

---

[71] N 67 above.
[72] N 69 above.
[73] Case C-126/01 *Ministre de l'Economie, des Finances et de l'Industrie v GEMO SA*, pending, Advocate General Jacobs delivered his opinion on 30 April 2002, paras 117 *et seq*.

service, which would not result in a negative effect on competition between the service provider and his competitors.

Advocate General Léger's argument in favour of the more formal approach in the *Altmark Trans* case are not convincing. First, Article 86(2) may still play a role in the state aid context where it cannot be determined with certainty that a compensation will always match exactly the costs for providing a public service but where the particular form of compensation is nevertheless the most efficient way of ensuring that the public service obligation is discharged. In addition, Article 86(2) continues to play an important role in other areas of competition law. Advocate General Léger's second argument speaks more in favour of the state aid approach than against it. Furthermore, removing the control of public financing out of the Commission's scope if there is merely an adequate compensation allows the Commission to allocate its resources cost-effectively. Where the beneficiary receives no undue economic advantage there is no competition problem, and thus no room for regulatory supervision. It is inefficient to bother the Commission with no-issue cases simply for the sake of extensive regulatory control and to waste time and money in administrative proceedings where it is evident from the outset that the Commission will clear the 'aid'.

The circumstances in which Advocate General Jacobs requests a modification of the effects-based approach are precisely the circumstances in which state funding is not appropriate compensation for the public service obligation. This involves the cases where it is not clear from the outset that the state funding is intended as a *quid pro quo* for a clearly defined public service obligation. *Ferring*[74] was such a borderline case since the tax advantage in favour of the medicinal wholesale distributors was granted in a separate law after the public service obligation had been imposed. However, the obligations imposed were clearly defined; moreover, it was clear from the circumstances of the case (e.g. *travaux préparatoires*) that there was a strong link between the tax exemption and these obligations.

In *Banco Exterior de España*[75] the conditions of the compensation approach were not met. The Court of Justice was correct in holding that the tax exemption granted to all public banks amounted to state aid as there was clearly no link between the tax exemption and the alleged public service obligation of administering the public provision of credit. Such a link is necessary to establish whether or not a state measure confers an undue economic advantage. When identifying the economic advantage, a comparison must be made between the beneficiary's financial situation before and after the adoption of the state measure. If, as a result of the measure, the beneficiary's situation has improved, the measure clearly constitutes an economic advantage. If it has not improved, the measure does not constitute an economic advantage. The fact that the beneficiary is exposed to other unrelated economic disadvantages is irrelevant. Only where a measure links state funding with a public service obligation will the measure as a

---

[74] N 67 above.        [75] N 68 above.

whole not confer an advantage (provided the funds net out the costs of the public service obligation).

## III. Conclusion

State aid control currently suffers from many of the same defects which characterized the early phases of anti-trust enforcement, in particular in relation to Article 81, namely a vast over-inclusion, analysis by pigeon-holing, and legal uncertainty.

In our view, the developments of competition policy under Article 81 may provide important lessons for state aid policy. Two aspects in particular deserve to be highlighted. The first is to transform the concept 'restriction of competition' into an independent element of Article 87(1), in other words an element which has to be established independently of 'gratuitous benefit', 'state resource', and 'specificity'. While Article 81 cannot be used as a carbon-copy for state aid control, many of the same questions arise. In particular, the question of the goal of state aid control will have to be addressed in more detail. In parallel, the other elements of Article 87(1) should be interpreted more in line with an effects-based competition policy. This will require a considerable narrowing of the concept of specificity.

# 3

# The Financial Assistance Granted by Member States to Undertakings Entrusted with the Operation of a Service of General Economic Interest

CESARE RIZZA*

## I. Introduction

The interplay between the Treaty rules on State aid and Article 86(2) EC lies at the heart of the stimulating debate, involving the regulated industries in which incumbent operators are granted financial advantages by public authorities in order to compensate for the cost of public service constraints imposed upon them, which has been developing following the judgments delivered by the EC courts of law in the *FFSA* and '*CELF*' cases[1]. The Court of First Instance (the 'CFI') and at least implicitly the Court of Justice (the 'ECJ') initially endorsed the principle, which A.G. Jacobs dubbed the 'State aid approach' in his recent Opinion in the pending *GEMO* Case,[2] that the fact that an aid measure is merely

---

* An edited version of this article was first published in 9 *Colum. J. Eur. L.* (2003).

[1] See Cases T-106/95, *FFSA and Others/Commission* [1997] ECR II-229, C-174/97 P, *FFSA and Others/Commission*, [1998] ECR I-1303, and C-332/98, *France/Commission* ('CELF') [2000] ECR I-4833. See also C.Quigley & A.M. Collins, *EC State Aid Law and Policy* (2003), pp. 45–48, 118–20, and A. Alexis, Services publics et aides d'État: Évolution récente de la jurisprudence, in *Rev. D. Union Eur.*, n, 1/2002, p. 63. The Treaty rules on State aid are applicable to the grant of public financial assistance to providers of general interest services only to the extent that such services constitute economic activities and the measure in question is liable to affect trade between Member States [cf., e.g., Commission Decisions of August 23, 2002 (State aid C 54/2000—Italy; Tax measures for banks and banking foundations), as reported in Commission press release IP/02/1231, holding that certain fiscal measures introduced in 1998 and 1999 in favour of banking foundations fell outside of the scope of State aid control rules because the foundations' activity of managing own assets and using the proceeds to donate grants to not-for-profit entities was not an economic activity; and of December 21, 2000 (State aid N 258/2000—Germany; Leisure pool Dorsten), as reported in Commission press release IP/00/1509, holding that an annual DM 2 million grant for the private operator of an open-air swimming pool in Dorsten (North Rhine-Westphalia) did not constitute State aid because, since the amenity was used by the inhabitants of the town and the surrounding area and its catchment area did not extend to the nearby Netherlands, there was practically no likelihood of intra-Community trade being affected. Germany had notified the Commission of the measure, seeking at the same time a Commission decision to approve the subsidy in question without opening proceedings]. Moreover, according to the *de minimis* rule, State support of up to a total of €100,000 per undertaking over any three year period does not constitute State aid within the meaning of the EC Treaty.

[2] See Opinion delivered on April 30, 2002, in Case C-126/01, not yet reported in the ECR, para 95.

intended to offset the extra costs of the public service tasks assumed by the beneficiary undertaking cannot prevent it from being classified as aid within the meaning of Article 87 EC, although that factor may be taken into account when considering whether the measure in question is 'shielded' from application of the EC Treaty competition rules pursuant to Article 86(2) EC.[3] This principle, however, was called into question by the recent *Ferring* ruling,[4] in which the ECJ (Sixth Chamber) held that aid exists only if and to the extent that the economic advantage which State funding of a SGEI provides to the beneficiary undertaking(s) exceeds appropriate remuneration for the cost of providing the service in question (the 'compensation approach' in A.G. Jacobs' language). It may seem ironic that the ECJ's redefinition of the boundaries of Articles 87 and 86(2) EC comes precisely at a time when the Commission, reacting to the concerns expressed by the European Council in 2000 and in 2001, has committed itself to exploring ways of increasing legal certainty in the sphere of services of general interest.[5]

It is extremely important to note at the outset of this analysis that the debate between the 'State aid approach' and the 'compensation approach' is not merely

[3] Under Article 90(2) of the EC Treaty (now Art. 86(2) EC), undertakings entrusted with the operation of a service of general economic interest (a 'SGEI') or having the character of a revenue-producing monopoly shall be subject to the rules contained in the Treaty in so far as the application of such rules does not obstruct the performance, in law or in fact, of the particular tasks assigned to them. The development of trade must not be affected to such an extent as would be contrary to the interests of the Community. According to the ECJ, this provision 'seeks to reconcile the Member States' interest in using certain undertakings, in particular in the public sector, as an instrument of economic or fiscal policy with the Community's interest in ensuring compliance with the rules on competition and the preservation of the unity of the common market. The Member States' interest being so defined, they cannot be precluded, when defining the services of general economic interest which they entrust to certain undertakings, from taking account of objectives pertaining to their national policy or from endeavouring to attain them by means of obligations and constraints which they impose on such undertakings' (see, e.g., Case C-157/94 *Commission v Netherlands* [1997] ECR I-5699, paras. 39 and 40). The application of Article 86(2) relies on a factual assessment of economic data and must be done by the judge dealing with the facts in the case at issue. The burden of proof of the justification (necessity and proportionality) of the restriction of competition at issue rests upon the party invoking the derogation (*id.*, at para. 51). Pursuant to the case law, loss of income is not in itself sufficient to satisfy the requirement to show obstruction for the purposes of Art. 86(2) (see, e.g., Case 41/83, *Italy v. Commission (British Telecommunications)* [1985] ECR 873, para. 33). However, it is not necessary to show that the financial balance or economic viability of an undertaking entrusted with a general interest mission would be threatened, but simply that it would not be possible for it to perform the particular tasks entrusted to it, defined by reference to the obligations and constraints to which it is subject (see, e.g., Case C-157/94, *Commission v. Netherlands (Electricity Imports)* [1997] ECR I-5699, para. 52).

[4] Case C-53/00 *Ferring* [2001] ECR I-9067.

[5] To that end, the Commission has begun studying, in close cooperation with the Member States, the possibility of adopting a regulation for the block exemption of certain State aid in the area of services of general interest. It has also committed itself to adopting a number of other measures to increase transparency [see Communication on services of general interest in Europe (OJ 2001 C 17/4), Report to the Laeken European Council on services of general interest (Oct. 17, 2001; COM (2001) 598 final), and Report to the Seville European Council on the status of work on the guidelines for State aid and services of general economic interest (June 6, 2002; COM (2002) 280 final)], including a Green Paper, to be published in the first quarter of 2003, discussing the option of adopting a framework directive [see Communication on the status of work on the examination of a proposal for a framework directive on services of general interest (Dec. 4, 2002; COM (2002) 689 final)].

theoretical but has material practical consequences: if, on the basis of the 'compensation approach', a given financing measure does not constitute State aid, the measure falls outside the scope of the State aid rules and need not be notified to the Commission. Moreover, a national court can decide that a State measure intended to offset the cost of public service obligations involves no State aid without having to wait for an assessment by the Commission of the compatibility of the measure.[6] Under the 'State aid approach' the same measure would constitute State aid which must be notified in advance to the Commission, the derogation in Article 86(2) EC being subject to the same procedural regime as the exemptions in Article 87(2) and (3) EC.

## II. THE 'STATE AID APPROACH' IN *FFSA*

*FFSA*[7] concerned alleged State aid offered to La Poste, which was the subject matter of a complaint by an association representing several insurance companies. These companies complained that the French public postal operator was afforded several benefits at the time of its reorganization and incorporation, in particular a series of *reductions in relation to local and communal taxation*. In proceedings for judicial review of a 1995 Commission's decision,[8] the CFI observed that Article 90(2) of the EC Treaty required the Commission to take into account the demands inherent in the particular tasks of the undertakings concerned and that public authorities of the Member States may in some instances have a degree of latitude in regulating certain matters, such as, in the case before it, the organization of public services in the postal sector. Therefore in

---

[6] Art. 87 EC gives the Commission *exclusive* competence Commission to exempt State aid (see Case 78/79 *Steinike & Weinlig* [1977] ECR 595, para 9). National courts, on the other hand, are involved in the system of reviewing State aid through the direct effect of the prohibition on implementation of planned aid laid down in the last sentence of Art. 88(3) of the EC Treaty : 'The Member State concerned shall not put its proposed measures into effect until [the procedure provided for in para 2] has resulted in a final decision'). According to case law, national courts must offer to individuals the certain prospect that all appropriate conclusions will be drawn from an infringement of that provision, in accordance with their national law, as regards the validity of measures giving effect to the aid, the recovery of financial support granted in disregard of that provision, and possible interim measures. While the national courts may, for that purpose, determine whether or not a national measure should be classified as State aid within the meaning of the Treaty, they may not rule on the compatibility of aid measures with the common market, the final determination on that matter being in the exclusive jurisdiction of the Commission, subject to review by the ECJ (see, in particular, Case C-143/99 *Adria-Wien Pipeline* [2001] ECR I-8365, paras 26–29).

[7] Case T-106/95, *FFSA and others/Commission* [1997] ECR II-229, paras 99–101, 167–178, 185–193.

[8] See Commission Decision of February 8, 1995 relating to a procedure implementing Article 88 of the EC Treaty (State aid NN 135/92: competitive activities of the French Post Office), OJ 262/11. The Commission decided not to treat these tax concessions as State aid as they were worth less than the economic burden of the public service constraints, such as the obligation to ensure post offices throughout the national territory and to operate at a loss a number of services imposed by the postal administration's terms of reference, principally as part of the government's regional development policy. The applicants sought the annulment of the Commission's decision and questioned the manner in which the Commission calculated additional public service costs.

its assessment of additional public service costs, involving an examination of complex economic facts, the Commission enjoyed even wider discretion than normal in applying the Treaty competition rules, comparable to that which it exercises when applying Article 87(3) EC.[9] This assessment of complex economic facts was one in which the reviewing court was limited to establishing the accuracy of the facts used and ensuring that there were no manifest errors in the assessment. The CFI found no such error and upheld the validity of the decision.[10]

With respect to the Article 90(2) assessment of the tax concession granted to La Poste, the CFI endorsed the 'State aid approach' that the ECJ had adopted in its 1994 judgment in *Banco Exterior de España*.[11] The CFI referred to the established case law, under which Article 87 EC is construed to mean that there are no distinctions among causes or aims of the State interventions, the latter being defined in relation to their *effects on competition*. Since the measure in question, although not taking the form of a transfer of State resources, placed an undertaking such as La Poste in a more favourable financial situation than other taxpayers, including the companies represented by the applicants, it constituted State aid. However, since Article 86(2) could be relied upon, *although the aid involved was still State aid within the meaning of Article 87*, the effect of the competition rules could nevertheless be curtailed. Therefore a prohibition on giving effect to new aid, inferred from Articles 87 and 88(2) and (3) read together,[12] could be declared inapplicable to the tax concession in question granted to La Poste.[13]

With respect to the applicants' claim that Article 86(2) EC had been incorrectly applied because, *inter alia*, the aid was unnecessary, the CFI held that the *Corbeau* case law, concerning the application of Articles 85 and 86 of the EC Treaty (now Articles 81 and 82 EC) could be applied, *mutatis mutandis*,

---

[9] It is well established case law that, the basic prohibition of State aid being neither absolute nor unconditional, Art. 88(3) EC confers on the Commission a wide discretion to declare certain aid compatible with the common market by way of derogation from the general prohibition laid down in Art. 87(1) thereof (see, e.g., Case C-143/99, note 6 above, para 30).

[10] Interestingly, in so doing it rejected the argument that the Commission wrongfully failed to take into account 'opportunity costs' (i.e., the real economic cost which La Poste was to pay in order to maintain its unprofitable post offices and thus fulfil its public service task) as well as the reference margin below which a post office should be closed. The CFI took the view that, '[i]n the absence of Community rules governing the matter, the Commission is not entitled to rule on the basis of public service tasks assigned to the public operator, such as the level of costs linked to that service, or the expediency of the political choices made in this regard by the national authorities, or La Poste's economic efficiency in the sector reserved to it' (para 108 of the judgment).

[11] See Case C-387/92 [1994] ECR I-877, para 21.

[12] Art. 88(3) EC requires prior notification to the Commission of any plans to grant or alter aids, at sufficient notice to enable it to submit its comments. The aid may not be implemented until the Commission adopts a decision to authorize it. Pursuant to the directly effective provision of Art. 88(3), an individual may seek relief in a domestic court of the Member State where aid has been granted without notification or put into effect before the Commission's decision.

[13] See also Case C-174/97 P, note 1 above, paras 31–34. The CFI later confirmed its endorsement of the 'State aid approach' in Case T-46/97 *Sociedade Independente de Comunicação/Commission (SIC)* [2000] ECR II-2125, para 84.

to the field of State aid.[14] As a result, the grant of State aid may, under Article 86(2), escape the prohibition in Article 87, provided that: (i) the sole purpose of the aid in question is to offset the extra costs incurred in performing the particular task assigned to the undertaking entrusted with the operation of a SGEI and (ii) the grant of the aid is necessary in order for that undertaking to be able to perform its public service obligations under conditions of economic equilibrium. According to the CFI, determining whether the aid is necessary entails a general assessment of the economic conditions under which the undertaking in question performs the activities *in the reserved sector*, without taking into account any of the benefits it may accrue in the sectors open to competition.

In *FFSA* the CFI also rejected the applicants' argument based on a cross-subsidy between the tax concession applicable in the reserved sector and non-reserved activities, such as insurance. According to the applicants, because La Poste had no analytical accounts it was impossible to determine that the tax concession in question did not, contrary to Community law, benefit its competitive activities. The CFI ruled that, where the aid concerned is granted to an undertaking of the kind contemplated in Article 86(2), the possibility of a cross-subsidy taking place is excluded to the extent to which the aid in question remains lower than the extra costs generated by the particular task attributed to the aid beneficiary. The CFI emphasized the Commission's discretion in deciding on the most appropriate method for ensuring that the competitive activities of La Poste did not receive any cross-subsidy and held that, on the basis of the information available at the time, the Commission could be reasonably certain of its conclusions.

## III. THE 'COMPENSATION APPROACH'

The question of the assessment of public funding of services of general interest under State aid control rules was resolved differently in the ECJ's *Ferring* judgment.[15] The ECJ was persuaded by A.G. Tizzano's Opinion of 8 May

---

[14] In Case C-320/91 *Corbeau* [1993] ECR I-2533, paras 13–19, the ECJ established a connection between the first two paragraphs of Art. 86 EC: a national measure contrary to Community law pursuant to Art. 86(1) may nonetheless be deemed compatible with the EC Treaty if it satisfies the conditions laid down in Art. 86(2), in particular if it is necessary to ensure the performance of the task of general economic interest assigned to the undertaking in question. Therefore, the exclusion of competition in a given market from potential new entrants who would tend to engage in 'cream-skimming', i.e. concentrating on the economically profitable businesses included within the universal service, can be justified in order to enable the monopoly to offset less profitable sectors against the profitable sectors and thus to perform its services of general interest in economically acceptable conditions (the ECJ, however, took the view that the exclusion of competition cannot be justified with respect to specific services severable from the SGEI in question if provision of those services does not compromise the latter's economic equilibrium).

[15] Case C-53/00, note 4 above, paras 21–33. See A. Bartosch, 'The relationship between public procurement and State aid surveillance: The toughest standard applies?', 39 *CML Rev.* (2002), 551–576, at 564–566. The *Ferring* case concerned the compatibility with Arts. 87, 86(2),

2001, and held that, *leaving aside the public service obligations in question*, not assessing on wholesale distributors the tax on direct sales was equal to granting them a tax exemption. The economic advantage conferred upon wholesale distributors was granted through the use of State resources and made wholesale distributors better able to compete with the other distribution channel. However, according to the ECJ, provided that the tax corresponded to the additional costs actually incurred by wholesale distributors in discharging their public service obligations, not assessing them for the tax could be regarded as compensation (in the French original, *contrepartie*) for the services they provided. Moreover, provided there was the necessary equivalence between the exemption and the extra costs incurred (it was left to the referring court to decide whether that condition was satisfied) wholesale distributors would not be enjoying any real advantage for the purposes of Article 87(1) EC. That being the case, the tax would not amount to State aid because its only effect would be to put distributors and laboratories on an equal footing.[16] By contrast, should the referring court conclude that the advantage for wholesale distributors in not being assessed for the tax on direct sales of medicines *exceeded the additional costs* that they bore in discharging their public service obligations, such advantage would not be covered by the derogation laid down in Article 86(2) EC. The ECJ held that, in those circumstances, the advantage in question could not be regarded as necessary to enable the undertakings concerned to carry out the particular tasks assigned to them, and therefore would not be covered by such derogation.

and 49 EC of French legislation imposing upon pharmaceutical laboratories a contribution to the financing of the national health insurance scheme, levied on direct wholesale sales of branded pharmaceuticals to pharmacies. This tax on direct sales was designed to rebalance the conditions of competition between laboratories and wholesale distributors of medicines, only the latter being required under French law to have permanently at their disposal an adequate stock of medicinal preparations, sufficient to meet the requirements of a specific geographical area, and to deliver requested supplies within a very short time over the whole of that area, so that the population as a whole would be guaranteed an adequate supply of medicines at all times.

[16] As authority for this proposition, the ECJ referred to its judgment in Case 240/83, *Association de Défense des Brûleurs d'Huiles Usagées (ADBHU)* [1985] ECR 531, para 18), a preliminary ruling on the interpretation and validity of Council Directive No 75/439/EEC on the disposal of waste oils. In *ADBHU* the ECJ was asked to assess the validity of Arts. 13 and 14 of said Directive, which provided that any undertakings required by the State to collect and/or dispose of waste oils offered to them by holders could be granted indemnities (not exceeding annual uncovered costs actually recorded by each such undertaking, taking into account a reasonable profit) for the services rendered. The ECJ held that those indemnities were consistent with the requirements of free competition, and in particular with the Treaty rules on State aid control. In one short *attendu*, the ECJ reasoned that, as the Commission and the Council had rightly argued in their observations, the indemnities at issue did not constitute State aid but rather consideration for the services performed by the collection or disposal undertakings. In my view, in *ADBHU* the ECJ confined itself to assessing whether the factors cited by the referring judge affected the validity of the Directive at issue, and did not provide a full-blown interpretation of the notion of State aid under Art. 87. Moreover, in 1985 when the judgment was rendered, the possible interaction between Arts. 87 and 86(2) EC was virtually unexplored territory. Therefore, the reference to the *ADBHU* judgment in *Ferring* appears to be rather daring, bearing in mind the extreme caution usually exercised by the ECJ in its citation of authorities.

Although the ECJ did not expressly rule on the question of whether failure to give advance notice of the State measures at issue to the Commission could be deemed to render the aid illegal based on Article 88(3) EC, the ECJ's approach in *Ferring* implies that the Article 86(2) derogation could be applied directly by national courts to the granting of new State financing to providers of services of general interest, *including any unnotified measure*. This would represent a development in the law since the EC courts have not ruled to date on the question of whether national courts can validly apply the provision in question so as to permit the grant of State aid, bypassing the Commission's review.[17]

## V. FERRING'S SHORTCOMINGS

I believe that the ECJ's approach in *Ferring* results in essence in negating the function and relevance of Article 86(2) EC with respect to the control of State aid because it entails that any advantage conferred upon undertakings through public resources in order to compensate them for the cost of public service obligations be necessarily characterized, depending on its relative magnitude *vis-à-vis* such extra costs, either as a legitimate measure falling outside the scope of Article 87 EC (no advantage, thus no aid) or as a disproportionate and unjustifiable subsidy.

A.G. Léger took a similar critical view in his subsequent Opinion in the pending *Altmark* case.[18] A.G. Léger criticized the compensation approach followed in *Ferring* not only because it deprives Article 86(2) EC of any useful role in the analysis of State funding of services of general interest, but also because it blurs the conceptual distinction between the issue of *characterization of a State measure as aid* and the issue of its *justification*.[19] In this respect, it may

---

[17] On the other hand, it is an established principle that national jurisdictions are empowered to apply the combined provisions of Art. 86(2) *and other, directly applicable, Treaty rules*, such as Arts. 49, 81, and 82 EC (see Cases C-260/89, *Elliniki Radiophonia Tiléorassi* [1991] ECR I-2925, paras 33 and 34; and C-393/92, *Almelo* [1994] ECR I-1477, paras 50 and 51). Within this framework, the provisions of Art. 86(2) EC may be relied on by individuals before national courts in order to obtain a review of compliance with the conditions which they lay down (see Cases C-320/91, note 14 above, para 20, and C-218/00 *Cisal* [2002] ECR I-691, para 19).

[18] C-280/00 *Altmark Trans* (Opinion of A.G. Léger delivered on 19 March 2002, not yet reported in the ECR, paras 61–98, in particular para 82). See also Opinion of A.G. Léger delivered on January 14, 2003, in Case C-280/00 *Altmark Trans* (not yet reported in the ECR; '*Altmark II*'). A.G. Léger suggested that the ECJ rule, *inter alia*, that financial compensation granted to a public passenger transport undertaking to offset the cost of public service obligations constitutes aid within the meaning of Art. 87(1) EC, without prejudice to the possibility of that measure being exempted under the derogations provided in the Treaty and, particularly, under Arts. 73 and 86(2) EC.

[19] See *Altmark I* para 76–85. In *Altmark II* (see note 18 above, paras 31–46) A.G. Léger elaborated further upon the notion of 'advantage' for the purposes of Art. 87 EC. He reasoned that in *Ferring* the ECJ adopted what could be described as a 'net' definition of aid (or the 'real' advantage theory), as opposed to the 'gross' notion of aid (or the 'apparent' advantage theory), which is enshrined in the Treaty rules on State aid control (in particular, in Arts. 87(2) and (3) and 73 EC). Under the latter approach, the advantages conferred by the public authorities and what the recipient has to contribute in return must be examined separately: the existence of such contribution is of

be interesting to draw a parallel with the application of Article 86(2) EC in combination with the Treaty competition rules applying to undertakings.[20] In the latter context, the EC courts of law have never ruled that, if it is established that an agreement in restraint of competition, abusive conduct by a dominant undertaking, or the grant of certain exclusive rights excluding competition by other economic operators is necessary and proportionate to the objective of ensuring the provision of a SGEI in conditions of economic and financial stability, such a finding is sufficient for that anticompetitive conduct or grant of exclusive rights to fall outside of the scope of the relevant Treaty rule altogether. The EC courts' assessment invariably focuses on the existence of a *justification* of the (otherwise illegal) conduct or State measure in question, which would render it compatible with the EC Treaty.

Furthermore, according to A.G. Léger, it is doubtful that the test of 'necessary equivalence' between the value of the State measure and the extra public service costs, established by the ECJ in paragraph 27 of the *Ferring* ruling, can function as an appropriate shortcut for the assessment of whether the performance of the recipient undertaking's task would be frustrated by the application of the State aid control system. Professor Nicolaides, too, has opined that the *Ferring* test makes it virtually impossible for the Commission and the national courts to assess whether the grant of State compensation to public service providers fulfils the necessity and proportionality requirements laid down in Article 86(2) of the EC Treaty. In his view, public compensation can be deemed to represent a legitimate option only when it can be shown that the service obligations imposed upon the undertakings entrusted with a public interest task would otherwise cause a reduction in the supply of the relevant service to a socially unacceptable level. On the other hand, even where such obligations are prescribed by the law or another act of public authority, it is far from obvious that the entrusted undertakings have been *forced* to engage in the provision of the public services in question, and the compensation offered by public authorities is thus necessary. Indeed, the beneficiary undertakings might have provided those services voluntarily (i.e. without expecting any financial assistance from the State) in the pursuit of their competitive activities simply by expanding the services already supplied to their regular customers and sharing fixed costs with those services. Therefore, the fact that public compensation covers the incremental cost of producing the public service (i.e. the full extra cost associated with it)— irrespective of whether this cost would be avoided, even in part, in the absence of the State compensatory measure—is likely to distort competition between the

---

no relevance for determining whether the State measure constitutes aid and comes into consideration only at a later stage of the analysis, for assessing whether the aid is compatible with the common market.

[20] I.e., the prohibition on restrictive agreements, decisions, and concerted practices laid down in Art. 81 EC, the ban on abuse of market power laid down in Art. 82 EC, and the prohibition on State measures incompatible with the Treaty, which favour public undertakings or undertakings granted special or exclusive rights by a Member State, laid down in Art. 86(1) EC.

beneficiaries and non-entrusted undertakings that may wish to offer similar services. In addition, competition among beneficiary undertakings is distorted to the extent that the least efficient firms (i.e. those with the highest internal cost structure) receive proportionally larger subsidies.[21]

In his Opinion in *Altmark* (see note 18 above) A.G. Léger also addressed the concern that the compensation approach may virtually shelter State funding of services of general interest from the necessary control by the Commission. As noted above, although in *Ferring* the ECJ did not expressly rule on the question of whether failure to give advance notice of the State measures at issue to the Commission could be deemed to render the aid illegal based on Article 88(3) EC, it follows from the ECJ's judgment that any measures offsetting the cost of public service obligations are no longer subject to the obligation of notification as provided for in Article 88(3) since they do not constitute aid within the meaning of Article 87(1) (for the same reason, existing measures need no longer be held under constant review by the Commission as provided for in Article 88(1) and (2) EC). In his Opinion in *Ferring*, A.G. Tizzano took issue with the CFI's statement in *FFSA* according to which the assessment of additional public service costs, involving an examination of complex economic facts, implies the exercise of broad discretionary powers. A.G. Tizzano opined that no discretionary assessment is involved in the application of the Article 86(2) derogation to State measures aimed at offsetting the public service extra costs borne by certain undertakings. Therefore, as far as such aid measures are concerned, the prior notification requirement laid down in Article 88 EC is essentially formal in nature. A.G. Tizzano thus suggested, as a secondary line of reasoning,[22] that *even under the State aid approach*, although Article 87 EC alone is not directly applicable,[23] a national court could directly declare that new financing granted to an undertaking entrusted with the operation of a SGEI is permissible State aid, inasmuch as the measure in question is aimed solely at offsetting the extra costs incurred in performing the particular task assigned to the beneficiary

---

[21] See P. Nicolaides, Distortive Effects of Compensatory Aid Measures: A Note on the Economics of the Ferring Judgment, in *ECLR*, 2002, p. 313.

[22] The *main* solution proposed by A.G. Tizzano in his *Ferring* Opinion, which was accepted by the ECJ, was based on the proposition that the concept of aid requires the grant of an economic advantage and an ensuing distortion of competition; no such economic advantage (and thus no distortion of competition) exists where State funding is confined strictly to offsetting an objective disadvantage imposed by the State on the recipient, such as the public service obligations imposed on wholesale distributors by the French legislation at issue (see paras 60–63 of the Opinion).

[23] Indeed, the involvement of national courts in the system for review of State aids established by the Treaty is the result of the direct effect that the prohibition on implementation of planned aid laid down in the last sentence of Art. 88(3) EC has been held to have, without prejudice to the national court's power, when it is seized of a request that it should draw the appropriate conclusions from an infringement of such a prohibition, to interpret and apply the concept of aid in order to determine whether a State measure introduced without observance of the preliminary examination procedure ought to have been subject thereto. Where the national court entertains doubts, it may seek clarification from the Commission or refer a question to the ECJ for a preliminary ruling on the interpretation of Art. 87 EC (see Case C-39/94, *Syndicat Français de l'Express International v. La Poste* [1996] ECR I-3547, paras 39 and 49–51).

undertaking. In such a case, even failure to give advance notice of the granting of the aid to the Commission could not render the aid illegal because the national judge could apply Article 86(2) in combination with Article 88(3) EC. As a result, the Member State involved and the beneficiary undertaking would be shielded from the adverse consequences of their breach of the notification and standstill obligations imposed by the latter provision, although the Commission could bring infringement proceedings against that State pursuant to Article 232 EC.

In my view, this proposition confuses the issue of a State measure's substantive compatibility with the common market with the issue of its legality with respect to the procedural requirements imposed upon Member States by the Treaty rules on State aid control.[24] I concede that in such situation, under the 'State aid approach', although the public funding involved is still State aid within the meaning of Article 87(1) EC, application of the Article 86(2) derogation, *which becomes relevant only if the State measure in question is not found to be compatible with the common market under Article 87(3) EC*, renders the aid permissible. However, even State aid measures that the Member State concerned deems to be compatible are subject to the general prohibition on giving effect to new aid. Indeed, Article 88 EC places on the Commission a specific duty to monitor aid and imposes on the Member States specific obligations precisely in order to facilitate the Commission's task and to prevent *faits accomplis* for that institution, with a view to ensuring the effectiveness of the prohibition on incompatible aid.[25]

## V. The interplay between the Article 86(2) derogation and the procedural requirements imposed upon Member States by the Treaty rules on State aid control in '*CELF*'

The 'compensation approach' thus results in virtually introducing a blanket exemption from the State aid control's procedural requirements for State funding of services of general interest. This result, which the *Ferring* judgment implicitly supports, is in my view inconsistent with the ruling delivered in 2000 by the ECJ in the '*CELF*' case.[26] France challenged by way of a direct action the legality of a 1998 Commission decision holding that the annual grants from the French

---

[24] See Case C-354/90 '*Salmon*' [1991] ECR I-5505, para 16, holding that the Commission's final substantive decision does not have the effect of regularizing *ex post facto* any national implementing measures of *unnotified* aid, which were invalid because such measures had been taken in breach of the prohibition laid down by the last sentence of Art. 88(3) EC. The opposite result, on one hand, would impair the direct effect of that prohibition and disregard the interests of individuals to be protected by national courts; on the other hand, it would have the effect of according a favourable outcome to the non-observance by the Member State concerned of its procedural requirements under Art. 88(3) and would deprive that provision of its effectiveness.

[25] See Case C-143/99, note 6 above, paras 23–25.

[26] Case C-332/98, *France/Commission* [2000] ECR I-4833.

Ministry of Culture to the Coopérative Française d'Exportation du Livre Français (CELF) for the handling of small orders of books in the French language constituted aid within the meaning of Article 87(1) EC but was, despite France's failure to notify the aid to the Commission, compatible with Article 87(3)(d) (aid granted to promote culture and heritage conservation). France asked the ECJ to annul the contested decision insofar as Article 86(2) EC was not applied. The applicant disputed, notably, the Commission's conclusion that there was no need to consider CELF's State-aided activities in the light of Article 86(2), since the application of Article 87 resulted in the grants at issue being considered legitimate, and thus would not obstruct the performance by CELF of the task of handling small orders. According to the French government, State aid covered by Article 86(2) EC requires, by its very nature, special treatment *in regard to procedural matters*. In particular, the obligation to suspend temporarily the implementation of that aid is necessarily and automatically inapplicable in the case of aid for undertakings entrusted with the operation of a SGEI, in order to avoid disruption of the service provided.

The ECJ relied on its settled case law, which holds that the principle enshrined in the final sentence of Article 88(3) EC[27] is a means of safeguarding the machinery for review laid down by that provision, which in turn is essential to ensure the proper functioning of the common market. Therefore, according to the ECJ, even if the Member State concerned takes the view that the aid measure is compatible with the common market, that fact does not entitle it to defy the clear provisions of Article 88 EC. The ECJ made clear that the purpose served by Article 88(3) is not a mere obligation to notify but an obligation of prior notification, which necessarily implies the suspensory effect required under the final sentence of that provision. Therefore, the obligations of notification and suspension laid down therein cannot be disjoined from one another. That conclusion, according to the ECJ, was particularly evident where, as in the case at hand, the aid was at no time notified to the Commission.

## VI. Advocate General Jacobs's suggestion in *GEMO* that the 'compensation approach' to State remuneration of general interest services be restricted to cases in which providers are selected in accordance with general public procurement rules

To complicate things further, a third approach (which could be described as a fine-tuned variant of the 'compensation approach') to the matter of the assessment of State funding of services of general interest under State aid control rules was recently put forward by Advocate General Jacobs in his Opinion, delivered

---

[27] See note 6 above.

on 30 April 2002, in *GEMO*.[28] The *GEMO* case, actually pending before the Sixth Chamber, was referred to the ECJ for a preliminary ruling by the Administrative Court of Appeal, Lyon. It concerns a 1996 French law establishing a public service for the collection and disposal of animal carcasses and dangerous slaughterhouse waste, intended to cover the approximately 10 per cent of animal material not intended for human consumption which is considered to be hazardous. The system established by the French legislation is (i) compulsory, (ii) operated by private carcass disposal undertakings, which are remunerated by the State under contracts awarded after public procurement procedures, while the service is provided free of charge to the main beneficiaries, namely farmers and slaughter-houses, and (iii) financed through a meat purchase tax imposed mainly on meat retailing supermarkets. The ECJ was requested to interpret Article 87 EC with a view to establishing whether the State measure at issue, which was not notified to the Commission pursuant to Article 88 EC, contained aid in favour of, *inter alia*, carcass disposal undertakings selected and paid by the State for the operation of the service in question.

A.G. Jacobs took the position that neither the 'compensation' nor the 'State aid approach' provided for an ideal solution in all cases involving State financing of services of general interest. The A.G. proposed that the ECJ base its assessment: (i) on the nature of the link between the financing granted and the general interest duties imposed by the State upon the undertaking(s) entrusted with the operation of a SGEI, and (ii) on how clearly those duties are defined. In his view, any cases in which the financing measures are manifestly intended as a direct *quid pro quo* for clearly defined general interest obligations (e.g. public service contracts awarded after public procurement procedures) should be analysed according to the 'compensation approach'. Recourse to the 'State aid approach' should thus be confined to cases where the link between State funding and the general interest obligations imposed is either not direct or not manifest, or the general interest obligations are not clearly defined in the State measure at issue, and the necessity of the advantage granted for the purpose of offsetting the extra costs of the beneficiary undertaking is only alleged by public authorities at a later stage, when the measure is analysed under State aid control rules.

In the framework of the carcass disposal system at issue in *GEMO*, the French State awarded, in accordance with general public procurement rules, service contracts of a maximum duration of five years to specialized undertakings for the purpose of the operation of the public service in question. Therefore, according to A.G. Jacobs, since in such a system the remuneration that those undertakings received was directly and manifestly linked to clearly defined obligations that they had to fulfil under the public service contracts in question, the payments to be made by the State constituted State aid only if and to the

---

[28] See above note 2. A.G. Jacobs's analysis was endorsed by A.G. Stix-Hackl in the Opinion she delivered on 7 November 2002, in Joined Cases C-34/01 to C-38/01 *Enirisorse* (not yet reported in the ECR, paras 153–165) as well as by Quigley & Collins, note 1 above, pp. 369–370.

extent that they exceeded appropriate remuneration, to be defined with reference not to the costs of providing those services, but to the remuneration that carcass disposal providers would receive from any third party on a normally functioning market.

## VII. Final remarks

It seems logical to expect that the Sixth Chamber of the ECJ will postpone the adoption of its decision in the *GEMO* case until the full Court judgment in *Altmark* is delivered. In addition, the oral procedure in the latter case was reopened by Order of 18 June 2002, and the ECJ invited the parties to the main proceedings, the Member States (six of which actually took part in the new hearing),[29] the Council, and the Commission to submit their observations on the *Ferring* judgment. On 14 January 2003 A.G. Léger delivered his second Opinion in the *Altmark* case, which predictably affirmed his former analysis.[30]

The Commission, too, has called a halt to the drafting of its long-awaited guidelines on state aid and services of general economic interest, expressly reserving judgment until the *Altmark* ruling is delivered.[31] Nonetheless, on 10 July 2002 the Commission decided to initiate, pursuant to Article 88(3) EC, the preliminary examination of the French carcass disposal system, with respect, *inter alia*, to the possible aid element inherent in farmers' and slaughter-houses' receiving the service free of charge, the selection process of the entrusted undertakings by public authorities, and the level of public compensation.[32]

In my view, the solution proposed by A.G. Jacobs may present the same problems as the 'compensation approach' without providing any real advantage

---

[29] Namely Denmark, France, Germany, Spain, the Netherlands, and the United Kingdom.

[30] See note 18 above. A.G. Léger suggested that the Court should rule that: (i) financial advantages granted by the authorities of a Member State to offset the cost of the public service obligations they impose on an undertaking constitute State aid, (ii) measures instituting such advantages are subject to the notification and suspension obligations laid down in Art. 88(3) EC, and (iii) Art. 86(2) EC does not have direct effect in the field of State aid.

[31] See Report to the Seville European Council, note 5 above, paras 10–17 (announcing the projected adoption of a 'text' by the Commission by the end of 2002, aimed at 'clarify[ing] the methods for calculating compensation, notably in connection with public contracts, in order to avoid excess compensation' and noting that, 'if *Ferring* is upheld, a text, the legal form of which would be defined at the appropriate time, would still help to increase legal certainty, in particular as regards the methods for calculating compensation and the arrangements for selecting the firms to be entrusted with the operation of general economic interest services'; see paras 17 and 14). The Commission, however, has been continuing its works concerning other issues in this area. A meeting with Member States' experts for discussing the conditions governing the operation of SGEIs was held on December 18, 2002, on the basis of a working paper drawn up by DG Competition [see Non-paper: Services of general economic interest and state aid (12 Nov. 2002) and Report from the Commission on the state of play in the work on the guidelines for state aid and services of general economic interest (SGEIs) (27 Nov. 2002) COM (2002) 636 final)].

[32] See State Aid C 49/2002—France, Commission press release IP/02/1031 of July 10, 2002.

*vis-à-vis* the 'State aid approach' or otherwise advancing legal certainty.[33] Indeed, as conceded in paragraph 129 of the *GEMO* Opinion, the suggested distinction between the two categories of measures 'might not always be easy to draw'. As noted by A.G. Léger in *Altmark II*, the '*quid pro quo* approach', to the extent that it prescribes to assess whether a public service contract was awarded after a public procurement procedure[34] and the nature and content of the beneficiary undertaking's obligation have been specified by law, regulation, or contractual provisions, departs from the case law, under which State aid must be defined by reference solely to the effects of the measure, not to criteria of a purely formal or procedural nature. That an SGEI is awarded as a result of a fair, transparent, and non-discriminatory procedure—in particular, on the basis of an open tender—with respect to the services to be provided and the amount of compensation, should only be relevant in the context of the assessment of the necessity and proportionality of the State's intervention, for the purpose of authorizing the aid granted through that compensation as compatible with the common market.

As noted, the main consequence of characterizing planned State financing of a SGEI as a *quid pro quo* for clearly defined general interest obligations, providing the beneficiary undertaking(s) with an economic advantage not exceeding the public service's additional costs, is that such a planned measure will not amount to State aid, and thus will not be subject to the prior notification and standstill obligations laid down in Article 88(3) EC. Therefore, in my view, it is obvious that under the new *GEMO* approach Member States would be tempted to use a new '*quid pro quo* exception' as a basis for abstaining from notifying an even larger number of financing measures than it is already the case.[35] As a result' this approach, if endorsed by the ECJ, would present the danger inherent in any

---

[33] See P. Nicolaides, The New Frontier in State Aid Control: An Economic Assessment of Measures that Compensate Enterprises, in *Intereconomics*, 2002, p. 190, in particular pp. 194 and 195. As an alternative method for dealing with the issue of compensatory measures under the Treaty's State aid rules, the author emphasizes the importance of calculating the minimum necessary amount of public financial assistance that would lead to the desired increase in supply of a given general interest service, and proposes that the obligation to provide the service in question be auctioned with a view to identifying the firm(s) that, having lower operating costs than their competitors, would be willing to offer the service while receiving in compensation the lowest possible subsidy. Since State measures offering compensation of extra costs through an auctioning procedure would simply remove the cost disadvantage imposed by the public service obligations, they would fall outside of the scope of Art. 87(1) EC.

[34] '[A]part from the case of a public service contract concluded after an award procedure, none of the parties was able to provide a single specific example of this kind of link between State financing and public service obligations. In fact, the sole concrete and "operational" criterion which can be set in the context of the *quid pro quo* approach is the requirement of a public service contract concluded after an award procedure. The various parties concur, however, in admitting that such a requirement is disproportionate' (*Altmark II*, see note 18 above, para 86 and footnote 97).

[35] Cf. Nicolaides, note 33 above, pp. 191 and 194 (stating that the *Ferring* judgment as well as A.G. Jacobs' approach in *GEMO* make it 'both very feasible and likely' that, as long as the various costs borne by enterprises can be disguised as vague obligations imposed by public authorities in the context of some policy of providing services of general interest, then Member States will be able to escape the net cast by the proposed redefinition of what constitutes aid).

solution aimed at granting the very parties upon which a prior notification obligation is imposed, a certain discretion in assessing whether the requirements triggering that obligation are met in any specific case. Indeed, failure to notify planned aid inevitably carries with it the risk that a measure that could adversely affect competition within the common market might be implemented.

Indeed, the possibility of invoking the derogation under Article 86(2) EC in the area of State aid control presents difficulties that are unknown in the context of *ex post* control by the Commission of the conduct covered by Articles 81 and 82, namely the risk of depriving the Community system of enforcement of competition rules of its practical effect. In the latter context, if the Commission decides that the conditions for application of Article 86(2) are fulfilled, the undertaking responsible, which would otherwise be judged guilty of a breach and ordered by decision immediately to end the prohibited practice and could also possibly be fined for previous breaches, will be shielded by the derogation in question from enforcement of the substantive rules. However, the situation is completely different where the derogation under Article 86(2) is invoked by a Member State granting aid in order to evade the standstill obligation. The purpose of the preventive control assigned to the Commission in the State aid area, as in the case of the provisions laid down by the Community legislature for controlling concentrations between undertakings having a Community dimension,[36] is to prevent competition on the internal market from undergoing, through *faits accomplis*, unlawful distortions whose elimination, to reinstate the *status quo ante*, either by unscrambling the capital and assets of merged companies or recovering funds paid to the beneficiary in the form of aid, might prove extremely difficult, if not impossible.

With respect to the application of the Article 86(2) derogation by the Commission to a general interest service provider benefiting from public resources, as a *quid pro quo* for the performance of its public service obligations, two alternative solutions are theoretically possible. The first is to construe Articles 87 and 88, in combination with Article 86(2) EC, in the sense that the Commission can decide whether the derogation is applicable only in the context of its final decision on the substantive compatibility of the measure. I concede that this option is not without shortcomings since, regard being had to the specific nature of any aid measures designed to ensure the continuous and flexible operation of the service by the beneficiary undertaking, the late application of the derogation risks having little or no practical effect.

Under the second option, the Commission's decision must be confined to the formally establishing *ex post facto* a breach of the standstill obligation already committed by the Member State involved, based on the finding that the measure in question was in fact not eligible for the derogation that was already relied upon. This solution, thus, entails giving any national authorities wishing to grant

---

[36] See Council Regulation (EEC) No 4064/89 of 21 December 1989 on the control of concentrations between undertakings (OJ L 395, p. 1), as amended.

aid on the basis of Article 86(2) the power to assess and decide for themselves whether to suspend implementation of the planned measure, pending the outcome of the examination procedure. This result contrasts manifestly with the ECJ's case law concerning the Treaty rules applying to undertakings, according to which the application of Article 86(2) EC is not left to the discretion of the Member State that has entrusted an undertaking with the operation of a SGEI. Article 86(3) assigns to the Commission the task of monitoring such matters, under the supervision of the ECJ.[37] There is no reason why a different principle should apply to State aid control. Moreover, since no aid can be deemed properly introduced unless it has been subject to preliminary examination, for which Article 88 EC gives sole jurisdiction to the Commission, any Member State knowingly putting itself in a position of illegality cannot benefit from any derogation to the general rules of procedure.

In *GEMO* A.G. Jacobs justified his proposed solution by stating that the *destination* of the products that the State (or emanations of the State) obtain for consideration on the market should not figure in the assessment of the existence of an economic advantage distorting competition. In particular, according to A.G. Jacobs, the outcome of the State aid control analysis should be identical irrespective of whether the State, acting in its capacity as public authority, purchases services *to be provided to the public* (e.g. waste disposal services) or acts *iure privatorum*, purchasing on the market goods or services *for its own direct use and benefit* (e.g. room cleaning services). In both cases, in his view, the arrangement between the State and the service provider, involving mutual rights and obligations, should be examined as a whole and the existence of aid should be admitted only to the extent that the price paid by the State exceeds the market price or appropriate remuneration.

It is submitted that the parallel drawn by A.G. Jacobs with the State aid case law concerning commercial transactions on preferential terms entered into by public authorities is of limited usefulness here. This analogy seems to disregard the fact that the drafters of the Treaty chose—without prejudice to the Member States' power to designate which services they consider to be of general economic interest, taking into account objectives pertaining to their economic or fiscal policy, as well as to decide freely whether to provide such public services themselves, directly or indirectly, or to entrust their provision to third parties—to make the selection of such third-party providers and compensation for their public service obligations subject to a number of requirements. Under the special regime applicable to undertakings entrusted with the operation of a SGEI—irrespective of whether the assignment of the public interest tasks takes

---

[37] See Case 41/83 *Italy/Commission* [1985] ECR 873, para 30. In the context of such assessment the Member States' interest in using certain undertakings, in particular in the public sector, as an instrument of economic or fiscal policy must be reconciled with the Community's interest in ensuring compliance with the rules on competition and the preservation of the unity of the Common Market (see Case C-202/88, *France/Commission* [1991] ECR I-1223, para 12).

place by law[38] or another act of public authority (such as a concession agreement), or by a contract concluded with the competent public authority—the party invoking the Article 86(2) derogation, i.e. the national authorities granting aid and/or the beneficiary undertaking, must prove *not only* that the State is behaving like an ordinary economic operator in a like commercial transaction (i.e. that it is not using its powers to confer a pecuniary advantage thereon by foregoing the profit which it could normally realize)[39] *but also and above all* that the service in question genuinely constitutes a SGEI[40] and that its financing by the State does not affect the development of trade to an extent contrary to the interests of the Community. To the extent that it does not allow any scrutiny of the latter elements, the new *GEMO* approach shares the same shortcomings of the 'compensation approach' *tout court*.[41]

A.G. Jacobs' position in *GEMO*, like A.G. Tizzano's in *Ferring*, may have been motivated primarily by a different concern. A.G. Jacobs emphasized that, under the 'State aid approach', the notification and standstill requirements in Article 88(3) EC may seriously disrupt the provision of services of general interest through private undertakings, to the extent that it may be difficult or even impossible to wait for prior authorization by the Commission with regard to the provision of certain services (e.g. disposal of toxic waste or ambulance services; see paragraph 115 of the Opinion). This concern, however, may have been overemphasized. Indeed, without prejudice to the future adoption of a block exemption regulation in this area[42], under the established *Lorenz* case law,[43] the Commission—in the course of the preliminary stage of the procedure for reviewing aid, which is intended to allow it to form a *prima facie* opinion of whether the aid schemes notified to it are in partial or complete conformity with

---

[38]  In such a case, compensation may consist, e.g. in granting annual subsidies or preferential fiscal treatment to the beneficiary undertaking or lowering its social security contributions.

[39]  See Case T-14/96 *BAI/Commission* [1998] ECR II-139, paras 71–82.

[40]  According to F. Blum-A. Logue, *State Monopolies under EC Law*, Wiley's (1998), p. 23, a SGEI must satisfy essential needs of the population. It should be remembered that since Art. 86(2) permits, in certain circumstances, derogation from other rules of the Treaty, the definition of those undertakings that can take advantage of it must be interpreted strictly (see Case 127/73 *BRT (II)* [1974] ECR 313, para 19). In his Opinion in the *GEMO* case A.G. Jacobs assumed that the collection and disposal of animal carcasses amounted to a SGEI, based on public health considerations, without any elaboration upon this point.

[41]  Under the more radical approach adopted by A.G. Léger in *Altmark II* (see note 18 above, paras 19–27) the private operator criterion formulated by the EC courts of law applies only in situations where the intervention of the State is of an economic nature, not where it forms part of the exercise of public powers, as it is the case for the financing of public services. Indeed, it is for the public authorities to define the services that are to be made available to the community as well as to take the necessary measures to ensure their functioning and financing. Therefore, '[i]t is not correct to compare cases where the State purchases goods or services on its own account with those where it "acquires" services which are made available directly to the collectivity (namely public services). In the former case, the State conducts itself in a way which a private operator may adopt with a view to profit; whereas, in the latter case, the State acts as a public authority.'

[42]  See note 5 above. See also *Altmark II* (see note 18 above, paras 70–74).

[43]  See Case 120/73 *Lorenz* [1973] ECR 1471, para 4. See also Case C-99/98 *Austria/Commission* [2001] ECR I-1101, paras 72–74.

the Treaty—must act diligently in order to offer Member States the required legal certainty, and inform them quickly as to the compatibility with the Treaty of particular aid, which may be a matter of urgency.

If after being informed by a Member State of a plan to grant aid aimed at offsetting the extra costs borne by one or more undertakings for complying with certain public service obligations, the Commission fails to initiate the contentious procedure within two months, the Member State concerned may, after giving prior notice to the Commission, put the aid in question into effect, whereupon it will come under the system for existing aid.[44] It is submitted that, where the Commission is notified of a financing measure that is manifestly intended as a direct *quid pro quo* for the general interest obligations clearly defined in the entrusting act, the examination procedure will be fairly straightforward, making it normally unnecessary to initiate the *inter partes* procedure provided for by Article 88(2) EC, which is not subject to time limits and which is inevitably lengthened by the participation of complainants and interested third parties.[45]

---

[44] Moreover, according to the case law, for the purposes of the preliminary phase, in order for a notification to be regarded as complete and thus cause the two-month period to begin to run, it is sufficient if it contains, either from the beginning or once the Member State has replied to questions raised by the Commission, such information as will enable the Commission to form a *prima facie* opinion of the compatibility of the aid with the Treaty. Because of the nature of the preliminary examination procedure, the question whether a notification is complete, and consequently whether the Commission is entitled to request further information, must not be construed in such a way as to impose upon the Member State at that stage an obligation to provide exhaustive information. In any event, it is unacceptable for the Commission, if it has sufficient information to carry out its preexamination, artificially to prolong that preliminary procedure by repeatedly asking new irrelevant questions, particularly if it does so on each occasion shortly before expiry of the two-month period (see Case 99/98, note 43 above, paras 53–66).

[45] Pursuant to Art. 7(6) of Council Regulation (EC) No 659/1999 of 22 March 1999, laying down detailed rules for the application of Article 88 EC (OJ L 83, p. 1), the Commission shall as far as possible endeavour to adopt a decision to close the formal investigation procedure within a period of 18 months from the opening of the procedure.

# 4

# Decentralization, Effectiveness, and Modernization: Contradictions in Terms?

MALCOLM ROSS

## I. Introduction

Decentralization as both goal and process in the context of EC law takes various forms, although usually falling within one of two camps. The first, more politicized, approach treats it as a rallying cry in selecting the relevant law to be applied as between national or EC rules. On this view, decentralization patrols the boundaries of the Treaty and may even demand repatriation of particular powers to national decision-makers and institutions. A second, less constitutionally confrontational, model treats decentralization as a process of localized application designed to render EC rules more effective. The debate in this scenario is not about which law to apply, but only who should do it. Of course, these two approaches may be combined, and indeed confused—most notably in the reception given to the Treaty concept of subsidiarity.[1]

Recent developments in competition law largely reflect the second model of decentralized enforcement.[2] To take the most obvious example, the fundamental overhaul of the enforcement procedures relating to Articles 81–82 EC contemplates switching from an *a priori* notification system to an *ex post facto* control using national courts and competition authorities as well as the Commission. This change, it is claimed,[3] not only addresses the workload of the Commission by enabling it to concentrate on significant cartels but also integrates local enforcement agencies into a mature system based on established legal principles and clear parameters for Community action. As is well known, the theoretical distribution of institutional responsibility in the Treaty had already been eroded

[1] Art 5(2) EC. Subsidiarity addresses which level of authority is better placed to take action, but can only apply in cases where there is a shared competence between the EC and Member States. It has no application in the event of an exclusive EC competence: see Advocate General Fennelly in Case C-376/98 *Germany v European Parliament and Council* [2000] ECR I-2247. For possible reforms in subsidiarity management, see report of the working party established by the Convention on the Future of Europe; http:european-convention.eu.int/ (last visited on 31 October 2002).

[2] Although the EC Merger Regulation attempts to divide EC law regulation and national law competence using economic size and multi-State impact as the entry criteria.

[3] *White Paper on Modernisation of the Rules Implementing Arts 85 and 86* [now 81 and 82], April 1999.

by the case law giving direct effect to Article 81(1)[4] and a range of legislative and informal devices adopted by the Commission to offset the backlog of individual exemption applications.[5] To some extent, therefore, the Draft Regulation[6] only confirms and extends trends possessing significant pedigree already.[7] However, Article 3 of the Draft Regulation also encroaches upon fundamental competence questions by providing for the exclusive application of EC competition law rules to agreements and abusive practices that affect inter-state trade instead of the previous parallel existence of national and Community rules.[8] In short, decentralization in the general competition law field envisages a model in which the same but exclusive set of rules is applied by a range of agencies: Commission, national competition authorities, and national courts.

Any discussion of the decentralization of State aid law needs to take account of this background, if only to ascertain whether the same conditions prevail. At first sight, the notion of decentralization seems singularly inappropriate in relation to Articles 87–89 EC, at least as far as the justifications for that process in other areas of competition law and policy are concerned. Three strikingly different features of the State aid context should all should sound warning bells against swift or unconditional endorsement of any stampede towards decentralization.

The first obvious difference is that by definition the State aid rules specifically concern assistance provided by the State rather than the market conduct of private undertakings. To the more cynical observer, downloading responsibility for calling Member States to account to the level of their own national courts might not seem the smartest move towards guaranteeing effective and consistent enforcement across the Union. This reservation is not so much based on the risk of cheating,[9] but expresses healthy scepticism concerning the willingness of national courts to carry out complicated balancing of values in a Community-wide context.[10] Secondly, the suitability of the latter task for national application may be doubted. There are significant qualitative policy differences that shape the weighing of justifications for State aid when compared to the scheme of Articles 81–82. Again, the *raison d'être* of establishing an EC regime for State

---

[4] Case 127/73 *BRT v SABAM* [1974] ECR 62.

[5] Such as successive block exemption Regulations for the purposes of Art 81(3), plus Notices in areas such as Minor Agreements and Market Definition.

[6] COM (2000) 582 Final.

[7] The huge literature includes C-D Ehlermann, 'The modernization of EC antitrust policy: A legal and cultural revolution' (2000) 37 CMLRev 537; D Gerber, 'Modernising European competition law: a developmental perspective' [2001] ECLR 122.

[8] This proposal is not without critics, acknowledged by A Schaub, speech on 'Developments of European Competition Law' 19 April 2002; http://europa.eu.int/comm/competition/ (last visited on 31 October 2002).

[9] It will, of course, normally be the national court of a defendant Member State that is vested with the responsibility of adjudicating claims for damages brought by individuals under the *Francovich* principle.

[10] Nobody appears seriously to be suggesting that national courts should become arbiters of Art 87(3) criteria, but a role is placed upon them already by Art 86(2) in relation to undertakings entrusted with services of general economic interest.

aid was not just to moderate the impact of national discretion on market liberalization but also to allow the pursuit of other Treaty objectives to trump the rules of the marketplace. At first sight, the balancing function inherent in the latter situation might appear to be more easily and appropriately vested in the Commission (as formally recorded in Article 87(3)) rather than in national bodies. Whilst assessment of potential breaches of Articles 81 and 82 may require some broader considerations to be weighed,[11] the essential tasks occupy familiar judicial territory in so far as they engage questions of discrimination, restrictive effects, and fair dealing in the context of acceptable 'normal' or 'workable' competition[12].

On a third, practical, level it should be pointed out that whilst many aspects of State aid law have been clarified it might be misleadingly optimistic to describe the definition of aid as endowed with the certainty and clarity of the general principles of Articles 81–82. The current controversy, pending in two cases before the Court of Justice,[13] over the characterization of support given by Member States in the context of the delivery of public services, is only one illustration of significant doubt.

However, despite these distinguishing features of State aid law and policy, the Court of Justice has already ensured that the centralized Treaty model, requiring prior notification by States to the Commission for evaluation, presents only a partial picture of State aid regulation. In one early line of authority, the Court[14] sanctioned resort by individuals to national courts for protection of the procedural obligation upon Member States to notify, set out in Article 88(3) EC. Since ascertaining breach of that obligation presupposes analysis of whether a measure is an aid in the first place, national courts have accordingly become exponentially embroiled in aid cases in relation to the scope of the Treaty. The other, much more recent, path of case law has seen the invocation of Article 86(2) EC as a defence in aid cases in addition to the *lex specialis* provisions reserved to the Commission in Article 87(3). These two proliferating strands of Treaty interpretation suck national courts into questions of both scope and justification in relation to the State aid rules. Determining the place of Article 86(2) in the aid regime is one of the keys to the direction and focus of decentralization so far as the role of national courts is concerned. It is argued below that, contrary to frequent denials by the Court itself of any 'rule of reason' within Article 87(1) a similar function has in fact come to be performed by Article 86(2) for certain aid cases, with potentially inconsistent and unpredictable results.

[11] Art 81(3) includes references to economic progress and consumers' fair share of benefits.

[12] This paradigm statement of the link between competition and the single market imperative came from the Court of Justice in Case 26/76 *Metro v Commission (No 1)* [1977] ECR 1875 at 1904.

[13] Case C-280/00 *Altmark Trans GmbH, Regierungspräsidium Magdeburg v Nahverkehrsgesellschaft Altmark GmbH* and Case C-126/01 *Ministre de l'économie, des finances et de l'industrie v GEMO SA*, in which Advocate Generals Léger and Jacobs respectively have attacked the ruling of the Court's Sixth Chamber in Case C-53/00 *Ferring* [2001] ECR I-9067. For a detailed consideration of these cases, see Rizza above.

[14] Case 120/73 *Lorenz* [1973] ECR 1471.

Accordingly, this paper addresses some wider ramifications of the decentralization of State aid enforcement not dwelt on in detail elsewhere in this
volume.[15] In particular, it examines the extent to which the *sui generis* character
of the EC regime governing State aid has succumbed to more general pressures
and principles affecting and driving competition law at large. These trends
comprise, *inter alia*, the greater responsibility devolved to national courts, the
assumption that injured competitors will be active putative guardians of the
Treaty, the enhanced presence of block exemptions together with 'soft law'[16]
techniques of guidance and direction, and the emergence of EC principles for
steering and monitoring remedies in domestic law. Moreover, analysis of these
decentralizing tendencies will show they cannot be limited to a vacuum
of pragmatism sealed by the need for effective enforcement. Instead, they
contain, but may mask, deeper concerns of principle relating to the boundaries
of EC law and the mechanisms used to patrol them. To this extent, State aid
decentralization can be analysed against three important but more general and
familiar concerns of EC law development: the separation (or not) of questions
of scope and justification in relation to Treaty prohibitions, the relationship
between the goals of decentralization and the judicially created principle of
effectiveness,[17] and the necessary preconditions for modernization. These are
dealt with in turn below.

## II. Conceptualizing aid: conflating scope and justification?

The pattern of negative integration chiselled into the Treaty rules on free movement and competition hardly needs rehearsing.[18] Basic prohibitions against
unacceptable measures or behaviour are almost universally set against exceptions indicative of Treaty values.[19] Equally well documented has been the
refinement of this simplistic approach by the Court of Justice, establishing
more prohibitions and also more exceptions as both markets and players responded to the single market imperative. The initial paradigm step, taken in

---

[15] It therefore consciously avoids repetition of the more detailed examinations of national case law
provided in the papers by James Flynn and Kelyn Bacon below.

[16] For the many functions and guises of 'soft' law, see L Senden & S Prechal, 'Differentiation in and
through Community Soft Law' in B de Witte, D Hanf, & E Vos (eds), *The Many Faces of Differentiation in EU Law* (Intersentia, 2001), 181.

[17] Developed by the Court of Justice in relation to the procedural autonomy of Member
States whilst respecting the obligation to protect EC rights for individuals; the other element in the
usual dual mantra, equivalence, is less likely to arise given the paucity of national systems for
regulating State aid.

[18] An excellent recent collection of critical material can be found in C Barnard & J Scott (eds), *The
Law of the Single European Market, Unpacking the Premises* (Hart, 2002).

[19] Although the tax rules, for example, do not contain stated exemptions. The result has been to
make the gate-keeping of Art 90(1) depend on whether taxes are objectively justifiable, and hence non-
discriminatory.

*Cassis de Dijon*,[20] combined Treaty expansion and derogation enlargement so skilfully that commentators spent years trying to decide which was the more accurate analysis[21] of the Court's approach. Today's received wisdom almost universally treats *Cassis* public interest requirements[22] as exceptions, implying that without making out a recognized head of interest a Member State or other relevant actor[23] would infringe a Treaty prohibition. Indeed, the Court itself in its more recent case law appears to conceive of public interest considerations as derogations rather than limitations defining the scope of the initial prohibition.[24] The resulting arrangement is a regime established in EC law that balances 'home State' and 'host State' models of regulatory competence.[25] Through its interpretation of Article 28 and other free movement rules of the Treaty, the Court has combined both competence allocation and decentralized enforcement to the point where market regulation (and re-regulation) occurs via competition between national regimes. The Court has been prepared in principle to assess the validity of the host State's regulatory choices in an evolving context which is open, as a result of judicial insistence upon the rule of reason, to 'permeation by factors of considerable social and political breadth'.[26]

In the context of State aid a tension is being played out that is similar in kind though not in form. In theory, the aid rules could be a further lever in the trader's toolkit to prise open markets subject to local State protection. However, the methodology of the single market case law, subjecting local rules restrictive of market access to Community justification, is not so easily or transparently applicable to State aid. Indeed, the Court has seemingly tried to keep the lid on the scope of Article 87(1), perhaps realizing that provision's potential ability to unseat any measure conferring market advantage upon selected undertakings or sectors. Attempts to extend the reach of the aid rules into myriad manifestations of State regulatory activity have usually failed to convince the Court of Justice. For example, it has restricted the notion in Article 87(1) of 'any means whatsoever' to intermediaries for the State such as public undertakings. In other words the phrase has been taken to constitute an anti-avoidance device encompassing disguised arms of the 'State' rather than an amplification of the concept of 'aid'.[27]

---

[20] Case 120/78 *Rewe Zentrale v Bundesmonopolverwaltung für Branntwein* [1979] ECR 649, although the approach was presaged in Case 8/74 *Dassonville* [1974] ECR 837.

[21] See A Arnull, *The European Union and its Court of Justice* (OUP, 1999) ch 7.

[22] Today these heads apply across the fundamental freedoms although not always expressed in the same terminology or policy concerns; see J Snell, *Goods and Services in EC Law* (OUP, 2002) esp pp 186–192.

[23] Depending on which Treaty rule is being invoked: Case C-281/98 *Angonese* [2000] ECR I-4139 makes explicit that private bodies may fall foul of Art 39 EC.

[24] See J Snell, n 22 above.

[25] See S Weatherill, 'Pre-emption, harmonisation and the distribution of competence to regulate the internal market' in C Barnard and J Scott (eds), n 18 above, 41.

[26] Ibid, p. 49.

[27] Joined Cases C-72/91 and C-73/91 *Sloman Neptun Schiffahrts AG v Seebetriebsrat Bodo Ziesemer der Sloman Neptun Schiffahrts AG* [1993] ECR I-887; Joined Cases C-52/97, C-53/97, and C-54/97 *Viscido and others v Ente Poste Italiane* [1998] ECR I-2629.

The Court has been similarly averse to arguments which try to import measures 'of equivalent effect' to an aid into the scope of Article 87(1). In one of its
most recent judgments in the area[28] it gave short shrift to the Commission's
argument that the duty of solidarity imposed on Member States by Article 10 EC
could be invoked to define the scope of Article 87(1) by way of analogy to the
case law[29] linking Article 10 to the prohibition contained in Article 81(1). The
Commission's position had explicitly invoked the need to preserve the effectiveness of the State aid rules as the teleological justification for bringing within their
scope support measures which are decided upon by the State but financed by
private undertakings. Unlike Advocate General Jacobs, who only rejected the
point after careful examination,[30] the Court peremptorily concluded that the
second paragraph of Article 10 cannot be used to extend the scope of Article 87
to conduct by States that does not fall within it.[31]

This question-begging stance points to one of the most difficult areas of State
aid law, one of huge relevance to decentralization. The Court's failure to unravel
the relationship between the scope of aid and any justification for it invites
amplification of confusion should enforcement responsibilities be widened to
include agencies other than the Commission. Certainly, opportunities abound
within Article 87(1) for invoking justifications as part of the process of establishing an aid. As pointed out by Kelyn Bacon in this volume,[32] there is a
justificatory element attached to the assessment of market conditions when
applying the hypothetical investor test, in so far as commercial justifications
may exist for particular benefits.[33] She also notes that the selectivity element of
Article 87(1) can give rise to confusing or even erroneous use of justificatory
arguments, especially when national courts try to apply the rather opaque
concept of 'inherent' attributes or logic of a general system. Bacon nevertheless
adheres to the view that the proper application of this test involves establishing a
justification of ostensibly differential treatment which renders it a general measure and accordingly outside Article 87(1).

However, it is submitted that the 'inherent' doctrine (if this rather easy
formulation merits such a lofty description) is more accurately seen as a species
of either remoteness or proportionality. The Court may well be alive to this
problem, offering in recent examples at least case-specific reasons for rejecting
the 'inherent' arguments that are so attractive to Member States. In *Adria-Wien*

---

[28] Case C-379/98 *Preussen Elektra AG v Schleswag AG* [2001] ECR I-2099, para 65.

[29] In particular, Case C-2/91 *Meng* [1993] ECR I-5751, para 14.

[30] see para 180 *et seq* of Opinion.

[31] It may not be entirely coincidental that the Court also dodged the problematical free movement
aspect of *PreussenElektra*. Advocate General Jacobs had boldly invited it to reconsider the whole issue
of whether only indistinctly applicable measures could take the benefit of *Cassis*-type public interests.

[32] Cf the discussion of 'advantage' by M Ross, 'State aids and national courts: definitions and other
problems: A case of premature emancipation?' (2000) 37 CMLRev 401.

[33] For a very recent application, see the CFI's annulment of the Commission's reasoning in Case
T-98/00 *Linde AG v Commission* (judgment 17 October 2002), holding that the impugned arrangement had in fact been the behaviour of rational operators in a market economy, motivated primarily
by commercial considerations and having no regard for economic or social policy objectives (para 49).

*Pipeline*,[34] for example, Advocate General Mischo had accepted that a tax rebate granted only to undertakings whose activity consisted primarily in the manufacture of goods was not an aid. The Court, rejecting that Opinion, observed that no justifications were apparent from the nature of the general scheme set up by the Austrian rules. In particular, undertakings supplying services could incur similar energy taxes yet not be entitled to the rebate. Any ecological arguments were equally doomed on the basis that energy consumption by service providers was just as damaging to the environment so that relief for one sector could not be justified. The Court's approach in *Adria-Wien Pipeline* has been adopted and applied subsequently by the Court of First Instance,[35] but it remains to be seen whether national courts will maintain the same vigilance against attempts to employ circular reasoning to justify selective measures.

Probably the clearest approximation to the 'rule of reason' mix of scope and justification analysis is to be found in the problematical relationship between the State aid rules and Article 86(2) EC. The general developments of interpretation in the latter area have been well documented elsewhere.[36] The central issue here is whether, and on what basis, State support to enable undertakings to deliver their public service obligations constitutes an aid. The European Courts have followed an inconsistent path culminating in the two decisions currently pending. In some cases, notably *FFSA*,[37] the approach has been to treat financial and other logistical support as an aid within the meaning of Article 87(1) EC but capable of justification. In situations involving undertakings providing services of general economic interest, it has seemed that Article 86(2) is a possible source of justification.[38] On the other hand, the Court of Justice in *Ferring*[39] decided that where the alleged aid is merely a compensatory amount to cover the extra costs incurred by an undertaking in discharging its essential public service function, there is no aid at all. The significant implication for regulatory purposes is, of course, that there is no EC regime of control at all in the latter example. Something falling outside the EC Treaty in the first place requires neither notification nor justification against Treaty criteria.

It is this facet of the *Ferring* judgment that has caused consternation in some quarters. The Court of Justice currently has the chance to review the jurisprudence in this area in two pending cases: *Altmark Trans*[40] and *GEMO*.[41] Both

[34] Case C-143/99 *Adria-Wien Pipeline GmbH and Wietersdorfer & Peggauer Zementwerke v Finanzlandesdirektion für Kärnten* [2001] ECR I-8365.

[35] Joined Cases T-346/99, T-347/99, & T-348/99 *Disputación de Álava and others v Commission* (judgment, 23 October 2002), esp paras 50–64.

[36] See A Arnull, A Dashwood, M Ross, & D Wyatt, *Wyatt & Dashwood's European Union Law* (Sweet & Maxwell, 4th ed, 2000) pp 719–727.

[37] Case T-106/95 *FFSA v Commission* [1997] ECR II-229, upheld on appeal, C-174/97P [1998] ECR I-1303.

[38] Although Art 86(2) does not give relief from Art 88(3), the requirement of prior notification of aid; see Case C-332/98 *France v Commission* [2000] ECR I-4833.

[39] Case C-53/00 *Ferring v ACOSS* [2001] ECR I-9067.

[40] Case C-280/00, n 13 above, Opinion of 19 March 2002.

[41] Case C-126/01, n 13 above, Opinion of 30 April 2002.

cases have already received full and robust Opinions from Advocates General Léger and Jacobs respectively. Advocate General Léger criticizes the Court for its approach in *Ferring*, which he considers to have deprived Article 86(2) of any substantial meaning in the context of State aid. He tellingly observes[42] that the *Ferring* judgment conflates the questions of scope and justification, with the result that Article 86(2) can never be invoked. If the amount of support is less than the costs of discharging public service obligations then there will be no aid according to *Ferring*. If, on the other hand, the sum involved exceeds the compensatory figure to meet obligations then *Ferring* expressly precludes the measure from being justified.[43] The result of this erroneous analysis, in the view of Advocate General Léger, is to offend the status of Article 86(2) as 'the central Treaty provision for reconciling Community objectives',[44] in other words balancing the 'Member States' interest in using certain undertakings as an instrument of economic, fiscal or social policy with the Community's interest in ensuring compliance with the rules on competition and the preservation of the unity of the common market'.[45]

Advocate General Jacobs is less strident in *GEMO* in his attack on the *Ferring* approach. Nevertheless, he clearly has grave reservations about the wisdom of its general application as a doctrine. His preferred solution represents an attempt to reconcile the existing case law and to clarify for the future, rather than break with the past in the way called for by Advocate General Léger. Thus, for Advocate General Jacobs, two lines of approach can be distinguished according to factual situations.[46] For one group, where there is a 'direct and manifest' link between the support granted by the State and particular, well defined public service obligations to be performed by the undertaking, he endorses the *Ferring* reason based on the concept of compensation and not aid. However, where the financial link is not so direct or the obligations of the undertaking are less clear, Advocate General Jacobs prefers to apply the aid rules.

Of course, as Advocate General Jacobs himself acknowledges, his two-tier construction invites problem cases on the borderline. It might also be added that his proposal does not address the central conceptual problem about the nature of State aid. The 'compensation' analysis is, it is submitted, not a special fact scenario but a manifestation of the rather dangerously multi-layered 'inherent' line of reasoning mentioned above. In other words, the *Ferring* judgment can perhaps be read as a statement that where State support equals the amount of extra cost in discharging functions then that amount is no more than inherent in the nature of the system. Even if, as argued above, the latter inquiry demands an application of the Community law test of proportionality, the exercise is hardly

---

[42] Para 76.

[43] *Ferring* judgment, para 32: 'that advantage, to the extent that it exceeds the additional costs mentioned, cannot, in any event, be regarded as necessary to enable [the undertakings] to carry out the particular tasks assigned to them'.

[44] *Altmark* Opinion, para 80

[45] Ibid.

[46] Paras 115–132 of *GEMO* Opinion.

free from doubt. As a Commission insider has observed[47] national authorities within the same Member State and of different Member States may apply different criteria to calculate the proportionality of the compensation. Quantifying the additional costs of providing a service of general interest could be affected by whether this means incremental costs in cases where the provider is engaged in other services or whether stand-alone costs of the public service should be measured. Other imponderables[48] include whether to include in a costs structure the indirect advantages that accrue from being entrusted with a service of general interest, such as reputation. Taking 'compensation' cases out of the ambit of Article 87(1) altogether excludes not only *ex post facto* supervision but also prior notification to the Commission and, with it, the latter's authority to draw up guidelines or firmer rules about methodology of compensation assessment that would lend transparency and rationality to proportionality.

Above all, it is submitted, the main danger in the Court's approach in *Ferring* is to assume what ought instead to be argued, namely the value of general interest services and their compatibility in their particular execution with the rules of the Treaty. Put differently, the rationale of *Ferring* could be the assumption that the giving of a cost-discharging amount is no more than the proportional implementation of a legitimate aim as already recognized in EC law by Article 86(2) and, it is argued further below, Article 16 EC. However, the bald terms of the judgment in *Ferring* can equally be read as a repatriation of powers to Member States without any supervision at Community level.

The significance of this line of case law in relation to arguments about the decentralization of State aid law is thus immense, extending beyond the obvious importance of identifying the boundaries of Article 87(1). The outcome of the two pending cases will have huge implications for the other strands of political and legal development that have been emerging as regards the proper relationship between EC and national responsibilities in relation to the delivery of public services. Since its first Communication on the topic in 1996[49] the Commission has been developing a strategy in relation to public services. This was based initially on identifying principles (equality, universality, continuity, and adaptability) and practices (fair prices, openness in funding, and scrutiny). Its 2000 Communication[50] went further in setting out a notion of services of general interest[51] based upon Treaty neutrality as to the ownership of public service providers but with Treaty control exercised through the mechanisms of Article 86(2) and proportionality.

---

[47] Grespan, 'An example of the application of State aid rules in the utilities sector in Italy' Competition Policy Newsletter October 2002, Commission's competition website.

[48] Ibid, p 22, n 4.

[49] OJ 1996 C281/03.

[50] OJ 2001 C17/04.

[51] The terminology is important; note the dropping of the adjective 'economic' in contrast to the wording of Article 86(2) EC.

By the time of the Laeken Council at the end of 2001 the Commission had reached a position[52] embracing two paths: developing an EU legislative framework for aid to services of general interest and, much more controversially, indicating a willingness to pursue a benchmarking regime to supervise the quality of delivery of services. As far as aid was concerned, the proposal at Laeken was in terms of a block exemption, if needed, under the normal Treaty rules of Articles 87–88 EC for certain categories of aid. In relation to the more ambitious benchmarking concept, the Commission merely set out its view of the need for a culture of evaluation and feedback on public service delivery Europe-wide. In other words, the idea was for a 'best practice' framework to identify principles for the operating standards to be expected of public services. Not surprisingly, the Laeken Council gave the go-ahead to take the aid proposal further but completely ignored the benchmarking references. The Commission accordingly prepared further material in relation to State aid for services of general interest for the Spanish Presidency summits of 2002 at Barcelona and Seville.

Clearly, as the Commission itself acknowledged in its Report to the Seville Council,[53] upholding *Ferring* would demolish the need for any block exemption legislation. There is, however, a paradox in the Court's position. On one hand, excluding compensatory support from the regime of Article 87(1) altogether (and indeed the Treaty) would clearly rehouse public service delivery within the remit of Member States, even where it affects inter-state trade. Yet, oddly, the second limb of *Ferring* prevents there being any assessment of the justification for excessive compensation by recourse to Article 86(2). This not only removes the mechanism that would provide the closest matching of competition and wider concerns under the Treaty, but also rules out such concerns being examined by national courts. Leaving aside for the moment the potential structural inconsistency in reserving Article 87(3) criteria to the Commission whilst permitting individuals to invoke Article 86(2) before national courts in State aid cases, the fact remains that the Court has had no qualms in the past about allowing national courts to adjudicate under Article 86(2) in other circumstances involving services of general economic interest and market failures.[54]

Depending on the Court's reaction to the Opinions in *Altmark Trans* and *GEMO*, the legal position on aid to public services could strangle at birth the development of Article 16 EC. As argued at length elsewhere,[55] textual and teleological arguments may be made to give this provision (introduced into the EC Treaty by the Treaty of Amsterdam) an interpretation that decouples

---

[52] Report to the Laeken European Council COM (2001) 598.

[53] Paras 10–15.

[54] Although the national court will encounter difficult market assessment questions as a result. See Case C-475/99 *Ambulanz Glockner v Landkreis Sudwestpfalz* [2001] ECR I-8089.

[55] M Ross, 'Article 16 EC and services of general interest: From derogation to obligation?' (2000) 25 ELRev 22.

the treatment of public services from the competition and market rules of the Treaty. On this view, Article 16 can sustain an autonomous, *communautaire* contribution to the regulation of public services by both underlining their importance in the shared values of the Union and shaping essential minimum standards of quality in their provision.

In this respect, it is particularly noteworthy that Advocate General Jacobs specifically drew attention to this wider context in *GEMO*, observing that an advantage of his proposed two-tier view of aid to services of general interest was that 'it gives appropriate weight to the importance now attached to services of general interest, as recognised in Article 16 EC and in Article 36 of the EU Charter of Fundamental Rights, while avoiding the risk of circumvention of the State aid rules'. These considerations, whilst not articulated by the Advocate General in quite these terms, also play to another thread in standard decentralization arguments: the protection and involvement of individuals. Of course, this is problematic in relation to the two provisions identified by Mr Jacobs. It is difficult to see how Article 16 could satisfy directly effective criteria and the history of the Charter's legal status is already notorious.[56] However, if Article 86(2) remains applicable before national courts seised with State aid and public services issues, this provision may yet offer the most likely stimulus for further refinement of broader openings for emerging citizenship forged in recent cases.[57] Should the Court uphold and generalize the whole of the *Ferring* approach it could kill off a whole rich vein of Community law development in the field of territorial cohesion.

## III. Effectiveness as an Enforcement Principle

It is all too easy to treat decentralization and effective enforcement as intertwined goals and processes with a high degree of mutual dependence. Involving more agencies to enforce EC law, so the argument runs, both empowers those agencies and opens up further mechanisms, incentives, and opportunities for effective enforcement. There is an almost glib assumption that decentralization brings about better enforcement whilst, conversely, increasing and honing the tools of enforcement will ensure effective decentralization by embedding a culture of responsibility and legal awareness among practitioners, businesses, and individuals alike. More empirical evidence, especially about the former proposition and the vagaries of litigation strategies, is needed to make

[56] The Charter (OJ 2000 C364/01) was 'solemnly proclaimed' alongside the Treaty of Nice. The Charter has been embraced with various degrees of passion by Advocates General but studiously ignored by the Court. For a classic illustration of these approaches, see Case C-353/99P *Council of the European Union v Heidi Hautala* [2001] ECR I-9565.

[57] The Court's most recent pronouncement holds that Article 18(1) EC is directly effective: Case C-313/99 *Baumbast and R v Sec State Home Dept*, judgment 17 September 2002. It had previously declared that Union citizenship was 'destined to be the fundamental status' of nationals of the Member States in Case C-184/99 *Grzelczyk* [2001] ECR I-6153.

these claims sound entirely convincing.[58] For the moment, however, it is clear that the State aid enforcement regime is being pulled along in the wake of more general developments in relation to remedies and the conceptual analysis of enforcement.

In particular, the question to be addressed is whether the ruling by the Court of Justice in *Courage v Crehan*[59] is of any relevance to State aid law. Reactions to this judgment have ranged from hailing it[60] as the new (horizontal) *Francovich*, creating a distinct *communautaire* entitlement to damages against private parties, to near-dismissal[61] as just one more manifestation of the familiar effectiveness principle in the bag marked procedural autonomy. Of course[62] the factual circumstances of *Crehan* are not easily transplanted into the typical arrangement of parties in a State aid case. The strict point in *Crehan* was a very narrow one, involving the extent to which a party to a contract found to be illegal in domestic law by virtue of its violation of an EC rule (Article 81) could claim damages against the other contracting party. Although the Court of Justice gave an affirmative answer to this, national courts were also given a blessing to deny damages to a party who is found to bear significant responsibility for the distortion of competition in question. This part of the judgment[63] was explicitly linked to the principles of equivalence and effectiveness.[64]

Of more interest to State aid lawyers are earlier passages in *Crehan* contained in paragraphs 19, 26 and 27:

19. . . . Just as it imposes burdens on individuals, Community law is also intended to give rise to rights which become part of their legal assets. Those rights arise not only where they are expressly granted by the Treaty but also by virtue of obligations which the Treaty imposes in a clearly defined manner on individuals and on the Member States and the Community institutions . . .

26. The full effectiveness of Article 85 [now 81] of the Treaty, and, in particular, the practical effect of the prohibition laid down in Article 85(1) would be put at risk if it were not open to any individual to claim damages for loss caused to him by *a contract or by conduct* liable to restrict or distort competition.

27. Indeed, the existence of such a right strengthens the working of the Community competition rules and discourages agreements or practices, which are frequently covert,

---

[58] Noting in particular the proposed changes to enforcement of Arts 81 and 82 EC. It is not self-evident that the assumption that individuals and firms will choose litigation strategies is necessarily well founded, especially with variations across and within States as to access to courts, costs, and legal cultures. The inevitable speculation is that decentralization will favour certain types of litigant in particular circumstances; see generally, C Kilpatrick, T Novitz, & P Skidmore (eds), *The Future of Remedies in Europe* (Hart, 2000).

[59] Case C-453/99 [2001] ECR I-6297.

[60] A Komninos, 'New prospects for private enforcement of EC competition law: *Courage v Crehan* and the Community right to damages' (2002) 39 CMLRev 447.

[61] See O Odudu and J Edelman, 'Compensatory damages for breach of Article 81' (2002) 27 ELR 327.

[62] As noted by James Flynn below.

[63] N 59 above, para. 31.

[64] The Court only cites *Palmisani*, although this is not an obvious choice: see A Komninos, n 60 above.

which are liable to restrict or distort competition. From that point of view, *actions for damages before the national courts can make a significant contribution to the maintenance of effective competition* in the Community [emphases added].

Two points are immediately striking about these passages. First, they appear before the references to the principles of equivalence and effectiveness, suggesting in the ordinary course of things that the Court was identifying the general before moving to the particular and that therefore some wider principles are being divulged here.[65] Secondly, they are wide enough to embrace the State aid rules when regard is had to the major purpose, characteristics, and enforcement weaknesses of the latter. Since Articles 87–88 EC form part of the competition rules there is no need to strive to show that *Crehan* covers all breaches of the Treaty before trying to make sense of it in a State aid context.

So, assume for the moment that *Crehan* can be read as a judgment of two halves, the first creating a general, primary, prima facie entitlement in EC law, the second authorizing a departure from it in a particular national scenario subject to the EC principles of equivalence and effectiveness. Even if this is holds force, does it affect State aid law? Clearly, a straight factual transplant ends in a blind alley: the two equivalent parties are presumably the State and the beneficiary of the aid. The State is not ordinarily in a weak bargaining position,[66] and the beneficiary is hamstrung by previous case law from the Court of Justice that points to the prudent businessman being obliged to take care to ensure that aid is lawful.[67] However, if *Crehan* does represent the creation of a horizontal right in damages for private parties, at least when arising in competition law situations, other scenarios also require consideration.

The first of these is the potential liability of a beneficiary of aid to aggrieved competitors. According to previous case law[68] the machinery for reviewing State aid established by Article 88 does not impose any specific obligation on the recipient of aid, since it is for the Member State to notify any aid, and it is also the addressee of the Commission's subsequent decision on the matter. Yet it is also apparent that the Court of Justice has not ruled out the prospect of non-contractual liability of recipients to injured third parties under national law.[69] It is therefore hard to see how *Crehan* can apply to actions by competitors against beneficiaries since there is no violation of Community State aid rules by the latter. In the absence of a revised legislative position at EC level concerning the duties of beneficiaries when aid is granted, the position will remain that litigants in different Member States will be entitled to varying degrees of legal protection depending on national provision.

---

[65] This style is reminiscent of the Court's reasoning in *Francovich* itself, cited in *Crehan* in support of para 19 of that judgment.

[66] See James Flynn's paper below, discussing Case C-294/90 *British Aerospace and Rover v Commission* [1992] ECR I-493.

[67] Case C-5/89 *Re Bug-Alutechnik: Commission v Germany* [1990] ECR I-3437.

[68] Case C-39/94 *SFEI v La Poste* [1996] ECR I-3547.

[69] Ibid, para. 75; also see Case C-390/98 *Banks* [2001] ECR I-6117, a case decided on the same day as *Crehan* by an almost identically constituted Court, para 80.

The other scenario to be discussed is that of competitor as regards Member State, though again this looks to yield minimalist outcomes. A *Francovich* action in damages is possible in any event, assuming that the conditions of that liability are met. The interest posed by *Crehan*, therefore, is whether it constitutes a short-cut to a remedy without going through the *Francovich* hoops, especially the requirement that there has been a 'serious breach' by the State.[70] Just as the *Francovich* principle was itself refined in later cases, there is presumably more to be told by the Court in relation to individual liability with the result that hitherto undisclosed restrictions may be revealed in future cases. It may yet prove significant that the language of *Crehan* is directed towards the better protection of individual rights and is not linked exclusively in principle with the identification of particular defendants.

However, in the short term it is hard to envisage *Crehan* inspiring much by way of additional litigation tools for aggrieved competitors in the face of unlawful aid. In the State aid context there is the added complication that national legal systems may not offer redress or supervision of aid transactions at all. Of course, this does not prevent litigants having recourse to the 'normal' standards of EC supervision of national procedural rules and remedies.[71] However, the lack of specific national frameworks may perhaps explain the Court's willingness in the past to set out its own procedural principles regarding limitations to enforcement and recovery actions in respect of State aid.[72]

## IV. Conditions precedent for modernization

The Commission's former Director-General of Competition has noted that modernization of State aid law presents challenges which have 'some similarities to anti-trust',[73] notably the speedy disposal of routine cases to clear the Commission's decks for more important problems. In particular, he points to the value of the general procedural regulation[74] and subsequent block exemptions,[75]

---

[70] Acknowledging that 'serious' may not necessarily be an unduly onerous obstacle to a claim; see Opinion of Advocate General Jacobs in Case C-150/99 *Sweden v Stockholm Lindöpark Aktiebolag and others* [2001] ECR I-493 for an argument that serious means clear, rather than an expression of gravity.

[71] I.e. that national rules must not be less favourable than those governing similar domestic actions (principle of equivalence) and that they do not render practically impossible or excessively difficult the exercise of rights conferred by Community law (principle of effectiveness); these principles were reiterated by the Court in *Crehan*, n 59 above, para 29.

[72] See Dougan, 'Enforcing the single market' in C Barnard and J Scott (eds), n 18 above, ch 6, esp pp 173–179.

[73] Schaub, 'Developments of European competition law', conference speech of 19 April 2002, located on Commission competition website, at p11.

[74] Regulation 659/99 [1999] OJ L83/1.

[75] Already in relation to training aid (Reg 68/2001) and aid to small and medium-sized enterprises (Reg 70/2001). A third proposal is firmly advanced in relation to aspects of employment aid affecting recruitment of disadvantaged categories of worker and the additional costs of employing disabled workers.

describing the latter as of benefit not only to the Commission but also the national, regional, and local administrations in Member States.[76] This section is concerned with whether the *acquis communautaire* on State aid law is fit for modernization.

Whether the Director General's view is misplaced, even blind, optimism depends on a number of factors. It is submitted that the assumptions and mechanisms for securing the single market do not necessarily hold sway for State aid law. This is not to deny that State aid has anything to do with the single market. Indeed, as the Court has very recently reiterated, Article 88 'is essential for protecting the proper functioning of the common market'.[77] But its location in the competition rules of the Treaty may not make that connection immediately obvious with the result that national courts are at risk of losing sight of market integration concerns.[78] Block exemptions will commit national courts to more aid inquiries but with, it seems, less clear guidance as to the outer boundaries of Article 87(1). In addition to the concerns about selectivity, compensation, and justification discussed above, there remain other controversial areas such as the relevance of *de minimis* and the measurement of the inter-state trade requirement. Although these are dealt with at greater length by other contributors to this volume,[79] the necessary observation here is that Commission practice and judicial doctrine have not always been entirely *ad idem*. For the moment, the Court seems content to rule that the Commission 'is bound by the guidelines and notices that it issues in the area of supervision of State aid where they do not depart from the rules in the Treaty and are accepted by the Member States'.[80]

Mention has already been made of the foreclosing effect that might occur in the event of looser decentralization of normative issues in relation to the development of Article 86(2) and Article 16 as regards services of general interest. Accordingly, any plans for the creeping decentralization or modernization of State aid law should not just subsume this area of activity within competition law for some technically more efficient system of desk-clearing for the Commission's convenience. Extremely significant normative changes are occurring within State aid policy on at least two levels: first, within the competition framework as to the appropriate economic criteria to be deployed for measuring the existence of notifiable aid, and secondly, wider issues relating to the nature and source of legitimizing criteria for defending the grant of aid. These two strands of development are themselves potentially in tension, in so far as any

[76] Above, n 73, p12.
[77] Case C-143/99 *Adria-Wien Pipeline and Wietersdorfer & Peggauer Zementwerke v Finanzlandesdirektion für Kärnten*, at para 25.
[78] A similar observation has been made about modernization of the general principles of EC competition law; see Albors-Llorens, 'Competition policy and the shaping of the single market' in C Barnard and J Scott (eds), n 18 above, ch 12 at 330–331.
[79] Particularly R Plender, above.
[80] Case C-351/98 *Spain v Commission* (judgment 26 September 2002); cf C-382/99 *Netherlands v Commission* (judgment 13 June 2002) where the formulation was that in so far as guidelines do not contradict Treaty rules, the policy rules they contain are to be followed by the Commission.

preoccupation with turning State aid assessment into an economic measurement may divert attention away from the policy goals pursued by Community regulation of aid provision. In a recent policy document[81] the Commission attaches considerable importance to establishing economic indicators to measure the effectiveness of State aid in achieving its purposes and the impact of aid upon competitive conditions. Indeed, it is considering to what extent economic criteria should be taken into consideration in the design of State aid procedures. Even with the increasingly ubiquitous Guidelines and Notices to underpin such explanations, it may be asked whether economic deconstruction of aid definition in this fashion is susceptible to simultaneous application by national courts.

The Court of Justice has also contributed to this tension through mixed messages in its interpretation of the boundaries of Article 87(1). As Dougan has argued convincingly in a broader view of the single market,[82] its preferred scheme (if it has one) for modernizing and decentralizing enforcement of EC law lacks transparency and, possibly, coherence. It has avoided imposing any model of uniformity but has not always been consistent in the rigour with which it applies the review tools of equivalence and effectiveness. An 'enforcement deficit' may arise through undesirable inequalities in the standards of judicial protection available to economic undertakings across the Union.[83]

## V. Conclusions

Evaluation of the European Union since the Treaty of Maastricht has concentrated upon general phenomena and tendencies. The early focus upon subsidiarity, citizenship, and constitutionalism has now extended to close analysis of decentralized enforcement and differentiation. These concepts share dual capacities, being invoked as both ends and means according to the agenda of the day or of the author. As descriptors these labels are evidence of a state of affairs in governance or constitutional evolution that avoids encapsulation against more constraining criteria. In the increasingly multi-layered but unplanned European architecture, the absence of design is replaced by component structures formed of materials characterized by flexibility and permeability to cope with internal and external stresses.

This chapter has tried to show in outline the risks associated with treating these phenomena as self-justifying or inevitable processes without reference to the goals they serve or affect. State aid law has a purpose, albeit a changing one. In a revealing statement, the Commission has observed: 'The principal objective of State aid is to resolve market failures in various economic sectors, to support

---

[81] *Communication from the Commission to the Council*, Progress report concerning the reduction and reorientation of State aid, COM (2002) 555 final, 16 October 2002.

[82] Above, n 72.

[83] Dougan, n 72 above, at p 179.

national, regional or Community policy objectives or reduce the potential social cost of structural changes that are occurring throughout European economies'.[84]

In other words, State aid control is an instrument to pursue a mixed set of goals, the balancing of which is a complex, normative function. Despite the decrease in levels of aid and the stated commitment of Member States to reducing them further,[85] considerable challenges remain. In addition to the public services question discussed above, the Commission has identified particular concerns arising from newly liberalized sectors, especially energy, telecommunications, and postal operations, pointing out[86] that government measures not previously considered as constituting State aid may, in the wake of deregulation, acquire this characteristic. Any abandonment of Treaty supervision, by limiting further the scope of Article 87(1) or excluding the operation of Article 86(2), would run counter to effective monitoring of those concerns. Similarly, too much decentralization in terms of enforcement responsibility may be, at the very least, an invitation to inconsistent or misguided resolution of State aid problems.

Historically, there has been a strong centralized tendency in the Treaty model of State aid control, reinforced by some aspects of the Court's case law in relation to the recovery of unlawful aid.[87] It is perhaps odd that calls for modernization and decentralization of State aid law should be appearing at a time when the larger issues that need resolution could be undermined by such developments. Differentiation is perhaps today's buzz word among Euro-lawyers, at least in the academic sphere. In the field of State aid law, a differentiated pattern of supervision and apportionment of enforcement responsibilities distinct from the trend under Articles 81–82 might demand the retention of an unfashionably strong level of centralized control.

[84] Ninth Survey on State Aid in the European Union, COM (2001) 403, para 22.
[85] Ibid, paras 7 and 45.
[86] Ibid, para 53.
[87] See Dougan, n 72 above, at p 174 in relation especially to legitimate expectations and defences of passing on.

# 5

# State Aid and Obstacles to Trade

ANDREA BIONDI and PIET EECKHOUT

## I. Introduction

State aid law and policy are playing an ever stronger and more central role in the European Union's quest to establish and maintain a well functioning internal market. In the current stage of market integration, we are past the days of obvious obstacles to trade resulting from disparities in its regulation. The case law of the Court of Justice[1] and extensive harmonization of legislation have supplied the tools to take such obstacles apart. There is, in addition, a well established 'private' competition policy on cartels, abuse of dominant position, and mergers. It is true that that policy is facing a radical overhaul, but that is at the level of organization, procedure, and enforcement, rather than concepts.

State aid policy, by contrast, continues to struggle to define its role, script, and movements on the internal market scene. Essential concepts are still not fully clarified, and vital choices of policy remain to be made. One need only refer to the debates on financing through State resources,[2] and on services of general economic interest.[3] Some of the causes for these indeterminacies may lie in the inherent and ever increasing difficulties in locating the boundary between the public and the private in modern European societies. States are redefining their economic role, acknowledging the benefits of a market-based approach to previously monopolized economic activities, yet actively engaging with the future organization and operation of such activities through taxation, regulation, and subsidies. The abandonment of monopolies therefore goes hand in hand with active intervention, reflecting the growing and varied demands which society places on the public sphere. Yet such active intervention risks interfering with competition between companies, whether public or private, in ways that are considered unacceptable from the perspective of an increasingly integrated internal market. It is an inherent tension that cannot easily be resolved. In the absence of stronger common policies or policy harmonization in such vital areas as utilities, transport, broadcasting, and education, it befalls State aid policy to arbitrate, and to determine the appropriate spheres for the public and the private. The legal tools are essentially those of the 1957 EEC Treaty, constructed with mechanics which may have worked well at the time, but definitely work less well in the current environment of transformation of the State's function.

---

[1] Hereafter ECJ.    [2] See Plender above.    [3] See Rizza and Ross above.

The purpose of this chapter is to contribute to the debate on the evolution and development of State aid policy, by looking at its intercourse with the free movement side of the internal market. State intervention in the economy and in the internal market is, in areas where common European policies are lacking, essentially subject to two types of control. The first is that regulation and taxation may not create unjustified obstacles to trade in goods or services nor to free movement of persons, companies, or capital. The second is that States may not grant unapproved aids which distort competition in the internal market. The *prima facie* and traditional view may be that those are distinct types of control. However, much like in the case of the public–private divide it is increasingly difficult to locate and determine the boundaries. Closer study reveals that the two types of restraint essentially overlap, thereby requiring deeper analysis of their respective spheres and interaction.

This chapter looks at three dimensions. First comes a discussion of the policy rationales of the law on free movement and of State aid law. One may term this the political economy of the two systems. Second on our list is the delineation of free movement and State aid law, as identified in the case law. Where are State measures located? Is the policy overlap reflected in legal overlap, or does the case law attempt to create at least legal clarity by defining clear boundaries? The third topic which we address relates to the policy justification for what would otherwise be illegal measures. Free movement law operates on the basis of a broad definition of what constitute barriers and obstacles, counterbalanced by an equally broad approach to justification, with proportionality as the judicially modulated lynchpin. In the context of State aid there is the obvious approval process, enabling the Commission to authorize certain types of aid. However, the definition of what constitutes State aid increasingly bears traces of a prohibition-and-justification approach. That definition is of course in the courts' hands, which calls for a comparison with justification issues in the free movement context. The informed reader may recall *Wouters*,[4] in which the ECJ developed a unified approach to justification in the context of Articles 81 and 82 EC, and of free movement, respectively. Are we also moving towards such a unified approach towards justification as regards free movement and State aid? That question and others related to the definition of a State aid, its delineation with free movement law, and relevant justification analysis, are also explored below.

## II. Political economy

At first sight the policy rationales of free movement and State aid law may appear disconnected, even if there is general agreement that they complement each other in the pursuit of a functioning internal market. Free movement law is concerned with removing obstacles in areas of regulation and taxation. The *Dassonville*

---

[4] Case C-309/99 *Wouters* [2002] ECR I-1577.

formula, still celebrated as laying down the basic formula for free movement of goods, addresses State measures which are capable of hindering cross-border trade.[5] *Cassis de Dijon* emphasized that indistinctly applicable market regulation is caught by Article 28 EC, thereby moving the law beyond discrimination, but the ECJ made allowance for justification on the basis of non-economic public policies.[6] The *Keck and Mithouard* saga identified market access as the central concern of free trade law.[7] Case law on free movement of services, persons, and capital essentially follows the trade-in-goods approach, banning both discrimination against foreigners and obstacles. Here too there is emphasis on market access.[8] With respect to taxation, discrimination against foreign products is prohibited under Article 90 EC, the purpose of which is to avoid protectionist taxes.[9] In other areas of free movement taxation comes within the general approach, and is therefore subject to the prohibition of discrimination and of obstacles. In a nutshell, the language of free movement is one of discrimination, obstacles, and market access.

State aid, by contrast, is about undistorted competition, a concept which does not play a significant role in the case law on free movement. It is true that Article 87 EC requires that the aid affect trade between Member States, but that requirement is in the nature of a jurisdictional criterion which is easily satisfied. There is no express requirement of finding an obstacle to trade, or of identifying in what way market access is impeded.

And yet closer analysis reveals that the political economy of free movement and State aid are more entangled than appears on the surface. It is remarkable that in the case law on free trade in goods, and more generally on free movement, there is so little reference to the notion of undistorted competition.[10] As true border measures disappear, nearly all of the contested market regulation is internal, and the idea of undistorted competition between domestic and foreign economic actors could easily be more central to the judicial reasoning within free movement law. One need only refer to the partial equivalent of Articles 28 and 90 EC in WTO law, i.e. Article III GATT on national treatment, to see that in the GATT and WTO case law it is characterized as fundamentally aiming at equality of competitive conditions.[11] The rule of non-discrimination in WTO law (effectively a free-trade rule) contains a clear undistorted-competition element.

---

[5] Case 8/74 *Dassonville* [1974] ECR 837.

[6] Case 120/78 *Rewe-Zentrale AG v Bundesmonopolverwaltung für Branntwein* [1979] ECR 649.

[7] Joined Cases C-267 and 268/91 *Keck and Mithouard* [1993] ECR I-6097, see also C-34, 35, & 36/95 *KO v De Agostini* [1997] ECR I-3843 and C-405/98 *KO v Gourmet International Products* [2001] ECR I-1795.

[8] Case C-384/93 *Alpine Investments* [1995] ECR I-1141; Case C-451/93 *Bosman* [1996] ECR I-4921; Case C-54/99 *Eglise de Scientologie* [2000] ECR I-1335.

[9] Case 168/78 *Commission v France (Whisky/Cognac)* [1980] ECR 347.

[10] See in general Mortelmans 'Towards convergence in the application of the rules on free movement and on competitition?' 38 CMLRev (2001) 613.

[11] WTO Appellate Body, *Japan—Taxes on Alcoholic Beverages*, WT/DS8/AB/R, WT/DS10/AB/R, WT/DS11/AB/R, 4 October 1996 and *EC—Measures Affecting Asbestos and Asbestos-containing Products*, WT/DS/135/AB/R, 12 March 2001, para 97.

However, one does not need to dig too deep in EC free movement law to find the competition element. The emphasis on market access may lead to references to undistorted competition. An example is Advocate General Jacobs' analysis in *Leclerc-Siplec*, where he spoke of the guiding principle *'that all undertakings which engage in a legitimate economic activity in a Member State should have unfettered access to the whole of the Community market, unless there is a valid reason for denying them full access to a part of that market'*.[12] It is but a small step from this principle to the idea that all undertakings are entitled to undistorted competition.

More significant perhaps is the case law on Article 95 EC, the central provision on harmonization of legislation ('approximation') regarding the establishment and functioning of the internal market. It is common knowledge that this provision complements free movement law, by enabling the European Union to harmonize in areas where otherwise obstacles would remain because Member States are entitled to derogate from the free movement principle, either under express Treaty provisions or under the judge-made exceptions inaugurated by *Cassis de Dijon*. However, the case law on Article 95 EC, as confirmed in the constitutional *Tobacco Advertising Directive* case, does not merely refer to the removal of obstacles to trade. In its judgment in that case the ECJ recalled that Article 95 EC permits the adoption of measures which are intended to improve the conditions for the establishment and functioning of the internal market, whilst denying that the article vested in the Community legislature a general power to regulate the internal market. Measures must genuinely contribute to such improvement, i.e. they must either contribute to eliminating obstacles to free movement or they must purport to eliminate an appreciable distortion of competition.[13] It is clear from the case law that the elimination of obstacles and the removal of competition distortions are alternative bases for taking legislative action under Article 95 EC.

The reference to undistorted competition highlights that State measures do not only interfere with a properly functioning internal market by creating obstacles to free movement, but also by distorting competition between undertakings competing in the internal market. What remains unresolved is whether State measures of the latter kind are caught by the Treaty provisions on free movement. In other words, is it possible to challenge national legislation on the basis of e.g. Article 28 EC on the sole basis that such legislation distorts competition in the internal market? The case law does not directly deal with that question. It is none the less obvious that there is a dimension of competition between domestic and foreign undertakings in important strands of free-movement case law. *Cassis de Dijon* itself was concerned with competition between domestic and foreign alcoholic drinks producers, and the mutual recognition idea can be easily

---

[12] Case C-412/93 *Leclerc-Siplec v TF1 Publicité and M6 Publicité* [1995] ECR I-179, para 41 Opinion.

[13] Case C-376/98 *Germany v EP and Council* [2000] ECR I-8419.

connected to notions of undistorted competition. A case such as *PreussenElektra*, in the grey zone between free movement and State aid, also throws up a competition element on the internal market side (competition between domestic and foreign producers of green electricity) even if the ECJ did not satisfactorily deal with that element.[14]

In much the same way as there is a competition element in the free-movement case law, so there is an obstacle-to-trade element in State aid law. The effect of a State aid on intra-Community trade is not confined to the jurisdictional criterion in Article 87 EC. Such aid may create problems of market access for other Member States' undertakings, and the case law intuitively takes the market-access and obstacles-to-trade issues on board.

Against that background we can now examine exactly how the Treaty provisions on free movement, in particular those dealing with goods, and those on State aid are delineated in the case law.

### III. DEFINING THE BOUNDARIES BETWEEN STATE AID AND FREE MOVEMENT: A RECONSTRUCTION OF THE ECJ CASE LAW

The relationship between free movement of goods and State aid provisions has always been examined in terms of generality/speciality and complementarity/exclusivity. In particular the main questions have been identified as follows:

a) whether the wide notion of restriction to trade elaborated by the ECJ with reference in particular to the definition of 'measures having equivalent effect' could be stretched so as to include an aid within the meaning of Article 87 EC;
b) whether the two sets of provisions should be considered mutually exclusive.

The leading authority in this area is still the *Iannelli v Meroni* judgment delivered as long ago as 1977.[15] The case mainly concerned the question whether a national court could be allowed, when asked to rule on a certain system of State aids, to take into account the possible violation of Article 28 as well. The Court's reply was comprehensive.

First the Court dealt with the question whether 'obstacles to trade' covered by other provisions of the Treaty could be absorbed by Article 28 (or better by the wide interpretation of that provision given by the Court itself). The ECJ first acknowledged that an aid regime is likely to have at least an indirect effect on trade. However, the following elements should have also been taken into account: the particular purpose of specific Treaty provisions, their position in the general context of the Treaty aims, and their respective fields of application.

The purpose and context of the State aid regime were identified by the Court as consisting of: (a) the non-mandatory nature of Article 87; the article provides

[14] Case C-379/98 *PreussenElektra AG v Schleswag AG* [2001] ECR I-2099; see below.
[15] Case 74/76 *Iannelli v Meroni* [1977] ECR 557, at para 10.

in fact for a series of exceptions, and confers on the Commission a wide discretion to accept a State aid in derogation of the paragraph 1 prohibition; (b) the transfer to the Commission of full responsibility to carry out an analysis of whether a national measure had to be considered as contrary to the internal market. The purpose and context of the free movement provisions were instead: (a) their mandatory and explicit and unconditional nature; and (b) their direct invokability before national courts. Thus the Court concluded that:

*the effect of an interpretation of Article 30 (now Art. 28) which is so wide as to treat an aid as such within the meaning of Article 92 (now Art. 87) as being similar to a quantitative restriction referred to in Article 30 would be to alter the scope of Articles 92 and 93 of the Treaty and to interfere with the system adopted in the Treaty for the division of powers by means of the procedure for keeping aids under constant review as described in Article 93.*[16]

The distinction between State aid and free movement provisions is therefore not functional, but rather, one could say, 'constitutional'. In other words, the allocation of competence as provided by the Treaty, *Commission-State Aid v Individuals—Free Movement* makes it impossible to use them interchangeably. However, the assumption upon which the entire reasoning is based is the recognition that both sets of rules are pursuing an identical aim, namely that of ensuring the free movement of goods under normal conditions of competition.[17]

The prohibition contained in the free movement provisions against any possible obstacle to the free flow of goods and the prohibition contained in Article 87(1) EC of aid which distorts or threatens to distort competition have then the same legal consequence: that the national measure in question is incompatible with Community law.[18] Only by keeping in mind this functional identity can one fully understand the approach towards the question of the mutual exclusivity of the two sets of provisions.

As is well known, in *Iannelli* the Court, contrary to the Opinion of AG Warner, held that:

*Those aspects of aid which contravene specific provisions of the Treaty other than Articles 92 (now Art. 87) and 93 (now Art. 88) may be so indissolubly linked to the object of the aid that it is impossible to evaluate them separately so that their effect on the compatibility or incompatibility of the aid viewed as a whole must therefore of necessity be determined in the light of the procedure prescribed in Article 93. Nevertheless the position is different if it is possible when a system of aid is being analysed to separate those conditions or factors which, even though they form part of this system, may be regarded as not being necessary for the attainment of its object or for its proper functioning.*[19]

---

[16] Case 74/76 *Iannelli v Meroni* [1977] ECR 557, at para. 12.

[17] See Case 17/81 *Pabst & Richarz* [1982] ECR 1331; Case 17/84 *Commission v Ireland* [1985] ECR 2375; Case 103/84 *Commission v Italy* [1986] ECR 1759; Cases C-78/90 to C-83/90 *Compagnie Commerciale de l'Ouest* [1992] ECR I-1847; Case C-17/91 *Lornoy* [1992] ECR I-6523; Cases C-113/00 and C-114/00, *Spain v Commission* [2002] ECR I-7657.

[18] Case C-21/88 *Du Pont de Nemours Italiana* [1990] ECR I-889, AG Opinion, paras 11–13.

[19] *Iannelli*, above n 15, at para 14.

In this latter case, the national court was allowed to take into account possible violations based on free movement provisions.

This 'severability' test has been severely criticized for lacking clarity and for its difficult application.[20] However, when looked at in the above context, the test is clearly aimed at ensuring the effective application of EC law and at the dismantling of possible national barriers. In the vast majority of cases where the issue of the relationship between State aid and free movement had been raised, the Court invariably managed to spell out how a particular contested measure could be severed from a general State aid regime, and thus be made subject to scrutiny under the free movement provisions. The *Buy Irish* judgment[21] is a good example. The case concerned an advertizing campaign financed by the Irish Government, and aimed at promoting sales of Irish products. AG Capotorti in a very strong Opinion argued that such a campaign should not have been considered as a measure having equivalent effect, as the contested measures were '*in the nature not of barriers or obstacles to trade established by the public authorities but rather of public aid whereby it sought to give domestic producers a competitive advantage over foreign producers*'.[22] The Court held instead that the mere fact that the campaign itself was directly financed by State resources did not mean that it could escape the prohibitions laid down in Article 28. Behind this very curt reply again lies the assumption that State aid and free movement provisions serve the same purpose. The Court identified the substitution of domestic products for imported products on the Irish market as the true Government intention: an intention which was both anti-competitive and liable to hinder trade.

The same approach was adopted in *Commission v France*, a case concerning a tax advantage granted to newspaper publishers on condition that the newspapers were printed in France. The ECJ replied once again that '*the provisions relating to the free movement of goods, the repeal of discriminatory tax provisions and aid have a common objective, namely to ensure the free movement of goods under normal conditions of competition*'.[23] Thus, the mere fact that a national measure can be defined as an aid could not rule out the applicability of the prohibition on obstacles to trade. The effect on market access therefore undoubtedly plays a role in the assessment of State aid.

A final recent example is AG Jacobs' Opinion in *GEMO*, where distortion of competition and effect on trade between Member States are examined in one breath. Jacobs points out that the provision free of charge in France of the service of the collection and disposal of animal carcasses and slaughterhouse waste reduces the price of French meat exports to other Member States by relieving the meat export sector from costs which it would normally have to bear.

---

[20] P. Oliver, *Free Movement in the European Community*, London, IV ed, 2003, at p 107, citing A. Dashwood, Case note, in ELR (1977) 367.

[21] Case 249/81 *Commission v Ireland* [1982] ECR 4005.

[22] Ibid, p. 4031.

[23] Case 18/84 *Commission v France* [1985] ECR 1339.

Conversely, meat imports from other Member States, which have to bear the costs of the disposal of dangerous animal material in their State of origin, are made more difficult: through the meat purchase tax at the retail stage those meat imports have to contribute to the costs of disposing of waste produced by their French competitors.[24]

In conclusion, it could be argued that the test used by the Court does not really focus on the possible severability of the State aid/free movement aspects, but rather on ensuring the effective application of EC law to national measures which could constitute an obstacle to trade. As has been observed the Court was prompt in reacting to the 'unattractive nature'[25] of the mutual exclusivity argument. In *Buy Irish* and in *France v Commission*, neither aid had been notified by the Member States. Accepting the defence argument that Article 28 was not applicable would have left the breach of Community law unsanctioned.

Such a 'bias' in favour of the application of free movement provisions implies a further consequence: the enhancement of the role of national courts which were given the green light to be involved, albeit indirectly, in reviewing State aid regimes. It should be stressed once again that the *Iannelli* case was really about the jurisdictional powers of the Italian courts. The ECJ replied that by identifying the conditions under which Article 28 could be applicable, the national court was then directly entitled to protect individuals' rights which could have been violated by the imposition of a measure contrary to the principle of free movement of goods. It is also worth noting that most of the cases where the Court found in favour of a possible application of free movement provisions concerned non-notified aids. In those circumstances the only possibility for national courts (and thus for individuals) to review a system of aid arose in the Article 88 scenario, namely because of the failure of a Member State to wait for the Commission approval before enforcing it.[26]

The link between free movement/State aid and the question of allocation of competence between national courts and the Commission is apparent even in more recent decisions. The *Nygård* judgment[27] concerned a levy imposed by Denmark on the production of live pigs for export. The national court had no doubts about the compatibility of such a measure with the free movement of goods. It was, however, unsure whether the authorization, granted by the Commission under Article 87(3) of the Treaty to the Danish scheme of production levies, could preclude it from setting aside a levy used to finance authorized aid. The ECJ repeated that the correct institutional arrangement proscribed that the decision whether an aid scheme was compatible with the internal market was a matter which the Commission alone was competent to determine.[28] However, it

---

[24] Case C-126/01 *Ministre de l'Economie, des Finances et de l'Industrie v GEMO*, Opinion of 30 April 2002, nyr, para 84.

[25] Oliver, n 20 above, at p 108.

[26] Case 120/73 *Lorenz* [1973] ECR 1471.

[27] Case C-234/99 *Niels Nygård v Svineafgiftsfonden* [2002] ECR I-3657.

[28] *Lonroy*, n 17 above, and Case C-72/92 *Scharbatke* [1993] ECR I-5509.

also recognized that national courts have full responsibility in checking whether any other directly effective provisions might have been violated, especially '*with a view to remedying, if necessary, infringements of Community law which have not been confirmed in the procedure provided for under Article 88 of the Treaty*'.[29] Therefore, whilst the compatibility of an aid is still a Commission responsibility, national courts also need to carry out an assessment of an economic and social nature, and in particular as for '*the assessment of the manner in which the revenue generated by a domestic parafiscal charge is allocated, the national courts are best placed to collate the necessary information and to carry out the assessments required in that regard*'.[30]

Thus, even if a scheme has been authorized by the Commission, a national court may carry out an assessment of whether certains conditions may constitute a violation of free movement provisions in order to protect individual rights which would not otherwise be protected.

## IV. Definition, delineation, and justification

If it is clear that the political economy of State aid and of free movement are interconnected, the question of justifications to possible violations of the two sets of provisions arises next.

The 'old' case law of the Court immediately clarified that when confronted with national measures which were openly of a distinctly applicable nature, such as in *Buy Irish* or *Commission v France*, the aid argument could not be used as justification to derogate from the application of either Article 28 or Article 90. The *Du Pont des Nemours* judgment[31] is particularly illustrative. In that case the Italian Government tried to 'justify' the imposition of a fixed quota of public contracts to undertakings established in the south of Italy by simply arguing that such a measure had to be considered as an 'aid'. The Court, having qualified this measure as a measure having equivalent effect to a quantitative restriction, held that the Treaty rules on State aids could not be used to frustrate the scope of Article 28. Thus, as made explicit in AG Lenz's Opinion, once Article 28 applies, derogations from the principle of free movement of goods must be interpreted restrictively, and as they are expressly enumerated in Article 30.[32]

However, in the light of the functional identity of State aid and free movement provisions discussed above, the more interesting question is whether some of the principles elaborated so far as regards the possible grounds available to Member States to justify a breach of free movement provisions could be applied to the field of State aid. Without dwelling on the *vexata questio* whether the distinction between Treaty derogations and other grounds of justification is still valid, or

---

[29] *Niels Nygård*, above n 27, at para 60.
[30] Ibid, para 61.
[31] *Du Pont*, n 18 above. See also Case 103/84 *Commission v Italy* [1986] ECR 1759.
[32] *Du Pont*, n 18 above, at p 910.

whether the ECJ uses them interchangeably,[33] it is becoming increasingly apparent that the ECJ tends to treat the question of justifications in a unitary approach. First, the Court clarified that breaches of the four freedoms can be justified under the principle of 'overriding public interests' provided that four conditions are satisfied: 'they must apply in a non-discriminatory manner; they must be justified by imperative requirements in the general interest; they must be suitable for securing the attainment of the objective which they pursue; and they must not go beyond what is necessary in order to attain it'.[34] Secondly, in *Wouters*[35] the Court applied the same reasoning on the question of justifiability to a possible distortion of competition and to a free movement of services issue. As regards the competition rules, it clearly did so at the level of the threshold question whether a particular type of conduct is caught by the Treaty provisions. The same trend might be detected in the field of State aid, in particular in cases at the borders of the definition of what constitutes an aid. Other contributors in this volume point to the case law on the financing of services of general economic interest as an example of a possible transplant of a rule of reason in the field of State aid law.[36] The full debate currently before the ECJ is described in those contributions, and need not be analysed here. Suffice it to say that the ECJ's approach in *Ferring*[37] resembles the rule-of-reason approach of *Cassis de Dijon*: any public service policy may justify what is effectively a subsidy, by conceptualizing the subsidy as not constituting a State aid, provided it does not go beyond compensation for the provision of the service in question. It is clear that such a test would effectively need to function in the same way as standard issues of justification in free movement law. For one thing, the principle of proportionality would need to apply to the question of determining whether the subsidy is purely compensatory. By contrast, the so-called State aid approach, defined in case law of the Court of First Instance and advocated by AG Léger in *Altmark Trans*,[38] is predicated on the concept that financing services of general economic interest requires justification under Article 86(2) EC. Proportionality would of course again apply, but it would seem that the institutional approach would be markedly different. The Commission monitors the application of Article 86(2), and it is not clear whether there would be any remaining territory for national courts, other than in cases of non-notified aid. The constitutional and institutional issues discussed above therefore find themselves replayed in this debate.

---

[33] For a discussion see AG Jacobs' Opinion in Case C-379/98 *PreussenElektra v Schleswag*, n 14 above and Oliver, 'Some further reflections on the scope of Articles 28–30' (1999) 36 CMLRev, 783, at 804–806.

[34] Case C-55/94 *Gebhard* [1995] ECR I-4165, at para 37 and Case C-390/99 *Canal Satélite Digital*, judgment of 22 January 2002, nyr.

[35] N 4 above.

[36] See Rizza and Ross above.

[37] Case C-53/00 *Ferring* [2001] ECR I-9067.

[38] Case C-280/00 *Altmark Trans GmbH, Regierungspräsidium Magdeburg v Nahverkehrsgesellschaft Altmark*, Opinions of 19 March 2002 and 14 January 2003, nyr.

It is also interesting to reflect on what the consequences of either approach, compensation or State aid, could be for the delineation of the Treaty's free movement and State aid provisions. The questions here relate not so much to the free movement of goods, but rather to the free provision of services. Let us take the facts of *GEMO*,[39] where the State compensates the public service obligations imposed on carcass disposal undertakings. Assuming that the compensation approach prevails, the legal conclusion of the State aid question is that there is no such aid. The next point seems to be whether the measure at issue could be considered a restriction on the freedom to provide services, in so far as it affects carcass disposal undertakings established in other Member States. If the Treaty's State aid provisions are inapplicable, there would seem to be no barrier whatsoever to applying the provisions on services. The outcome of such application would seem to be that the State should not discriminate against service suppliers from other Member States.[40] This may mean that the State cannot simply impose the public service obligation on its own companies, and then compensate them for that. Again, there would be no State aid, so there would clearly be no defence in arguing that the scheme is in some way compatible with the Treaty.

By contrast, it is not clear whether the Treaty provisions on freedom to provide services would apply within the context of the State aid approach to financing of public services. It may not be possible to sever the effect on free movement from the overall assessment under Article 86(2) EC, which would constitute an argument for locating the analysis of such financing only within the framework of the Treaty provisions on State aid and services of general economic interest.

At another level of the relationship between State aids and free movement, the *PreussenElektra* judgment[41] needs to be analysed. The case concerned a German law which imposed an obligation on electricity distributors to purchase electricity produced from renewable energy suppliers within their area at fixed minimum prices, and required upstream suppliers to compensate them. The law was apparently based on environmental concerns, specifically the promotion of renewable energy sources. The Court was confronted with two questions. The first was whether the purchase obligation amounted to an aid even if this obligation did not involve a transfer of state resources, and the second was whether it could be considered as a measure having equivalent effect. The Court reaffirmed its *Sloman Neptun* acquis, and restated that only advantages granted directly or indirectly through State resources were to be considered aid within the meaning of Article 87(1).[42] It then found that the obligation imposed on private electricity suppliers to purchase electricity produced from renewable

---

[39] N 24 above.

[40] Case C-260/89 *ERT* [1991] ECR I-2925, Case C-353/89 *Commission v Netherlands* [1991] ECR I-4069 and Cases C-27/90, 281/90, and 289/90 *Commission v Netherlands* [1992] ECR I-5833.

[41] *PreussenElektra* n 14 above.

[42] Joined Cases C-72/91 and C-73/91 *Sloman Neptun v Bodo Ziesemer* [1993] ECR I-887; See also Joined Cases C-52/97, C-53/97, and C-54/97 *Viscido* [1998] ECR I-2629.

energy sources at fixed minimum prices did not involve any direct or indirect transfer of State resources to undertakings which produced that type of electricity. The Court concluded that, although the purchase obligation was imposed by statute and conferred an undeniable advantage on certain undertakings, that was not sufficient to confer upon it the character of State aid. On the possible violation of Article 28, the judgment states that the measure was at least potentially an obstacle within the meaning of Article 28, since it favoured German electricity and discouraged undertakings from importing electricity from other Member States. However, one had to look at the 'aim' of the measure. Since growth in the use of renewable energy sources was 'among the priority objectives' of the Community, since environmental protection had to be integrated into other Community policies, and since the German measure was also designed to protect the health and life of humans, animals, and plants within the meaning of Article 30 EC, the law was not incompatible with Article 28. Moreover, the Court noted, the nature of electricity was such that once it has been allowed into the transmission or distribution system it was difficult to determine its origin and the source of energy from which it was produced.

This judgment has been subjected to various criticisms,[43] especially as regards the very restrictive notion of aid adopted and the Court's failure to clarify explicitly whether a clearly discriminatory measure, where based on environmental concerns, may still be justified by reference to a mandatory requirement. However, we wish to focus on the relationship between the first and second parts of the judgment. The Court's approach may be explained perhaps with reference to the idea that, although the whole scheme did certainly have an anti-competitive effect and constitute an obstacle to trade, it could none the less be justified as it was deemed to pursue an objective of public interest. The general test on justification would then be that EC prohibitions do not apply to restrictions which are essential in order to attain the legitimate aims which they pursue. As AG Cosmas argued in his Opinion in *Deliège*, a case on the compatibility of rules of professional sporting associations, '*the idea is that rules which, at first sight, reduce competition, but are necessary precisely in order to enable market forces to function or to secure some other legitimate aim, should not be regarded as infringing the Community provisions on competition*'.[44] Such a reconstruction seems to confer on Member States a considerable degree of leeway, a margin of appreciation confirmed also by the disappointing lack of any discussion by the Court on the proportionality of the measure at stake in *PreussenElektra*. The Court simply concluded its judgment by stating that the measure should not be considered as incompatible with Article 28. It made no mention of the questions whether the system laid down by German legislation was appropriate for securing the attainment of the objective of environmental protection and whether it

---

[43] See in particular Rubini, in Diritto Comunitario e degli Scambi Internazionali, 3/2001, 473 and Bronckers & Van Der Vlies in [2001] ECLR 458.

[44] Joined Cases C-51/96 and C-191/97 *Christelle Deliège* [2000] ECR I-2549, Opinion, para 110.

went beyond what was necessary. It is important to stress that AG Jacobs, having accepted that environmental concerns had to be taken into account in interpreting the Treaty provisions on the free movement of goods, expressed serious doubts about the proportionality of the system. In particular, he could not find any reason why electricity from renewable sources produced in another Member State would not contribute to the reduction of greenhouse gas emissions in Germany to the same extent as electricity from renewable sources produced in Germany. Secondly, the necessity to exclude producers in other Member States of electricity from renewable sources was at least questionable. As argued by the same Advocate General elsewhere, the approach towards justifications should be based on a unitary concept, namely whether the ground invoked is a legitimate aim of general interest and, if so, whether the restriction *'can properly be justified under the principle of proportionality. In any event, the more discriminatory the measure, the more unlikely it is that the measure complies with the principle of proportionality.'*[45] A proper assessment of proportionality therefore also serves as an indirect guarantee for controlling state measures. As mentioned in the Opinion of AG Jacobs in *PreussenElektra*, the risks derived from the inapplicability of the State aid rules to undertakings which are financed through private resources should not be exaggerated as the undertakings required to finance such measures *'will use all legal and political means at their disposal to combat the measures in question'.*[46] However, the full protection of these individual rights in national law depends also on the clarity of guidance from Luxembourg.

Nor is the Court's reference to the nature of electricity, and the difficulties of identifying its origin once it is on the grid, terribly convincing, in particular in the light of its own case law. In *Outokumpu*[47] the Court looked at Finnish excise duties on electricity. As regards domestic electricity the tax system differentiated in accordance with environmental considerations. However, as regards imported electricity there was a flat-rate system, where the rate was set between the highest and lowest domestic rates and corresponded to the average rate levied on electricity of domestic origin. The Finnish authorities sought to justify this on the basis that it was not possible to determine the origin of imported electricity once it had entered the distribution network, so that it was not possible to apply the tax differentiations. The Court did not accept this defence, which it characterized as irrelevant 'practical difficulties', and simply established that in at least some cases imported electricity was taxed more highly than similar domestic electricity. This was sufficient to establish a violation of Article 90 EC.

If one compares this judgment with *PreussenElektra* the rules on discriminatory taxation appear stricter than those on regulatory obstacles to trade. Article 90 EC is not accompanied by an express Treaty provision permitting derogation,

[45] Case C-136/00 *Rolf Dieter Danner*, judgment of 3 October 2002, nyr. Opinion para 40.
[46] N 14 above, para 158.
[47] Case C-213/96 *Outokumpu* [1998] ECR I-1777. See further Van Calster, 'Greening the EC's State Aid and Tax Regimes', [2000] ECLR, 294.

nor did the Court accept that environmental considerations could be argued in the broad approach of *PreussenElektra*, where the Court appeared to have no problems with the clear discrimination against foreign suppliers of green electricity. It is therefore questionable whether there is currently a coherent approach to justification issues in the areas of taxation and regulation, respectively. What a Member State may be able to achieve through regulation (such as compelling electricity distributors to purchase a certain amount of green electricity only with domestic suppliers) it cannot achieve by way of differential taxation of domestic and imported green electricity. In fact, the tax system in *Outokumpu* appeared on the whole less discriminatory than the German legislation in *PreussenElektra*.

Moreover, if one brings the State aid dimension into the equation, the difference in approach between taxation and regulation becomes even more disturbing. In *PreussenElektra* the Court confirmed that regulatory measures which lead to subsidization by private companies are not caught by the State aid rules. By contrast, taxation is of course generally subject to the State aid disciplines.[48] If Germany had attempted to achieve its environmental goals by giving subsidies to domestic green electricity producers, there would have been little doubt that there was a State aid, and the Commission would have been able to supervise the scheme. If Germany had attempted to achieve those goals by taxing green electricity at a lesser rate than imported electricity, Article 90 EC would have applied, and the environmental objective would not have been able to save the measure, at least not if *Outokumpu* continues to be good law.

Whilst we agree with the boundaries which the Court drew around the State aid concept in *PreussenElektra*, the case none the less shows that care should be taken to achieve a consistent approach to the internal market, where obstacles to trade and distortions of competition ought to be addressed in such a way that the validity of national measures does not depend on the type of governmental measure, but rather on its effects on trade and competition.

## V. CONCLUSION

This chapter perhaps raises more questions than it manages to answer. The analysis in any event shows that the relationship between State aid law and general internal market law deserves further study and reflection. That is partly due to the fact that State aid law is still, despite the age of the Treaty, in a phase of conceptual uncertainty. However, its juxtaposition with free-movement law may also enrich the latter, and reveals certain problematic features and conceptual uncertainties in that area too. Perhaps the time has come to attempt to construct an even more unified theory of the internal market, connecting not only the various strands of free movement, but also competition and State aid law. This is clearly an important and broad agenda for further academic reflection and research.

---

[48] See Quigley below.

# 6

# Recent Developments in Commission State Aid Policy and Practice

## MARIA REHBINDER[1]

## I. INTRODUCTION

When European State aid control was introduced as a key pillar of the European Community competition discipline in the Treaty of Rome, the main responsibility for this task was placed on the European Commission. Of course, obligations were also imposed on Member States to notify all intended aid measures and to refrain from implementing them prior to Commission approval. A relatively broad margin of discretion for the Commission to approve aid which contributes to Community objectives was provided by the Treaty. Within this framework Community State aid law has developed through the jurisprudence of the European Courts and the practice of the Commission.

The European Courts have played an important role in clarifying the limits of European State aid control and in recent years the ECJ has delivered several crucial judgements clarifying the concept of State aid. The European Courts also had an important role in the development of procedural rules for State aid control, although this has diminished somewhat in recent years following the codification of procedural rules in the State aid procedural regulation.

The jurisprudence of the Courts is relatively well known to lawyers interested in State aid law and landmark decisions such as *Preussen-Elektra*,[2] *Ferring*,[3] and *Stardust*[4] are discussed in the literature. Commission practice, as it is embodied in Commission soft law, appears to be less well known outside the Commission and the Member States' authorities dealing with State aid matters. This is even more true of the practical functioning of the Commission State aid control system. The objective of this Chapter is to provide some highlights on these aspects of the State aid discipline.

In this Chapter I first deal with recent developments of Commission soft law. I explain two very different initiatives aimed at reinforcing and modernising State aid control: the multisectoral framework, and the communication on risk capital. I also briefly comment on recent Commission texts on specific forms of

---

[1] The views expressed are the author's own and should not be interpreted as representing the position of the European Commission.
[2] Case C-379/98 *PreussenElektra AG v Schleswag AG* [2001] ECR I-2099.
[3] Case C-53/00 *Ferring* [2001] ECR I-9067.
[4] Case C-482/99 *France v Commission* [2002] ECR I-4397.

aid, and notably on the Notice on direct business taxation. The second part of the Chapters concerns the experiences to date of procedural reform.

Before turning to these subjects, I would make two introductory remarks on State aid policy and the development of the State aid control system in general. First, recent developments in Commission practice reflect the main line of State aid policy as set out by the Prodi Commission. The Commission is determined to keep tight control over State aid, with the objective of reducing distortions of competition. Commissioner Monti has also made clear that strict State aid policy is one of his political priorities. This Commission policy, which aims at reinforcing State aid control, together with modernizing State aid rules, translates itself into a number of different initiatives, not all of which are covered in this Chapter.

Secondly, a few words are needed about the development of the State aid control system. In this respect, the general trend is a development towards a more transparent and rule-based system, with the increased involvement of Member States (and very recently the national Courts). One element contributing to this trend is that the Commission, in the mid-nineties, modified its view on the desirability of secondary legislation in the form of Council regulations based on Article 89 of the Treaty. Previously the Commission had been hesitant in this respect, because several earlier proposals to the Council had not been adopted. This change of approach has resulted in the adoption of the procedural regulation,[5] and the enabling regulation[6] which enables the Commission to adopt block exemptions for certain types of horizontal aid.

## II. Guidelines clarifying compatibility criteria

### A. Aid for Community objectives

Within the scope of the derogations included in Article 87, the Treaty provides a relatively broad margin of discretion for the Commission to consider aid compatible with the Common Market. The underlying principle is that any distortion of competition resulting from State aid should be balanced against the benefit that the aid can have in contributing to important Community objectives.

Over time the assessment criteria for many types of aid have, in practice, become well established and have been incorporated by the Commission in an increased body of soft law. This soft law has, to a large extent, consisted of guidelines aimed at defining the criteria against which the Commission assesses the compatibility of State aid measures for 'traditional horizontal' objectives.[7] It

[5] Council Regulation no 659/99 laying down detailed rules for the application of Article 93 EC, *OJ* L 83, 27.03.1999, p.1–9.

[6] Council Regulation (EC) No 994/98 on the application of Articles 92 and 93 of the EC Treaty to certain categories of horizontal aid, *OJ* L 142, 14.5.1998, p.1–4.

[7] Soft law can be called guidelines, framework, notice, or communication, which does not affect their status. However, guidelines and frameworks often focus on compatibility criteria for traditional types of aid whereas texts that focus on certain forms of aid (e.g. fiscal aid, guarantees) have more often been called notices.

includes objectives such as regional development, supporting small and medium-sized companies, employment, environment, research and development, and training. The main control method involves determining eligible expenses and maximum allowable aid intensities.

The Commission guidelines have been adopted for specific time periods and are reviewed periodically. Aid for traditional horizontal objectives is today largely covered by the enabling regulation and is, accordingly, potentially appropriate for inclusion in block exemptions in the context of these periodic reviews.

The periodic reviews provide an opportunity to modify soft law in the light of developments in the Common Market and State aid policy. Two recent examples are the new multisectoral framework[8] and the communication on risk capital.[9] The key objectives of the reform introduced by the multisectoral framework are a reduction of aid levels and simplification. The communication on risk capital, for its part, is dealing with a new type of aid measure (and Community objective?) and it underlines an economic approach.

These two recent texts highlight one of the main challenges for developing the State aid discipline in relation to the compatibility criteria. It is not always easy to combine the objective of a strict rule-based approach with flexibility to consider an economic assessment of individual aid measures.

## B. Regional investment aid for large projects and to sectors with structural problems (the multisectoral framework)

The Commission has recently completed a radical reform of the rules that limit aid both to large regional investment projects and to the sensitive manufacturing sectors. Such aid can be particularly distortive and give rise to subsidy races between 'poor' regions to attract large investment projects from multinational enterprises. In such cases, the amount of aid granted results in a distortion of competition that is unlikely to be outweighed by a positive impact on regional development.

To address these issues, in 1997 the Commission adopted a multisectoral framework, reducing aid ceilings for large projects. The reduction of the aid ceiling depended on the capital intensity, the market share of the company, the situation of the relevant market, and the degree of indirect job creation. In addition, for the so-called sensitive sectors such as the automotive industry and the synthetic fibres sector, special guidelines have been in place for a long time.[10]

The recent evaluation of the first multisectoral framework concluded that the rules were too complicated, with too heavy an administrative procedure and, perhaps most important, insufficient reduction of aid levels to prevent unjustified

---

[8] Communication from the Commission: Multisectoral framework on regional aid for large investment projects, *OJ C 70, 19.03.2002, p.8–20*

[9] Commission Communication on State aid and risk capital *OJ C 235, 210.8.2001, p. 3–11.*

[10] Special rules also apply to steel and shipbuilding as well as coal, transport, agriculture, and fisheries. These sectors are not covered by the multisectoral framework.

distortions of competition. Therefore, in February 2002 the Commission adopted a new framework that will replace the old one as from 1 January 2004. It represents a radical simplification of the rules and ensures an effective limitation of the aid authorized for large-scale projects. The new framework has the following features.

1. *It is based on the normal rules or maximum aid intensities for regional investment.*

2. *Normal regional aid ceilings are reduced automatically according to the size of the investment. For eligible costs above 50 million euros, only 50 per cent of the aid ceiling can be granted; for costs above 100 million euros, only 34 per cent of the aid ceiling of the region may be granted. For example, in an area with a regional aid ceiling of 20 per cent a project with an investment totalling 100 million euros could obtain 15 million euros of aid. In this way the new framework for the first time uses project size to determine allowable aid. There is a small bonus for projects that are co-financed from the European structural funds, which intends to strengthen the cohesion within the Union.*

3. *Sectoral rules are integrated in the general framework. The Commission intends to establish a list of sectors suffering from structural problems. No aid at all will be authorized for these sectors, with the possible exception of a fast-growing niche market within the sector.*

4. *The new rules significantly simplify the notification obligation for large regional investment projects. Individual notification is only necessary for cases where the aid exceeds the permissible aid level for projects of 100 million euros in the region concerned. Therefore the number of cases that will be scrutinized by the Commission is reduced.*

5. *The Commission assessment criteria for notified projects are much simpler than before and are based on competition considerations. The Commission will look at the situation of the specific sector concerned. If a notified project reinforces a high market share (i.e. more than 25 per cent) or increases capacity in a non-growing sector by more than 5 per cent, no aid at all will be authorized. If the market share and capacity do not constitute such problems, the aid that can be authorized is calculated in the way described above.*

It should be added that the new multisectoral framework includes a separate chapter on steel, which prohibits regional investment aid in this sector. A separate Communication, adopted at the same time as the multisectoral framework, includes a prohibition of rescue and restructuring aid to the steel industry, but allows closure aid under certain conditions.[11] With this Communication, the Commission continues strict control of State aid to the steel sector following the expiry of the ECSC Treaty in July 2002.

---

[11] Communication from the Commission: Rescue and restructuring aid and closure aid for the steel sector, *OJ C 70, 19.03.2002, p. 21.*

## C. Risk capital

The State aid discipline must be able to respond to developments in the Common Market and changes in Community policy priorities. This may be possible without entirely changing the basic approach, as has been the case for the multisectoral framework. The new framework continues to be based on the normal regional aid rules and the maximum aid ceilings established in the regional maps. The limitation continues to operate as a reduction of these maximum aid intensities.

Recently, however, the traditional approach has proved problematic in dealing with some measures aiming to promote risk capital. In the late 'nineties the Commission was confronted with a new type of measure that Member States wanted to introduce, notably in the context of the European Structural Funds. This was at the time when the European Council was underlining the importance of the 'new economy' and many papers were published comparing the venture capital markets in Europe and the US which pleaded for measures to encourage the development of European Risk Capital markets in order to reach levels comparable to those in the US.

It may not come as a surprise that such policy priorities became a problem in the context of the State aid rules: the problem is that risk capital is not linked to an eligible cost. How to find such aid compatible and how to set criteria for control? Moreover, how to assess aid to co-investors? Or aid at the level of risk capital funds?[12] In order to clarify its policy for assessing risk capital measures, the Commission has responded with a new type of soft law and the compatibility criteria in the risk capital communication differ from those of traditional guidelines. The communication strongly underlines the need to establish the presence of a *market failure* as a criterion for authorizing aid.

The following criteria are provided for assessing compatibility:

1. *a 'safe harbour' for transactions below certain levels (1 million euros in Article 87(1)(a) regions; 750,000 euros in (c) regions; 500,000 euros in other regions);[13]*
2. *above these levels there is a need to prove market failure: the aid must be proportionate to the market failure and must minimize distortion; and*

---

[12] The traditional approach to State aid control is reflected in a set of principles and assumptions, embodied both explicitly and implicitly in the Commission's soft law. They include *inter alia* the following: (1) State aid is granted for a specific purpose, which can be expressed concretely in the form of the *eligible costs* for achieving that purpose; (2) State aid measures that are not in the form of grants must be given an *aid value* in order to assess compatibility; (3) the compatibility of an aid measure depends primarily on the aid intensity, which is measured in grant equivalents (aid in relation to the 'eligible' costs); and (4) operating aid is normally forbidden. Additionally, it is often implicit in the traditional approach that: (5) aid is granted to the entity benefiting from the aid. These elements of the traditional approach posed problems for risk capital measures, which are normally in the form of capital injections that are not provided for a specific purpose and cannot be measured in grant equivalents.

[13] The justification given is that for small transactions the argument that market failure exists through high transaction costs is more persuasive.

3. *additional compatibility criteria are expressed as 'positive' and 'negative' elements to be taken into account.*

The experience with this new type of approach is limited so far and suggests that the 'safe harbour' has been the most important element of the risk capital communication. However, the instrument provides for a potentially interesting test of basing compatibility on the concept of a market failure and it allows a more flexible approach than the traditional guidelines. On the other hand, transparency and predictability cannot be as high as is the case for *traditional* soft law.

The risk capital communication should not be interpreted as a complete change of the traditional approach. In the communication the Commission confirms its belief that there are, in general, good reasons for the 'eligible costs' approach, which provides certainty, predictability, and a basis for limiting aid and for ensuring equal treatment. The Commission also underlines that a departure from the traditional approach entails the risk of accepting operating aid, which is considered as one of the most distortive types of aid.

## III. NOTICES CLARIFYING THE APPROACH TO SPECIFIC FORMS OF AID

### A. Recent texts

As mentioned above, Commission soft law aims mostly at clarifying the margin of discretion that the Commission has in assessing the compatibility criteria authorizing State aid. In particular, this margin relates to balancing distortions of competition against Community objectives, rather than to the interpretation of the notion of State aid, which is an objective concept. Nevertheless, some soft law focuses primarily focuses on the evaluation of the aid character of specific measures and the aid intensity of specific forms of aid. Recent examples of this type of soft law are the notice on guarantees[14] and the notice on State aid and direct business taxation.[15]

Although it is clear that the State aid assessment should in principle be the same, irrespective of the form in which State aid is provided, certain issues typically arise when assessing certain types of measures. For financial measures, the most important element of the notion of State aid is whether there is a benefit to the company as compared to normal market conditions. The notice on guarantees provides criteria for assessing this. To date, however, not many Commission decisions give concrete interpretation on the criteria provided in the notice, under which public guarantees do not constitute aid. The key issue in

[14] Commission notice on the application of Articles 87 and 88 of the EC Treaty to State aid in the form of guarantees, *OJ C 71, 11.03.2000, p. 14–18.*

[15] Commission notice on the application of the State aid rules to measures relating to direct business taxation, *OJ C 384, 10.12.1998, p. 3–9.*

this respect concerns the acceptable level of premiums on state guarantees.[16] The recent landmark decisions of the Commission concerning guarantees to German public banks deal with a very specific German guarantee system.

For fiscal measures the most important element of the concept of State aid is, in practice, the selectivity criterion, which is also considered in the notice on business taxation. Before commenting shortly on fiscal aid, it must be emphasized that, following the evaluation of whether financial or fiscal measures constitute State aid, the compatibility of the aid should be assessed according to the normal rules on aid for horizontal, regional, or other objectives. Although fiscal and financial measures often take the form of operating aid, and are therefore normally forbidden, this is not necessarily the case. Many types of compatible aid measures can be provided through guarantees or the tax system, if the intensity of the aid can be calculated and the objective is an accepted Community objective.

## B. Notice on direct business taxation

Fiscal aid has recently been high on the agenda of the State aid Community including the Commission, the European Courts, national Courts, and complainants. One of the several factors contributing to this is closely linked to the notice on direct business taxation. This is, of course, the implementation of the Code of good conduct for business taxation agreed by the European Member States in December 1997. This Code provides for a definition of harmful tax competition in the field of business taxation and includes stand still and rollback provisions for such measures. A group has been established in the Council framework to oversee the implementation of the Code.

At the time when the Code of Conduct was agreed, it was already clear that some of the measures that the Code would cover are also covered by Community State aid rules. However, it was also clear that the Code group and State aid assessment would not necessarily coincide. The criteria of the Code are targeted at very specific harmful measures intended, notably, to attract mobile financial investment.

In the context of the agreement on the tax package, which included the Code, the Commission committed itself to the strict application of State aid rules. It undertook to draw up guidelines on the application of the State aid rules relating to direct business taxation. These were intended to provide guidance for the State aid assessment of the package of tax measures identified by the Code of Conduct group. Therefore, it was clear that the notice should give guidance on the key distinction between general measures and State aid. In this respect, the notice provides some general remarks on the distinction between State aid and general measures. It notes that the fact that some firms or some sectors benefit

---

[16] Furthermore the notice deals with the sometimes very difficult issue of establishing who is really benefiting from an aid measures. The notice explains that the aid beneficiary is usually the borrower, who can obtain better financial terms for a loan than those available for him on the financial markets without the guarantee. It is, however, recognized that it can, in certain circumstances, be the *lender* that benefits from the aid.

more than others from some of the tax measures does not necessarily mean that they are caught by the State aid rules.[17]

The notice also deals with the difficult theory that a derogation can be allowed if this is in line with the nature or general scheme of the system. It underlines that a distinction must be made between, on one hand, the external objectives assigned to a tax scheme (in particular regional and social) and, on the other, the objectives inherent in the tax system itself. Measures to avoid international double taxation are mentioned as an example of inherent features, because tax should only be paid once. The notice also assumes as an inherent feature of a profit tax to be that it should be levied on profits. All this might appear self-evident. More significant perhaps is the example of certain exemptions to the rules which are considered difficult to justify by the logic of the tax system. The example given in the notice is 'if non-resident companies are treated more favourably than resident ones or if tax benefits are granted to head offices or to firms providing certain services (for example, financial services) within a group'.[18]

Another factor contributing to the recent high profile of fiscal aid is no doubt the adoption of environmental taxes in most Member States. As new taxes, these are being very carefully scrutinized from the State aid point of view. They also pose very difficult assessment problems. One such problem is to establish the objectives of environmental taxes in order to assess whether derogations are in the nature of the tax system. It might not be always easy to agree which measures are consistent with a corporate tax system, but at least such taxes are well established and there is some degree of consensus on what a normal profit tax system should look like.[19] In the field of environmental taxes, there is much more variety and less consensus at this stage. The scope of the tax base, as to different energy products, is also a difficult issue. In some Member States the tax base has developed step by step from the harmonized excises on mineral oils by adding taxation on other energy products. Other states have totally reformed their environmental taxes, setting clear environmental objectives.

## IV. PROCEDURAL REFORM

### A. Block exempted aid

The system of block exemptions is primarily a procedural reform that introduces derogation from the general obligation to notify aid measures. Because of the

---

[17] See point 14 Two examples are given. First, measures designed to reduce the taxation of labour of all firms, which inevitably have a relatively greater effect on labour-intensive industries than capital-intensive industries. Another example provided is that tax incentives for environmental, R&D, or training investment favour only firms which undertake these investments, but again do not necessarily constitute State aid.

[18] See point 26 of the notice.

[19] Defining the normal tax system was a very popular subject in the 'eighties in the tax expenditure literature, and several countries introduced tax expenditure budgets as annexes to their State budgets.

practice of approval requirements for aid schemes, the notification obligation has never required that each individual aid award by national authorities be notified to the Commission. Nevertheless, one key element of the functioning of State aid control was modified by the adoption of the first block exemptions. For aid measures covered by these exemptions, the *ex ante* control by the Commission has been replaced by *ex post* control.

The first block exemptions adopted by the Commission covered aid to SME, training aid, and *de minimis* aid.[20] The first two measures clarify criteria under which aid to SMEs and training aid can be considered compatible with the Treaty and exempted from the notification obligation. The nature of the block exemption on *de minimis* aid is slightly different, as it defines a global amount of financial support per beneficiary (100,000 euros over three years) which is not considered to constitute a State aid within the meaning of Article 87(1) and is therefore entirely exempted from the State aid rules of the Treaty.

The use of block exemptions has been considered appropriate only when certain conditions are fulfilled. First, the criteria that the Commission applies for judging compatibility should be well established and not in need of significant modifications. Secondly, the use of block exemptions requires that the compatibility criteria can be expressed very precisely in a legal text.

In line with this approach the content of the first three block exemptions follow existing practice. They largely translate the criteria of the earlier guidelines into the more effective and reliable legal form of a regulation. With the introduction of the block exemptions the earlier guidelines for training and SME aid, as well as the notice on *de minimis* aid were abolished. However, the notification obligation has not been completely removed. The new training aid and SME aid regulations provide for notification of larger aid amounts, which the Commission intends to assess on the basis of the criteria provided in the regulations.

The conditions for the use of block exemptions mean that they cannot be expected to cover all horizontal aid in the short term. The recent environmental aid guidelines are a case in point, concerning the two conditions for adopting block exemptions.[21] The Commission also decided not to use the system of block exemptions for research and development aid when the guidelines were recently renewed. However, a block exemption for aid for job creation, which will replace the employment aid guidelines, is expected to enter into force soon.

Following the adoption of the first block exemptions there has been an immediate and significant decrease in the number of notifications of aid

[20] Commission regulation (EC) No 70/2001 on the application of Articles 87 and 88 of the EC Treaty to State aid to small and medium-sized enterprises, *OJ L 10, p. 33–42*; Commission Regulation (EC) No 68/2001 on the application of Articles 87 and 88 of the EC Treaty to training aid, *OJ L 10, 13.01.2001, p. 20–29*; and Commission regulation (EC) No 69/2001 on the application of Articles 87 and 88 of the EC Treaty to *de minimis* aid, *OJ L 10, 13.01.2001, p. 30–32*.

[21] Community guidelines on State Aid for Environmental protection, *OJ C 37, 3.2.2001, p. 3–15*.

schemes to the Commission. In 2001 the number of notifications was down approximately 30 per cent compared with 2000. However, the overall effect on the workload of the Commission will depend on several factors. First, the individual notification obligation for large aid awards is retained and it is not clear how many such notifications will be made. Additionally, Member States might consider the block exemptions as a 'safe harbour', and continue to notify the elements of aid schemes which do not strictly comply with the criteria of the block exemptions.

Because block exemptions are directly applicable, it is important to note that they strengthen the role of national courts. Complainants can go to national courts if their competitors have received aid that does not respect all the conditions of block exempted aid.

## B. The procedural regulation

The procedural regulation codifies, for the first time, State aid procedures in one single binding text. The regulation clarifies the four different procedures used depending on the type of aid: (1) notified aid, (2) unlawful (unnotified) aid, (3) misuse of aid, and (4) existing aid schemes. Already this clarification of the different types of aid procedures is contributing to increased transparency and legal certainty as far as State aid procedures are concerned. After the adoption of the block exemptions a new category of aid has emerged, which is block exempted aid.

An important objective of the procedural regulation was to strengthen the controlling powers of the Commission. In this respect, the provisions of the regulation that reinforce the notification obligation and the standstill clause of the Treaty are of particular interest. The Treaty provides an obligation to notify all plans to grant aid and the standstill clause prohibits the Member State from putting aid into effect until the Commission has authorized it. Many of the new procedural rules can contribute to the respect of these cornerstones of State aid control. However, the procedural regulation has not changed the fact that the Commission has no real sanctions for breach of the notification obligation. The rules on unnotified aid simply aim to restore the competitive situation *ex ante* before the unlawful aid was granted.

I want to comment on the following key aspects of State aid procedures in the light of the procedural regulation:

(1) speeding up Commission procedures;
(2) ensuring that Commission decisions are based on correct and complete information;
(3) restoring the *ex ante* competitive situation when unnotified aid has been granted;
(4) monitoring and control of compliance with Commission decisions.

## C. Speeding up Commission procedures

The Commission is often criticized for the lengthiness of State aid procedures. It is true that the examination of State aid cases can sometimes take a very long time. However, it is important to stress that the problems are of a different nature for notified and unnotified aid.

When an aid is notified to the Commission, the Member State concerned normally has a clear interest in speeding up the Commission decision and is ready to co-operate. Legal time limits for Commission decisions can, in such a situation, be effective in speeding up procedures. Indeed, the procedural regulation reinforces the two-month time limit for the Commission to conclude the initial investigation procedure. It clarifies the 'Lorenz procedure' that is available to the Member State. If no decision has been taken within the two-month time limit, the Member State may put the notified measure into effect, after giving prior notice to the Commission.

However, in practice the problem is that the two-month time period can only start to run from the receipt of a complete notification. If a notification is incomplete, the Commission will request additional information and a new two-month period starts to run from the receipt of that information. The regulation reinforces the position of a Member State which considers that the Commission is requesting too much information. To this end, it provides that a Member State may declare that it considers the notification complete and to request the Commission to take a decision. It appears that Member States have not yet actively explored this option.

The regulation also provides that the Commission may consider a notification withdrawn if the Member State does not provide complete information. The Commission has so far only used this option in a few cases. As long as the standstill clause is respected, no distortion of competition has occurred. However, incomplete notifications result in lengthy procedures and contribute to less efficient case-handling.

In practice the most important contribution to speeding up the initial first phase procedure for notified aid could result from the adoption of a standard notification form on the basis of Article 27 of the procedural regulation. The form can help to clarify, in detail, the information necessary for the assessment.

The regulation also provides for a time limit of eighteen months for closing the investigation procedure by a final decision. This cannot be expected to have considerable incentive effect on the Commission to conclude an examination of notified aid. The eighteen-month time limit is simply too long. Recent Commission practice shows that it is possible to close an investigation procedure within approximately six months with full co-operation from the Member State. The problem with setting time limits is that there should be a distinction between delays resulting from the Commission case handling and delays caused by Member States. Even eighteen months may be too short if the Member State does not co-operate.

The procedural regulation does not provide any time limits for unnotified aid. In such cases Member States have rarely requested the Commission to take a rapid decision. The practical problem for the Commission is the receipt of sufficient information on which to base its decision.

## D. Ensuring complete and correct information

The problem of ensuring complete information is, again, of a very different nature, depending on whether aid is notified or unnotified. A notification form should solve most problems for notified cases of traditional aid. The experience with the notification form of the multisectoral framework is, in this respect, encouraging. Such a form will have to allow for adaptations for different types of aid, reflecting the different types of information required.

In cases of unnotified aid the Member State might not, for obvious reasons, be very eager to provide information to the Commission. The procedural regulation therefore provides for an information injunction, which aims to ensure that the Commission receives the necessary information to deal with such cases. The consequence of an information injunction is that the Commission is entitled to take a decision on the information available if the Member State does not provide the information requested.

The potential for strengthening the information basis by information injunctions remains to be confirmed. The Commission has recently increased the use of such injunctions. However, it is not clear that this has resulted in a significant improvement in the information provided by Member States. The main effect appears to be that the Commission is in a better legal position, in taking decisions on the basis of incomplete information. In this context, it should be noted that the Commission is not generally empowered to undertake inspections in Member States. The novelty introduced by the procedural regulation concerns on-site inspections to monitor *ex post* compliance with Commission decisions.

## E. Restoring the ex ante competitive situation

Ensuring that aid which has been unlawfully granted is reimbursed in an efficient manner is crucial for the credibility of a State aid discipline based on a notification obligation and a standstill clause. The first thing to note is that the regulation empowers the Commission to take some provisional measures as soon as it learns about plans to grant unnotified aid. The Commission can issue a suspension injunction to suspend unlawful aid until the Commission has decided on compatibility; and it can issue a provisional recovery injunction under certain conditions. In rare cases the Commission has made use of a suspension injunction. However, the recovery injunction has not so far been used. The conditions are restrictive and in practice the Commission does not have enough information at this early stage.

The procedural regulation introduced some new elements concerning reimbursement of illegal aid. It has transformed the earlier option of requesting recovery into an obligation on the Commission to order recovery when taking a negative decision on unlawful aid.[22] However, even before the adoption of the procedural regulation, the practice of DG Competition was systematically to order recovery when taking final negative decisions. The Commission also required interest to be paid from the award of the aid until its effective reimbursement. Therefore the procedural regulation mainly confirmed existing practice.

Following a negative decision by the Commission on illegal aid, it is crucial that the recovery decision is executed efficiently. In this respect the procedural regulation provides that recovery shall be effected without delay and in accordance with the procedures under the national law of the Member State concerned, provided that they allow the immediate and effective execution of the Commission's decision. In the event of a procedure before national courts, the procedural regulation provides that a Member State must take all necessary steps which are available in their respective legal systems, including provisional measures, without prejudice to Community law.

The Commission's practice in following up recovery decisions has certainly been strengthened in the last two years. Clear rules and new internal reporting practices have been established for follow-up by DG Competition. If a Member State refuses to comply with the recovery decision, the Commission will refer the case to the Court of Justice. Normally, however, Member States do not refuse to co-operate with the Commission to ensure recovery according to national procedures. It also appears that they normally take the steps which are available in their respective legal orders in the event of a procedure before national courts.

One key problem is that the national procedures are very slow. So far the potential provided by the procedural regulation to question the primacy of national procedures that do not allow for immediate and effective execution have not been explored by the Commission. From any point of view, it is clear that relying on national procedures for recovering aid effectively creates unequal treatment between Member States.

Another aspect of recovery is that negative decisions often come late in the lifetime of companies in difficulties. These difficulties have already resulted often in the insolvency of the company. The recovery claim does not normally have high priority in insolvency procedures.

In some cases, circumvention of a forthcoming recovery decision has been attempted by creating new legal entities to take over the assets of the undertaking subject to the recovery decision. The Commission has recently been vigilant in reacting to such transactions and has extended the recovery obligation to the new legal entity taking over assets. However, it is emphasized that this only applies in clear situations of circumvention.

---

[22] The rare exceptions are: if recovery would be contrary to a general principle of Community law and the 10-year limitation.

## F. Monitoring

Monitoring of compliance with the Commission decisions is an important element of a credible State aid control system. The procedural regulation introduced a new element in this respect by providing for on-site monitoring visits to the aid beneficiary in cases where serious doubts exist about compliance with a Commission decision. This new provision has not yet been used in practice. However, similar monitoring has already been normal practice in some cases of aid to the sensitive sectors. The Commission cannot therefore be expected to hesitate in using the new provision, should there be doubts about the compliance with Commission decisions.

The success of the block exemptions depends heavily on the efficiency of the monitoring and control system that has been introduced. Member States have to provide to the Commission summaries of exempted aid schemes and individual aid awards, with a view to publication in the Official Journal. They are also required to record and compile all information on the exempted aid and to supply the Commission with annual reports.

In this context, it should be stressed that interested parties have a significant role to play in ensuring compliance with the block exemptions through the national courts, due to the direct applicability of the block exemption regulations. Upon action brought against such aid, it will be up to national courts to judge whether the conditions of a block exemption regulation are fulfilled.

Finally, I would like to note that some procedural questions have not been resolved by the procedural regulation, and obviously remain to be clarified. Therefore, the jurisprudence continues to play a significant role.

## V. Futher modernization of the State aid discipline

The key objectives of the modernization project, that has so far resulted in the procedural regulation and the block exemptions, continue to guide the State aid policy of the Commission. Further efforts will be made to increase the transparency and efficiency of procedures and to focus resources on the most distortive types of State aid. The experiences with the procedural regulation and the block exemptions provide a basis on which to build, as the Commission State aid control is facing the challenge of enlargement.

Increased transparency is pursued not only by clarifying the Commission practice in soft law and adopting secondary law on the basis of Article 89; the Commission has also put into place a State aid register and a scoreboard to increase the transparency of the cases decided by the Commission and the State aid policy of Member States. These instruments will be further developed.

At the national level, increased transparency should also help to activate the role of national courts in State aid control. They have an important role to play, not only in the context of the block exemptions, but more broadly in reinforcing the standstill clause of the Treaty. In an enlarged Community with many more Member States, the enforcement of State aid law must become, to a larger extent than it is today, a responsibility shared by the Commission and the national courts.

While the Commission pursues its modernization project, Member States are currently discussing their national State aid policies in the Council. As part of the so-called Lisbon agenda, the European Council has underlined the objectives of reducing and reorienting State aid from undesirable objectives to desirable ones. Discussions are expected to continue in the Council on these issues.

# 7

# State Aid Regulation in Candidate Countries: The Case of Poland

ANNA FORNALCZYK

## I. STATE AID MONITORING AND TRANSITION PROCESS

Market-oriented reforms, which have been carried out in candidate countries since the beginning of the 1990s, require radical changes in undertakings' attitude to financial disciplines and a simultaneous reduction of State activity in the economy. State intervention in a market economy is treated as an exception from market regulation and is subjected to formal restrictions aimed at effective spending of public money.

In the system of the centrally planned economy the State played the role of the main 'entrepreneur', while the regulatory function of the market was inactivated in its task of identifying the volume and structure of supplies and the allocation of production factors according to optimum efficiency of their utilization. In that period domestic producers were protected against competitive imports, which gave them the advantages of manufacturing at high costs, at poor quality, and with low innovation of production. Economic failures were financed by public resources or in the form of cross-subsidies within the framework of multi-plant undertakings. The undertakings got used to poor financial discipline, with active participation by the State in providing them with easily accessible money from the State budget or non-budgetary resources. This has been characterized as a soft budget constraint, which should be eliminated during the transformation process.[1]

The scope of aid from the State and from financial institutions connected with it in a market economy is different from the scope of State aid and competence of financial institutions in a centrally planned economy. It only seems that we are dealing with the same forms of aid (tax holidays and allowances, forbearances, debt forgiveness, subsidies, etc.) and the same financial institutions (budget, tax, subsidy, loan, etc.). In fact the objectives, forms, methods of creation and spending of public resources, and the rules of state interference in the economy

---

[1] J. Kornai, Economics of Shortage, North Holland Publ, Amsterdam, 1980; J. Neneman, M. Sowa, Soft Budget Constraints in Poland, in: Economic Growth, Restructuring and Unemployment in Poland. Theoretical and Empirical Approach, ed. By S. Krajewski, T. Tokarski, Uniwersity of Lodz, Lodz 2002, p. 105–129.

are different in the two systems. The transition to a market economy requires the preparation of new rules and forms of granting State aid.

Economic benefits from State aid for undertakings, sectors, and regions release the function of market mechanisms, putting the beneficiaries of such State aid into a better market position. This infringes the principles of competition, which have become a significant element of market reforms carried out in candidate countries in the 1990s. This, for instance, results in limiting the scale of elimination of inefficient undertakings from the market. Intervention in market mechanisms has usually been explained by social and political reasons. However, the long-term economic effectiveness of such actions is questionable. This particularly applies to the restructuring of the economy that has to increase the competitiveness of the economy in international markets.

Undertakings enjoying State aid must be aware that this is a temporary and targeted intervention, the results of which will be verified by the market during the implementation of the aid scheme and after its completion. State aid cannot be treated as the source of resources to support the existence of permanently inefficient undertakings. Being aware of that is also important for the State administration, which grants State aid. Granting State aid, according to binding law on the monitoring of State aid, is an exceptional means used to solve problems, important from an economic and social point of view, which result from the economic transformation.

The fact that in candidate countries numerous institutions were granting State aid and the—to a large extent—discretionary nature of their decisions were the reasons why criteria to grant aid were unclear before the implementation of State aid legal regulation. Making State aid transparent should be understood as making the use of taxpayers' money more transparent.

In countries with developed market economies, State aid focuses on the realization of objectives important for the development of the economy as a whole which either cannot be financed by private investors (e.g. development of infrastructure, R&D) or are not included in micro-economic calculations of private investors (e.g. protection of the environment). In the theory of economics this is called 'market failures' and these are the fields where State intervention is acceptable. State aid can also be used to restructure undertakings or regions in an especially difficult economic situation.

State aid cannot permanently eliminate the competition from the market, creating a temporarily privileged position for some undertakings to solve economic and social problems in a sector of the economy or in a region. Aid granted by the State or through State resources should improve the economic performance of an undertaking or help to eliminate inefficient operators from the market. Public resources should be engaged to alleviate the social consequences of a company liquidation (benefits for unemployed, funds for retraining of the staff, funds for start-ups).

Generally, State aid can be applied as an element of macro-economic policy of the State in the market economy. It can be linked with activities to reduce unemployment, stabilize the economy, encourage economic growth, change economic structures, and adjust companies to the requirements of competition in the international market. The realization of these objectives requires their translation into given aid schemes with allocated public resources; this is indispensable to realize them in a defined time frame. The way of utilization of these means by the beneficiaries and the evaluation of results are achieved thanks to State aid; they constitute important elements in assessing of the efficiency of the economic policy of the State.

Liberalization of economic co-operation in the world is the reason why the economic impact of State aid is subject to verification of its impact on competitive international markets. Protection of competition in the world market results in an increasingly restrictive approach to State aid, which is reflected in the provisions of international treaties concerning economic co-operation between their signatories.

## A. Premises and rules of State aid monitoring in candidate countries

The need for State aid monitoring does not only result from international obligations of candidate countries (accession negotiations with the European Union, membership of the WTO). The monitoring of State aid is also a relevant element of stabilization of the economy, by means of: budget deficit reduction,[2] public debt reduction, counteracting inflation, making public expenditure more transparent, and improved efficiency of the collection of taxes and other liabilities.

It is worth noting that the efficiency of these activities is interdependent. The reduction of budget deficit and public debt has a significant influence on lowering the inflation rate. An increase in the collection of taxes and liabilities towards special funds influences the level of the budget deficit, while public expenditure transparency helps with efficiency improvement. As a rule, State aid distorts competition creating favourable conditions for some enterprises. However, it is important that it should be limited in time, degressive, and targeted at restoring an enterprise's ability to operate in a competitive market.

Tightening public expenditure discipline creates a friendly climate for reducing the tax burden on entrepreneurs, which enables economic growth and the creation of jobs. That is particularly important in an economy in which sunset sectors are being restructured and unemployment is growing due to the reduction of the number of jobs in these sectors.

Reducing the tax burden allows the reduction of the dead-weight loss of the tax.[3] That loss from the point of view of buyers and sellers of goods amounts to

---

[2] Credibility of the Exchange Rate Policy in Transition Countries, CASE, Warsaw 2001.
[3] Stiglitz Joseph E., Economics of the Public Sector. Second Edition, W.W. Norton & Company, New York, London, 1988, ch.17; Varian, Hal R. Intermediate Microeconomics. A Modern Approach. Third Edition, 1993, ch. 16.

an income for the State. The ultimate result of taxpayers' profit and loss accounts depends on the efficiency of public expenditure.

State aid distorts competition by creating different conditions of operation for different entrepreneurs, because only some of them are the beneficiaries of aid. This means that State aid distorts Pareto efficiency. Justification for such deviation from the principles of effective allocation of resources in the economy are the market failures, appearing especially in the transformation economies characterized by: the need for restructuring whole sectors, rising unemployment rates, polluted natural environment, weak development of small and medium-sized enterprises, and insufficient technical infrastructure for the creation of a modern economy. Directing public money to support the transformation processes of the economy requires monitoring by an administrative body which is not an aid granter, and by Parliament through the enforcement of budgetary laws.

State aid monitoring should concentrate on estimating the influence of aid on competition distortions in markets relevant (both geographically and product-wise) to its beneficiaries, and on calculating the efficiency of the use of public funds granted to enterprises for the realization of tasks included in the support programmes. Because of that, the least efficient kind of aid is named operational aid in a European Union context.

The above arguments show that legal regulations and State aid monitoring are a compromise between Pareto efficient allocation of resources and the need for spending public money on undertakings to support the restructuring of economies in candidate countries.

## B. Association requirements

The Europe Agreements set up competition rules in trade between candidate countries and member countries of the European Union. The so-called competition provision of the Agreement provides, among others, that 'any State aid which distorts or threatens to distort competition by favouring certain undertakings or the production of certain goods' is incompatible with the proper functioning of the Agreements insofar as it may affect trade between the Community and candidate countries.

The competition provision of the Agreement contains a derogation clause, which allows grants of State aid compatible with the provisions of the Europe Agreement, provided that it is addressed to promote economic development or to fight unemployment (sectoral, regional, or horizontal aid) within monitored aid schemes which meet the requirement of transparency of such State activity.

The competition provisions of the Europe Agreement contain rules to ensure transparency of State aid, annual reporting to the other Party about the aid granted, and—upon request by one Party—the provision of information on aid schemes and particular individual cases of State aid. The Agreement does not oblige candidate countries to notify aid schemes, as is the case for the Member

States of the EU. The State aid provisions of the Agreement are designed to prepare candidate countries for notification requirements after being granted the status of Member of the European Union. This status shall, while imposing notification requirements, allow the candidate countries to benefit from structural funds at the disposal of the Commission.

State aid monitoring should help to create a database to meet the information criterion resulting from the Europe Agreement. It should be remembered that this requirement concerns State aid which affects or may affect trade between candidate countries and Member countries. Thus, by realizing the internal need to discipline public spending, candidate countries will be prepared to meet one of the most important conditions of association with the European Union. Access to the experiences resulting from the application of the Community regulations on State aid would allow the candidate countries to avoid many misunderstandings and would facilitate association negotiations.

All candidate countries have laws regulating State aid. The difference lies in the competent authority for monitoring State aid. In four countries (the Czech Republic, Latvia, Lithuania, and Poland) these competencies were granted to the competition agencies. In Bulgaria, Estonia, Slovakia, and Hungary this role is played by the State aid department of the Ministry of Finance, and in Slovenia a Commission for State aid operates. In Romania the monitoring of State aid has been carried out by the Competition Office, which is responsible for producing an inventory and reporting on State aid issues, and the Competition Council, which is responsible for the authorization of State aid.

The regulations on State aid are new in the candidate countries, and thus the case law is insufficient to evaluate the effectiveness of enforcement. It should be stressed at this point that due to the requirements of the negotiations these regulations are already in force in the candidate countries, while they have not existed in the EU Member States.

## II. The case of Poland

The European Agreement on the association of Poland with the European Union was signed on 16 December 1991 and will come into force in February 1994. Article 63 of the Agreement contains competition rules applicable in trade contacts between Poland and the EU.[4]

The Agreement obliges Poland to create a transparent database on State aid granted to enterprises and to provide the European Commission on request with basic information on planned and realized aid programmes. Publishing annual reports on State aid is not required by the Agreement, but results from Poland's intention to maintain a good climate in accession negotiations. It is worth

---

[4] Pomoc publiczna dla przedsiębiorstw w Unii Europejskiej i w Polsce (State Aid for Entrepreneurs in European Union and in Poland), ed. by: A. Fornalczyk, UKIE, Warsaw 1998.

mentioning that the obligation concerning information is bilateral: Poland also has a right to request information from the Commission on aid granted by Member Countries in case of distortions of trade among signatories of the Agreement.

Annual reports on State aid allow the realization of the above-mentioned internal reasons for aid monitoring, and prepare Poland for operating consistently within the rules resulting from Articles 87 and 88 EC, once Poland joins the European Union.

## A. Polish regulations on State aid

Poland formally met the requirements of the Agreement by passing the State Aid Act on 30 June 2000, which entered into force on 1 January 2001 (Dz. U. No. 60 item. 704) and the newest State Aid Act on 27 July 2002, which entered into force on 6 October 2002 (Dz. U. No 141 item. 1177). The Act is accompanied by implementing regulations laying down detailed rules on the notification, granting, and monitoring of State aid to entrepreneurs. The State Aid Acts were prepared in compliance with European Union regulations.

When assessing the degree of harmonization of State aid regulation in Poland with EU rules, one should bear in mind their temporary nature and the difficulties of harmonizing national State aid law to the European Union standards. Polish State aid law is focused not only on distortion of competition in trade with Member countries of the EU but also on distortion within the Polish market. The main issue for the law has been to strengthen the discipline of public spending.

## B. Organization of State aid monitoring

According to the Polish State Aid Act, the President of the Office for Competition and Consumer Protection (OCCP) is responsible for State aid control in Poland. That control concerns projects of legal acts, decisions, and agreements, on which the granting of State aid will be based. Other tasks of the OCCP President are the collection, recording, and processing of data and the estimation of the efficiency and effectiveness of granted aid. That is consistent with the above-mentioned arguments for aid monitoring as a tool for tightening public finance discipline in the important area of support for enterprises.

Reports on State aid have been published since 1996. Generally, the successive reports on State aid granted in Poland between 1996–2000 specify amounts and describe the legal basis for their granting. Institutions granting aid were not obliged to gather such data, nor to report the amounts of aid, aid beneficiaries, and the efficiency of granted aid. The State Aid Act requires the collection of information and analysis of data, the calculation of efficiency, and the influence on competition in markets relevant for the beneficiaries' operations.

## C. Types of aid instruments identified in the Polish Report

In accordance with the State Aid Act, the Report on State aid awarded to entrepreneurs in Poland in 2000 (further: the Report) uses the following types of State aid, classified according to their character:[5]

(i) *operations on taxes* tax reliefs, deferred payments and payments by instalments of tax and tax arrears, waivers of tax arrears and tax obligations;

(ii) *operations on liabilities towards funds* deferred payments and payments by instalments, debt waivers;

(iii) *operation on credits* soft loans, loans with conditional debt waiver clauses, State guarantees;

(iv) *equity participation* capital injection, temporary acquisition of shares for future resale, equity swaps; and

(v) *subsidies.*

In conformity with European Commission guidelines, the above-mentioned types of aid have been classified into four groups, labelled A, B, C, and D with suffix 1 or 2, characterizing the source of financing for the aid (representing respectively budget expenditure and tax expenditure).

In accordance with EU rules, aid has been classified according to the principal purposes for which it is given or the sector to which to it is directed (objectives of State aid):

(i) horizontal aid: research and development, environmental protection, small and medium-sized enterprises, trade, energy saving, foreign investment, employment, training, rescue and restructuring, investment aid, operational aid, privatization, other objectives;

(ii) sectoral aid: steel, shipbuilding, transportation, mining of coal and lignite, ore mining, other mining and quarrying, motor vehicle industry, air transport, post, financial services, and other;[6] and

(iii) regional aid.

The report includes data concerning absolute values of aid. The structure of awarded aid, classified into types and objectives, is also included.

The total value of aid granted in 2000 amounted to EUR 1,924.7 million (based on an average 2000 exchange rate of 1 euro = PLN 4,0069) and constituted about 4.6 per cent of value added in industry and about 1.1 per cent of gross national product in comparison with 1.5 per cent in 1999. The value of aid per person employed in industry was about 599 euros per person employed, in comparison with 616 euros in 1999.

[5] See: Jastrzębska D., Wozniak B., Wspieranie przedsiębiorstw ze środków publicznych w Polsce w latach 1995–1997 (Support for Enterprises from Public Sources in Poland in 1995–1997), Bank i Kredyt, 1999.

[6] Needs for restructuring of the Polish industry have been analysed in: Chances and Threats of the Polish Industry as a Result of Association of Poland to European Union), ed.: A. Cylwik, Center for Social and Economic Research (CASE), Warsaw 1999.

Table 7.1 Shows how State aid was granted and distributed between the different categories of aid.

Group A was the most significant category of aid in the period between 1996 and 2000. It is worth underlining that subgroup A2 (tax exemptions) included the majority of aid until 2000; in that year subsidies exceeded tax exemptions. In other categories of aid the shares were as follows: in group B (equity participation) 1.5 per cent group C ('soft loans') constituted 11.4 per cent; and group D (guarantees) constitued 2.6 per cent of all aid granted. In 2000 the total number of beneficiaries of State aid was 98,085.[7] The most active institutions granting aid were respectively: fiscal organs (67,833 beneficiaries, i.e 70 per cent of all beneficiaries) and Social Insurance Institutions (18,434, i.e. 19 per cent).

The distribution of State aid granted in Poland in 2000, divided into budget and tax expenditure, was as follows:

*(i)*   47.3 per cent of the total value of aid constituted budget expenditure (subsidies), and
*(ii)*  52.7 per cent of the total value of aid constituted tax and fund liabilities expenditure.

In the previous years the proportions were: in 1997 31.3 per cent and 68.7 per cent; in 1998 34.5 per cent and 65.5 per cent; and in 1999 34.9 per cent and 65.1 per cent. The conclusion is that tax expenditure has been preferred over budget expenditure in State aid. Such a situation is usually explained by lack of budget funds for the support for entrepreneurs and the simplicity of granting State aid through taxes and other budget liabilities. However, the policy of preferring operations on taxes distorts competition and makes the estimation of negative and positive effects of aid difficult: fortunately, we notice the continuing rise of the share of budget expenditure.

*Table 7.1: Distribution of State aid granted to enterprises in 1996–1999 (percentages)*

|            | 1996 | 1997 | 1998 | 1999 | 2000 |
|------------|------|------|------|------|------|
| TOTAL      | 100  | 100  | 100  | 100  | 100  |
| Group A1   | 19.3 | 20.4 | 25.7 | 32.8 | 46.0 |
| Group A2   | 61.7 | 59.5 | 50.2 | 53.2 | 38.5 |
| Group B1A  | 0.0  | 0.1  | 0.1  | 2.1  | 1.3  |
| Group B2A  | 0.6  | 0.3  | 0.3  | 0.5  | 0.2  |
| Group C1A  | 5.6  | 9.1  | 7.8  | 7.3  | 9.6  |
| Group C2A  | 10.2 | 8.8  | 15.0 | 0.9  | 1.8  |
| Group D1A  | 2.6  | 1.7  | 1.0  | 3.2  | 2.6  |

*Source*: Polish Report on State Aid, 2000

---

[7] Not including aid granted by the Ministry of Finance.

## 1. Subsidies (group A1)

The value of aid granted in the form of subsidies from the State budget amounted to 885 million euros. 50,000 entrepreneurs were beneficiaries of such aid. Table 7.2 shows how the subsidies were allocated.

Fifty-five per cent of group A1 aid constituted sectoral aid, directed mainly to coal mining (45 per cent) and transport (13 per cent). It is worth mentioning that the limitation of subsidies to entrepreneurs has been treated since the beginning of the Polish transformation as one of the important goals of the tightening of soft budget constraints inherited from the centrally planned economy.

The analysis of data concerning the value and the distribution of subsidies, broken down in terms of sectors of the economy, indicates that aid was mainly directed to coal mining and to the national railway. Sixty-eight per cent of subsidies was directed to coal mining, of which 74 per cent was allocated to employment restructuring. Ninety-five per cent of aid to the transport sector was assigned to investment in the national railway. From the Report's figures it appears that subsidies to passenger transport were not included, which exemplifies the underestimation of the value of aid granted in 2000. It is worth emphasizing the lack of subsidies for regional aid.

## 2. Operations on taxes and budget liabilities (groups A2, C2)

Operations on taxes and budget liabilities constituted the second main type of aid granted in 2000. That share of the total aid granted in 1999 was 40.3 per cent. The main aids in that group were tax reliefs and waivers of liabilities to funds, mainly the Social Security Fund (SSF). Waivers from the SSF amounted to PLN 145 million, almost 50 per cent of the total value of waivers. More than 25 per cent of waivers were directed to coal mining, 12 per cent to construction, 11 per cent to the steel sector, and 8 per cent to the synthetic fibres industry.

## 3. Equity participation (group B)

Equity participation represents a very small share of total aid granted in 2000, i.e. 5 per cent. Eighty-five per cent of such aid was spent on capital injection. The high dynamics of that form of aid is a result of its rare use at the beginning of

*Table 7.2:  Distribution of subsidies; breakdown of objectives of aid in 1996–1999*

| | Share (in %) | | | | |
|---|---|---|---|---|---|
| | 1996 | 1997 | 1998 | 1999 | 2000 |
| TOTAL | 100 | 100 | 100 | 100 | 100 |
| 1.  Sectoral aid | 72.6 | 83.7 | 87.9 | 63.7 | 55.7 |
| 2.  Horizontal aid | 27.4 | 16.3 | 12.1 | 35.9 | 43.8 |
| 3.  Regional aid | 0.0 | 0.0 | 0.0 | 0.0 | 0.0 |
| 4.  Unidentified | – | – | – | 0.4 | 0.5 |

*Source*: Polish Report on State Aid, 2000

reform. The sources of the capital were governmental agencies and environmental protection funds. The distribution of equity participation aid is shown in Table 7.3.

### 4. Operations on credits (groups C1 and D)

The long list of funds and agencies financing preferential credits and credit waivers (group C1) is included in the Report, as well as aid granted in the form of deferrals and the rescheduling of liabilities toward budget and funds (group C2).

Aid granted by agencies supporting the agriculture sector dominates group C1 (over 22 per cent of total aid granted in that form). Credit support for entrepreneurs employing disabled persons and investing in environmental protection are also relevant.

State aid in the form of credit guarantees (group D) accounted in 2000 for 2.6 per cent of total aid. One hundred and forty enterprises were beneficiaries of such aid. It is worth mentioning that guarantees are usually not treated as a form of State aid. It is considered that this form of aid does not employ public funds. The State Treasury granted more than 70 per cent of the total value of that form of aid, mainly concerning large credits from international financial organizations (IMF, World Bank). The second position, with a 25 per cent share, was taken by the State agency regulating supply on the agricultural products market.

### D. Objectives of State aid granted in Poland in 2000

Thirty per cent of total state aid granted to enterprises in 2000 had sectoral objectives, of which 70 per cent was directed to coal mining. Horizontal objectives constituted nearly 64.6 per cent of aid, one of whose main objectives was employment restructuring (social shields, training) which constituted abut 30 per cent of total aid.

Table 7.4 shows the distribution of aid in 2000, broken down according to objectives. One may assume that employment aid was at the same time a sectoral type of aid (coal mining restructuring). The share of regional aid in the total value of aid amounted to little more than statistical error, i.e. 3.7 per cent. Noticing expanding regional differences in economic development, this situation should undergo radical and rapid change.

*Table 7.3:* *Distribution of equity participation as a form of aid 1996–2000*

| Group | Type of aid | Share (in %) | | | | |
|-------|-------------|------|------|------|------|------|
| | | 1996 | 1997 | 1998 | 1999 | 2000 |
| | Equity Participation | 100 | 100 | 100 | 100 | 100 |
| B1 A | Capital Injections | 1.4 | 23.2 | 17.2 | 81.8 | 85.0 |
| B2 A | Equity Swap | 98.6 | 76.8 | 82.8 | 18.2 | 5.0 |

*Source*: Polish Report on State Aid, 2000

*Table 7.4:   Distribution of State aid granted in 2000; breakdown according to objectives*

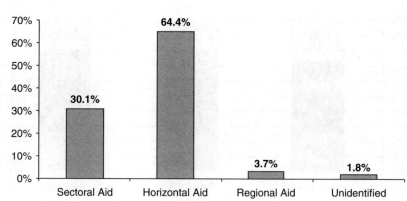

*Source*: Report on State Aid in Poland, 2000, p. 10

As a result of poor compliance with State aid monitoring obligations, only subsidies can be broken down according to the objectives of aid. This results from the Budgetary Law containing such data. From the analysis of those figures it appears that the main beneficiaries of that form of aid were coal mining and transport, including railways.[8] Subsidies for horizontal objectives were also mainly directed to the coal mining sector.

### E.  Comparison with the EU

In EU countries subsidies constitute the main instrument of aid. The detailed breakdown of the aid can be found in Surveys on State Aid prepared by the Commission of the European Communities. The biggest difference between Poland and the EU average is the dominance of tax aid over other types of aid instruments in Poland. See Table 7.5.

How can the Polish digression from the EU pattern be explained? In our opinion, there are several factors contributing to the different distribution of State aid in Poland compared to the EU. Those factors are: ideology, pressure, convenience, non-transparency, and flexibility in granting aid; these are discussed below.

### 1. Ideology

During the period of the planned economy, subsidies were extremely common. Their share in general government expenditure amounted in the last year of the Communist regime to almost 13 per cent in Poland.[9] The subsidies were directed

---

[8]  See: Budzet 2000 (Budget 2000), BRE Bank, Case, Warsaw 2000.
[9]  Bratkowski, A., Fiscal Policy in Poland under Transition, CASE, Warsaw, 1995

*Table 7.5:　State aid granted to enterprises in the EU 1992–1997 (breakdown into types of aid)*

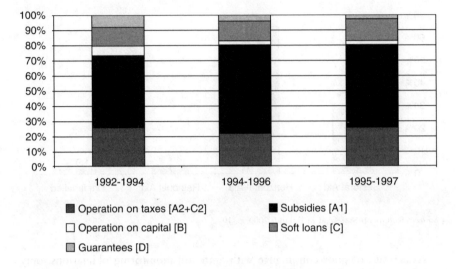

*Source*: Surveys on State aid in the European Union in the manufacturing and certain other sectors.

at products, rather than producers, and therefore one can hardly classify them as State aid. This was a result of the rigid and fundamentally distorted price structure. Generally necessities (foodstuffs, housing, energy, etc.) were cheap and therefore had to be subsidized. One of the key elements of the shift to a market economy was the liberalization of prices, and in consequence of the new price structures the 'demand' for subsidies weakened. The subsidies to products were to some extent replaced by the social transfers to the poor. In 1995 the share of subsidies in general government expenditure dropped to 2.2 per cent in Poland.[10] The government was reluctant to use subsidies, which are to some extent treated as a Communist instrument. Definitely, farmers are big advocates of subsidies. An argument concerning ideology does not directly justify such a high share of tax expenditure in the total amount of State aid, but describes the reasons of aversion to the alternative instrument, i.e. budget expenditure.

## 2. Pressure

Most of the State aid transferred to enterprises by the tax system is in our opinion not intentional. If the enterprise cannot meet its tax obligations, it can seek a tax relief or the like. If the enterprise were profitable, it would not have been given the aid. This means that such aid is an acknowledgement of the fact that some companies do not meet their obligations. Therefore State aid is a sign of the

[10] EBRD Transition Report 2000, EBRD 2000.

weakness of the government rather than a sign of its care for the economic development of the country.

The main beneficiaries of aid are large State-owned enterprises, in which strong resistance to restructuring and privatization exists. In case of lack of financial liquidity such an entity has to take a number of steps. As it does not want to restructure (threat of reduction of employment) it wants to improve its situation in the short term. Because it does not have the possibility to obtain credit it stops paying its liabilities. The volume of inter-firm credit is limited; it has to pay salaries to workers as well. Only budget liabilities are left, so the enterprise stops paying its taxes and liabilities towards funds. The State, bearing in mind the social costs of bankruptcy of such a large enterprise, allows this situation, and that becomes an incentive for other economic entities to engage in similar behaviour.

### 3. Convenience

From the legal and bureaucratic point of view it is easier and faster to transmit the aid through taxes than through any other instrument. From the point of view of costs of transfer, tax expenditure seems to be cheaper than budget expend-iture. Granting of State aid *ex post* is simply a recognition of tax arrears toward the State. It does not involve any cost connected with the preparation of a restructuring programme, nor with the monitoring of the restructuring pro-cesses. Taking into account the character of most aid granted in this way and the situation of its beneficiaries, it appears that such aid is of an occasional character and will have to be granted again to enable the survival of the enterprise on the market. It appears that convenience and high speed of granting go along with high costs in the long term.

### 4. Non-transparency

It is relatively easy to calculate the total value of all subsidies granted to an enterprise, sector, or region. In the case of tax instruments a special methodology is required, as well as practice to assess it correctly even for a single firm. Therefore policy-makers could give more aid than they are supposed or allowed to do. That lack of transparency has been used by policy-makers seeking sup-port, e.g. from labour unions.

### 5. Flexibility and volume

The total amount of aid is set in the Budget Law and, although there is plenty of room for manoeuvre in the allocation of aid within the special funds, the upper limit cannot be exceeded. The Budget Law has no provision regarding the amount of tax concessions, therefore policy-makers may use their discretionary power and grant substantial aid to certain enterprises, which is of great import-ance when taking into account the strong power of labour unions in Poland. Needless to say that this is also more prone to abuse.

The transition process may have influenced the choice of the type of aid instrument. The State-owned companies that are privatized or go bankrupt usually owe substantial amounts in unpaid taxes and social security contribution payments. If an enterprise is insolvent, there is often no chance of payment of these arrears. In such circumstances the government has no choice but to write off the unpaid amounts. If a company with unpaid taxes and other payments towards budget or para-budget institutions is to be privatized, then either these payments are waived or the price of the company is lowered, as the buyer will have to pay taxes and other payments. In such a situation, the cancellation of the debt is more transparent and offers security for the buyer.

Generally budget subsidies seem to be superior to tax subsidies with respect to economic efficiency and transparency. Therefore changes in the aid structure, namely the reduction of the relative importance of the tax expenditure in favour of direct subsidies, is a positive phenomenon. If this trend continues, then the Polish aid distribution pattern will converge with the EU pattern.

## III. Conclusions

(i)   State aid monitoring in Poland and in other candidate countries results mainly from the need to tighten the discipline of public finance.

(ii)  The European Agreement obliges candidate countries to ensure the transparency of data concerning State aid in order to guage its influence on trading conditions among them and with Member States of the EU. As pointed out above, this results in broader State aid monitoring in Poland than appears from accession obligations.

(iii) The first Polish State Aid Act entered into force on 1 January 2001, the second on 6 October 2002. The Act is accompanied by regulations concerning detailed rules of notifying, granting, and monitoring of State aid to entrepreneurs. The two Acts were prepared in compliance with European Union regulations.

(iv)  The person in charge of State aid control is the President of the OCCP. The President of the OCCP is responsible for: enforcing the legal rules of State aid grants in Poland; collection, recording, and processing the data and and analysis of efficiency and effectiveness of granted aid. The reports on State aid prepared in Poland since 1996 have been used mainly for negotiation purposes.

(v)   The forms of State aid identified in Polish practice include: operations on taxes, operations on budget liabilities, soft loans, equity participation, and subsidies.

(vi)  The total value of aid granted to entrepreneurs in 2000 amounted to almost 2,000 million euros, and was 15 per cent lower than in 1999. The value of aid per person employed in the industry was about 600 euros per person employed. In 2000 the total number of beneficiaries of State aid was 98,000.

*(vii)*  Group A was the most significant among the categories of aid granted in 2000. The amount of subsidies in 2000 was for the first time higher in group A1 than group A2 (tax exemptions).

*(viii)*  Aid granted in the form of subsidies was mainly directed to coal mining and to the national railway. Forty-five per cent of subsidies were directed to coal mining, and 74 per cent of this to employment restructuring. Ninety-five per cent of aid directed to the transport sector was assigned to investments in the national railway.

*(ix)*  Operations on taxes and budget liabilities constituted the second largest category of aid granted in 2000: 40 per cent of all aid granted in 2000. The main instruments in that group were tax reliefs and waivers of liabilities to funds.

*(x)*  Equity participation represents a very small share of total aid granted in 2000, less than 3 per cent. Eighty-five per cent of that form of aid was spent on capital injections.

*(xi)*  Soft loans were mainly used as a support for entrepreneurs employing disabled persons or investing in environmental protection. The main beneficiaries of such aid were coal mining, the machine and fibre industries, transport (railway), and construction.

*(xii)*  Thirty per cent of total State aid granted to enterprises in 2000 had sectoral objectives, of which 60 per cent were directed to coal mining. Horizontal objectives constituted nearly 64 per cent of aid, mostly aimed at employment restructuring (social shields, training). The share of regional aid in the total value of aid granted was a mere 3.7 per cent.

*(xiii)*  The biggest difference between aid in Poland and average aid figures for the EU is the dominance of tax aid over other types of aid instruments in Poland (except in 2000). There are several factors contributing to the different distribution of State aid in Poland compared to the EU. Those factors are: ideology, pressure, convenience, non-transparency, and flexibility in granting.

# 8

# The International Context of EC State Aid Law and Policy: The Regulation of Subsidies in the WTO

## LUCA RUBINI[1]

### I. INTRODUCTION

The European Commission has recently observed that 'as state aid policy in the European Union evolves, it has to account for the international context and, in particular, the multilateral obligations imposed by WTO rules: the WTO Agreement on Agriculture and the WTO Agreement on Subsidies and Countervailing Measures'.[2] It is in the light of this statement that the subject of this chapter hopes to find its proper position in this book. The chapter attempts to look beyond the boundaries of the EC by focusing on the set of rules that regulate government subsidization to enterprises in the WTO.

The interconnection of various legal systems is a typical characteristic of the contemporary world. Inevitably, EC law and WTO law are also increasingly linked with each other.[3] This seems, however, to be contradicted by some recent statements in the case law of the Community Courts. In *Portugal v Council* the Court of Justice made it clear that WTO law as such does not have direct effect in the Community legal system.[4] A few months later the Court of First Instance found that 'the reference to the concept of "subsidy" within the meaning of the WTO Agreement on Subsidies and Countervailing Measures has ... no relevance whatsoever to the classification of the measure in question as State aid within the meaning of Community law'.[5] In the light of these findings, it is easy to be

[1] I would like to thank Professor Piet Eeckhout, Dr Markus Krajewski, and Giuseppe Conte for their helpful comments.

[2] Ninth Survey on State Aid in the European Union (2001) paragraph 12. For the text of the WTO Agreement and of all its instruments referred to in this paper see *The Results of the Uruguay Round of Multilateral Trade and Negotiations: The Legal Texts* (1994).

[3] The clearest example is the possibility that a Community rule is found to be in breach of WTO law.

[4] Case C-149/96 *Portugal v Council* [1999] ECR I-8395, paragraph 36 *et seq.*

[5] Case T-55/99 *Confederación Española de Transporte de Mercancías v Commission* [2000] ECR II-3207, paragraph 50. See also Case C-351/98 *Spain v Commission* [2002] ECR 1–8031, paragraph 44; Case C-409/00 *Spain v Commission*, Judgment of 13 February 2003, nyr, paragraph 56.

tempted into concluding that the regulation of subsidies in the WTO and that of state aids in the EC proceed on different paths, and that a comparative insight into the two systems would not be useful.

It is submitted that this is not the case. Generally speaking, despite differences, comparisons are always enriching.[6] Further, the lack of direct effect does not necessarily mean that WTO law does not produce any effect in EC law. If the Commission's statement, whereby state aid law and policy have an international context to consider which the EC have to 'uphold and respect',[7] is to be taken seriously, EC law should be interpreted 'as much and as far as possible' consistently with the WTO obligations of the Community.[8] The benefits of a comparative exercise should not be overlooked also from another perspective. Clashes between EC law and WTO law are inevitable considering that the same measure may simultaneously be subject to the rules of either system and that their determinations can differ from each other. It is thus hoped that a better understanding of WTO law would somewhat contribute to reducing the possibilities of conflicts.

This chapter attempts to sketch the main features of the WTO regulation of subsidies concentrating in particular on some of the main issues concerning the definition and the categories of subsidy. Special attention is paid to the SCM Agreement as it represents the most comprehensive discipline of subsidies and countervailing duties in the WTO. When possible, I also attempt to draw brief tentative parallels with the EC regulation of state aids. Finally, a note on style: the exposition of the various issues is often accompanied by extensive passages from the reports of the Panels and the Appellate Body. That is the best way to convey the flavour of the sophisticated legal reasoning of WTO law, and to render it more familiar to EC lawyers who are indeed used to a more concise style.

## II. The discipline of subsidies in the GATT/WTO: An overview[9]

Only two provisions in the GATT agreement explicitly regulate subsidies. Article VI provides for the possibility for the importing country to impose

---

[6] P Eeckhout, 'Constitutional concepts for free trade in services' in G de Bùrca and J Scott, *The EU and the WTO: Legal and Constitutional Issues* (2001) 211.

[7] First Survey on State Aid in the EC (1989) page 2.

[8] P Eeckhout, 'Judicial enforcement of WTO law in the European Union: Some further reflections' (2002) Journal of International Economic Law 91. Cf also the Opinion of Advocate General Alber in Case C-93/02P *Biret International SA* v *Council*, and Case C-94/02P *Etablissements Biret et Cie. SA v Council*, delivered on 15 May 2003, where he concluded that an infringement of WTO law, where the Community has failed to implement a decision of the WTO Dispute Settlement Body within the prescribed period, could found a claim for damages against the Community. A recent comprehensive work on the impact of WTO law on EC law is F Snyder, 'The gatekeepers: The European Courts and WTO law' (2003) CML Rev 413.

[9] For a general overview of subsidy rules see JH Jackson, *The World Trading System: Law and Policy of International Economic Relations* (2nd ed, 1997), ch 11; MJ Trebilcock and R Howse, *The*

'countervailing' duties on subsidized imports that cause or threaten material injury to an established domestic industry or materially retard its establishment. Article XVI provides for a duty to notify all subsidies increasing exports of or reducing imports to the subsidizing country and a consultation procedure for limiting subsidization that causes serious prejudice to other contracting parties. Further, the contracting parties are required to 'seek to avoid' the grant of subsidies on the export of primary products, or, in any event, to guarantee that their application does not result 'in that contracting party having more than an equitable share of world export trade in that product'. Export subsidies to 'any product other than a primary product resulting in the sale of that product at a price lower that the comparable price charged for the like product in the domestic market' are prohibited.

GATT law does not provide for an express definition of subsidy. From the beginning, however, various forms of state intervention have been regarded as subsidies. In 1961 a Working Party drafted a list of measures considered as forms of export subsidies,[10] which *inter alia* included direct subsidies, the remission and exemption of direct taxes and social welfare charges, the sale of raw materials at prices below world prices, and the grant of export credits. The list was not considered exhaustive and thus it did not limit the 'generality of the provisions' of GATT Article XVI. This quite comprehensive approach can be compared with the contemporary wide interpretation of the notion of state aid adopted by the Court of Justice in the EC.[11]

In 1979 the Tokyo Subsidies Code, the first general comprehensive multilateral discipline on subsidies and countervailing duties, was adopted.[12] Track I of the Code expanded the obligations of GATT Article VI on the use of countervailing duties regulating in detail the procedures leading to the imposition of countervailing duties and the concept of material injury. Track II dealt with the discipline on the grant of subsidies that might affect international trade. It reinforced the prohibition on export subsidies, introduced a regulation of domestic subsidies, and developed the notification obligation under GATT Article XVI providing that, after a complex consultation, the adoption of 'such

---

*Regulation of International Trade* (2nd ed, 1999), ch 8. For a more technical exposition see McGovern, *International Trade Regulation* (1994, looseleaf updated every six months), chs 11 and 12, and M Benitah, *The Law of Subsidies under the GATT/WTO System* (2001). See also GC Hufbauer and J Shelton Erb, *Subsidies in International Trade* (1984); JHJ Bourgeois (ed), *Subsidies and International Trade: A European Lawyer's perspectives* (1991); CD Ehlermann and M Everson (eds), *European Competition Law Annual 1999: Selected Issues in the Field of State Aids* (2001); K Adamantopoulos and MJ Pereyra-Friedrichsen, *EU Anti-Subsidy Law and Practice* (2001).

[10] GATT Working Party Report of 19 November 1960 on the Provisions of Article XVI:4, BISD 9S/185 (1961) 186–187.

[11] Case 30/59 *De Gezamenlijke Steenkolenmijnen in Limburg* v *High Authority* [1961] ECR 1, at pp. 19 and 27.

[12] Agreement on Interpretation and Application of Articles VI, XVI, and XXIII of the General Agreement on Tariffs and Trade, GATT, BISD 26 Supp. 56 (1980). Its impact was however somewhat reduced because it was not binding on all GATT Members but only on its signatories.

countermeasures as may be appropriate' can be authorized. The Code, however, did not feature any definition of subsidy.

It is worth noting that the Tokyo Subsidies Code showed an ambivalent attitude towards subsidies, recognizing on one hand that they may be used to promote important objectives of social and economic policy, and on the other that they may cause adverse effects to the interests of other signatories. This ambivalence was particularly evident in the discipline of domestic subsidies. Article 11 combined the recognition of the important goals pursued by governments with the use of subsidies with a subsequent invitation on the contracting parties to avoid that such practices cause an adverse impact on international trade. Interestingly, that provision listed some of the justifications of subsidies[13] and also exemplified their possible forms.[14] Finally, by underlining that subsidies are normally granted either regionally or by sector, Article 11 already hinted at the fact that they should benefit specific enterprises or industries.

The WTO Agreement includes a new discipline on subsidies, the Agreement on Subsidies and Countervailing Measures ('SCM Agreement'). The SCM Agreement presents several new features as compared with the previous discipline of the Tokyo Code. Unlike the Tokyo Subsidies Code, it is binding on all WTO Members. For the first time a comprehensive definition of subsidy is introduced along with the concept of specificity. The actual discipline of subsidies is different according to their category (prohibited, actionable, or non-actionable). The SCM Agreement provides for a special, more favourable treatment, such as grace periods and exemptions, for developing countries and economies in transition.[15] Notification and surveillance procedures are enhanced.[16] As regards remedies, two tracks can be followed: the dispute settlement option or the countervailing duty procedure. Both are possible although only one remedy can be applied.[17] It is known that the dispute settlement system is an innovation of great importance of the WTO Agreement.[18] The Panels and the Appellate

---

[13] To eliminate industrial, economic, and social disadvantages of specific regions; to facilitate the restructuring, under socially acceptable conditions, of certain sectors, especially where this has become necessary by reason of changes in trade and economic policies, including international agreements resulting in lower barriers to trade; generally to sustain employment and to encourage retraining and change in employment; to encourage research and development programmes, especially in the field of high-technology industries; to implement economic programmes and policies to promote the economic and social development of developing countries; to redeploy industry in order to avoid congestion and environmental problems.

[14] The provision refers to 'government financing of commercial enterprises, including grants, loans or guarantees; government provision or government financed provision of utility, supply distribution and other operational or support services or facilities; government financing of research and development programmes; fiscal incentives; and government subscription to, or provision of, equity capital'.

[15] Art 27 and Art 29 SCM.

[16] Art 25 and Art 26 SCM.

[17] See footnote 35 to Art 10 SCM.

[18] '... dispute settlement has become a matter of compulsory jurisdiction for all WTO Members. It is this compulsory character that distinguishes it from all other existing international dispute settlement systems': CD Ehlermann, 'Six Years on the Bench of the "World Trade Court": Some Personal Experiences as Member of the Appellate Body of the World Trade Organisation' (2002) Journal of World Trade 605, 607.

Body review complaints regarding subsidy programmes adopted by the Members. Depending on the category of subsidy, they may recommend the removal of the effects caused by the subsidy or even its withdrawal. They may also review domestic countervailing duty laws and their application by domestic agencies.

Subsidies are explicitly regulated also in the Agreement on Trade in Services (GATS). Article XV, however, principally calls upon the Members to enter into negotiations with a view to developing the necessary multilateral disciplines to avoid trade-distortive effects. Any Member that considers itself to be adversely affected by a subsidy of another Member can request consultations. More substantive obligations can be found in the Agreement on Agriculture which permits both export and domestic subsidies on certain agricultural products but subjects them to certain defined limitations and to reduction commitments.

An important issue is that of the relationship between GATT Article XVI and the SCM Agreement and other provisions of WTO law such as those on National-Treatment Obligations,[19] on monopolies and exclusive service suppliers,[20] on technical barriers to trade,[21] on investment,[22] and on government procurement.[23] Thus, for example, GATT Article III and the WTO rules on subsidies focus on different problems: 'Article III prohibits discrimination between domestic and imported products while the SCM Agreement regulates the provision of subsidies to enterprises'.[24] GATT Article III does not apply to subsidies that are granted *exclusively* to domestic producers[25] 'so long as they do not have any component that introduces discrimination between imported and domestic products'.[26] By contrast, GATS Article XVII prohibits discriminatory behaviour also with respect to service suppliers. It is however important to note that GATS Article XVII operates differently from GATT Article III. It only applies if Members have specifically committed a certain sector to that discipline and only subject to the limitations and exceptions they have specified.[27] That said, it has to be asked whether the grant of a subsidy exclusively to domestic suppliers may amount to a prohibited practice under GATS Article XVII.[28] If this is so, then how should the Member which, for example, subsidizes one or more enterprises that perform a public service, and has bound itself to national treatment commitments without providing for any explicit 'condition

---

[19] Cf Art III GATT and Art XVII GATS.     [20] Cf Art VIII GATS.
[21] Cf the Agreement on Technical Barriers to Trade.
[22] Cf the Agreement on Trade-Related Investment Measures.
[23] Cf the plurilateral Agreement on Government Procurement.
[24] WTO Panel Report, *Indonesia: Certain measures affecting the automobile industry* ('Indonesia—Automobile industry'), WT/DS54/R, WT/DS55/R, WT/DS59/R, WT/DS64/R, adopted on 23 July 1998, paragraph 14.33.
[25] Cf Art III:8(b) GATT.
[26] Panel Report, *Indonesia: Automobile industry* (n 24 above) paragraphs 14.43 and 14.45.
[27] For example, the EC listed subsidies as an exception from all their national treatment obligations.
[28] M Krajewski, 'Public services and Trade Liberalisation: Mapping the Legal Framework' (2003) Journal of International Economic Law 341.

or qualification', accord a treatment 'no less favourable than that it accords to its own like services and service suppliers'? Admittedly, it could fulfil its national treatment obligation in two ways: either by extending the subsidy to the foreign service supplier, or by ceasing to subsidize its domestic supplier(s).

### First parallels between the GATT/WTO and the EC

In the GATT system, for a long time, the only substantial remedy was the unilateral power of contracting parties to impose countervailing duties. This power has been progressively regulated to avoid abuses. This heavy reliance on unilateral measures cannot be found in the EC, which constitutes 'a new legal order of international law',[29] based much more on the 'commonality' of the European enterprise rather than the 'reciprocity' of Member States' interests.[30] EC law does not confer on Member States that claim to be prejudiced by subsidies granted by another Member State the power to take unilateral defensive actions. Further, the grant of an aid cannot be justified by the fact that similar subsidies are granted by other Member States.[31] Admittedly, this principle is also applicable in WTO law. In the GATT era, the *DISC* Panel took note of:

the United States' argument that it had introduced the DISC legislation to correct an existing distortion created by tax practices of certain other contracting parties. However, the Panel did not accept that one distortion could be justified by the existence of another one and considered that, if the United States had considered that other contracting parties were violating the General Agreement, it could have had recourse to the remedies which the General Agreement offered. On the other hand, the fact that tax practices of certain other countries had been in force for some time without being the subject of complaints was not, in itself, conclusive evidence that there was a consensus that they were compatible with the General Agreement.[32]

GATT/WTO law only permits, under certain conditions, the imposition of compensatory duties on subsidized imports, not the conferral of subsidies to one's own domestic industry.[33] Article 32.1 SCM provides that 'no specific

[29] Case 26/62 *Van Gend en Loos* [1963] ECR 1, page 12; see also Opinion 1/91, delivered pursuant to the second subparagraph of Article 228(1) of the Treaty, on the draft agreement on the establishment of the EEA [1991] I-6079, paragraph 21.

[30] The principle of reciprocity *inadimplenti non est adimplentum*, whereby a party injured by the failure of another party to perform its obligations should be entitled to withhold the performance of its own, does not apply in the relations between Member States. It is for the Community to enforce Community law. Cf Joined Cases 90 and 91/63 *Commission v Luxembourg and Belgium* [1964] 635, page 631; Case C-146/89 *Commission v United Kingdom* [1991] ECR I-3557, paragraph 47. See also Case 52/75 *Commission v Italy* [1976] ECR 277, paragraph 11.

[31] Case 78/76 *Steinike and Weinlig* [1977] ECR 595, paragraph 24; Case T-214/95 *Vlaams Gewest v Commission* [1998] ECR II-717, paragraph 54.

[32] GATT Panel Report, *US Tax Legislation (DISC)* ('DISC'), issued on 12 November 1976 (L/4422, BISD23S/98), paragraph 79.

[33] Cf WTO Panel and Appellate Body Reports, *Brazil—Export financing programme for aircraft* ('Brazil—Export financing'), WT/DS46/R and WT/DS46/AB/R, both adopted on 20 August 1999, paragraph 7.26 and paragraph 185 respectively.

action against a subsidy of another Member can be taken except in accordance with the provisions of GATT 1994, as interpreted by this Agreement'. The Panel in *US— Subsidy Offset* thus made it clear that US legislation which provided that the proceeds of antidumping and countervailing duties should have been distributed to affected domestic producers was a 'specific action against a subsidy' contrary to SCM Article 32.1.[34]

In the EC 'new' aids are scrutinized by the Commission prior to their implementation.[35] Member States are under an obligation to communicate any proposed new aid or alteration of existing aid to the Commission before its implementation. The effectiveness of this preventive control is guaranteed by national courts' powers to order the recovery of state aids granted 'illegally', ie without having being notified to and approved by the Commission. This power derives from the direct effect of the 'standstill obligation' in the last sentence of EC Article 88(3).[36] That prohibition gives rise to subjective rights in favour of individuals that national courts are bound to safeguard. In particular, national courts must offer the certain prospect that all the necessary inferences will be drawn, in accordance with their national law, as regards the validity of measures giving effect to the aid, the recovery of financial support granted in disregard of that provision, and possible interim measures.[37] As national courts and the Commission fulfil complementary and separate roles, the fact that the Commission is investigating a given aid measure does not release the national courts from their duty to safeguard the rights of individuals in the event of a breach of the prohibition of implementation.[38] Further, even when the Commission eventually approves the aid as compatible with the common market, that decision does not have the effect of regularizing *ex post facto* the invalid measure, since otherwise the direct effect of that prohibition would be impaired and the interests of individuals would be disregarded.[39] The Court of Justice has repeatedly underlined that any other interpretation would have the effect of according a favourable outcome to the non-observance by the Member State concerned of the last

[34] WTO Panel Report, *US—Continued dumping and subsidy offset 2000 Act* ('US—Subsidy Offset'), WT/DS217/R and WT/DS234/R, adopted on 27 January 2003, paragraph 7.7 *et seq*.

[35] 'Existing' aids are subject to the constant review of the Commission pursuant to Article 88(1) EC and Regulation (EC) No 659/1999 of 22 March 1999 laying down detailed rules for the application of Article 93 of the EC Treaty (Regulation No 659/1999) OJ L83, 27 March 1999, 1. Article 1(b) and (c) of Regulation No 659/1999 provide the definitions of 'new' and 'existing' aids.

[36] 'The Member State concerned shall not put its proposed measures into effect until this procedure has resulted in a final decision'.

[37] Cf Case C-354/90 *Fédération Nationale du Commerce Extérieur des Produits Alimentaires and Syndacat National des Négotiants et Transformateurs de Saumon* v *France* ('FNCE') [1991] ECR I-5505, paragraph 12.

[38] Case C-39/94 *SFEI* v *La Poste* [1996] ECR I-3547, paragraphs 41 and 44.

[39] Case C-354/90 *FNCE* (n 38 above) paragraph 16. It is also interesting to note that, under Art 14.1 of Regulation No 659/1999 (n 35 above), which codifies the previous practice, also the Commission shall order the recovery of any unlawful aid but only when it adopts a negative decision.

sentence of Article 93(3), now 88(3), and would deprive that provision of its effectiveness.[40]

The situation in the WTO is different. The notification and surveillance system provided for under WTO law is not as effective as that in the EC. Although the notification obligations under GATT Article XVI:1 and the SCM Agreement could, in theory, be enforced by use of the dispute procedures,[41] the only sanction that bears some resemblance to those in the EC system was that provided for non-actionable subsidies that were not notified as provided in the SCM Agreement.[42] In such a case they could be proceeded against as though they were actionable and subject to countervailing procedures, at least until their non-actionable status was established.[43] Further, WTO law does not have direct effect in the domestic legal systems of many of its Members so that national courts cannot safeguard any right arising from it.[44] The fact is that, although it is true that the new dispute settlement system has strengthened the WTO inter-national obligations on subsidies, there is still a considerable difference between WTO law and EC law with regard to remedies. EC law flatly prohibits state aids that are 'not compatible with the common market' and, if they have been granted, imposes their retroactive recovery. WTO law provides prohibitions only in fairly limited cases, requiring in those cases that Members should 'neither grant nor maintain' prohibited subsidies. In case of breach, the remedy is the withdrawal of the subsidy. Generally, however, the SCM Agreement merely requires that the Members avoid causing, through the use of subsidies, adverse effects to the interest of other Members. Subsidies that produce such effects are actionable and the remedy against them is either the removal of their adverse effects or their withdrawal. The interpretation of the expression 'withdraw the subsidy' under Article 4.7 of the SCM[45] was at issue in the *Brazil—Export financing* and in the *Australia—Automotive Leather* disputes. In the former, the Appellate Body held that such withdrawal 'refers to the "removal" or "taking away" of [the] subsidy'.[46] But it is in the second dispute that a crucial point with respect to the interpretation of SCM Article 4.7 was clarified. According to the Panel: 'where any repayment of any amount of a past subsidy is required or made, this by its very nature is **not** a purely prospective remedy. No theoretical construct allocating the subsidy over time can alter this fact. In our view, if the

---

[40] Case C-354/90 *FNCE* (n 37 above) paragraph 16; see also Case C-39/94 *SFEI v La Poste* (n 39 above), paragraphs 45 and 69.

[41] McGovern (n 9 above) paragraph 11.35.

[42] Cf Art 8.3 SCM.

[43] Cf Art 10 SCM, footnote 35.

[44] For the position in US law see Jackson (n 9 above) 96–97; for the EC see Eeckhout (n 8 above) passim.

[45] 'If the measure in question is found to be a prohibited subsidy, the Panel shall recommend that the subsidising Member withdraw the subsidy without delay...'

[46] WTO Appellate Body Report, *Brazil—Export Financing Programme for Aircraft Article 21.5 I* ('Brazil—Export Financing Article 21.5 I'), WT/DS46/AB/RW, adopted on 4 August 2000, paragraph 45.

term "withdraw the subsidy" can properly be understood to encompass repayment of **any** portion of a prohibited subsidy, "retroactive effect" exists'.[47]

After considering the principles of Article 31 of the Vienna Convention on the Law of Treaties[48] and the principle of effectiveness, the Panel concluded that: 'based on the ordinary meaning of the term "withdraw the subsidy", read in context, and in light of its object and purpose, and in order to give it effective meaning, [ ... ] the recommendation to "withdraw the subsidy" provided for in Article 4.7 of the SCM Agreement is **not** limited to prospective action only but may encompass repayment of the prohibited subsidy'.[49]

The repayment, however, does not imply that interest should be paid as, according to the Panel, the remedy at issue is not 'intended to fully restore the *status quo ante* by depriving the recipient of the prohibited subsidy of the benefits it may have enjoyed in the past. Nor do we consider it to be a remedy intended to provide reparation or compensation in any sense.'[50] It is not clear whether the remedy of the repayment should apply with respect to actionable subsidies for which SCM Article 7.8 alternatively provides for the 'removal of the adverse effects' or the 'withdrawal of the subsidy'. The indications of the Panel in *Australia—Automotive Leather* in this respect are not clear.[51] The *Australia—Automotive Leather* implementation Panel report was the first ruling to recommend a retroactive remedy in WTO law. Although its impact for the development of WTO law might be considerable, it seems that Panels and the Appellate Body in subsequent disputes have carefully avoided applying that drastic remedy.[52] It would be interesting to enquire why that has been so. That

---

[47] WTO Panel Report, *Australia—Subsidies Provided to Producers and Exporters of Automotive Leather Article 21.5* ('Australia—Automotive Leather Article 21.5'), WT/DS126/RW, adopted on 11 February 2000, paragraph 6.22 (the bold style is used in the original text).

[48] See below n 81.

[49] Panel Report, *Australia—Automotive Leather Article 21.5* (n 47 above), paragraph 6.39 (the bold style is used in the original text). It is noteworthy that the Panel (see paragraphs 6.30–6.31 and 6.41–6.42) confirmed that 'withdraw the subsidy' (which, as seen, was interpreted as a retroactive remedy) is different from 'bring the measure into conformity' in Article 19.1 DSU. Nevertheless, 'that a "retrospective" remedy might not be permissible under Article 19.1 of the DSU (a question which we do not here decide) does not preclude us from concluding, on the basis of the text of Article 4.7 of the SCM Agreement, that "withdraw the subsidy" is **not** limited to purely prospective action, but may encompass repayment of prohibited subsidies' (paragraph 6.42, the bold style is used in the original text).

[50] ibid, paragraph 6.49.

[51] ibid, paragraphs 6.28 and 6.23–6.24.

[52] Cf, for example, WTO Panel Report, *Canada—Measures Affecting the Export of Civilian Aircraft Article 21.5* ('Canada-Civilian aircraft Article 21.5'), WT/DS70/RW, adopted on 4 August 2000, paragraphs 5.47–5.48 which read: '. . . we are aware that the *Australia—Leather Article 21.5* panel recently found that a DSB recommendation to "withdraw" a prohibited export subsidy under Article 4.7 of the SCM Agreement "is *not* limited to prospective action only but may encompass repayment of the prohibited subsidy". However, Brazil has explicitly expressed the "hope" that the Panel does not consider itself bound to follow *Australia—Leather Article 21.5*. Indeed, Brazil "believes that the Panel in *Australia—Leather [Article 21.5]* reached a result that is not required by the language of the [SCM] Agreement" and "does not believe that this or any other Panel should follow *Australia—Leather [Article 21.5]*". In the light of these comments by Brazil, we consider that

attitude may depend on a certain degree of deference towards the parties to the dispute (and the discretion they enjoy in reaching a solution to it), on the fact that in the GATT/WTO remedies have usually been prospective,[53] or, more generally, on the inherent characteristics of a judicial system which is not as mature as, for instance, the EC one. But more definite conclusions would necessitate more comprehensive analysis. Whichever the case may be, it has rightly been noted that 'purely prospective remedies hardly constitute a deterrent effect against potential violators',[54] as is indeed witnessed by the experience in the EC and by the case law of the Court of Justice stressing the importance of guaranteeing the effectiveness of the prohibition on implementation in the last sentence of Article 88(3) EC, and of the recovery of any unlawful aid.

## III. THE DEFINITION AND CATEGORIES OF WTO SUBSIDY

The definition of a subsidy is very elusive. Economics, with its comprehensive notion,[55] is not sufficient to offer the required clarity. In fact most of the definitional difficulties stem from the fact that the whole area involves value judgements. Ultimately, what is involved is the confrontation between different philosophical, political, and societal conceptions of the role of state intervention in the economy. This is particularly apparent in an international organization that counts more than 140 countries where views diverge considerably not only between developed and developing countries but also within the former. Two different 'philosophical' attitudes on state subsidization can be identified.[56] The 'injury only school' considers that subsidies play an important role in correcting market failures and in achieving important goals, even if different from the maximization of economic efficiency. By contrast, the 'anti-distortion school' views the use of subsidies from a more negative perspective, considering the distortions produced to the detriment of the functioning of market forces and of

---

Brazil does not in fact want us to make any finding along the lines of *Australia—Leather Article 21.5*. The same is more obviously true of Canada. As noted above, we consider that a panel's findings under Article 21.5 of the DSU should be restricted to the scope of the "disagreement" between the parties. In the present case, therefore, we do not consider it necessary to make any finding as to whether Article 4.7 of the SCM Agreement may encompass repayment of subsidies found to be prohibited'. Cf also WTO Appellate Body Report, *US—Tax Treatment for 'Foreign Sales Corporations'* ('US—FSC'), WT/DS108/AB/R, adopted on 20 March 2000, paragraph 178.

[53] Cf Art 19.1 DSU. In fact *ex tunc* remedies were granted by some GATT panels in the fields of anti-dumping and countervailing duties: cf PC Mavroidis, 'Remedies in the WTO Legal System: Between a rock and a hard place' (2000) European Journal of International Law 763, 775 *et seq*.

[54] ibid 790.

[55] Cf P Low in Ehlermann and Everson (n 9) 103: 'any intervention that affects relative prices or the conditions of competition in a market can, at least in theory, be expressed as a subsidy or tax equivalent'.

[56] See JHJ Bourgeois, 'The GATT Rules for Industrial Subsidies and Countervailing Duties and the New GATT Round: The Weather and the Seeds', in Petersmann and Hilf (eds), *The New Gatt Round of Multilateral Trade Negotiations: Legal and Economic Problems*, vol. V, (1991) 231 *et seq*.

comparative advantages. As has been observed, 'both schools of thought admit
that subsidies can create or correct market distortions. They disagree, in practice, on what should be the basic attitude towards subsidies. Should they be
allowed, unless their trade distortive effects are proved, or should there be a
general, but rebuttable, presumption of the existence of such effects?'[57] In the
light of this, the statement of the Appellate Body, whereby it is 'unwise to attach
undue importance to arguments concerning the object and purpose of the SCM
Agreement' as the latter does not contain any express statement in that respect,[58]
can be appreciated.

As an invariable consequence of the lack of agreement in the area legal norms
are thus often elusive. Indeed, in some cases they are not adopted. A 1961 report
on the 'Operation of the Provisions of Article XVI' explains that 'it was neither
necessary nor feasible to seek an agreed interpretation of what constituted a
subsidy. It would probably be impossible to arrive at a definition which would at
the same time include all measures that fall within the intended meaning of the
term in Article XVI without including others not so intended. In any event the
Panel felt that the lack of a precise definition had not, in practice, interfered with
the operation of Article XVI'.[59]

Although the SCM Agreement has introduced a fairly elaborate definition of
subsidy, many important issues remain unclear. In some cases this is due to the
fact that divergences between the Members were not eliminated.[60]

Article 87(1) EC does not define what an aid is. However, it requires that a
state aid be 'granted by the State or through State resources', that it 'favours'
'certain undertakings or the production of certain goods' by 'distorting or
threatening to distort competition within the common market', and that it
'affects trade between Member States'. Article 87(3) provides for a list of often
generally phrased derogations. Some of the requirements of Article 87(1) EC are
similar to those provided for in the SCM Agreement, in particular the 'financial
contribution', the 'benefit', and the 'specificity'. The resemblance between the
two sets of rules is not so immediate when the effects of the measure are
considered. Compared to a single 'distortion' test in Article 87(1) EC, which is
nonetheless to be read in conjunction with the justifications in Article 87(3), the
SCM Agreement provides for separate and different trade impact standards
according to the various categories of subsidies.

---

[57] ibid 232.

[58] WTO Panel Report, *Canada—Measures Affecting the Export of Civilian Aircraft* ('Canada—
Civilian Aircraft'), WT/DS70/R, adopted on 20 August 1999, paragraph 9.119. The Panel tentatively
observed that 'as suggested by Canada [ . . . ] we consider that the object and purpose of the SCM
Agreement could more appropriately be summarised as the establishment of multilateral discipline
"on the premise that some forms of government intervention distort international trade, [or] have the
potential to distort [international trade]"'. By contrast, the purpose of EC state aid rules is to ensure
that 'competition in the internal market is not distorted' (Art 3(g) EC).

[59] Report of Panel on Subsidies, BISD 10S/201 (1962) 208.

[60] Significantly, the SCM Agreement (along with the Antidumping Agreement) has no preamble.

## A. The 'financial contribution' and the 'income or price support'

SCM Article 1.1 holds that, when reference is made to the concept of subsidy, the latter 'shall be deemed to exist' if there is either a 'financial contribution by a government or any public body' or 'any form of income or price support'. A financial contribution exists when:

  (i)   a government practice involves a direct transfer of funds (eg grants, loans, and equity infusion), potential direct transfers of funds or liabilities (eg loan guarantees);

 (ii)   government revenue that is otherwise due is foregone or not collected (eg fiscal incentives such as tax credits);

(iii)   a government provides goods or services other than general infrastructure, or purchases goods; or

 (iv)   a government makes payment to a funding mechanism, or entrusts or directs a private body to carry out one or more of the type of functions illustrated in (i) to (iii) above which would normally be vested in the government and the practice, in no real sense, differs from practices normally followed by governments.

Alternatively, the existence of 'any form of income or price support' which, according to GATT Article XVI:I, operate to increase exports or decrease imports of the product receiving the subsidy, has to be established.

Despite its elaboration, the 'financial contribution' requirement leaves many important interpretative issues open. For example, the provision presents contradictory indications on the exhaustive, or merely illustrative, nature of the list. Considering governments' ingenuity in devising new forms of assistance to their industries, one of the reasons why the GATT has been so reluctant to adopt a definition of subsidy, it has been pointed out that it would be unfortunate if the four clauses were found to constitute a comprehensive definition.[61] The Panel in the *US—Export Restraints* dispute has, however, held that the list is 'finite'.[62]

SCM Article 1.1(a)(1) refers to the practices carried out by either the 'government' or 'any public body' which, in the provision, are generally summed up in the expression 'government'. This alternative should be sufficiently inclusive to refer to the practices carried out by various levels of government. In *Canada—Dairy Products*[63] the Appellate Body held:

the essence of 'government' is, therefore, that it enjoys the effective power to 'regulate', 'control' or 'supervise' individuals, or otherwise 'restrain' their conduct, through the exercise of lawful authority. This meaning is derived, in part, from the *functions*

[61] McGovern (n 9 above) paragraph 11.313.
[62] WTO Panel Report, *United States—Measures Treating Export Restraints as Subsidies* ('US—Export Restraints'), WT/DS194/R, adopted on 23 August 2002, paragraph 8.73.
[63] WTO Appellate Body Report, *Canada—Measures Affecting the Importation of Milk and the Exportation of Dairy Products* ('Canada—Dairy Products'), WT/DS103/AB/R and WT/DS113/AB/R, adopted on 27 October 1999.

performed by a government and, in part, from the government having the *powers* and *authority* to perform those functions. A 'government agency' is, in our view, an entity which exercises powers vested in it by a 'government' for the purpose of performing functions of a 'governmental' character, that is, to 'regulate', 'restrain', 'supervise' or 'control' the conduct of private citizens. As with any agency relationship, a 'government agency' may enjoy a degree of discretion in the exercise of its functions.[64]

It is interesting to compare this approach, along with the use of an intermediary under point (a)(1)(iv), with the situation in the EC.[65]

A very controversial issue has always been whether a subsidy necessarily involves a 'cost to the government' or whether, on the contrary, what is exclusively required is the conferral of an advantage.[66] In the EC a similar controversy focuses on the interpretation of the expression 'granted by the State or through state resources' in Article 87(1)EC.

It is first necessary to establish what 'cost to government' means. This is an elusive concept that may refer only to expenditure or also to losses of public revenue, both being usually recorded in the public accounts. However, the expression 'loss of public revenue' can be intended in different ways, the more extensive including also opportunity costs in the form, for example, of foregone interests. No trace of such costs is usually found in the public accounts which only take note of actual expenditure (such as a transfer of resources) or potential expenditure (such as guarantees). Nevertheless, their inclusion in the concept of 'cost to government' seems to be the more correct in economic terms.

Whatever the exact meaning of the 'cost to government', GATT law did not provide a conclusive answer on whether it required it. For example, the various examples of export subsidies included in the Illustrative List of Export Subsidies provided arguments in both directions.[67] The two opposite views collided during the Uruguay Round negotiations.[68] The response to the argument that what matters is the distortive effect of the measure, and not its means of financing, was that, by omitting the 'cost to government' requirement, an indefinite number of measures would be caught. The wording of point (a)(1)(iv), which is vague enough to accommodate both views and leave the issue open, is the inevitable result of the gap between the two positions which could not be bridged. It was thus predictable that the matter would have been referred to the dispute settlement system. The issue was not raised in the context of the interpretation of the

---

[64] ibid paragraph 97.

[65] Cf for example Joined Cases 67, 68, and 70/85, *Van der Kooy* v *Commission* [1988] ECR 219, paragraph 35; and case C-482/99 *France* v *Commission* [2002] ECR I-4397, paragraphs 50 *et seq.*

[66] See, among others, MCEJ Bronckers and R Quick, 'What is a Counteravailable Subsidy under EEC Trade Law? [1989] in Journal of World Trade 23.

[67] Thus, some items simply refer to measures 'mandated' by governments (c) or 'government-mandated' (d). By contrast, other expressions used in other examples (such as 'provision', 'allowance', 'exemption', 'remission', 'deferral', 'drawback', and 'grant') seem to suggest the use of public resources. In this direction seems to lead, in particular, the closing Item (l) that refers to '*any other charge on the public account* constituting an export subsidy' (emphasis added).

[68] See TP Stewart (ed), *The GATT Uruguay Round: A Negotiating History (1986–1992)* (1993), 898.

'financial contribution', but rather of the definition of the 'benefit'. In the *Canada—Civilian Aircraft* dispute, the Panel rejected the argument that the notion of 'cost to government' is relevant in the interpretation of the term 'benefit' within the meaning of Article 1.1(b) of the SCM.[69] The Appellate Body confirmed this finding and went further, suggesting that a 'cost to government' is not implied even in the context of the 'financial contribution'.[70] It observed that

Canada insists that the concept of 'cost to government' is relevant in the interpretation of 'benefit'. We note that this interpretation of 'benefit' would exclude from the scope of that term those situations where a 'benefit' is conferred by a private body under the direction of government. These situations cannot be *excluded* from the definition of 'benefit' in Article 1.1(b), given that they are specifically *included* in the definition of 'financial contribution' in Article 1.1(a)(iv). We are, therefore, not persuaded by this argument of Canada.[71]

In the *US—Export Restraints* dispute[72] the Panel held that an export restraint could not be considered as a subsidy. In reducing the domestic price of the relevant products, the measure could confer a benefit to domestic buyers of those products without entailing any financial cost to the State that imposed it. However, the Panel determined that if the government does not direct the sale of the product at a lower price, the price decrease simply represents a consequence of the export restraint and the practice is not caught by subparagraph (iv) of Article 1.1(a)(1) of the SCM. The Panel made it clear that 'subparagraph (iv) has to do with the entrustment or direction by a government to a *private body* of one of the *government* "functions" identified in subparagraphs (i)–(iii)'.[73] In doing so, its aim is to avoid circumvention practices by acting through private bodies.[74] The Panel, however, did not address the 'cost to government' issue.

When governments adopt measures that mandate prices, such measures may constitute 'forms of income or price support' under SCM Article 1.1(a)(2). In this respect, a 1960 Panel report[75] concluded that, under GATT Article XVI, such 'price support' measures require a 'loss' to the government for being regarded as subsidies.[76] A similar conclusion should be reached for the forms of 'income

---

[69] WTO Panel Report, *Canada—Civilian Aircraft* (n 58 above) paragraphs 9.111–9.120.

[70] WTO Appellate Body Report, *Canada—Measures Affecting the Export of Civilian Aircraft* ('Canada—Civilian Aircraft'), WT/DS70/AB/R, adopted on 20 August 1999, paragraphs 149–161.

[71] ibid paragraph 161, emphases in original.

[72] Panel Report, *US—Export Restraints* (n 62 above).

[73] ibid paragraph 8.52.

[74] ibid paragraph 8.53.

[75] GATT Panel Report adopted on 24 May 1960 (Review pursuant to GATT Article XVI:5) BISD 9th Suppl 1961 page 188.

[76] ibid 191: ' the Panel discussed the circumstances under which a system which fixes domestic prices to producers at above the world price level might be considered a subsidy within the meaning of Article XVI. It was generally agreed that a system under which a government, by direct or indirect methods, maintains such a price by purchases and resale at a loss is a subsidy. [...] The Panel considered, however, that there could be other cases in which a government maintained a fixed price above the world price without resort to a subsidy. One such case might be that in which a government fixes by law a minimum price to producers which is maintained by quantitative

support'. If there is no financial outlay or loss the measure is not a subsidy. It therefore seems that different conclusions can be drawn for the 'financial contribution' and the 'income or price support'. In the former case a 'cost to government' is not necessary, whereas in the latter it is required.[77] In any event, it is clear that no interpretation should in fact eliminate the financial contribution as a legal element separate from the requirements of benefit or specificity.[78]

In the EC the definition of state aid necessarily implies the use of state resources. The Court has recently made it clear that

only advantages granted directly or indirectly through State resources are to be considered aid within the meaning of Article 92(1) [now 87(1)EC]. The distinction made in that provision between 'aid granted by a Member State' and aid granted 'through State resources' does not signify that all advantages granted by a State, whether financed through State resources or not, constitute aid but is intended merely to bring within that definition both advantages which are granted directly by the State and those granted by a public or private body designated or established by the State.[79]

It is interesting to compare this explanation to the very similar 'circumvention' argument used by the *US—Export Restraints* Panel cited above.

In a recent paper I have drawn attention to a curious paradox which arises from the comparison between the Appellate Body report in *Canada—Civilian Aircraft* on one hand and the Court of Justice decision in *PreussenElektra* on the other.[80] Although in both cases the provisions under examination (SCM Article 1.1(a)(iv) and EC Article 87(1) respectively) are vague, whereas the Appellate Body concluded that a 'cost to government' is not required, the Court of Justice held that the use of 'state resources' is necessary. The paradox arises, not because the two courts reached different conclusions, which is in fact to some extent reasonably predictable, but because the most restrictive position should have been that adopted by the Appellate Body. It is indeed known that WTO law should be interpreted with restraint,[81] particularly when the adoption of one

restrictions or a flexible tariff or similar charges. In such a case there would be no loss to the government, and the measure would be governed not by Article XVI, but by other relevant Articles of the General Agreement.'

[77] It is interesting to note that the Agreement on Agriculture does not always require a 'cost to government': see Article 9(1)(c) that talks of 'charge on the public account'.

[78] Panel Report, *US—Export Restraints* (n 62 above) paragraph 8.40.

[79] Case C-379/98 *PreussenElektra AG* v *Schleswag AG* [2001] ECR I-2099, paragraph 58.

[80] L Rubini, 'Brevi note a margine del caso PreussenElektra, ovvero come "prendere seriamente" le norme sugli aiuti di stato e la tutela dell'ambiente nel diritto comunitario' [2001] Diritto Comunitario e degli Scambi Internazionali 473.

[81] The WTO Agreement should be interpreted in accordance with the principles of the 1969 Vienna Convention on the Law of Treaties. Cf WTO Appellate Body Report, *US—Standards for Reformulated and Conventional Gasoline*, WT/DS2/AB/R, adopted on 20 May 1996. In particular, Article 31 of the Vienna Convention reads: 'a treaty shall be interpreted in good faith in accordance with the ordinary meaning to be given to the terms of the treaty in their context and in the light of its object and purpose'. Although the actual relationship between all these elements is not clear, the prevailing reading of this provision, by requiring, as seems natural, to start from the 'ordinary meaning of the words' inevitably puts a stress on this element. Only when the meaning of the text is equivocal or inconclusive, or when a confirmation is in any event desirable, is the assessment of the text followed by

interpretation may impose an obligation on a Member and when the vagueness of the text depends on the lack of agreement between the Members.[82] By contrast, the interpretation of EC law is usually much more purposive. This applies also for state aid rules, where the Court, considering the wording of Article 87(1) EC (which prohibits aids 'in any form whatsoever') and the objective in Article 3(g), has consistently held that the focus should be on the effect of the measure.[83]

## B. The benefit

Article 1.1(b) of the SCM provides that a subsidy shall be deemed to exist if a 'financial contribution' or a 'form of income or price support', as described above, confers a 'benefit'. Unlike the 'financial contribution' element, the 'benefit' concept is not developed at all in the SCM agreement. Indeed there was no agreement on its meaning, some seeking to refer to commercial benchmarks, others to the cost to the subsidizing government, and yet others to the recipients of the subsidy.[84] It has therefore been for the jurisprudence of the Panels and Appellate Body to construe it.

### 1. The benchmarks

In the *Canada—Civilian Aircraft* dispute the Panel underlined that 'the ordinary meaning of "benefit" clearly encompasses some form of advantage and does not include *per se* any notion of cost to government'.[85] The Appellate Body upheld the Panel's finding. It commenced its analysis with the ordinary meaning of benefit:

the dictionary meaning of 'benefit' is 'advantage', 'good', 'gift', 'profit' or, more generally, 'a favourable or helpful factor or circumstance'. Each of these alternative words or phrases gives flavour to the term 'benefit' and helps to convey some of the essence of that term. These definitions also confirm that the Panel correctly stated that 'the ordinary meaning of "benefit" clearly encompasses some form of advantage'. Clearly, however, dictionary meanings leave many interpretive questions open.[86]

The most crucial of these questions is that of the criteria to be used to establish the existence of a benefit. It is clear, according to the Panel and the Appellate

---

the analysis of the object and purpose of the treaty. This restraint finds support in Article 19.2 of the Dispute Settlement Agreement whereby 'the Panel and the Appellate Body cannot add to or diminish the rights and obligations provided in the covered agreement'. On the rules of interpretation followed by the Dispute Settlement Body cf Ehlermann (n 18 above) 615 *et seq*; and Trebilcock and Howse (n 9 above) 72–75.

[82] The principle *in dubio mitius* accords deference to the sovereignty of states. When various interpretations are possible, the meaning that is less onerous on the party assuming the obligation should be adopted.

[83] See *inter alia* Case 173/73 *Italy v Commission* [1974] ECR 709, paragraph 13.

[84] Low in Ehlermann and Everson (n 9 above) 114–115.

[85] Panel Report, *Canada—Civilian Aircraft* (n 58 above) paragraph 9.112.

[86] Appellate Body Report, *Canada—Civilian Aircraft* (n 70 above) paragraph 153.

Body, that the term benefit 'implies some kind of comparison. This must be so, for there can be no "benefit" to the recipient unless the "financial contribution" makes the recipient "better off" than it would otherwise have been, absent that contribution'.[87] The implied idea is that the benefit can be viewed as a sort of derogation. Two cases can however be distinguished.

On one hand, there are measures adopted by a government *qua* public authority for which, by definition, there are no clear equivalents in the marketplace. Significant examples are tax and social measures. Only governments impose and collect taxes and demand the payment of social contributions and then, with the resources raised, transfer benefits to the entitled categories. In all these cases, the appropriate yardstick to establish the existence of a benefit is whether the measure constitutes a *derogation from* what can be identified as *the rule otherwise applicable in the relevant field*. Article 1.1(a)(1)(ii) of the SCM refers to this form of 'financial contribution' when it mentions the case of government revenue *otherwise due* that is foregone or not collected and exemplifies this category with the case of fiscal incentives. On the other hand, we have those transactions which, in principle, could also be carried out by private agents in the marketplace. In these cases, it is possible to use commercial benchmarks testing government conduct against that of a hypothetical private agent. The assessment, which builds up on the test described above, thus focuses on whether the intervention *derogates from the commercial practice otherwise applicable in similar circumstances*.

i) The 'but for' test: The case of tax measures

The relevant test can be found in one of the forms of 'financial contribution'. In the *US—FSC* case[88] the Panel, called to interpret the expression 'otherwise due' in Article 1.1(a)(1)(ii) of the SCM, clarified:

[...] the WTO Agreement does not impose any general obligation on Members to levy taxes or duties, nor to levy them at a particular level [...] there is in the WTO Agreement no theoretical 'correct' benchmark for taxes that would represent the norm for taxes and duties 'otherwise due' [...] In accordance with its ordinary meaning, we took the term '*otherwise* due' to refer to the situation that would prevail but for the measures in question. It is thus a matter of determining whether, absent such measures, there would be a higher tax liability. In our view, this means that a panel, in considering whether revenue foregone is 'otherwise due', must examine the situation that would exist but for the measure in question. Under this approach, the question presented in this dispute is whether, if the FSC scheme did not exist, revenue would be due which is foregone by reason of that scheme[89].

The Appellate Body confirmed the Panel's finding:

---

[87] ibid paragraph 157; cf also the Panel Report, *Canada—Civilian Aircraft* (n 58 above) paragraph 9.112.

[88] WTO Panel Report, *US—Tax Treatment for 'Foreign Sales Corporations'* ('US—FSC'), WT/DS108/R, adopted on 20 March 2000, paragraphs 7.41–7.46.

[89] ibid paragraphs 7.43 and 7.45, emphasis in original.

we [ . . . ] agree with the Panel that the term 'otherwise due' implies some kind of comparison between the revenues due under the contested measure and revenues that would be due in some other situation. We also agree with the Panel that the basis of comparison must be the tax rules applied by the Member in question. [ . . . ] What is 'otherwise due' [ . . . ] depends on the rules of taxation that each Member, by its own choice, establishes for itself.[90]

It nonetheless felt that it should add:

the Panel found that the term 'otherwise due' establishes a 'but for' test [ . . . ] In the present case, this legal standard provides a sound basis for comparison because it is not difficult to establish in what way the foreign source income of an FSC would be taxed 'but for' the contested measure. However, we have certain abiding reservations about applying any legal standard, such as this 'but for' test, in the place of the actual treaty language. Moreover, we would have particular misgivings about using a 'but for' test if its application were limited to situations where there actually existed an alternative measure, under which the revenues in question would be taxed, absent the contested measure. It would, we believe, not be difficult to circumvent such a test by designing a tax regime under which there would be no general rule that applied formally to the revenues in question, absent the contested measures. We observe, therefore, that, although the Panel's 'but for' test works in this case, it may not work in other cases.[91]

The caveat arises from the known problems of interpretation of tax law concerning the determination of general rules and exceptions. In *US—FSC Article 21.5* the Appellate Body observed that:

in identifying the normative benchmark, there may be situations where the measure at issue might be described as an 'exception' to a 'general' rule of taxation. In such situations, it may be possible to apply a 'but for' test to examine the fiscal treatment of income absent the contested measure. We do not, however, consider that Article 1.1(a)(1)(ii) always *requires* panels to identify, with respect to any particular income, the 'general' rule of taxation prevailing in a Member. Given the variety and complexity of domestic tax systems, it will usually be very difficult to isolate a 'general' rule of taxation and 'exceptions' to that 'general' rule. Instead, we believe that panels should seek to compare the fiscal treatment of legitimately comparable income to determine whether the contested measure involves the foregoing of revenue which is 'otherwise due', in relation to the income in question.[92]

These problems are well known in EC law.[93] This is why both the Panel and the Appellate Body have indicated their preference for using benchmarks that are as close as possible to the language of the SCM Agreement. The *US—FSC* Panel

---

[90] Appellate Body, *US—FSC* (n 52 above) paragraph 90.

[91] ibid paragraph 91. Cf also the WTO Panel and the Appellate Body Reports, *US—Tax Treatment for 'Foreign Sales Corporations—Article 21.5* ('US—FSC—Article 21.5'), WT/DS108/RW and WT/DS108/AB/RW, both adopted on 29 January 2002, paragraphs 8.14–8.19 and 8.29 and paragraphs 90–92 respectively.

[92] Appellate Body Report, *US—FSC Article 21.5* (n 91 above) paragraph 91.

[93] Commission notice on the application of the state aid rules to measures relating to direct business taxation (1998) OJ C384/3, 10.12.98. See also W Schön, 'Taxation and State Aid Law in the European Union' [1999] CMLRev 911.

rejected the criteria ('deviation from or exemption to the generally applied rate or basis for collection'; 'not based on neutral or objective criteria, ie the exemption or exclusion as special or programmatic') suggested by the EC. The US underlined the complexities of distinguishing between 'general rules' and 'exceptions' and it pointed out that the adoption of these criteria would have created confusion with the separate issue of specificity. The Panel, although conceding that the two tests may well produce similar outcomes, rejected the EC test as not corresponding to the ordinary meaning of the words of the SCM Agreement.[94] For its part, as seen, the Appellate Body underlined its reservations about applying any legal standard 'in the place of the actual treaty language'.

ii) The marketplace

The marketplace is consistently used as benchmark to determine the existence of the 'benefit'. In this regard, in *Canada—Civilian Aircraft* the Panel held that: 'the only logical basis for determining the position the recipient would have been in absent the financial contribution is the market. Accordingly, a financial contribution will only confer a "benefit", ie an advantage, if it is provided on terms that are more advantageous than those that would have been available to the recipient on the market'.[95]

The Appellate Body upheld this interpretation: 'the marketplace provides an appropriate basis for comparison in determining whether a "benefit" has been "conferred", because the trade-distorting potential of a "financial contribution" can be identified by determining whether the recipient has received a "financial contribution" on terms more favourable than those available to the recipient in the market'.[96]

The Appellate Body[97] found support for its interpretation in SCM Article 14 which, pursuant to Article 31(1) of the Vienna Convention, represents relevant context of the term 'benefit'. That provision, which supplies guidelines for calculating the amount of the subsidy, refers to market criteria such as 'usual investment practice of private investors', 'comparable commercial loan which the firm could actually obtain on the market', and 'prevailing market condition'. The application of market criteria to define the benefit under SCM Article 1.1 has been consistently repeated in other cases.[98] The most appropriate yardstick for loans is thus the net interest margin (ie the difference between the borrowing and lending rate) whereas, when equity injections are concerned, it is the rate of

---

[94] See Panel Report, *US—FSC* (n 88 above) paragraph 7.46.
[95] Panel Report, *Canada—Civilian Aircraft* (n 58 above) paragraph 9.112.
[96] Appellate Body Report, *Canada—Civilian Aircraft* (n 70 above) paragraph 157.
[97] ibid paragraphs 155–158.
[98] WTO Panel Report, *US—Imposition of Countervailing Duties on Certain Hot-Rolled Lead and Bismuth Carbon Steel Originating in the UK* ('US—Lead and Bismuth), WT/DS/138/R, adopted on 7 June 2000, paragraph 6.64; WTO Panel Report, *US—Countervailing Measures concerning Certain Products from the European Communities* ('US—Countervailing Measures'), WT/DS212/R, adopted on 8 January 2003.

return on equity. In *Canada—Regional Aircraft*[99] one of the issues raised before
the Panel was whether the provision by a government of support not available in
the market necessarily confers a benefit. However, having found that, in the case
at hand, a market equivalent did in fact exist, the Panel did not address the
issue.[100]

In the EC also the market investor principle is used to assess whether the
public intervention in issue constitutes a state aid.[101]

The use of the market investor criterion has, however, also been subject to a
certain degree of criticism in the GATT/WTO and in the EC alike. It is said that,
by definition, when governments intervene in the economy they do so, not for
commercial considerations, but in the pursuit of public interest objectives. It is
therefore incorrect for governments to be equated to private investors who
pursue purely individualistic goals. Ultimately, it is argued, to assess the government behaviour against commercial criteria means to discriminate against them.
The 'private investor' criterion should therefore be substituted by a 'public
investor criterion', modelled on the public role of governments.

However, it seems evident that the use of commercial criteria is the more
natural yardstick for determining whether an advantage to a given enterprise or
industry has been given. As the Appellate Body has pointed out, the marketplace
is the best benchmark to assess the 'trade-distorting potential' of a financial
contribution. Public interest considerations, such as the need to create a level
playing field, to redistribute wealth, or to address in general market failures,
should therefore be taken into consideration with special provisions justifying
the grant of subsidies. In WTO law, that is what used to happen with the
category of 'non-actionable' subsidies. In the EC there are even more comprehensive and flexible rules to take account of socio-economic interests that may
compensate for distortions of competition, Articles 87(2) and (3) EC, and Article
86(2) EC. Under the latter provision, state aids could be justified when they are
necessary to avoid that the performance, in law or in fact, of the particular task
assigned to undertakings entrusted with the operation of services of general
economic interest is obstructed. The definition of the scope of application of
this provision in the State aid field, in particular with respect to the financing of
public services, is currently a hot topic.[102]

---

[99] WTO Panel Report, *Canada—Export Credits and Long Guarantees for Regional Aircraft*
('Canada—Regional Aircraft'), WT/DS222/R, adopted on 19 February 2002.

[100] See ibid paragraph 7.341.

[101] The case-law on the issue is abundant. An interesting analysis of the concept of 'normal market
conditions' in the postal sector is Case C-39/94 *SFEI v La Poste* (n 38 above) paragraph 54 et seq, and
Joined Cases C-83/01P, C-93/01P, and C-94/01P, *Chronopost et al v Commission*, Judgment of 3 July
2003, nyr, paragraph 31 et seq.

[102] Cf case C-53/00 *Ferring* [2001] ECR I-9067, and its 'fine-tuning' case C-280/00 *Altmark Trans*,
Judgment of 24 July, nyr. Cf also the Opinion of Advocate General Jacobs in Case 126/01 *GEMO*,
delivered on 20 April 2002. Generally speaking, the debate on the regulation of public services in the

Considering their importance, a brief digression on the regulation of public services in the WTO, and in particular on their financing, may be useful. Subsidization of services is not covered by the SCM Agreement. Although some doubts persist as to the precise scope of application of the GATS, it has been shown that, as the law now stands and on a proper interpretation of GATS Article 1(b) and (c), public services should be subject to it when provided 'on a commercial basis' (ie for profit) and 'in competition with one or more service suppliers'.[103] That established, however, the GATS does not provide for comprehensive regulation of subsidies. The only relevant provision is Article XV, which does not impose any immediate obligation, simply setting out a duty to enter into negotiations and to 'accord sympathetic consideration' to other Members' requests for consultation. Thus arguments on the need to offset the costs for performing public services have not been put forward in the WTO. In any event, Members are not completely free to grant subsidies to service suppliers, being still constrained by the other obligations of the GATS, in particular the national treatment obligation embodied in Article XVII of the GATS.[104]

## 2. Beneficiaries

The identification of the beneficiary of a subsidy—the undertaking or the product—is important. In the EC, Article 87(1) EC rather unsatisfactorily provides that the aid measure should favour 'certain undertakings or the production of certain goods'. However, the consistent reading is that the recipient company is the beneficiary. In the WTO, GATT Article VI refers to bounties or subsidies granted directly or indirectly to 'the manufacture, production or export of the merchandise'. The SCM Agreement is silent on this point, in particular in the 'definition' of Article 1.1. The Appellate Body thus clarified: 'a "benefit" does not exist in the abstract, but must be received and enjoyed by a beneficiary or a recipient. Logically, a "benefit" can be said to arise only if a person, natural or legal, or a group of persons, has in fact received something. The term "benefit", therefore, implies that there must be a recipient'.[105]

---

EC is currently particularly strong. The Commission has recently issued a discussion paper and other documents on services of general economic interest and state aids, all available on the website of the Competition Directorate (http://www.europa.eu.int/comm/competition, last checked on 27 June 2003). It is also worth recalling the recently introduced Article 16 EC which underlines the importance of public services in Europe.

[103] Krajewski (n 28 above).

[104] See Section II above. Another provision of the GATS that may become relevant is Article VIII which precludes Members from allowing monopoly service suppliers to use their monopoly power to negate their most-favoured-nation commitments and to undermine their specific market-access commitments. See Low in Ehlermann and Everson (n 9 above) 119.

[105] Appellate Body Report, *Canada—Civilian Aircraft* (n 70 above) paragraph 154.

This interpretation was confirmed in *US—Lead and Bismuth*[106] which also raised two other points of some importance, particularly in the context of privatizations. The first is whether, in the case of change of ownership of the undertaking that has been granted a 'non-recurring'[107] and 'untied'[108] subsidy, or indeed a transfer of its assets, it should be presumed that the benefit conferred by that subsidy has passed to the new owner. The second issue is whether the fact that a 'fair market value' has been paid for the 'productive assets, goodwill, and all other factors' employed by the successor companies in the production of the products at issue excludes the existence of a benefit for the new owners. Both the Panel and the Appellate Body rejected the possibility of using presumptions. They further concluded that if there has been payment of a 'fair market value', in the context of an 'arm's length' transaction and in full compliance with 'commercial considerations', then the buyer has not 'benefited' from the operation.[109] Significantly, however, the Appellate Body restricted its ruling to 'the particular circumstances of the case' and to 'the facts of the case'.[110]

In the recent *US—Countervailing Measures* dispute[111] the Panel was asked whether, with respect to a context similar to that in *US—Lead and Bismuth*, a distinction should be made between the 'benefit to the owners of the company' and the 'benefit to the company itself'.[112] The Panel, in rejecting the US' argument that the benefit 'reside' in the legal person or company and continue to accrue to it even if its ownership changes, significantly underlined that 'when someone purchases a company for fair market value, the purchase price includes the *value of the benefit* conferred to that company'. Therefore, 'for the purpose of benefit determination based on market criteria [ . . . ] there should be no distinction between the advantage or benefit conferred by the financial contributions to the company or to the shareholders, ie the owners of the company'.[113] The Appellate Body, however, felt it necessary to amend such findings. There may well be cases where the distinction between the company and its owners is indeed relevant.[114] The finding of the Panel should have been qualified. It should have been limited to the 'very narrow' set of circumstances at issue in that dispute and not predicated with respect to *all* cases. The Appellate Body also qualified the finding that privatizations at arm's length and for fair market value *always* exclude that the benefit is passed through. In particular it pointed out that:

---

[106] Panel Report, *US—Lead and Bismuth* (n 98 above) paragraph 3.66; see also the Appellate Body Report in the same dispute, WT/DS138/AB/R, adopted on 7 June 2000, paragraph 31.

[107] Provided on an irregular basis.

[108] Provided on a company basis and not directed at specific products.

[109] Panel Report, *US—Lead and Bismuth* (n 106 above) paragraph 3.81; Appellate Body Report, *US—Lead and Bismuth* (n 109 above) paragraph 68.

[110] Appellate Body Report, *US—Lead and Bismuth* (n 106 above) paragraph 74.

[111] Panel Report, *US—Countervailing Measures* (n 98 above).

[112] ibid, paragraph 7.40.

[113] ibid, paragraph 7.51.

[114] WTO Appellate Body Report, *US—Countervailing Measures concerning Certain Products from the European Communities* ('US—Countervailing Measures'), WT/DS212/AB/R, adopted on 8 January 2003, paragraphs 116–119.

the Panel's absolute rule of 'no benefit' may be defensible in the context of transactions between two private parties taking place in reasonably competitive markets; however, it overlooks the ability of governments to obtain certain results from markets by shaping the circumstances and conditions in which markets operate. Privatisations involve complex and long-term investments in which the seller—namely the government—is not necessarily always a passive price taker and, consequently, the 'fair market price' of a state-owned enterprise is not necessarily always unrelated to government action. In privatisations, governments have the ability, by designing economic and other policies, to influence the circumstances and the conditions of the sale so as to obtain a certain market valuation of the enterprise.[115]

The Appellate Body thus concluded that:

the Panel erred in concluding that '[p]rivatisations at arm's length and for fair market value *must* lead to the conclusion that the privatised producer paid for what he got and thus did not get any benefit or advantage from the prior financial contribution bestowed upon the state-owned producer. Privatisation at arm's length and for fair market value *may* result in extinguishing the benefit. Indeed, we find that there is a rebuttable presumption that a benefit ceases to exist after such a privatisation. Nevertheless, it does not *necessarily* do so. There is no inflexible rule *requiring* that investigating authorities, in future cases, *automatically* determine that a 'benefit' derived from pre-privatisation financial contributions expires following privatisation at arm's length and for fair market value. It depends on the facts of each case (emphases added).[116]

In the EC, too, similar issues have arisen. In *HJ Banks* the Court held that 'in principle, where a company which has benefited from aid has been sold at the market price, the purchase price reflects the consequences of the previous aid, and it is the seller of that company that keeps the benefit of the aid. In that case, the previous situation is to be restored primarily through repayment of the aid by the seller'.[117] The case law of the Court on 'share deal' cases (where the sale concerns the shares of the company that benefited from the aid) was recently analysed by Advocate General Tizzano in *Germany v Commission*.[118] He observed that the Court oscillates between two positions, requiring the repayment of the aid either by the company itself or by the seller of the shares (when the share price reflects the value of the aid granted); the buyer's liability is in contrast excluded when the share price is the market price.[119] With respect to 'asset deal' cases (where the sale concerns the assets of the company benefiting from the aid) it also seems that the guiding principle is the market price.[120]

The reference in SCM Article 1.1(a)(1)(i) to the 'direct' transfers of funds and liabilities is interpreted as a way to distinguish the scope of this provision from that of point (a)(1)(iv) which regulates the use of private bodies as

[115] ibid paragraph 124.       [116] ibid paragraph 127.
[117] Case C-390/98, *HJ Banks v Coal Authority and Secretary of State for Trade and Industry* [2001] ECR I-6117, paragraph 78.
[118] See the Opinion in Case C-277/00, delivered on 19 June 2003, paragraphs 75 et seq.
[119] ibid, paragraph 82.       [120] ibid, paragraph 98.

intermediaries.[121] It is thus unlikely that the mere passing of funds through a third party would take an arrangement outside the scope of the SCM Agreement.[122] Indeed, GATT Article VI:3 mentions 'subsidies granted . . . *indirectly*'. Also EC law strikes down state aids granted indirectly. Thus, for example, in *Germany* v *Commission* the Court held that a tax relief to individuals investing in companies situated in Berlin or in the new *Länder* constituted aid in favour of the companies.[123]

A case of indirect grant of subsidies is that of 'upstream' or 'input' subsidies. This occurs when a manufacturer of product A uses product B as input. Suppose that the government grants a subsidy to the manufacturer of the input product B. The latter will then be able to sell its product to A at a lesser price. The product A manufacturer is thus alleged to benefit from an indirect subsidy. The issue, of course, is to determine when the benefit granted to the input manufacturer 'passes through' to the downstream producer of A. According to the Panel in *US—Pork from Canada*,[124] the principal characteristic of an 'indirect subsidy' is that: 'subsidies granted to swine producers [must have led] to a decrease in the level of prices for Canadian swine paid by Canadian pork producers below the level they have to pay for swine from other commercially available sources of supply and that this decrease was equivalent to the full amount of the subsidy'.[125]

The Panel indicated that it was necessary, *inter alia*, to consider the degree to which swine were internationally traded, and the per unit cost of producing additional output of swine that the subsidies may have caused. In *US—Softwood Lumber* it was held that presumptions cannot be used to establish that a benefit has passed through: 'we are of the view that an authority may not assume that a subsidy provided to producers of the 'upstream' input product automatically benefits unrelated producers of downstream products, especially if there is evidence on the record of arm's-length transactions between the two'.[126] In this regard, US law seems to be more sophisticated in that it requires a more thorough analysis of whether the upstream subsidy has in fact passed through to the downstream producer. What has to be established is that the upstream subsidy confers a 'competitive benefit' on the downstream goods and that this has a 'significant effect' on the cost of manufacturing or producing the merchandise.[127]

---

[121] McGovern (n 9 above) paragraph 11.313.           [122] ibid.

[123] Case C-156/98 [2000] ECR I-6857, paragraph 26. Issues as to the identification of beneficiaries arise also in the context of state guarantees. The beneficiary of the guarantee is certainly the borrower who can obtain financing that it would not have had, at least on those conditions, but for the State's intervention. Under certain circumstances, however, it is also possible to regard the financial institution that borrows as beneficiary, in particular when the guarantee is given *ex post* in respect of a transaction already in existence and whose terms have not been amended.

[124] GATT Panel Report, in *US—Countervailing Duties on Fresh, Chilled and Frozen Pork from Canada* ('*US—Pork from Canada*') DS7/R-38S, BISD 38S/30 (1992), adopted on 11 July 1991.

[125] ibid paragraph 4.9.

[126] WTO Panel Report, *US—Preliminary Determinations with respect to Softwood Lumber from Canada* ('*US—Softwood Lumber*'), WT/DS236/R, adopted on 11 November 2002, paragraph 7.71.

[127] Cf Benitah (n 9 above) 269–272.

## C. Specificity

WTO law requires that a subsidy be specific to 'an enterprise or industry or group of enterprises or industries' in order to be subject to the provisions of the agreement.[128] The only relevant exception is that of export and local-content subsidies, which are prohibited without it being necessary to establish that they are specific. EC law features a similar requirement, providing that state aids must 'favour certain undertakings or the production of certain goods'.

Although, strictly speaking, specificity is not considered as one of the elements of the definition of a subsidy,[129] its determination is strictly linked to the issues concerning that definition. The rationale behind the specificity test is not fully evident. Although some suggest that specific measures are potentially more distortive than general ones, others point out that this argument is not completely sound from an economic standpoint. It therefore seems that this test is ultimately based on much more practical reasons, that is 'to avoid a painstaking review of all programmes and their eventual distortive potential'.[130]

SCM Article 2 comprehensively defines what is meant by specificity, in substance adopting the same three-tier specificity test developed in the application of US countervailing duty law whereby both the *purpose* and the *effect* of the government programme have to be examined.

The first part of the test is to assess whether the measure is *de jure* specific, ie whether 'the granting authority, or the legislation pursuant to which the granting authority operates, *explicitly* limits access to a subsidy to certain enterprises'.[131] This is not the case if the granting authority or the legislation establishes objective criteria or conditions on the eligibility for and the amount of the subsidy.[132] These criteria and conditions must be 'objective', which means 'neutral, which do not favour certain enterprises over others, and which are economic in nature and horizontal in application, such as the number of employees or size of enterprise'. Moreover, they must be 'clearly spelled out in law, regulation, or other official document, so as to be capable of verification', their eligibility must be automatic, and they must be strictly adhered to.[133]

The most interesting test, however, is that of *de facto* specificity which is established when, notwithstanding the appearance of being generally available,

---

[128] SCM Arts 1.2 and 2.    [129] cf SCM Arts 1.2 and 2.1

[130] A Beviglia Zampetti, 'The Uruguay Round Agreement on Subsidies: A Forward-Looking Assessment' [1996] Journal of World Trade 21.

[131] SCM Art 2.1(a). Emphasis added.

[132] SCM Art 2.1(b).

[133] Applying these criteria Adamantopoulos and Pereyra-Friedrichsen (n 9 above, 109) observe that aid to small and medium-sized Enterprises (SMEs) would not be specific under WTO law whereas it would be so, although it could be authorized if it meets certain conditions, in the EC. See Case C-351/98 *Spain* v *Commission* and Case C-409/00 *Spain* v Commission, both cited in note 5 above. In Case C-409/00 the Court held that the argument that the measure at issue established 'objective criteria of horizontal application' (possibly not qualifying as a subsidy under the SCM Agreement) was irrelevant. In the Court's view that circumstance 'can only serve to show that the aid at issue falls within an aid scheme and is not individual aid'.

the measure at issue is in fact limited to certain enterprises. Thus the *de facto* test does not focus on the legislation *per se* but on the actual disbursements made on the basis of that legislation.[134] Article 2.1(c) provides that:

if, notwithstanding any appearance of non-specificity resulting from the application of the principles laid down in subparagraphs (a) and (b), there are reasons to believe that the subsidy may in fact be specific, other factors may be considered. Such factors are: the use of a subsidy programme by a limited number of certain enterprises, the predominant use by certain enterprises, the granting of disproportionately large amounts of subsidy to certain enterprises, and the manner in which discretion has been exercised by the granting authority in the decision to grant a subsidy. In applying this subparagraph, account shall be taken of the extent of diversification of economic activities within the jurisdiction of the granting authority, as well as of the length of time during which the subsidy programme has been in operation.

A footnote to this indent reads that particular consideration will be given to 'information on the frequency with which applications for a subsidy are refused or approved and the reasons for such decisions'.

It is worth underlining that in EC law aid granted to an entire sector of the economy, such as the manufacturing sector, would be regarded as fulfilling the specificity test.[135] And the same conclusion would apply even if the sector is represented by 'all national products exported'.[136]

SCM Article 2 goes on to provide in paragraph 2 that 'a subsidy which is limited to certain enterprises located within a designated geographical region within the jurisdiction of the granting authority shall be specific. It is understood that the setting or change of generally applicable tax rates by all levels of government entitled to do so shall not be deemed to be a specific subsidy for the purposes of this Agreement.' According to that provision, if a regional government wishes to introduce, say, tax inducements to attract investments, they are entitled to do so, as their measures will not be considered as a specific subsidy (provided that they do not target 'certain enterprises'). This is so even if the shortfall for the public revenue is made good with funds from the central government.[137] However, should an identical measure be adopted by a central government in favour of one of its regions, then that subsidy could be deemed to be specific. It is interesting to note that, in the EC, the Court of Justice made it clear that 'measures adopted by intra-state entities (decentralised, feder-ated, regional or other) of the Member States, whatever their legal status and description, fall, in the same way as measures taken by the federal or central authority, within the ambit of Article 92(1) [now 87(1)] of the Treaty, *if the conditions laid down in that provision are satisfied*'.[138] That seems to mean that

---

[134] Panel Report, *US—Subsidy Offset* (n 34 above) paragraphs 7.106 *et seq.*
[135] Case C-143/99 *Adria-Wien Pipeline* [2001] ECR I-8365, paragraph 55.
[136] Joined Cases 6 and 11/69 *Commission v France* [1969] ECR 523, paragraphs 20 and 21.
[137] McGovern (n 9 above) paragraph 11.313.
[138] Joined Cases T-127/99, T-129/99, and T-148/99 *Territorio Histórico de Álava—Diputación Foral de Álava* v *Commission* [2002] ECR II-1275, paragraph 142 (emphasis added); Case 248/84 *Germany* v *Commission* [1987] ECR 4013, paragraph 17.

the operation of the tax power by intra-state authorities does not *per se* fulfil the specificity test. What is important is to establish that the conditions under Article 87(1) EC, including specificity, are present.

According to Article 2 of the SCM, any determination of specificity shall be clearly substantiated on the basis of positive evidence. This would exclude the possibility of using presumptions.[139]

The determinations of whether a benefit has been conferred and whether this benefit is selective are strictly interconnected. This is particularly apparent in the EC, where the language of derogation described above in the context of the analysis of the benefit is used to distinguish between selective state aids and general measures. However, it has been argued that the two issues are logically distinct, and that the derogation test operates more naturally when the existence of the advantage is under examination.[140] The use of a derogation test to assess specificity could produce incorrect results. Establishing whether a measure does favour 'certain enterprises or group of enterprises' or 'certain undertakings or the production of certain goods' is very problematic as even measures that are generally available will inevitably produce a differential impact. A clear example are general infrastructures that inevitably end up being used more by some users than by others. The provision of general infrastructures is, however, expressly considered as not constituting a financial contribution under Article 1.1(a)(1)(iii) of the SCM. The real issue in the selectivity assessment is therefore the determination, through the criteria in SCM Article 2, of the 'degree of intensity' of the said differential impact. On this basis, even an infrastructure that appears to be general may in fact be regarded as a specific financial contribution if it is established that in fact it, for example, *mainly* benefits certain enterprises.

## D. The categories of subsidies

One of the most significant characteristics of the regulation of subsidies in the GATT first and in the WTO afterwards is the 'taxonomy approach': subsidies are divided into various categories in accordance to the different impact they allegedly produce on international trade. From this perspective, EC state aid law, with its single, general clause of 'distortion on competition', seems simpler. Upon closer scrutiny, however, it becomes clear that the interplay between the Article 87(1) prohibition and the Article 87(2) and (3) and Article 86(2) justifications also results in an elaborate treatment of various types of aids.

Further, although WTO law does not expressly provide for an 'across the border' test, this requirement can be implicitly read into the relevant discipline. It is indeed evident that WTO law should be concerned only if the effects of the measures at issue are not confined to the jurisdiction of the granting Member but have an impact on international trade. It has nonetheless been suggested that, for the sake of 'judicial economy', it would be advisable to introduce an express

---

[139] McGovern (n 9 above) paragraph 11.313.     [140] Schön (n 96 above) passim.

'distortion across the border' test to be determined in the preliminary stage of countervailing procedures when the existence of the subsidy is under examination.[141] A similar requirement is expressly provided in Article 87(1) EC as, to be caught by the discipline, state aids should affect trade between Member States.

## 1. Prohibited subsidies

This category includes two types of subsidies:

– subsidies contingent, in law or in fact, whether solely or as one of several conditions, upon export performance, including those included in the 'illustrative list of export subsidies' annexed to the SCM agreement ('export subsidies'); and
– subsidies contingent, whether solely or as one of several other conditions, upon the use of domestic over imported goods ('local-content subsidies').[142]

The distinction between export and domestic subsidies is a leitmotiv in the history of the international regulation of subsidies. The idea that export subsidies (to which are equated local-content subsidies) pose a special danger to international trade has always found unanimous support among the Members. Export subsidies are difficult to justify in terms of legitimate domestic policy objectives and raise serious concerns 'over the prospect of mutually destructive international export subsidy wars'.[143] As they are the most significant form of subsidies, the SCM Agreement does not require the establishment of any specificity or distortion: the occurrence of adverse effects is presumed. They are therefore simply prohibited: pursuant to Article 3.2 of the SCM, 'a Member shall neither grant nor maintain subsidies referred to in paragraph 1'.[144] The existence of 'material injury' only has to be determined when the imposition of countervailing duties is considered. In the EC, too, the fact that aid is available to all exported products does not preclude it from being specific.[145] Further, export and local-content aids are subject to stricter regulation. For example, the recent Commission Regulation 69/2001 on the application of Articles 87 and 88 EC to *de minimis* aid[146] expressly provides that the regulation, and hence the exemption it concedes, does not apply to ' . . . (b) aid to export-related activities, namely aid directly linked to the quantities exported, to the establishment and operation of a distribution network or to other current expenditure linked to the export activity; (c) aid contingent upon the use of domestic over imported goods'.[147]

The various criteria provided for in SCM Article 3 have been considered in some disputes. Attention has quite often focused on export subsidies and, in particular, on the definition of the contingency on export performance.

---

[141] Jackson (n 9 above, ch 9).          [142] SCM Art 3.1.
[143] Trebilcock and Howse (n 9 above) 207.
[144] From the procedural point of view, the SCM Agreement provides for a fast procedure, whereby the time periods applicable under the Dispute Settlement Understanding are halved.
[145] See Joined Cases 6 and 11/69 *Commission v France* (n 136 above) paragraphs 20–21.
[146] OJ (2001) L10/30.          [147] ibid Art 1.

For export subsidies to exist SCM Article 3.1(a) requires that they are 'contingent, in law or in fact, . . . upon export performance'. *De jure* contingency refers to those cases where the grant of the subsidy is made *legally* contingent on export performance. By contrast, as explained in footnote 4 to SCM Article 3.1(a), *de facto* contingency concerns those cases where the bestowal of the subsidy is '*in fact tied to actual or anticipated exportation or export earnings*'.[148] Crucially, the second sentence of footnote 4 makes it clear that 'the mere fact that a subsidy is granted to enterprises which export shall not for that reason alone be considered to be an export subsidy within the meaning of this provision'.

In the *Canada—Civilian Aircraft* dispute the Appellate Body dealt with the interpretation of SCM Article 3.1(a) and of footnote 4.[149] It held that contingent means, as the Panel had found, 'conditional', 'dependent for its existence on something else'.[150] Then it noted that, whereas *de jure* contingency between the subsidy and export performance is evident from the words of the relevant measure,[151] *de facto* contingency 'must be inferred from the total configuration of the facts constituting and surrounding the granting of the subsidy, none of which on its own is likely to be decisive in any given case'.[152] In particular:

the facts 'must demonstrate' that the granting of a subsidy is *tied to* or *contingent upon* actual or anticipated exports [footnote omitted]. It does *not* suffice to demonstrate solely that a government granting a subsidy *anticipated* that exports would result. The prohibition in Article 3.1(a) applies to subsidies that are *contingent* upon export performance. [ . . . ] There is a logical relationship between the second sentence of footnote 4 and the 'tied to' requirement set forth in the first sentence of that footnote. The second sentence of footnote 4 precludes a panel from making a finding of *de facto* export contingency for the sole reason that the subsidy is 'granted to enterprises which export'. In our view, merely knowing that a recipient's sales are export-oriented does not demonstrate, without more, that the granting of a subsidy is tied to actual or anticipated exports. The second sentence of footnote 4 is, therefore, a specific expression of the requirement in the first sentence to demonstrate the 'tied to' requirement. We agree with the Panel that, under the second sentence of footnote 4, the export orientation of a recipient may be taken into account as *a* relevant fact, provided that it is one of several facts which are considered and is not the only fact supporting the finding.[153]

Further, the Appellate Body, reversing the Panel, rejected the possibility of using presumptions founded on how close the subsidy brings the product to sale in the export market to establish 'export contingency'. In its words, 'while we agree that this nearness-to-the-export-market factor *may*, in certain circumstances, be a relevant fact, we do not believe that it should be regarded as a legal presumption. It is, for instance, no "*less . . . possible*" that the facts, taken

---

[148] Emphasis added.    [149] Appellate Body Report, *Canada—Civilian Aircraft* (n 70 above).
[150] ibid paragraph 166.
[151] This may occur either explicitly or by necessary implication. See WTO Appellate Body Report, *Canada—Certain measures affecting the automotive industry* ('Canada—Automotive industry'), WT/DS139/AB/R, WT/DS142/AB/R, adopted on 19 June 2000, paragraph 100.
[152] Appellate Body Report, *Canada—Civilian Aircraft* (n 70 above) paragraph 167.
[153] ibid paragraphs 171 and 173, emphases in original.

together, may demonstrate that a pre-production subsidy for research and development is "contingent ... in fact ... upon export performance"'.[154]

According to the Appellate Body, SCM Article 3.1(b) also implicitly refers to *de jure* and *de facto* contingency.[155]

In WTO law, therefore, 'export contingency' is something more than mere 'export anticipation or orientation'. In this respect, the regulation of export aids in the EC seems to be stricter. In the *Tubemeuse* case[156] the Court held that it is possible that export aid (at issue were aids to an undertaking that exported 90 per cent of its production *out of* the Community) affects intra-Community trade as 'it was ... *reasonably foreseeable* that Tubemeuse would redirect its activities towards the internal Community market'.[157] The difference between this language, which refers to a mere 'propensity' to affect trade and competition, and the 'export contingency' required by WTO law is clear.

The illustrative list in Annex I of the SCM Agreement provides some examples of export subsidies. Importantly, measures that fall within the list are deemed to be export subsidies[158] while measures that are considered in the Annex 'as not constituting export subsidies shall not be prohibited',[159] but are still subsidies.[160] In any event, the fact that a measure does not fall within one of the items of the illustrative list does not mean that it is permitted.[161]

One of the most interesting types of export subsidies, which has provoked major disputes under the GATT and the WTO, concerns favourable tax treatment, in the form of tax deferrals or exemptions, for income generated by export transactions.[162] In this field, it is important to distinguish between direct and indirect taxation. Hence, according to item (e) of the illustrative list, 'the full or partial exemption, remission, or deferral specifically related to exports, of direct taxes or social welfare charges paid or payable by industrial or commercial enterprises' amounts to an export subsidy. A deferral does not amount to an export subsidy where, for example, appropriate interest charges are collected.[163] Further, item (e) does not 'limit a Member from taking measures to avoid the double taxation of foreign-source income earned by its enterprises or the

---

[154] ibid, paragraph 174.

[155] Appellate Body Report, *Canada—Automotive Industry* (n 151 above) paragraphs 138 *et seq*.

[156] Case C-142/87 *Belgium* v *Commission* [1990] ECR I-959.

[157] ibid paragraph 38.

[158] Panel Report, (*Brazil—Export Financing Article 21.5 I*), WT/DS46/RW, adopted on 4 August 2000, paragraph 6.31.

[159] SCM Art 3.1(a), footnote 5.

[160] Appellate Body Report, *US—FSC* (n 52 above) WT/DS108/AB/R, paragraph 93.

[161] WTO Panel Report, *Brazil—Export Financing Programme for Aircraft Article 21.5 II* ('Brazil—Export Financing Article 21.5 II'), WT/DS46/RW/2, adopted on 23 August 2001, paragraphs 5.272–5.275.

[162] See the GATT Panel Report, *DISC* (n 32 above). See also the GATT Panel Reports, *Income tax practices maintained by France*, BISD 23S/114; *Income tax practices maintained by Belgium*, BISD 23S/127; *Income tax practices maintained by the Netherlands*, BISD 23S/137. All these reports were adopted, along with the DISC report, in 1981 and accompanied by an Understanding (*Tax legislation*, BISD 28S/114, 7–8 December 1981). In the WTO, see the Panel Report, *US—FSC* (n 88 above) and Appellate Body Report, *US—FSC* (n 52 above).

[163] Pursuant to footnote 57 of the illustrative list.

enterprises of another Member'.[164] By contrast, only the exemption or remission, in respect of the production and distribution of exported products, of indirect taxes *in excess of* those levied in respect of the production and distribution of like products when sold for domestic consumption shall be considered as an export subsidy.[165] In general, WTO Members are free to adopt any tax system of their choice (such as a 'worldwide' or 'territorial' system) provided that it complies with WTO obligations.[166] If, however, a Member decides as a general principle to tax income arising from foreign economic processes, it will then be prohibited from exempting selectively certain limited categories of that income.[167]

We have seen that arguments that an unlawful tax practice is necessary to remove an existing distortion are not generally accepted.[168] The Panel in *US—FSC* held that a Member cannot justify a tax exemption on the basis that this is necessary to compensate companies for disadvantages created by its tax system as compared with that of other countries.[169] Similarly, in *Italy* v *Commission*[170] it was alleged that an exemption from social contribution charges was not intended to confer a competitive advantage on the textile industry, but merely to make up for the handicap faced by the latter as compared with other industries and with the textile industries of other Member States.[171] The Court replied that the aim of Article 87 EC is 'to prevent trade between Member States from being affected by benefits granted by the public authorities which, in various forms, distort or threaten to distort competition by favouring certain undertakings or the production of certain goods. Accordingly, Article 92 [now 87] does not distinguish between the measures of State intervention concerned by reference to their causes or aims but defines them in relation to their effects'.[172] The Court pointed out that, whatever the situation is, 'the point of departure [against which to assess the existence of an aid] must necessarily be the competitive position existing in the Common market before the adoption of the measure at issue'. It is inevitable that this position is the result of numerous factors, including different levels of social charges among the industries in the various Member States. 'The unilateral modification of a particular factor of the cost of production in a given sector of the economy of a Member State may have the effect of disturbing the existing equilibrium'. Thus state aid cannot be justified on the grounds set out above. Indeed, 'generic distortions resulting from differences

---

[164] ibid.

[165] Item (g) of the list (emphasis added). Further, according to footnote 1 to the SCM Agreement, 'the exemption of an exported *product* from duties or taxes borne by the like product when destined for domestic consumption, or the remission of such duties or taxes in amounts not in excess of those which have accrued, *shall not be deemed to be a subsidy*' (emphasis added).

[166] Appellate Body Report, *US—FSC* (n 52 above) paragraphs 90 and 179.

[167] Panel Report, *US-FSC* (n 88 above) paragraphs 7.92 and 7.119. Cf the Appellate Body Report, *US—FSC* (n 52 above) paragraphs 99 and 120.

[168] Panel Report, *DISC* (n 32 above).

[169] Panel Report, *US—FSC* (n 88 above) paragraph 7.122.

[170] See n 83 above.    [171] ibid paragraph 12.    [172] ibid, paragraphs 13 and 17.

between the tax and social security systems of the different Member States have to be addressed by harmonisation measures taken at the Community level'.

In the WTO, too, we find statements that recall the Court of Justice's finding that state aid is defined on the basis of its effects and not its causes or aims. In *US—Softwood Lumber*[173] the Panel had to determine whether stumpage rights on standing timber provided for in certain Canadian provinces could be regarded as a financial contribution. It stated:

we wish to note that we do not deny that the Canadian provinces may well be pursuing broader forestry management policy goals in addition to ensuring the appropriate exploitation of the forestry resources when entering into stumpage arrangements with the harvesting companies. Indeed, it is normal that when a government makes a financial contribution, including where it provides a subsidy, that there is a mix of policy objectives. However, the fact of the matter remains that, from the harvesting company's point of view, the only reason to enter into such tenure or licensing agreements is to cut trees for processing or sale.[174]

If a measure is found to be a prohibited subsidy its 'withdrawal without delay' must be recommended.[175] As we have seen,[176] the withdrawal of prohibited subsidies requires their repayment even with respect to the past.

### 2. Actionable subsidies

Subsidies are 'actionable' if they cause 'adverse effects' to the interests of other Members. Article 5 SCM provides:

no Member should cause, through the use of any subsidy [...] adverse effects to the interest of other Members, ie:
(a) injury to the domestic industry of another Member;
(b) nullification or impairment of benefits accruing directly or indirectly to other Members under GATT 1994 in particular the benefits of concessions bound under Article II of GATT 1994;
(c) serious prejudice to the interest of another Member.

Under this category (and under that of 'non-actionable' subsidies), we find what, under the Tokyo Code, were called 'domestic' subsidies.

Whereas 'prohibited subsidies' cannot be granted or maintained,[177] with respect to actionable subsidies the Members should merely *avoid to cause*

---

[173] Panel Report, *US—Sofwood Lumber* (n 126 above).

[174] ibid, paragraph 7.16.

[175] SCM Art 4.7. The discipline for compliance is more stringent than that generally provided under WTO law. Cf Art. 21.3 of the of the Understanding on Rules and Procedures governing the Settlement of Disputes which also refers to a 'reasonable period of time'. Cf also SCM Art 7.9 which, with regard to actionable subsidies, contemplates a six-month period.

[176] See Section II above, 'First parellels between the GATT/WTO and the EC'.

[177] SCM Art 3.2. See also WTO Appellate Body Report, *Brazil—Export Financing Article 21.5* (n 46 above), paragraph 45. WTO Panel Report, *Australia—Automotive Leather Article 21.5*, (n 47 above) paragraphs 6.19 *et seq*. See also Appellate Body, *Brazil—Export Financing* (n 33 above) paragraph 191.

adverse effects. Admittedly, if these effects are removed the Member may continue to grant the subsidy. In the presence of actionable subsidies, the DSB may determine that the subsidy 'should be withdrawn' *or* that 'appropriate steps' should be taken 'to remove the adverse effects'. In the event that 'appropriate steps' to remove those effects or to withdraw the subsidy have not been taken, and that the parties have not agreed on some form of compensation, the DSB may authorize countermeasures 'commensurate with the degree and nature of the adverse effects'.[178] It is not clear if, as in the case of prohibited subsidies, the withdrawal of actionable subsidies requires their repayment.[179] By contrast, in EC law, irrespective of whether they are 'export' or 'domestic', state aids that are incompatible with the common market are simply prohibited and have to be recovered.

Finally, it is useful to note that both WTO and EC law regulate not only actual distortion caused by the subsidy or the state aid but also the threat thereof. In the WTO, determinations of threat of injury are 'to be based on facts and not merely on allegation, conjecture or remote possibility. The change in circumstances that would create a situation in which the subsidy would cause injury must be clearly foreseen and imminent'.[180] Crucially, in such cases, the 'application of counter-vailing measures shall be considered and decided with special care'.[181]

We can now turn to the three tests of 'adverse effects', devoting particular attention to the injury requirement.

The term 'nullification or impairment' has the same meaning as in the relevant provisions of GATT 1994. The scope of Article XXIII:1 is potentially very wide, as it refers to any measure, 'whether or not it conflicts with the provisions' of the GATT, or to 'the existence of any other situation' causing 'nullification or impairment'. However, as is underlined by Article 5(b) of the SCM, GATT practice has mostly confined the recourse to this concept to those cases where a Member that has given a tariff concession acts in a way that denies the competitive advantages that other Members could reasonably expect.[182] With specific regard to subsidies, GATT Article II:4 could thus be construed as providing for a general prohibition against the use of subsidies to inhibit imports into the subsidizing country when that country has bound its tariff on the product concerned.[183]

With regard to the 'serious prejudice to the interests of another Member', Article 6 provides a thorough elaboration. The resulting discipline is quite complex. The first paragraph of Article 6 originally laid down some presumptions. A 'serious prejudice' was deemed to exist when (i) the subsidization exceeded a certain percentage of the product value (that was normally 5 per cent); (ii)

---

[178] SCM Art 7.9.
[179] See Section II above, 'First parallels between the GATT/WTO and the EC'.
[180] SCM Art 15.7.
[181] SCM Art 15.8.
[182] McGovern (n 9 above) paragraph 2.271.
[183] JH Jackson, *World Trade and the Law of GATT* (1969), Chapters 15 and 16.

in case of subsidies to cover operating losses of an industry or an enterprise;[184] and (iii) when debt was directly forgiven, or when grants to cover that debt were given. Article 6.1. lapsed in the year 2000.[185] Despite these presumptions, the subsidizing country was allowed to put forward a rebuttal demonstrating that the subsidy had not produced any of the effects described in Article 6.3 of the SCM.

Article 6.3 sets out the following circumstances:

a)  displacement or impediment of imports of a like product of another Member into the subsidising Member's market;[186]

b)  displacement or impediment of exports of a like product of another Member from a third country market;

c)  significant price undercutting of the subsidized product as compared with the price of a like product of another Member, significant price suppression, depression, or lost sales in the same market;

d)  increase in the world market share of the subsidizing Member in a particular subsidized primary product.

These circumstances have a double relevance for the determination of serious prejudice. On one hand, if one of them is established serious prejudice *may* arise. On the other hand, if it is proved that none of them is present then *no* serious prejudice may be established with regard to Article 6.3. It is interesting to refer to the *Indonesia— Automobile Industry* dispute,[187] and in particular to the analysis of the notion of 'like product' and of the concepts of displacement or impedance and of price undercutting under, respectively, Article 6.3 (a) and (c).

The concept of 'injury to the domestic industry' is used in the same sense as in the context of countervailing duty procedures where it is thoroughly elaborated.[188] The general provision is GATT Article VI:3, whereby 'no contracting party shall levy any [ . . . ] countervailing duty on the importation of any product [ . . . ] unless it determines that the effect of [ . . . ] subsidisation [ . . . ] is such as to cause or threaten material injury to an established domestic industry.'

SCM Article 15 specifies this provision. In particular, paragraphs 1, 2, 4, and 5 thereof read:

a determination of injury [ . . . ] shall be based on positive evidence and involve an objective examination of both (a) the volume of the subsidised imports and the effect of the subsidised imports on prices in the domestic market for like products and (b) the consequent impact of these imports on the domestic producers of such products.

---

[184] Unless, in the latter case, they were a non-recurrent measure and were given merely to provide time for the development of long-term solutions and to avoid acute social problems.

[185] See the analysis of non-actionable subsidies below.

[186] Displacement or impediment resulting in serious prejudice as provided in points (a) and (b) of Art 6.3 is excluded if one of the circumstances in SCM Art 6.7 is present.

[187] Panel Report, *Indonesia—Automobile Industry* (n 24 above).

[188] Cf SCM Arts 15 and 16.

With regard to the volume of subsidised imports, the investigating authorities shall consider whether there has been a significant increase in subsidised imports, either in absolute terms or relative to production or consumption in the importing Member. With regard to the effect of the subsidised imports on prices, the investigating authorities shall consider whether there has been a significant price undercutting by the subsidised imports as compared with the price of a like product of the importing Member, or whether the effect of such imports is otherwise to depress prices to a significant degree or to prevent price increases, which otherwise would have occurred, to a significant degree. No one or several of these factors can necessarily give decisive guidance.

The examination of the impact of the subsidised imports on the domestic industry shall include an evaluation of all relevant economic factors and indices having a bearing on the state of the industry, including actual and potential decline in output, sales, market share, profits, productivity, return on investments, or utilisation of capacity; factors affecting domestic prices; actual and potential negative effects on cash flow, inventories, employment; wages, growth, ability to raise capital or investments and, in the case of agriculture, whether there has been an increased burden on government support programmes. This list is not exhaustive, nor can one or several of these factors necessarily give decisive guidance.

It must be demonstrated that the subsidised imports are, through the effects [as set forth in paragraphs 15.2 and 15.4][189] of subsidies, causing injury within the meaning of this Agreement. The demonstration of a causal relationship between the subsidised imports and the injury to the domestic industry shall be based on an examination of all relevant evidence before the authorities. The authorities shall also examine any known factors other than the subsidised imports which at the same time are injuring the domestic industry, and injuries caused by these other factors must not be attributed to the subsidised imports. Factors which may be relevant in this respect include, *inter alia*, the volumes and prices of non-subsidised imports of the product in question, contraction in demand or changes in the patterns of consumption, trade restrictive practices of and competition between the foreign and domestic producers, developments in technology and the export performance and productivity of the domestic industry.

Despite its high sophistication, the language of this provision is often indeterminate. In particular, serious problems have arisen in the interpretation of the causation standard. It has been noted that 'there is no precise definition in the Uruguay Round Agreement of "cause", beyond a list of factors that may be examined, leaving the appropriate standard to the discretion of the investigating authorities'.[190] Such indeterminacy depends on the fact that 'each provision is drafted in such a way as to refer to another and this interrelation and interdependency forms an almost closed loop'.[191] Indeed, all relevant provisions (Article VI of the GATT and Article 15, paragraphs 1, 2, 4, and 5 of the SCM) attribute a language of causality alternatively to *subsidized imports* or to *subsidization*. The most difficult issue is raised by the link between 'effects of the subsidy' and 'paragraphs 2 and 4' made by footnote 47 in Article 15:5 of the SCM. As a result, two constructions of the causation standard seem possible.

---

[189] The text between brackets appears in a footnote in the original text.
[190] Trebilcock and Howse (n 9 above) 211. Cf Benitah (n 9 above) 281 *et seq*.
[191] Benitah (n 9 above) 281.

A determination of injury to the domestic industry may be made even though the adverse effects depend not on the subsidization but rather on imports' competition. Support of this reading has been found in the Panel Report in the *Atlantic Salmon* dispute. Applying the virtually identical provisions of the Tokyo Code, the Panel noted that the expression 'through the effects of subsidies' refers to the effects set forth in the paragraphs on volume increase, price effects, and impact on industry. On this basis, it then concluded that that expression does not require proof that subsidization is the cause of the injury, but merely that the subsidized imports are the cause.[192] Along this line of reasoning it has been underlined that 'the primary focus of the WTO rules on subsidies is on producer interests and access to foreign markets',[193] no reference being made to consumers' interests or to a broader welfare standard.[194]

However, 'injury to the domestic industry cannot be equated to distortion of competition. Injury to competitors is not the same as injury to competition'.[195] Indeed situations can be imagined where subsidized imports prove popular with purchasers, and therefore injure the domestic industry, for reasons other than price, for example quality.[196] It has thus been suggested that, maybe through a progressive judicial interpretation, the injury test (as well as the other two types of adverse effects provided for in Article 5 of the SCM) should be construed so as to guarantee what is seen as the underlying aim of the GATT/WTO system, the safeguarding of 'normal competition':

> what would be important to prove is that the subsidy has indeed provided the recipient firm or firms with an artificial competitive advantage, affecting its cost and revenue structures, and that this action has distorted the normal competitive process, resulting in injury to the domestic industry. Consideration of this link appears to be missing in the causation analysis, which remains undefined in the Agreement, and would thus have no bearing on the possibility of obtaining a remedy.[197]

Despite the difficulties in defining the purpose of the WTO system, and of subsidy rules in particular, this 'competition-oriented' interpretation seems to be in line with the wording, object and purpose of Article 15 of the SCM. The first sentence of SCM Article 15:5 expressly sets out the object of the determination and, in doing so, it defines the relationship between subsidized imports and subsidization. According to that passage, 'it must be demonstrated that the subsidised imports are, *through the effects of subsidies*, causing injury within the meaning of this Agreement'.[198] It is indeed quite reasonable to require such a

---

[192] Cf GATT Panel Report, *US—Imposition of Countervailing Duties on Imports of Fresh and Chilled Atlantic Salmon from Norway* ('Atlantic Salmon'), SCM/153, adopted on 28 April 1994, paragraphs 328 *et seq*.
[193] Low in Ehlermann and Everson (n 9 above) 120.
[194] ibid 116.
[195] Beviglia Zampetti (n 130 above) 23.
[196] See McGovern (n 9 above) paragraph 12.415.
[197] Beviglia Zampetti (n 130 above) 24.
[198] SCM Art 15.5, first sentence (emphasis added). Cf SCM Art 19.1.

causal link, as the object of the SCM Agreement is to regulate subsidies and responses to them. With respect to the latter, if there is no subsidy then there cannot possibly be any countervailing duty.[199] SCM Article 21.1 is clear on this point, expressly stating that 'a countervailing duty shall remain in force only as long as and to the extent necessary to counteract *subsidisation which is causing injury*'.[200] Therefore if the injury depends on factors other than subsidization no determination of injury should be made. SCM Article 15.5 indeed requires the examination of 'any known factors other than the subsidised imports which at the same time are injuring the domestic industry' and makes it clear that 'the injuries caused by these other factors must not be attributed to the subsidised imports'. Among these factors, 'competition between the foreign and domestic producers' is also included.

This 'competition-oriented' interpretation would also contribute to safeguarding the system's coherence. Indeed, GATT Article VI and the SCM Agreement concern *subsidies* and responses to *subsidized* imports. The need to provide, under certain (exceptional) circumstances, 'import relief' to the domestic industry should be addressed by safeguard mechanisms,[201] and not by subsidy rules.

## 3. *Non-actionable subsidies*

Originally, the SCM Agreement provided that some types of subsidies were neither actionable nor countervailable either because they were non-distortive or because they served economic and social objectives of overriding importance. However, this category lapsed in the year 2000 as it was not possible to reach a consensus to extend their application (along with that of Article 6.1) according to Article 31,[202] mainly because of developing countries' concerns about the alleged imbalance of those provisions in favour of developed countries.[203] It is regrettable that those provisions could not be extended, even for a limited period of time, to allow further experience on their application to be gained and consideration of possible amendments to address developing countries' concerns. However, the risk of letting those provisions lapse was underlined as, after that, it would have been extremely difficult 'to resurrect the key concept of non-actionability' and, in any event, to start again from scratch.[204] Although

---

[199] Cf Panel Report, *US—Lead and Bismuth* (n 98 above) paragraphs 6.48 *et seq.*

[200] Emphasis added. Cf GATT Article VI:3 and footnote 36 to SCM Article 10 which read that countervailing duties are levied for the purpose of offsetting any subsidy.

[201] GATT Art XIX and the Agreement on Safeguards.

[202] 'The provisions of paragraph 1 of Article 6 and the provisions of Articles 8 and 9 shall apply for a period of five years, beginning with the date of entry into force of the WTO Agreement. Not later than 180 days before the end of this period, the Committee shall review the operation of those provisions, with a view to determining whether to extend their application, either as presently drafted or in a modified form, for a further period'.

[203] See the minutes of the regular meeting of the Committee on Subsidies and Countervailing Measures held on 1–2 November 1999 (G/SCM/M/24) and of the special meeting held on 20 December 1999 (G/SCM/M/22).

[204] The representative of the Canadian government warned about the risk of 'throwing the baby out with the bath water'. Cf also the Doha ministerial decision of 14 November 2001, Implementation-related issues and concerns, (section 10, paragraph 2) which includes the proposal of some countries

these provisions are not in force any more, it is useful to expose and comment them briefly for their significance, in particular in view of a brief parallel with EC law.[205]

SCM Article 8.2 referred to the following three categories of non-actionable subsidies:

(a)  subsidies for research activities conducted by firms or by higher education or research establishments on a contract basis with firms if, in particular, the assistance does not cover more than given amounts depending on whether the activity is of 'industrial research' or 'pre-competitive development', and if it is limited to certain classes of costs;

(b)  subsidies in favour of disadvantaged regions given pursuant to a general framework of regional development and non-specific within eligible regions provided that the region is clearly definable, it is considered as disadvantaged on the basis of neutral and objective criteria such as income or GDP per capita and the unemployment rate;

(c)  subsidies to promote adaptation of existing facilities to new environmental requirements imposed by law and/or regulations which result in greater constraints and financial burden on firms, provided that the assistance is *inter alia* a one-time non-recurring measure, limited to 20 per cent of the cost of adaptation, directly linked to and proportionate to the plan of reduction of nuisances and pollution, and is available to all firms that can adopt the new equipment or production processes.

SCM Article 8.3 provided that, whenever a subsidy programme fell within one of those three categories, it should have been notified 'in advance of its implementation' to the Committee. A system of yearly updates of the notifications, including, in particular, information on modification of the subsidy programmes, was also envisaged. Further, upon request by a Member, the Secretariat and the Committee should have reviewed the notifications to determine whether the conditions and criteria laid down above had been met.

Interestingly, Article 9 provided that if a subsidy programme complying with the criteria above (and hence being in principle 'non-actionable') was causing '*serious* adverse effects' to the domestic industry of a Member, such as to cause damage that would have been difficult to repair, consultations could be requested. If no mutually acceptable solution was reached, the matter was referred to the Committee that could have recommended the modification of the programme to remove the effects. It must be noted that the trade-impact standard under that provision was stricter than that provided for 'actionable subsidies'.

that subsidies with 'legitimate development goals' in developing countries (including support for regional growth, technology research and development, production diversification, and development and implementation of environmentally sound methods of production) should not have to face countervailing measures or other actions from other governments. During the course of the negotiations, members were urged to exercise due restraint with respect to challenging these measures.

[205] See Section IV below on 'Final parallels between WTO and EC law'.

## IV. FINAL PARALLELS BETWEEN WTO AND EC LAW

We have seen that the regulation of subsidies in WTO law does not necessarily embrace a full competition analysis as it may also be construed as a relief mechanism providing protection to the domestic industry from the competition of foreign products. The adoption of a competition standard in the interpretation of the adverse effects test would, however, represent the most correct solution. This seems to be true although a full welfare analysis, focusing on the conditions of competition in the market and the market failure that a subsidy intervention is designed to address, is unlikely to prosper in the WTO as it would inevitably involve going beyond the narrow national context.[206] This is indeed what happens in the EC, where a state aid may be declared as compatible with the common market if, despite distorting competition, it contributes to the achievement of a Community objective set out in Article 87(3) of the EC. Crucially, this scrutiny is exercised centrally by the Commission which, in doing so, enjoys a wide discretion.[207]

The situation in the WTO contrasts with that in the EC, where any state aid that distorts or threatens to distort competition by favouring certain undertakings or the production of certain goods is prohibited. It has been pointed out, however, that the attitude that prevails in Community law is that any state aid of significance is automatically deemed to fall within the scope of Article 87(1) of the EC.[208] For this reason, it was argued a few years ago that whereas EC law was already concerned with the *potential* effects of the aid at issue, GATT law focused on the *actual* effects of the subsidy, thus intervening only at that level.[209] In the *Philip Morris* case the Court of Justice rejected the claim that the Commission should define the relevant product market. It also held that, if the state aid strengthens the position of an undertaking as compared with that of other undertakings competing in intra-Community trade, the latter must be regarded as affected by that aid. More recently, however, the Court of First Instance annulled a Commission decision on the ground that it should have analysed the distortion of competition in relation to a more specific product market.[210] Indeed, the need to use more economic analysis in state aid law is increasingly strongly advocated.[211] The alleged distortion of competition should thus be

---

[206] Low in Ehlermann and Everson (n 9 above) 115.

[207] It should be noted however that, even in the area of state aids, there is a trend towards the decentralization of this control as evidenced by the adoption of the 'exemption regulations' in the areas of *de minimis* aid, training aid, aid to SMEs, and, more recently, employment aid.

[208] FY Jenny, 'Competition and State Aid Policy in the EU' [1998] Fordham Corporate Law Institute 84.

[209] Coccia (in Bourgeois, n 9 above).

[210] Case T-155/98 *SIDE* v *Commission*, Judgment of 28 February 2002, paragraph 71.

[211] S Bishop, 'The European Commission's Policy Towards State Aid: A Role for Rigorous Competitive Analysis [1997] European Competition Law Review 85; Jenny (n 208 above) 75. The importance of a secure anchorage of competition decisions (including those on state aids) to economic analysis has recently been emphasized by the Commission itself. Cf Commissioner Monti's article in *The Economist* of 9 November 2002.

assessed on a case-by-case basis using the technical tools that are common in antitrust law, in the first place the definition of the relevant product market, with any necessary adjustments.[212]

With respect to justifications, we have seen that the category of 'non-action-able' subsidies has lapsed. However, if we compare for a moment the regulation emerging from those provisions with that in the EC, we see that EC law also recognizes that, under certain circumstances, state aids for research and development, regional, and environmental goals should be justified as 'compatible with the common market'.[213] The close examination of the criteria and conditions in EC law, and their parallel with WTO regulation, is, however, beyond the scope of this paper. In any event, what differentiates Community law from WTO law is the fact that in the former the existence of the general idea of 'compensatory justification' allows one to justify state aids that pursue important aims which are deemed to correspond with the 'Community interest'. The criteria in Article 87(3) EC (and also Article 86(2) ) EC are very general. The system is quite flexible and, as stated above, the Commission enjoys a wide discretion in assessing whether the aid is 'compatible with the common market'.[214] Several cases of 'horizontal', 'sectoral', and 'regional' aids, which go considerably beyond the three cases of subsidies that were non-actionable in the WTO, can be justified.

It is difficult to determine in a general way which is the strictest regulation of subsidies, that in the WTO or that in the EC. From the procedural standpoint, for example, while EC law seems to be more rigorous in its more efficient control and surveillance system and in its remedies for illegal and incompatible aids, only WTO law envisages the possibility of adopting unilateral defensive measures. If we turn to the substantive law, parallels are even much more difficult to draw. EC state aid law does not distinguish aids in favour of goods or services, whereas WTO regulation is still very much based on that distinction. Most interestingly, however, the comparison of the various requirements of the concept of subsidy and aid and of their categories does not offer univocal outcomes. Whereas WTO law seems to be stricter in some areas, EC law is more rigorous in others. A more precise assessment could, and arguably should be made. However, it would require a far more comprehensive analysis than space here allows.

---

[212] J Fingleton in Ehlermann and Everson (n 9 above) 57.

[213] Cf the Community guidelines on State aid for environmental protection OJ 2001 C37/03; Community framework for State aid for research and development OJ 1996 C45/05 amended by the Commission communication OJ 1998 C48/02; Guidelines on national regional aid OJ 1998 C74/09 as amended (see OJ 2000 C258/05).

[214] However, it must be noted that the application of Article 86(2) would not require the use of discretion if it were used for offsetting the costs of public services. Cf Advocate General Tizzano in his Opinion in Case C-53/00 *Ferring* (n 102 above) paragraph 79.

# 9

# The EEA State Aid Regime

MICHAEL SÁNCHEZ RYDELSKI[*]

## I. INTRODUCTION

The aim of the Agreement on the European Economic Area (hereinafter the 'EEA Agreement' or simply the 'EEA') is to guarantee the four fundamental freedoms, as well as equal conditions of competition for undertakings and non-discrimination between individuals in all eighteen EEA States.[1] The EEA Agreement contains basic provisions, which are drafted to reflect as closely as possible the corresponding provisions of the EC Treaty. These provisions include elements governing the free movement of goods, persons, services and capital, competition, and other common rules, such as public procurement and State aid. The task of controlling State aid is one of the most important means of safeguarding that equal conditions of competition within the EEA are not distorted by actions of States. In the field of State aid, the powers to control the EFTA States that are members to the EEA Agreement (hereinafter the 'EFTA States'), are vested with the EFTA Surveillance Authority (hereinafter the 'Authority'). The powers of the Authority mirror the extended competencies of the European Commission (hereinafter the 'Commission') in this area. This means that the EFTA States are subject to the same strict State aid control, exercised by a supranational body, as the Member States in the European Community (hereinafter the 'Community'). Close co-operation between the Commission and the Authority ensures that diverging policies between the 'two pillars' of the EEA will not exist.

The objective of this Chapter is to focus on the State aid provisions of the EEA legal framework and to clarify issues related to State aid which are specific to the EEA Agreement. This Chapter describes the tasks of the Authority to control State aid and highlights the limits of the Authority's competence to assess State aid to certain sectors, such as fisheries, falling outside the scope of the EEA Agreement. The Chapter finally provides some examples of jurisprudence of the EFTA Court in relation to State aid cases. Questions concerning the interpretation of the State aid rules which are common to the EC Treaty are therefore not dealt with in this Chapter.

---

[*]The author expresses in this contribution his personal views and not those of the EFTA Surveillance Authority.

[1] Norberg/Hökborg/Johansson/Eliasson/Dedichen, EEA Law—A Commentary on the EEA Agreement, First Edition, Stockholm 1993; Blanchet/Piipponen/Westman-Clément, The Agreement on the European Economic Area (EEA), First Edition, Oxford 1994.

## II. Background

The EEA Agreement entered into force on 1 January 1994.[2] The Contracting Parties to the EEA Agreement were initially the Community, the European Coal and Steel Community, and the then twelve EC Member States, on one hand, and five EFTA States, namely Austria, Finland, Iceland, Norway, and Sweden, on the other.[3] On 1 January 1995 Austria, Finland, and Sweden joined the Community and left Iceland and Norway in the 'EFTA pillar' of the EEA Agreement. The number of EFTA States was subsequently brought to three when, on 1 May 1995, the EEA Agreement entered into force for the Principality of Liechtenstein.

The objective of the EEA Agreement is to establish a dynamic and homogeneous[4] European Economic Area, based on common rules and equal conditions of competition. To this end, the four fundamental freedoms of the internal market, as well as a wide range of accompanying Community rules and policies, are extended to the participating EFTA States. Secondary Community legislation, in areas covered by the EEA Agreement, are brought into the EEA by means of direct reference to the relevant Community acts in the respective Annexes to the EEA Agreement.

The EEA Agreement implies that two separate legal systems are applied in parallel within the EEA (the 'two-pillar structure').[5] On one hand, the EEA Agreement applies to relations between the EFTA States and the Community, as well as between the EFTA States themselves. On the other hand, Community law applies to relations between the EC Member States. This being the case, for the EEA to be homogeneous, the two legal systems must develop in parallel and be applied and enforced in a uniform manner. To this end, the EEA Agreement provides for decision-making procedures intended to ensure the integration into the EEA of new secondary Community legislation (into the respective Annexes to the EEA Agreement). It also provides for a surveillance mechanism to ensure the fulfilment of obligations under the EEA Agreement and uniform interpretation and application of its provisions.

The task of ensuring that new Community legislation is extended to the EEA in a timely manner rests, in the first place, with the EEA Joint Committee, a committee composed of representatives of the Contracting Parties.[6]

---

[2] The Agreement on the European Economic Area was published in: OJ 1994 L 1, page 3. An updated version of the Agreement on the European Economic Area can be obtained from the website of the EFTA Secretariat (www.efta.int).

[3] Norberg/Hökborg/Johansson/Eliasson/Dedichen, pages 33 *et seq.*

[4] On homogeneity see for example Part VII, Chapter 3, Section 1 of the EEA Agreement.

[5] This follows, *inter alia*, from Articles 108 and 109 EEA.

[6] On the EEA Joint Committee see Part VII, Chapter 1, Section 2 of the EEA Agreement. Blanchet/Piipponen/Westman-Clément, page 27; Norberg/Hökborg/Johansson/Eliasson/Dedichen, page 121.

### III. The EFTA Surveillance Authority

While the introduction of new rules within the EEA is thus entrusted to a joint body, the surveillance mechanism, to ensure correct application of these rules, is arranged in the form of a two-pillar structure, with two independent bodies. The Commission supervises the Member States of the Community, whereas the Authority supervises the EFTA States.[7] Although the EEA Agreement already foresaw the foundation of the Authority, its concrete establishment was undertaken by the Agreement between the EFTA States on the Establishment of a Surveillance Authority and a Court of Justice (hereinafter the 'Surveillance and Court Agreement').[8] The Surveillance and Court Agreement contains basic provisions governing the Authority's organization and lays down its tasks and competences.[9]

#### A. General Surveillance Responsibilities

The Authority ensures that the EFTA States respect their obligations under the EEA Agreement, and that enterprises abide by the rules relating to effective competition. The general surveillance responsibilities are laid down in Articles 108 and 109 EEA. According to Article 108(1) EEA, the 'EFTA States shall establish an independent surveillance authority [ . . . ] and procedures similar to those existing in the Community' to ensure the fulfilment of obligations under the EEA Agreement. The main task of the Authority is thus to ensure that EEA rules are properly enacted and applied by the EFTA States. The EFTA States are obliged to notify the Authority of their transposition of EEA provisions into national law. If a State does not transpose and/or apply the EEA rules correctly, the Authority will intervene. The Authority may eventually initiate infringement proceedings, which, as a last step, may bring the matter before the EFTA Court.[10]

#### B. Surveillance in the Field of State Aid

The surveillance of the Authority in the field of State aid fully corresponds with the procedure of the Commission in this field. The Authority keeps all systems of existing aid in the EFTA States under constant review and, where relevant, proposes appropriate measures to ensure the compatibility of such aid with the EEA Agreement. The EFTA States may not introduce new aid or alter existing

---

[7] This follows, *inter alia*, from Articles 108 and 109 EEA.

[8] The Agreement between the EFTA States on the Establishment of a Surveillance Authority and a Court of Justice was published in: OJ 1994 L 344, page 1. The Agreement can also be obtained via the website of the EFTA Secretariat (www.efta.int).

[9] Further information on the Authority can be obtained from the Authority's website (www. efta.int).

[10] Article 31 of the Surveillance and Court Agreement. Norberg/Hökborg/Johansson/Eliasson/Dedichen, pages 217 *et seq.*

aid without first having been authorized by the Authority. Where aid has been granted and paid out without such authorization, the Authority may instruct the Government concerned to recover from the recipient the whole or part of the aid received. The procedural EEA State aid provisions are described in the subsequent section.

## IV. THE EEA STATE AID PROVISIONS

The EEA State aid provisions aim at ensuring that conditions of competition are equal and not distorted by State measures favouring certain industries or enterprises.[11] Due to its distortive effects, State aid is, in principle, considered incompatible with the functioning of the EEA Agreement, unless it fulfils certain conditions under which aid is or may be exempted from the general ban on State aid. The EEA State aid provisions reflect the corresponding Community rules.

### A. The Basic Substantive Provisions

The rules on State aid are contained in Part IV, Chapter 2 of the main part of the EEA Agreement, as well as in Annex XV and Protocols 26 and 27 to the Agreement. The basic substantive provisions on State aid are found in Article 61 EEA. Article 61 EEA is, with some technical adaptations, identical in substance to Article 87 EC. The main rule in Article 61(1) EEA is that aid granted by EC Member States, EFTA States, or through State resources which distorts or threatens to distort competition by favouring certain undertakings or production of certain goods and which affects trade between the EEA Contracting Parties is incompatible with the EEA Agreement. The second and third paragraphs of Article 61 EEA add certain exception clauses to this main rule. Article 61(2) EEA replicates the provisions of Article 87(2) EC and declares that the same categories of aid shall be considered compatible with the functioning of the EEA Agreement. Article 61(3) EEA basically copies the provisions of Article 87(3) EC, with the exception of Article 87(3)(d) EC, laying down the categories of aid which may be considered to be compatible with the functioning of the EEA Agreement.

Furthermore, Article 63 EEA refers to Annex XV to the EEA Agreement, which contains secondary Community legislation and other *acquis* in the field of State aid adopted by the Commission up to 31 July 1991. More specifically, Annex XV lists, *inter alia*, Commission and Council Directives in the field of State aid, as well as various frameworks, letters from the Commission to the EC Member States, Commission communications, and even extracts from

---

[11] Blanchet/Piipponen/Westman-Clément, pages 229 *et seq.*; Norberg/Hökborg/Johansson/Eliasson/Dedichen, page 554; Evans, EC Law of State Aid, First Edition, Oxford 1997, page 3; D'Sa, European Community Law on State Aid, First Edition, London 1998, paras. 2–10 *et seq.*; Hancher/Ottervanger/Slot, EC State Aids, Second Edition, London 1999, para. 3–009.

the Commission Annual Reports on Competition Policy. The listing puts an obligation on both the Commission and the Authority to take due account of them in the EEA context, which is important with regard to the uniform application of the provisions in the main Agreement. Annex XV therefore ensures that the *acquis* in the field of State aid is interpreted in conformity by both surveillance authorities. It placed an obligation on the Authority, upon the entry into force of the EEA Agreement, to adopt corresponding acts. As regards EEA relevant acts adopted by the Commission after 31 July 1991, the Authority has to adopt, after consultation with the Commission, corresponding acts in order to maintain equal conditions of competition.[12]

## B. The Procedural Provisions

In the field of State aid, the powers of the Authority mirror the extended competencies of the Commission in this area. The general description of the surveillance obligations and powers of the Authority, laid down in Articles 108 and 109 EEA, are supplemented by specific provisions applicable in the field of State aid.

Article 62 EEA provides that all existing systems of State aid in the territory of the Contracting Parties, as well as any plans to grant or alter State aid, shall be subject to constant review as to their compatibility with Article 61 EEA. According to Article 62(1) EEA, this review shall be carried out: (a) as regards the EC Member States, by the Commission; (b) as regards the EFTA States, by the Authority according to the rules set out in an agreement between the EFTA States establishing the Authority. Both surveillance authorities have therefore their own decision-making autonomy. The attribution of cases depends on the State which is proposing the aid measure.

Article 62(1)(b) EEA further specifies that the Authority is entrusted with the powers and functions laid down in Protocol 26 EEA. This Protocol reads as follows:

The EFTA Surveillance Authority shall, in an agreement between the EFTA States, be entrusted with equivalent powers and similar functions to those of the EC Commission, at the time of the signature of the Agreement, for the application of the competition rules applicable to State aid of the Treaty establishing the European Economic Community, enabling the EFTA Surveillance Authority to give effect to the principles expressed in Articles 1(2)(e), 49 and 61 to 63 of the Agreement. The EFTA Surveillance Authority shall also have such powers to give effect to the competition rules applicable to State aid relating to products falling under the Treaty establishing the European Coal and Steel Community as referred to in Protocol 14.

The competences of the Authority thus envisaged in the EEA Agreement are laid down in the Surveillance and Court Agreement. In a manner similar to that in

---

[12] See the General Note No. II in Annex XV. Concerning the adoption of corresponding acts (State Aid Guidelines) by the Authority, see above in section III.B.

Article 109 EEA, Article 5 of the Surveillance and Court Agreement lays down the general monitoring functions of the Authority, providing that the Authority shall, *inter alia*, ensure the fulfilment by the EFTA States of their obligations under the EEA Agreement and the application of the rules of the EEA Agreement on competition.

Concerning the Authority's competence in the field of State aid, Article 24(1) of the Surveillance and Court Agreement specifies:

The EFTA Surveillance Authority shall, in accordance with Articles 49, 61 to 64 and 109 of, and Protocols 14, 26, 27, and Annexes XIII, section I(iv), and XV to, the EEA Agreement, as well as subject to the provisions contained in Protocol 3 to the present Agreement, give effect to the provisions of the EEA Agreement concerning State aid as well as ensure that those provisions are applied by the EFTA States.

This Article contains an enumeration of the provisions on State aid of the EEA Agreement, the application of which the Authority is to ensure. It is drafted in a similar way as Protocol 26 EEA, specifying not only the general State aid provisions in Article 61 EEA, but also provisions related to specific fields, including Article 49 EEA (transport sector) and Protocol 14 EEA (ECSC steel industry).

Article 24(2) of the Surveillance and Court Agreement further states that '[i]n application of Article 5(2)(b) [of the Surveillance and Court Agreement], the EFTA Surveillance Authority shall, in particular, upon the entry into force of this Agreement, adopt acts corresponding to those in Annex I'. In this respect, the Authority has adopted a number of procedural and substantive rules in the field of State aid, incorporating most of the principles, as well as guidelines and frameworks, developed in the context of the EC State aid rules. For this purpose, the Authority has made a certain number of adaptations to the text of the non-binding acts which have been, in principle, only of a technical nature, as it could not, due to the homogeneity requirements, change the substance of the rules contained in the acts. These Guidelines are published in the Official Journal of the European Communities.[13]

The primary procedural rules are set out in Article 1 of Protocol 3 to the Surveillance and Court Agreement. Article 1 of Protocol 3 sets out the procedures for the examination of new and existing aid. These provisions are comparable to Article 88 EC. Article 2 of Protocol 3 to the Surveillance and Court Agreement lays down the principles concerning the establishment and functions of an EFTA Advisory Committee on aid granted for transport by rail, road, and inland waterway, a Committee which also exists on the EC side. Decisions of the Authority are published in the Official Journal of the European Communities and can also be obtained from the Authority's website.[14]

[13] Procedural and Substantive Rules in the Field of State Aid. Adopted and issued by the Authority on 19 January 1994. Published in: OJ 1994 L 231, page 1, and EEA Supplement to the OJ 1994 No 32, page. The State Aid Guidelines were last amended on 18 December 2002, not yet published. The State Aid Guidelines can also be obtained via the website of the Authority (www.efta.int).

[14] Under the section 'State aid Registry'.

## C. Co-operation between the Commission and the Authority

As mentioned above, both the Commission and the Authority have their own decision-making autonomy. With a view to ensuring a uniform surveillance in the field of State aid throughout the territory covered by the EEA Agreement, Article 62(2) EEA states that the Commission and the Authority shall cooperate in accordance with the provisions set out in Protocol 27 EEA. To this end, Protocol 27 EEA lays down the principles according to which the Authority and the Commission shall co-operate in order to ensure uniform application of the State aid rules. According to this Protocol, it is provided, *inter alia*, that the Commission and the Authority have an obligation to exchange information and views on general policy issues and inform each other on all decisions as soon as they have been taken.[15] Finally, Article 64 EEA contains provisions on dispute settlement in relation to State aid cases. This Article covers situations where one of the surveillance authorities considers that the implementation of the rules contained in Articles 61 and 62 EEA or Article 5 of Protocol 14 EEA (ECSC steel) is not in conformity with the maintenance of equal conditions of competition within the EEA.

## V. THE SCOPE OF THE EEA AGREEMENT: STATE AID TO FISHERIES

It is important to recall that the product coverage of the EEA Agreement is limited in scope. It should be noted that there will probably be individual cases or schemes which will concern products both covered and not covered by the EEA Agreement. In this case, the Authority will examine only that part of the aid which supports products covered by the EEA Agreement. The dividing line is to be found in a case-by-case approach taking into consideration all specific elements related to the aid measure in question. In this context it should be mentioned that the question whether the Authority's competence covers the assessment of State aid to the fisheries sector has been an issue of frequent dispute.[16] State aid to the fisheries sector should therefore be taken as an example to delimitate the competence of the Authority in this sector.[17]

## A. Provisions of the EEA Agreement on State Aid to Fisheries

The starting point would be to examine whether a certain fish product falls within the product scope of the EEA Agreement. Article 8(3) EEA and Protocol 3

---

[15] Norberg/Hökborg/Johansson/Eliasson/Dedichen, page 233.

[16] See for example: EFTA Court, Case E-2/94 *Scottish Salmon Growers Association Limited* v *EFTA Surveillance Authority* [1995] Report of the EFTA Court. The judgment is available on the website of the EFTA Court (www.efta.int).

[17] Concerning processed agricultural products and forestry see: Blanchet/Piipponen/Westman-Clément, pages 243 *et seq.*

EEA define the products falling under the EEA Agreement. Article 8(3) EEA provides that

[u]nless otherwise specified, the provisions of this Agreement shall apply only to:

(a)   products falling within Chapters 25 to 97 of the Harmonized Commodity Description and Coding System, excluding the products listed in Protocol 2;
(b)   products specified in Protocol 3, subject to the specific arrangements set out in that Protocol.

In other words, Article 8(3) EEA limits the material scope of application of the EEA Agreement to the above products, unless otherwise specified in the Agreement. Fish and any fishery products, in so far as they do not fall under Chapters 25 to 97of the Harmonized Commodity Description and Coding System (HS) or are specified in Protocol 3, fall outside the general scope of application of the EEA Agreement.

To take one example, farmed Atlantic salmon, whether fresh, filleted, chilled, or frozen, falls in Chapter 3 of the HS, and for certain prepared salmon products Chapter 16.04 may also be relevant. These commodities are neither within the general product coverage defined in point (a) of Article 8(3) EEA nor does Protocol 3 EEA cover them. Hence these products fall outside the product coverage of the EEA Agreement as defined in Article 8(3) EEA. It follows that application to the salmon producing industry of the provisions of the Agreement, including the State aid provisions in Chapter 2 of Part IV, is excluded, 'unless otherwise specified'. Article 20 EEA provides that '[p]rovisions and arrangements that apply to fish and other marine products are set out in Protocol 9'.

Protocol 9 EEA on trade in fish and other marine products contains rules relating to customs duties and charges having equivalent effect, rules on quantitative restrictions on imports, rules of origin, as well as rules on State aid and competition. Concerning customs duties, Protocol 9 EEA is asymmetric in nature, as it does not provide for equal tariff concessions from all Contracting Parties. Concerning the above-mentioned example, under Protocol 9 EEA, the Community has not granted any tariff concessions to farmed Atlantic salmon or other salmon products. However, the absence of tariff concessions does not preclude the application of the State aid provisions of Protocol 9 EEA.

From the content of the provisions in Protocol 9 EEA, and the context in which reference to these provisions is set in the main body of the EEA Agreement, it emerges that Protocol 9 EEA in principle forms an independent, basic set of rules governing trade in fish and other marine products, separate from (except when otherwise provided) other provisions in Part II in the main body of the EEA Agreement. In other words, Protocol 9 EEA is in principle a *lex specialis* for fish and other marine products. The general rules of the EEA Agreement, including those on State aid set out in Chapter 2 of Part IV of the Agreement (Articles 61 to 64 EEA), are not applicable to the fisheries sector, except when explicitly so provided in the relevant articles of the main part of the Agreement (cf. Articles

21(4), 23, second paragraph, and 65(1) and (2) EEA) or in Protocol 9 EEA. Article 4 of Protocol 9 EEA contains the following provisions on State aid and competition:

1. Aid granted through State resources to the fisheries sector which distorts competition shall be abolished.
2. Legislation relating to the market organization in the fisheries sector shall be adjusted so as not to distort competition.
3. The Contracting Parties shall endeavour to ensure conditions of competition which will enable the other Contracting Parties to refrain from the application of anti-dumping measures and countervailing duties.

In the Joint Declaration on the agreed interpretation of Article 4(1) and (2) of Protocol 9 EEA, annexed to the Final Act of the EEA Agreement, the Contracting Parties have agreed on the following interpretation:

1. While the EFTA States will not take over the *acquis communautaire* concerning the fishery policy, it is understood that, where reference is made to aid granted through State resources, any distortion of competition is to be assessed by the Contracting Parties in the context of Articles 92 and 93 of the EEC Treaty and in relation to relevant provisions of the *acquis communautaire* concerning the fishery policy and the content of the Joint Declaration regarding Article 61(3)(c) of the Agreement.

Attention should also be paid to Article 6 of Protocol 9 EEA, which provides:

Should the necessary legislative adaptations not have been effected to the satisfaction of the Contracting Parties at the time of entry into force of the Agreement, any points at issue may be put to the EEA Joint Committee. In the event of failure to reach agreement, the provisions of Article 114 of the Agreement shall apply *mutatis mutandis*.

No reference is made in Articles 4 and 6 and the Joint Declaration which would make the State aid provisions in the main body of the EEA Agreement applicable. Hence, taking into account the provisions of Articles 8(3) and 20 EEA, and as neither the main Act nor Protocol 9 EEA provide otherwise, State aid rules in the Agreement applicable to the fisheries sector must be considered to be set out exhaustively in Protocol 9 EEA. It has to be noted that the other State aid provisions in Chapter 2 of Part IV are all related to Article 61 EEA. Thus, Article 62 EEA, which defines the division of responsibilities for the surveillance of State aid between the Commission and the Authority, explicitly refers to Article 61 EEA, when stating that '[a]ll systems of State aid [ ... ] shall be subject to constant review as to their compatibility with Article 61'.

Article 61(1) EEA makes its application conditional upon the absence of any other provisions in the EEA Agreement stating otherwise. In this respect, Article 4 of Protocol 9 EEA can be considered to form a derogation, as it provides that only '[a]id [ ... ] which distorts competition shall be abolished', whereas Article 61(1) EEA provides that 'any aid [ ... ] which distorts or threatens to distort competition [ ... ] shall [ ... ] be incompatible with the functioning of this Agreement'. Hence, according to its wording, Article 4(1) of Protocol 9 can be considered to form a *lex specialis* governing State aid for fisheries. It provides for only an *ex post* system of supervision where aid 'shall be abolished', whereas Article 61 EEA provides that aid 'shall [ . . . ] be incompatible [ . . . ]' and Article 62 EEA lays down a system of constant review of the compatibility of aids. No such system is foreseen in Protocol 9 EEA.

To summarize, State aid provisions applicable under the EEA Agreement to the fisheries sector are exhaustively set out in Protocol 9 EEA. Protocol 9 EEA is a derogation from the general rules of the EEA Agreement governing State aid, as it does not envisage a continuous surveillance and monitoring function, with e.g. advance notification obligations regarding aid plans. On the contrary, only an *ex post* system of assessment has been envisaged.

## B. Competence of the EFTA Surveillance Authority to assess State Aid to Fisheries

The competences of the Authority in the field of State aid have been dealt with above. As already mentioned, Article 24 of the Surveillance and Court Agreement contains an enumeration of the provisions on State aid of the EEA Agreement, the application of which the Authority is to ensure. Consequently, as there is no reason to consider that Protocol 26 EEA and Article 24 of the Surveillance and Court Agreement were not meant to exhaustively enumerate the Authority's powers in the field of State aid, the conclusion must be drawn that the provisions of the EEA Agreement and of the Surveillance and Court Agreement, which define the scope of the Authority's competences in the field of State aid, do not confer upon it the powers to assess State aid under Protocol 9 EEA.

The question remains whether competence to assess State aid to the fisheries sector is nevertheless conferred upon the Authority by the provisions in Protocol 9 EEA. As no direct answer can be found in Article 4(1) of Protocol 9 EEA, it is appropriate to seek guidance in the Joint Declaration on the agreed interpretation of Article 4(1) and (2) of Protocol 9 EEA, which has been quoted above. In this context it has to be borne in mind that Protocol 9 EEA is a compromise after difficult negotiations. In this situation, the textual interpretation should prevail, unless there are imperative factors speaking against that interpretation.

The Joint Declaration does not indicate that the functions and powers of the Authority, as explicitly defined in Protocol 26 EEA and Article 24 of the Surveillance and Court Agreement, are in any way extended to cover also the State aid provisions of Protocol 9 EEA. On the contrary it states quite clearly that 'any distortion of competition is to be assessed by the Contracting Parties'. The fact that the Joint Declaration regarding Article 61(3)(c) EEA is mentioned as one of the elements which the Contracting Parties in their assessment are to take into account does not alter the conclusion that it is not for the Authority to apply the State aid provisions of Protocol 9 EEA.

The same conclusion is furthermore supported by the formulation of Article 4(3) of Protocol 9 EEA, '[t]he Contracting Parties shall endeavour to ensure conditions of competition which will enable the other Contracting Parties to refrain from the application of [ . . . ] countervailing duties'. Finally, the language of Article 6 of Protocol 9 EEA, stating *inter alia* that '[s]hould the necessary legislative adaptations not have been effected to the satisfaction of the Contracting Parties at the time of entry into force of the Agreement, any points at issue may be put to the EEA Joint Committee', also reaffirms the above conclusion and makes it clear that the wording of the Joint Declaration is no coincidence. Therefore, the Authority lacks competence to assess State aid to the fisheries sector.

## VI. CASE LAW OF THE EFTA COURT

A two-pillar structure has also been established with respect to the judicial control mechanism, the EFTA Court operating as a parallel to the Court of Justice of the European Communities (hereinafter the 'European Court of Justice'). Decisions by the Authority in State aid cases may be challenged before the EFTA Court.

In this context, it is important to recall that Article 6 EEA declares that the relevant rulings of the European Court of Justice, given prior to the date of signature of the EEA Agreement, will govern the interpretation of the provisions of the EEA Agreement. Article 6 EEA is one of the basic provisions for ensuring a homogeneous EEA.[18] The rulings of the European Court of Justice delivered prior to the signature of the EEA Agreement thus constitute a source of EEA law in so far as the provisions of the EEA Agreement are identical in substance to provisions of Community law. Following the provisions concerning homogeneity (notably Article 6 EEA), the interpretation to be given to Article 61 EEA is one which has already been developed in the Community regarding Article 87 EC. The future case law of the European Court of Justice will be dealt with in a more complicated manner: through *inter alia* the mechanisms provided for in Articles 105 *et seq* EEA. Additionally, Article 3(2) of the Surveillance and Court Agreement obliges the EFTA Court and the Authority 'to pay due account' to the principles laid down by the relevant rulings of the European Court of Justice given after the signature of the EEA Agreement or of such rules of Community law which are identical in substance to the EEA Agreement. The obligation on the EFTA Court and the Authority to pay due account to future relevant case law of the European Court of Justice also concerns the provisions of Protocol 1 to 4 and the Annexes to the Surveillance and Court Agreement which are identical in substance to Community law.

The EFTA Court closely follows the case law of the European Court of Justice and the Court of First Instance. Two judgments of the EFTA Court concerning

---

[18] Norberg/Hökborg/Johansson/Eliasson/Dedichen, page 189.

State aid are of particular interest in this context, namely the *Husbanken* case and the case on Differentiated Social Security contributions.

## A. The Husbanken Case

In November 1995 the Norwegian Bankers' Association lodged a complaint with the Authority, requesting it to assess whether the framework conditions for the Norwegian State Housing Bank (hereinafter 'Husbanken') were in conformity with the EEA Agreement. Husbanken is a State institution governed by Act No. 3 of 1 March 1946 relating to the Norwegian State housing bank, as amended (*Lov om Den Norske Stats Husbank*). Husbanken forms part of the Norwegian housing policy. Husbanken's role in the Norwegian housing policy is to assist underprivileged groups of the population to become established in the market as house owners, and more generally to ensure good quality housing of moderate standards throughout the country. The role of Husbanken is, according to Section 1 of the Act, *inter alia*, to provide loans or loan guarantees in return for security in developed property and to channel support from central and local government to housing constructions and other housing projects. To this end, Husbanken provides, *inter alia*, loans with low interests to individuals for housing purposes.

The Norwegian Bankers' Association's (hereinafter 'the Association') complaint referred to Article 61 EEA, contending that the arrangement distorted competition to the detriment of credit institutions competing with Husbanken, and that the monopoly of subsidized lending constituted an economic barrier to free trade in financial services and affected cross-border trade. The Association further contended that the arrangement went beyond what was required by the interests of the population groups which the subsidies targeted, and beyond the scope of necessity implicit in Article 59 EEA (which corresponds to Article 86 EC) regarding public undertakings.

On 9 July 1997 the Authority adopted a Decision to close the case without any further action.[19] On 9 September 1997 the Association lodged an application with the EFTA Court for annulment of the Decision. The application for annulment was based on three pleas: that the Authority wrongfully did not commence formal proceedings concerning State aid; that the Authority infringed essential procedural requirements by not providing adequate reasons as required by Article 16 of the Surveillance and Court Agreement; and that the Authority wrongfully interpreted and applied Article 59(2) EEA.

As regards the *locus standi* of the Association, the EFTA Court noted that, according to the case law of the European Court of Justice,[20] 'parties concerned' within the meaning of Article 88(2) EC are those persons, undertakings, or

---

[19] Decision No. 177/97/COL.
[20] ECJ, Case C-225/91 *Matra* v *Commission* [1993] ECR I-3202, para. 18; Case C-328/82 *Intermills* v *Commission* [1984] ECR I-3809, para. 16 and Case C-198/91 *Cook* v *Commission* [1993] ECR I-2487.

associations whose interests might be affected by the grant of an aid, in particular competing undertakings and trade associations. The EFTA Court consequently concluded that the Association had *locus standi*.[21]

Concerning the substance of the case, the EFTA Court, in its judgment of 3 March 1999, although being in favour of the Authority's findings on many points, concluded that certain aspects of the Decision had not been considered to the extent necessary, and therefore decided to annul the Decision.[22] However, the EFTA Court did not alter the Authority's findings on the following points: the framework conditions for Husbanken involve State aid within the meaning of Article 61(1) EEA;[23] the aid was existing aid;[24] the Authority was under no obligation to open formal proceedings;[25] none of the exemptions in Article 61 EEA were applicable; Husbanken was an undertaking entrusted with the operation of services of general economic interest;[26] the Authority did not incorrectly interpret the EEA Banking Directives, in finding that these Directives did not apply to specialized house financing institutions such as Husbanken, nor did the Authority underestimate the effects of harmonization achieved through these Directives, as well as through primary and other secondary EEA legislation, when balancing the interests of the EEA with those of the Norwegian authorities;[27] the Authority is not under an obligation to ensure that Norway selects the least distortive means for the achievement of its housing policy goals; the appropriate test is that the means must not be disproportionate (a reasonable relationship between the aim and the means employed was satisfactory in this context). On the other hand, the EFTA Court found that the Authority did not adequately assess the effects of the aid on trade and the interests of the Contracting Parties in the context of Article 59(2) EEA.[28]

The EFTA Court noted that, in the application of Article 59(2) EEA, it was primarily for the Authority to assess whether certain services were 'services of general economic interest' within the meaning of Article 59(2) EEA. By referring to the case law of the European Court of Justice,[29] the EFTA Court concluded that, in this assessment, the nature of the undertaking entrusted with the services is not of decisive importance, nor was the question whether the undertaking was entrusted with exclusive rights. Rather the essence of the services deemed to be of general economic interest and the special characteristics

---

[21] By Decision of 12 June 1998 the EFTA Court declared the application admissible: EFTA Court, Case E-4/97 *Norwegian Bankers' Association* v *EFTA Surveillance Authority* [1998] Report of the EFTA Court, page 40.

[22] EFTA Court, Case E-4/97 *Norwegian Bankers' Association* v *EFTA Surveillance Authority* [1999] Report of the EFTA Court, page 3.

[23] Case E-4/97 [1999], page 3, para. 30.

[24] Ibid, para. 34.

[25] Ibid, para. 36.

[26] Ibid, para. 50.

[27] Ibid, para. 63.

[28] Ibid, paras. 67 to 70.

[29] ECJ, Case C-179/90 *Merci Convenzionali Porto di Genova* [1991] ECR I-5889, para. 27 and Case C-266/96 *Corsica Ferries France SA and Others* [1998] ECR I-3949, para. 45.

of this interest distinguished it from the general economic interest of other economic activities. In this context, the EFTA Court stated that it must also be kept in mind that it had been accepted by the Community judicature[30] that EC Member States could not be precluded from taking account of objectives pertaining to their national policy when defining the services of general economic interest which they entrust to certain undertakings.[31]

It is interesting to note that the EFTA Court, in the light of the Community case law[32] at the time, did not hesitate to conclude that the *Husbanken* system involved State aid at all, although the financial advantage only served to cover the 'extra costs' that the public service obligation created. Bearing in mind the new case law of the European Court of Justice[33] on the question whether compensation for costs created by public service obligations constitutes State aid at all, it will be interesting to see whether the EFTA Court will maintain its view on this point in future cases.

### B. The Case on Differentiated Social Security Contributions

Under the National Insurance Act of 28 February 1997 (*Folketrygdloven*) all persons residing or working in Norway are subject to a compulsory insurance scheme under which employees and employers pay social security contributions. The scheme covers benefits such as pensions, rehabilitation, medical care, wage compensation, and unemployment benefits. The contributions levied on employers are calculated on the basis of the individual employee's gross salary income. A system of regionally differentiated contribution rates ranging from zero to 14.1 per cent is in place, with the contribution rate depending on the zone where the employee has his or her registered permanent residence.

Having followed the procedure provided for in Article 1(2) of Protocol 3 of the Surveillance and Court Agreement, on 2 July 1998 the Authority rendered a Decision with regard to State aid in the form of regionally differentiated social security taxation.[34] The Authority concluded that the system involved State aid in the meaning of Article 61(1) EEA, but that the aid could be exempted according to Article 61(3)(c) EEA.

By an application of 2 September 1998 the Government of Norway brought an action under Article 36 of the Surveillance and Court Agreement for annulment of the Decision. The EFTA Court dismissed the application.[35]

---

[30] ECJ, Case C-202/88 *France* v *Commission* [1991] ECR I-1223, para. 12 and Case C-159/94 *Commission* v *France* [1997] ECR I-5815, para. 56.

[31] Case E-4/97 [1999], page 3, para. 47.

[32] Court of First Instance, Case T-106/95, *Fédération Française des Société d'Assurances (FFSA) and Others* v *Commission* [1997] ECR II-229.

[33] See contribution by Rizza, above.

[34] Decision No. 165/98/COL, OJ 1998 L 327, page 1.

[35] EFTA Court, Case E-6/98 *Government of Norway* v *EFTA Surveillance Authority* [1999] Report of the EFTA Court, page 74.

Norway submitted that the EEA Agreement did generally not cover tax measures and that the present system was part of the general tax system in Norway and was sufficiently general in nature as not to involve State aid.

On this point the EFTA Court concluded that, although tax systems of EEA/ EFTA States are not covered by the EEA Agreement, in certain cases such systems may have consequences that would bring them within the scope of application of Article 61(1) EEA.[36] In this context, the EFTA Court referred to the established case law of the European Court of Justice that the fiscal nature of a measure does not shield it from the application of Article 87 EC. Nor does Article 87 EC distinguish between the measures of State intervention by reference to their causes and aims but rather defines them in relation to their effects.[37] Thus, tax measures can also be caught by Article 61(1) EEA. The EFTA Court further found that the system of regionally differentiated social security contributions had to be seen as favouring certain undertakings within the meaning of Article 61(1) EEA, because of its geographical selectivity, unless it could be shown that the selective effect of the measure was justified by the nature or general scheme of the system itself.[38] The EFTA Court clarified, in line with the above case law of the European Court of Justice, that any direct or indirect discrimination which was to be considered justified should derive from the inherent logic of the general system and result from objective conditions within that general system. However, the Court concluded that these criteria were not satisfied in the present case.

The Norwegian Government also argued that the Authority misapplied Article 61(1) EEA, because it has failed to identify the aid that affects trade between Contracting Parties, since only this aid would be incompatible with Article 61(1) EEA.

However, the EFTA Court concluded on this point that when examining the compatibility with the EEA Agreement of aid granted in accordance with an existing aid scheme, a decision on the matter would relate to the scheme itself and not to individual aids granted under the scheme. In such a case the Authority may confine itself to examining the characteristics of the scheme in question in order to determine whether, by reason of the high amounts or percentages of aid, or the nature or the terms of the aid, it gave an appreciable advantage to recipients in relation to their competitors and was likely to benefit undertakings engaged in trade between Contracting Parties. In this context the EFTA Court referred to the case law of the European Court of Justice.[39] The EFTA Court went on to clarify that when State aid strengthened the position of an undertaking compared with other undertakings competing in intra-Community trade, the latter must be regarded as affected by that aid. For that purpose, it is not

---

[36] EFTA Court, Case E-6/98 *Government of Norway* v *EFTA Surveillance Authority* [1999] Report of the EFTA Court, page 74, para. 34.

[37] ECJ, Case 173/73 *Italy* v *Commission* [1974] ECR 709, para. 13.

[38] EFTA Court, Case E-6/98 *Government of Norway* v *EFTA Surveillance Authority* [1999] Report of the EFTA Court, page 74, para. 38.

[39] ECJ, Case 248/84 *Germany* v *Commission* [1987] ECR 4013, para. 18.

necessary for the beneficiary undertaking itself to export its products. By referring to the case law of the European Court of Justice,[40] the EFTA Court
concluded that where a Member State granted aid to an undertaking, domestic
production may, for that reason, be maintained or increased, with the result that
undertakings established in other Member States had less chances of exporting
their products to the market in that Member State.[41]

## VII. Conclusion

The EEA State aid regime is closely modelled on the provisions of the EC Treaty.
Both the Authority and the EFTA Court have applied and interpreted the
EEA State aid provisions in the light of the Commission's practice and the case
law of the European Courts. For example, in December 2001 the EC Council
Regulation laying down detailed rules for the application of Article 88 of
the EC Treaty (the 'Procedural Regulation'[42]) was incorporated into the EEA
Agreement (Protocol 26 thereto) as well as into the Surveillance and Court
Agreement (Protocol 3 thereto[43]). Protocol 26 EEA was amended so as to ensure
that the Authority would be entrusted with equivalent powers and similar
functions to those of the Commission. Protocol 3 to the Surveillance and
Court Agreement was amended by including the substantive rules laid down in
the 'Procedural Regulation'. These new procedural rules will enter into force
only after all EFTA States have made the necessary notifications in accordance
with Article 103 EEA and Article 49 of the Surveillance and Court Agreement. It
is to be hoped that the new procedural rules will finally enter into force in 2003.

With this close alignment to EC developments, the Authority and the EFTA
Court have over the years ensured that the State aid provisions of the EEA are
homogenously applied and interpreted, creating a level playing field for all
economic operators in the EEA. This close alignment will continue and the
EEA institutions have undertaken continuously to incorporate new developments of the 'EC pillar' into the 'EFTA pillar'.

---

[40] ECJ, Joined Cases C-278/92, C-279/92, and C-280/92 *Spain* v *Commission* [1994] ECR I-4103,
para. 40; Case 730/79 *Philip Morris* v *Commission* [1980] ECR 2671, para. 11; Case 102/87 *France*
v *Commission* [1988] ECR 4067, para. 19.

[41] EFTA Court, Case E-6/98 *Government of Norway* v *EFTA Surveillance Authority* [1999] Report
of the EFTA Court, page 74, para. 59.

[42] OJ 1999 L 83, page 1.

[43] Decision of the EEA Joint Committee No 164/2001 of 11 December 2001 as well as Agreement
between the EFTA States of 10 December 2001, amending Protocol 3 to the Surveillance and Court
Agreement.

# SELECTED AREAS

# 10

# General Taxation and State Aid

CONOR QUIGLEY QC

## I. Introduction

Approximately 25 per cent of all State aid is reckoned by the Commission to be
granted through the tax system. For the most part, this consists of tax breaks of
one sort or another, usually in the form of a derogation or exemption from a
standard rate or basis of assessment or in allowing a postponement in paying or
accounting for tax. Where there is a generally applicable tax rule, any derogation
from that rule which results in less tax being payable or in that tax being payable
in more favourable circumstances to the taxpayer must be examined in order to
confirm that the State aid provisions of the EC Treaty have been complied with.
In 1998 the European Commission published a notice on business taxation and
State aid in which it set out its policy in relation to identifying State aid within
the tax systems.[1] Since then the Commission has, aided at times by the European
Court of Justice, taken a rather more expansive view of the role which tax
measures play as a tool for the grant of aid. It is undoubtedly the case that
some general tax measures adopted by individual Member States or their regional authorities have led to a degree of distortion of competition, particularly
in relation to foreign investment decisions. This distortion could most effectively
be dealt with by the adoption of a European Commmunity fiscal policy entailing
a degree of harmonization of direct taxation provisions. Political movement in
this direction has, however, been at a snail's pace, with some Member States
making a point of fundamental principle out of their notions of tax sovereignty.
In the absence of such harmonization, Member States remain free to adopt the
tax systems that they consider most appropriate for their individual economies.
As a result, the Commission has turned to the State aid rules as the means by
which distortions of competition caused by differentiated tax provisions are to be
removed. Many general measures of taxation are considered by the Commission
to entail regional or sectoral implications, thereby triggering examination of the
measure for its compatibility with the common market. However, by exagger-
ating the extent of the scope of application of Article 87(1) EC to tax measures,
the Commission has caused unnecessary confusion in relation to such matters as
economic sovereignty, regional autonomy, free movement of capital, and the
status of tax relief for investments.

[1] OJ 1998 C384/3.

## II. General tax measures

General measures of economic policy are normally outside of the scope of application of Article 87(1) EC. Thus the provision by the State of infrastructure, such as roads, sewerage, hospitals, and universities, or the setting by the State of interest rates (outside of the eurozone) or of general rules of taxation have consistently been viewed by the European Commission as not giving rise to State aid. In its notice on business taxation and State aid, the Commission stated that tax measures that are open to all economic agents operating within a Member State are in principle general measures. This does not restrict the power of Member States to decide on the economic policy which they consider most appropriate and, in particular, to spread the tax burden as they see fit across the different factors of production. Provided that they apply without distinction to all firms and to the production of all goods, the following measures do not constitute State aid: tax measures of a purely technical nature (for example, setting rates of taxation, depreciation rules, and provisions to prevent double taxation or tax avoidance) and measures pursuing general economin policy objectives through a reduction of the tax burden related to certain production costs (research and development, environment, training, and employment).

This approach is based on the notion that these are generally applicable measures throughout the State and that they apply equally to all undertakings. A reduction in the rate of general taxation which applies across the board will also not give rise to State aid. Yet there is a conceptual problem in accepting this approach in the light of the definition of State aid given by the European Court of Justice in the seminal case of *Italy v Commission*[2] that aid arises where there has been an alteration in the pre-exising competitive position as between competiting undertakings. This conceptual problem is resolved by recognizing that that case concerned sectoral tax and social security advantages and that the principles enunciated in it may need to be modified as regards general taxation. On this basis, the notion that a reduction in general taxation in a given Member State does not result in State aid despite the effect on the pre-existing competitive position *vis-à-vis* competitors in other Member States derives from the fact that corporation tax is treated as a special factor in the costs of production. That factor is treated as a constant where it is an element of general taxation. Even if the rate of general taxation may be reduced, it remains constant as a factor in the State aid equation. On the other hand, where a proportion of the full tax is not charged on regional or sectoral grounds, the effect is to subject that constant to a variable.

In the normal case of regional or sectoral aid, any financial benefit granted by the State to an undertaking which is not also made available to competing undertakings will be regarded as altering the pre-existing competitive structure. Thus where a tax benefit, such as an exemption or accelerated capital allowance,

[2] Case 173/73, *Italy v Commission* [1974] ECR 709.

is made available only to certain undertakings on the basis of their economic activity or place of establishment, State aid has been granted on a sectoral or regional basis. Similarly, if the rate of tax charged in respect of a given economic activity or region is reduced by a Member State from that normally applicable under the general corporation tax regime to undertakings in the Member State concerned, a system of aid may be presumed to have been effected. In each of these cases, the undertakings benefiting from the reduced rates of taxation have had their competitive position *vis-à-vis* their competitors altered to their advantage. This applies equally whether those competitors are established in the same Member State, but which do not benefit from the reduction in taxation by virtue of their economic activity or place of establishment, or in other Member States where they are subjected to the applicable indigenous taxation system. In this respect, taxation is regarded as merely one of the costs of production to which any economically active business is subjected. The source of the taxation is irrelevant. If, for instance, the general rate of corporate taxation in France is, say, 35 per cent, but a specific provision is adopted reducing the tax on the profits of French textile manufacturers to 25 per cent, it will normally be considered that State aid has been given to these undertakings on the ground that their competitive position *vis-à-vis* textile manufacturers in other Member States has been altered. Textile manufacturers in those other Member States do not benefit from the French reduction. This is equally so regardless of the rate of tax applicable in the other Member States. On the other hand, if corporation tax in France is reduced across the board to 25 per cent, exactly the same economic consequences apply as regards the competitive position of textile manufacturers. Nevertheless, in this case no State aid is deemed to arise. It follows that in order to determine whether State aid is inherent in a reduction in taxation, the question is not whether a lower rate has been applied to the transaction in question than applied at a previous time, but whether the full rate applicable under the general system has been charged on the chargeable date.

## III. SECTORAL TAXATION

In its notice on business taxation and State aid, the Commission stated that the main criterion in applying Article 87(1) EC was that the measure provides in favour of certain undertakings in the Member State an exception to the application of the tax system. The common system applicable should therefore first be determined. The question must be posed whether special regimes of regional or sectoral taxation can be regarded, by virtue of certain characteristics, as being general systems, albeit only applicable within the region or sector concerned. Corporation tax applies to the profits made on business activities. Profits are calculated according to accepted accounting standards. The general notion is that a business will entail capital expenditure and operating expenses in order to make a profit. In the case of most economic activities, the same rules apply to determine profits and losses and the charges, such as depreciation, which may be offset prior to calculation of tax payable. However, not all business activity has this simplistic approach. For example, some activities may require huge capital investment with no profits coming on stream for several years. In such cases, the normal accounting approach of taxation may be unsuitable. The corporation taxation system may sometimes be adapted to accommodate this by specific provision within the corporate tax code. Exceptionally, an entirely separate corporate tax may be established, with structures and rates wholly different from those applicable under the general system. Such was the case for the taxation within the United Kingdom of profits from North Sea oil production.

The United Kingdom established Petroleum Revenue Tax (PRT) in place of corporation tax for profits on the supplies of oil products from the North Sea oil fields within its jurisdiction. At the time, the rate of corporation tax was 35 per cent PRT, however, was levied at 75 per cent, presumably in order for the Government to take as large a stake as possible in this natural resource. The setting of this rate of taxation, and any subsequent alteration to it, whether by way of increase or reduction, would have been regarded by all concerned, including the European Commission, as wholly within the economic sovereignty of the United Kingdom. There was no question of State aid. Moreover, the means of calculating the profits were different from those applicable under normal accounting principles. Profits and losses from oil and gas supplies were computed by reference to the price received or receivable for sales at arm's length or by ascertaining the aggregate market value for sales otherwise than at arm's length. The well known *ICI* case was concerned with whether an alteration introduced by the Finance Act 1982 to the method of calculating market value constituted State aid. Woolf J, in the High Court, held that it did not.[3] In any event, at no stage was it assumed that the PRT system as such could be regarded as entailing State aid merely because the tax rates and methods of assessing profits differed from those applicable under corporation tax generally. It is submitted that this would equally have been the case had PRT been established at 15 per cent rather than 75 per cent. The mere fact that PRT would have resulted in a lower rate of taxation than corporation tax is irrelevant once it has been established that the applicable system of taxation is within the economic sovereignty of the Member State.

The United Kingdom could, no doubt, have chosen to tax profits on petroleum production by means of special provisions within the Income and Corporation Taxes Act which would have operated as derogations from the normally applicable rules. In this case also, the economic effect of the rules would have been exactly the same, so that there is no economic reason to regard such provisions as giving rise to State aid. If that is the case, however, can it also be asserted that any sectoral rules applicable by way of derogation from the generally applicable code

---

[3] *R v Attorney General, ex parte ICI plc* [1985] 1 CMLR 588. On appeal, [1987] 1 CMLR 72, it was held that State aid did arise where the Revenue had underassessed the tax payable.

should also be treated as falling within the economic sovereignty of the Member States? The European Commission has been specifically prepared to accept such a view only in the case of agriculture and fisheries. Otherwise, the prevailing view appears to be that any derogation from the the the generally applicable rules will not constitute State aid only if it can be justified on the basis of the general scheme. However, the dividing line between derogations which are integral to a general system and those which are not is difficult to draw, whether in theory or practice. Special provisions applicable to small and medium-size businesses, for instance, may be justified where they result in lower administration costs for the business. In *Lunn Poly* the Court of Appeal correctly held that differential rates of travel insurance tax, where higher rates where charged on insurance sold by travel agents, would not amount to State aid to other companies effecting sales of insurance if the higher rate provisions were justified on grounds of tax avoidance. Tax avoidance measures form a legitimate and integral part of any tax system and, by their nature, may result in tax being charged according to criteria which do not apply in the normal course to those persons who are not suspected of avoiding the tax.[4] On the other hand, in *Adria-Wien Pipeline* the ECJ held that an exemption for the manufacturing industry in Austria from energy taxes could not be justified on financial or ecological grounds of the nature or general scheme of the energy tax law.

## IV. REGIONAL GENERAL TAXATION

The extent to which regional taxation falls within the scope of application of Article 87(1) EC is uncertain. On one hand, the Commission appears to take the view that regional taxation will constitute State aid where the level of general tax rates is lower than that applicable in the Member State generally. This approach may be criticized on the grounds that it fails to appreciate the nature of regional taxation, it dismisses regional autonomy as having fiscal consequences, and is overly centralized in its approach.

In the *Ramondín* cases, the Court of First Instance gave implicit support to the notion that regional autonomy in taxation will preclude the application of the State aid rules to general regional measures.[5] In Commission Decision 2000/795/EC the Commission had declared certain tax benefits granted by the Basque authorities to Ramondín SA as giving rise to unlawful State aid. The CFI dismissed an application for annulment of the decision on the ground that the Commission had correctly declared that the measure in question gave rise to

---

[4] *R v Commissioners of Customs and Excise, ex parte Lunn Poly* [1999] EuLR 653. In *Lunn Poly* the Court of Appeal held that there was no evidence to support the allegations of tax avoidance. The proportionality of the avoidance measures may also have to be taken into account in determining whether they are justified.

[5] Cases T-92/00 and T-103/00, *Territorio Histórico de Álava and Ramondín SA v Commission* [2002] ECR II-nyr.

a total benefit exceeding the regional investment aid limits set out in the regional aid guidelines. One argument that the applicants raised was that the tax-based benefits in question reflected a tax policy choice made by the Basque authorities, which had unlimited jurisdiction in tax matters under the Spanish Constitution. It was argued that the Commission, by considering the tax benefit to be selective State aid, was calling into question the legislative capacity of the Basque authorities. In its judgment the CFI side-stepped the conceptual issue and held that the applicant's argument was based on a misreading of the contested decision which had made no reference at all to the criterion of regional selectivity in order to establish that the measure in question constituted State aid. The CFI found, therefore, that the decision had no effect on the competence of the Basque authorities to adopt general tax measures applicable to the whole of the region concerned.[6]

It can be inferred, however, from the CFI's reasoning that it was sympathetic to the notion that regional authorities could have competence to adopt general tax measures. Indeed, this must be correct, given that several regions of certain Member States have been granted a measure of autonomy in recent years. In the United Kingdom new powers have been granted under the devolution programme to the legislative assemblies in Scotland, Wales, and Northern Ireland. The notion that the exercise of those powers to raise or lower general taxation within those regions should give rise to a presumption of State aid is inherently contradictory to the constitutional policy of devolution. Clearly, differential taxation may result as between different undertakings established in or operating in different regions. Similarly, when regional tax rates are lowered or raised, this will give result in an alteration to the pre-existing competitive structures between operators subject to tax within that region and operators elsewhere, whether within the same Member State or not. However, the very reasons which determine that differential tax systems as between Member States do not give rise to State aid considerations must surely apply equally to regional general taxation. By its nature, regional general taxation will not normally apply to undertakings which are neither established in or operating within the region. Those undertakings will, on the other hand, be subject to general corporate taxation in the region where they are based or where they carry on business. It may be that they are not subject to any autonomous regional taxation, but are solely within the scope of application of the general corporation tax of the State where they are situated. In either case, the State aid implications *vis-à-vis* regional taxation charged to their competitors should be the same.

Nevertheless, the Commission has taken a different approach. This was evident in the decision to open a formal investigation procedure into proposals for the reform of business taxation in Gibraltar in 2002.[7] The essential feature of the reform is the abolition of taxation of company profits. The general system of taxation will become a payroll tax, a business property occupation tax, and an

---

[6] Ibid, para 27.     [7] OJ 2002 C300/2.

annual company registration fee. In addition, the financial services and utilities sectors will be subject to top-up or penalty taxation on their profits. Companies will be subject to a payroll tax of £3,000 per employee per annum and a business property occupation tax (BPOT) in addition to property rates. The total liability for payroll and BPOT will be capped at 15 per cent of profits or £500,000 whichever is the lower, so that if a company makes no profit it will pay no tax. Financial services companies will pay an addition 8 per cent profits tax, although total taxation of these companies will also be capped at 15 per cent or £500,000. Utilities companies (telecoms, water, sewage, electricity, petroleum) will be charged a higher top-up tax at the rate of 35 per cent of profits in respect of utility services. Capital gains will not be treated as taxable profits.

In its decision following a preliminary assessment of the measures, the Commission concluded that it appeared that the criteria for the application of Article 87(1) EC were fulfilled. In particular, the measures afforded the beneficiaries a reduction in taxation and were therefore to be regarded as conferring a benefit. First, the requirement to make a profit before any payroll/property tax was incurred departed from the logic of a payroll tax system and could give an advantage to Gibraltar companies that made no profit. It is submitted that the Commission has put the cart before the horse in this respect. The Gibraltar authorities should be quite entitled, in the exercise of their fiscal sovereignty, to adopt the system of taxation which they feel is most appropriate for the circumstances of the Gibraltar economy. The fact that this might be labelled a payroll tax is, to a great extent, irrelevant in categorizing the tax as State aid. It is conceptually wrong to regard a new coherent system of taxation as a derogation from itself. Secondly, the Commission argued that the caps on tax liability for payroll tax and BPOT would confer an advantage on those companies that benefit most from them by limiting their tax liability. The 15 per cent cap would most likely apply to labour intensive companies or those with low profitability. The £500,000 cap would tend to apply to large companies. Again, this reasoning is questionable. On the face of it, the caps apply to any company fulfilling the specified criteria. Finally, the Commission takes issue with the proposed system on the ground that 'the whole of the Gibraltar economy (except utility companies) seems to be granted an advantage compared with companies in the United Kingdom as a whole'. The Commission's objection is that corporation tax in the United Kingdom is 30 per cent, whereas under the Gibraltar proposals, business taxes will be a maximum of 15 per cent with no tax on capital gains. Whilst the United Kingdom is responsible for the external relations of Gibraltar, it is surely questionable whether Gibraltar is to be treated as part of the United Kingdom for these comparative purposes. It is one thing to accept that trade between Gibraltar and Spain is, from a Community law point of view, trade between Member States (*ie* the United Kingdom and Spain); but it is quite another to regard Gibraltarian taxation as a derogation from the provisions applicable throughout the United Kingdom. In this respect, Gibraltar is entirely autonomous in its tax-raising powers.

## V. Low-tax jurisdictions

The problem of tackling distortions of competition caused by low-tax jurisdictions has become more urgent in recent years. When Ireland joined the European Community in 1973 its special regime of zero tax on export profits was deemed incompatible with the common market as being an export aid. Nevertheless, the Community at the time was sympathetic to the problems faced by Ireland in developing its economy, and in particular a broad manufacturing base. Accordingly, whilst export sales relief was phased out, a special rate of corporation tax was brought in at 10 per cent for manufacturing profits. This was allowed by the Commission as a general regional aid scheme applicable to Ireland as a whole which then constituted an Article 87(3)(a) EC region.[8] Over the years, and with the development within Ireland of a substantial services sector, the Commission changed its mind regarding the compatibiltiy of the 10 per cent rate for manufacturing profits with the common market. In 1998 it decided that the preferential treatment of manufacturing over services companies constituted operating aid which had to be eliminated. By agreement, the 10 per cent rate is being phased out to be replaced by a standard rate of 12.5 per cent for all corporate trading profits.[9]

Nevertheless, this low-tax policy remains a bone of contention with certain other Member States. Some baulk at the idea of billions of euros being given to Ireland from Community funds for the development of infrastructure, while profits generated within Ireland are repatriated to the United States having been subject to little or no corporate tax. Others worry that the success of the Irish economy in recent years will lead more countries into adopting a low-tax approach. Already, Hungary and Estonia are seeking to emulate the Irish experience. Other jurisdictions, such as Gibraltar and Luxembourg, are equally committed to attracting certain types of companies through a low-tax policy. In order to counteract this, the Council could adopt tax harmonization measures requiring tax rates to be set at particular rates. However, such legislation can only be adopted, at present, pursuant to Article 95 EC, which requires unanimity. No legislation harmonizing corporate tax rates has been proposed. Two reasons might explain this: first, the general reluctance of the Member States so far to legislate in corporate tax matters; secondly, those Member States pursuing low-tax policies will not, in any event, agree to legislating against such policies. Nevertheless, in the absence of such harmonization, there are alternative means by which Community law may play a role.

Apart from the State aid rules, which may only apply where the relevant criteria are fulfilled, the Community has competence to act in certain circumstances where distortion of competition arises. Where national provisions distort the conditions of competition in the common market, the Council, rather than having to act unanimously, may take action pursuant to Article 96 EC by

---

[8] 11th Report on Competition Policy.        [9] 28th Report on Competition Policy.

qualified majority. If the Commission finds that a difference in national provisions distorts the conditions of competition in the common market and that the resultant distortion needs to be eliminated, it must first consult the Member State concerned. If this consultation does not result in an agreement eliminating the distortion in question, the Council, acting by a qualified majority on a proposal from the Commission, is empowered to issue the necessary directives.

Despite this power being available, neither the Commission nor the Council has ever sought to act on it in order to challenge low-tax provisions causing distortion of competition. However, the Council has instead adopted a Code of Conduct for Business taxation which is directed at direct tax measures which affect, or may affect, in a significant way the location of business activities in the European Community. In particular, the Code of Conduct provides that tax measures which create a significantly lower effective level of taxation than that which generally applies in the Member State in question are to be regarded as potentially harmful. It is presumably on this basis that the Commission has taken its approach to the proposed reform of corporate tax in Gibraltar on the ground that the proposed 15 per cent cap is much lower than the 30 per cent corporation tax applicable in the United Kingdom. The Code of Conduct, however, is not a State aid measure as such, but is at this stage a voluntary code agreed by the Member States. It cannot be used as a means of extending the normal definition of State aid measures falling within Article 87(1) EC.

When assessing whether such measures are harmful account should be taken *inter alia* of:

- whether advantages are accorded only to non-residents or in respect of transactions carried out with non-residents;
- whether advantages are ring-fenced from the domestic market, so they do not affect the national tax base;
- whether advantages are granted without any real economic activity or substantial economic presence within the Member State offering such tax advantages;
- whether the basis of profit determination in respect of activities within a multinational group of companies departs from internationally accepted principles, notably those agreed within the OECD; and
- whether the tax measures lack transparency, including where statutory rules are relaxed at administrative level in a non-transparent way.

The Member States committed themselves not to introduce new tax measures which would be considered harmful within the meaning of the Code of Conduct and to examine their existing tax provisions with a view to eliminating any harmful measures as soon as possible. It may be noted that the Gibraltar proposals for tax reform, which have been contested by the Commission, are specifically stated by the Gibraltar authorities to comply with the Code of Conduct, particularly by abolishing previous discriminatory rules as between residents and non-residents. It may be noted that the Code of Conduct does not attempt to interfere with the right of Member States to set low rates of corporate taxation. Rather it is aimed at specific provisions in the tax code which have led to tax distortion. The success of the Code of Conduct remains to be evaluated in future studies.

## VI. INVESTMENTS, FREE MOVEMENT OF CAPITAL, AND STATE AID

An expansive interpretation of the scope of State aid to cover investments by private individuals benefiting from tax relief can give rise to significant problems in relation to the free movement of capital provisions in the EC Treaty. In *Germany v Commission*[10] the ECJ confirmed the Commission's decision that tax relief granted to individuals for investing in companies established in the former East Germany constituted State aid to those companies. It held that the origin of the advantage indirectly conferred on the companies was the renunciation by the German authorities of tax revenue which it would normally have received inasmuch as it was this renunciation which had enabled the investors to take up holdings in those companies on conditions which in tax terms were more advantageous. The fact that investors then took independent decisions did not mean that the connection between the tax concession and the advantage given to the companies had been eliminated since, in economic terms, the alteration of the market conditions which gave rise to the advantage was the consequence of the public authorities' loss of revenue. Moreover, because the tax relief was granted without any requirement as to how the money was spent in the hands of the company, it amounted to operating aid and so could not be considered as compatible with the common market as if it had been regional investment aid. It does not appear that any consideration was given by the ECJ in its deliberations in this case to the effect of the free movement of capital provisions as subsequently interpreted in *Verkooijen*.[11]

All restrictions on the free movement of capital and on payments between Member States and between Member States and third coutries are prohibited by Article 56 EC. Pursuant to Article 58(1)(a) EC, this prohibition is without prejudice to the right of Member States to apply the relevant provisions of their tax law which distinguish between taxpayers who are not in the same situation with regard to their place of residence or with regard to the place where their capital is invested. However, this exception only applies in respect of the relevant provisions of national tax law which were in force at the end of 1993, so that no new discriminatory provisions could be introduced after that date. It follows that Article 56 EC requires that no new restrictions are permissible on the place in which a person invests his capital. This applies to tax reliefs on investments by individuals. Thus, in *Verkooijen*, the ECJ held that where a

---

[10] Case C-156/98, *Germany v Commission* [2000] ECR I-6857.
[11] Case C-35/98, *Staatssecretaris van Financiën v Verkooijen* [2000] ECR I-4071.

Member State introduces a tax relief in relation to a shareholding held in companies established within its territory, it must equally apply that relief to shares held in companies established in other Member States. Joining the principles established in these cases together, however, leads to some confusion as regards the legality of tax reliefs which are aimed at encouraging private taxpayers to invest in underdeveloped regions. On one hand, tax relief granted to an individual conditional on investment in a company is to be regarded as operating State aid to the company. On the other hand, where relief is granted, it must be extended to cover shareholdings in companies in any Member State. The overall result appears to be to negate the efficacy of tax-based regional investments.

## VII. CONCLUSION: LIMITED DIRECT TAX HARMONIZATION IS DESIRABLE

It appears that the problems highlighted above could be resolved by the introduction of limited tax harmonization. All Member States presently operate a system of corporate taxation of business profits and double taxation treaties along the lines of the OECD model govern bilateral relations as between the Member States. Notions of accounting standards are also generally accepted. Company law has already been harmonized to a considerable degree by a series of directives. It should thus be relatively easy for the Member States to agree the outline of a harmonized basis for corporate taxation. Any derogation from such measures should be governed by the harmonization measures themselves. General measures should no longer be considered by the Commission to constitute State aid within the meaning of Article 87(1) EC. Rather State aid control would be applied solely to those derogating measures permitted by the harmonizing measures which favoured certain undertakings. Any further derogations would have to be agreed by the Council, as is the case with VAT, rather than by invoking the State aid rules. As to tax rates, a political decision will have to be taken at the level of the European Council. Either tax rates could be left out of the harmonization programme entirely, so that Member States retained the economic sovereignty inherent in deciding on the acceptable and desirable level of tax rates, or, as is the case with VAT, one or more bands of tax rates might be established, or a minimum level could be established. Ultimately it is a political choice. What is not satisfactory is for the present state of affairs to continue whereby the Commission interferes under the guise of the legal guardian of the State aid rules to control general rates of taxation.

# 11

# *State Aid and Public Undertakings with Specific Reference to the Airline Sector*

## KONSTANTINOS ADAMANTOPOULOS

### I. THE TREATY: NEUTRALITY AND EQUAL TREATMENT

Like so much else in the European Treaties, the regulation of public undertakings essentially involves a trade-off between a respect for the sovereignty and discretion of Member States and the necessity of ensuring the functioning of the common market.

Article 295 of the EC Treaty states that: 'The Treaty shall in no way prejudice the rules in Member States governing the system of property ownership'. This provision is the cornerstone of the Treaty's neutrality regarding the choices that a Member State may make between public and private ownership. It acknowledges the right of Member States to run a mixed economy and allows States to acquire and maintain shareholdings in private companies, to create and manage public undertakings, and even to nationalize entire sectors of the economy. The importance of this principle in the creation and development of the Communities right from their very creation ought not be underestimated. The Communities were inaugurated in a time when the ethos prevailing in the individual Member State regarding socio-economic models were far less convergent than they are today and when there was significantly less consensus on the role of the State *vis-à-vis* national economies. Indeed one might argue that any legal framework that can keep a renationalizing President Mitterand and a privatizing Prime Minister Thatcher 'under the same roof' must surely have something to be said for it.

Yet free competition has been the pulse of the internal market from its creation. The stated indifference of Article 295 of the EC Treaty regarding forms of ownership must be reconciled with the imperative of Article 3(g) of the EC Treaty whereby the Community commits itself to develop a 'system of ensuring that competition in the internal market is not distorted'. The threat posed by public undertakings to such a system is twofold.[1] First, there is the threat of a crossover between a State's role as a public authority and protector of

[1] On this point see Rose M. D'Sa *European Community Law On State Aid*, Sweet & Maxwell, 1998 p. 310.

public interest and its capacity as owner of the particular undertaking. Secondly there is the danger posed by the sheer quantum of the State's resources and the possibility that they could be used to distort competition. The subject of State aid is at the very heart of both these concerns.

The flip-side of the Treaty's neutrality between public and private ownership is the equal application of the competition rules to both public and private undertakings as indicated in Article 86(1) of the EC Treaty.[2] The consequence of this principle is the following. Should the State as owner of a public undertaking supply finance to a public undertaking in a manner inconsistent with its role of prudent owner of the undertaking (essentially in a manner that would not be replicated by a private owner), and instead inject capital out of motivations stemming from its role as a public authority and protector of the 'common good', then this is to be analysed with the confines of the Treaty articles relating to State aid and is to be treated in the same manner as would be aid granted by the State to a privately owned company.

## II. WHAT DO WE MEAN BY A 'PUBLIC UNDERTAKING'?

The Court of Justice has defined the concept of a 'public undertaking' by giving its approval to the criteria used in the Article 2 of Commission Directive 80/723 on the transparency of financial relations between Member States and public undertakings (hereafter referred to as the 'Transparency Directive' and to which we shall return[3]). The notion of a 'public undertaking' is thus taken to apply to:

[ . . . ] any undertaking over which the public authorities may exercise directly or indirectly a dominant influence by virtue of their ownership of it, their financial participation therein, or the rules which govern it.

A dominant influence on the part of the public authorities shall be presumed when these authorities, directly or indirectly in relation to an undertaking:

i. Hold the major part of the undertaking's subscribed capital; or
ii. Control the majority of the votes attaching to shares issued by the undertakings; or
iii. Can appoint more than half of the members of the undertaking's administrative, managerial or supervisory body.

Clearly this definition can be quite broad in its application. To cite just one example, the Commission held Credit Foncier de France (CFF), the French finance company, to be a public undertaking despite the fact that the shares in the company were divided between individual private shareholders and larger

---

[2] As confirmed by the Court of Justice in Case 78/76, *Firma Steinike und Weinlig v Federal Republic of Germany* [1977] ECR 595. An exception in this regard is made by Article 86(2) concerning 'services of general economic interest'. The significance of this exception will not be discussed in this chapter as it is dealt extensively by Rizza, above.

[3] Commission Directive 1980/723/EEC of 25 June 1980 on the transparency of financial relations between Member States and public undertakings, Official Journal 1980 /L 195/35. Cases 188–190/80 *France, Italy and the UK v Commission* [1982] ECR 2545.

private institutional investors. However, since the French government was entitled to appoint both the governor and deputy governors of the company as well as to be represented at the Annual General Meeting it was taken to have a dominant influence over the company and accordingly to be a public undertaking.[4]

## III. THE NECESSITY OF TRANSPARENCY

Perhaps the greatest threat of competition distorting aids comes not so much from high-profile restructuring or rescuing cash injections for public companies that come before the Commission from time to time but from the clandestine leaking of public funds to prop up ailing public companies. Detecting State aid given to public undertakings leads to a number of specific difficulties.[5] The relationships between the State and public undertakings tend to be complex and supervision can be difficult. Given the neutrality of the legal order regarding forms of ownership and the fact that the State should not be discriminated against when acting as an economic operator, it can at times be difficult to distinguish between the State's legitimate investment of capital in the form of the acquisition of a shareholding and the illicit provision of a State aid. Thirdly, as we have already seen, public undertakings may well be required to perform special duties of a social or 'public service' nature. Many of these duties may not be self-financing and will require the undertaking to be directly compensated by the State. The question of whether such services benefit from the exception from the competition rules found under Article 86 of the EC emphasizes the complexity and clear need for transparency arising from the relationship between public undertakings and the State coffers.

To take account of this necessity, in 1980 the European Commission issued the Transparency Directive (referred to above) which acknowledged not only the overriding need for transparent financial relations between public authorities and public undertakings but also the need to distinguish the role of the State as a public authority from its activities as a proprietor and investor. The Transparency Directive was said to be designed to 'ensure that the discipline of State aids is also applied in an equitable manner to public enterprise'.[6] Clearly the concept of transparency is closely related to that of equal treatment. The Transparency Directive obliges Member States to supply the Commission with all necessary information in order for the public funds supplied to public undertakings to 'emerge' clearly as well as the use to which they were put. The Transparency Directive emphasizes a number of financial transactions in particular which could well amount to a form of disguised State aid such as the setting off of

---

[4] 1996 OJ C 275/2.
[5] For a discussion of this point see Hancher, Ottervanger, and Slot, *EC State Aids*, Sweet & Maxwell, II ed. 1999, p. 137.
[6] EC Bulletin 1985, no.7/8, p.47. as cited by Hancher, Ottervanger, and Slot, p. 139.

operating losses, the provisions of grants without requiring repayment, the granting of preferential loans, the foregoing by the State of the normal returns on the funds supplied, and the provision by the State of compensation for financial burdens imposed by public authorities. The Member States must ensure that such information is kept at the disposal of the Commission for a period of five years.

The Transparency Directive has been amended a number of times, most significantly to extend the sectors covered (for our purposes it is worth noting that the Transparency Directive has covered transport since 1985) as well as to impose an obligation on Member States to file annual reports with the Commission on State intervention for public undertakings in the manufacturing sector having an annual turnover in excess of 250 million euro.

The spirit of the Transparency Directive is very much evident in the Commission's 1994 Guidelines on State aid in the aviation sector. While recognizing the fact that many European carriers are compensated by the relevant Member States for fulfilling socially desirable though economically unviable public service obligations, the Commission emphasizes that such compensation should not facilitate the covert granting of State aid. The costs and revenues relating to such services must be clearly accounted for and companies are obliged to keep accounting systems of sufficient sophistication so as to allow for a clear distinction to be made between the financing of public service functions and that of the company's other operations.

## IV. The concept of State aid and the market economy principle

We have already referred to the dichotomy between the State's dual capacities as a 'normal' investor and as a public authority and provider of State aid. The method of making this distinction is referred to as the market economy investor principle and identifies State aid as the provision of finance that could not be considered as the provision of equity capital according to standard company practice in a market economy.[7] In reality this is merely a specific example of what is referred to more globally as the market economy principle and applies not only to direct injections of capital but also to loans, loan guarantees, and other forms of public funding. The essential aim of the principle is to ensure that any 'advantage' within the meaning of Article 87(1) of the EC Treaty is recognized as being a State aid and is treated as such. Public entities are thus required to behave in the market as a private operator would, be it as an investor, lender, guarantor, etc. For a Member State claiming that an injection of capital or a loan guarantee is in fact a legitimate 'investment' and not therefore a State aid, the test is essentially whether the circumstances in which the guarantee was given or the

---

[7] Hancher, Ottervanger, and Slott p. 142.

investment made would be acceptable to an investor operating under normal market conditions. This involves an analysis of both the economic outlook of the public undertaking so as to obtain the prospects of a return on the investment and the terms of the transaction.

Yet second-guessing the decisions of a hypothetical market operator is in reality no more exact a science than Lord Denning's famous reference to the foresight of the 'man on the Clapham Omnibus'. Different investors pursue different strategies over different time frames with different hopes as to the outcome of their investments. Two judgments illustrate the Court of Justice's approach. In *ENI-Lanerossi*[8] the Commission had held that capital injections into a number of heavily loss-making subsidiaries of a publicly owned holding company involved in the clothing industry amounted to State aid. The Italian government responded by arguing that it was not unforeseeable that a private holding company might seek to compensate the loss of one of its members and thus that the injection did not constitute State aid. The Court held that a private investor might indeed make such an injection to prevent a subsidiary from folding out of considerations other than profit, such as to maintain the prestige of the company or to facilitate a company reorganization, and that this must be borne in mind when analysing a public authority's actions under the market investor test. However, on the facts the Court held that the conditions surrounding the Italian government's capital investment in this case were such that no private investor would have made it under normal market conditions. Similar reasoning was employed with a similar outcome in *Alfa Romeo*,[9] a decision handed down on the same day. While finding that the capital injection under discussion did amount to State aid, the Court emphasized that the behaviour of a private investor must not necessarily be always assumed to be that of one seeking a short-term return on his investment.

The market economy principle has become the bedrock of the Commission's approach to the identification of State aid to the public sector. They feature in the approach adopted by the Commission in a large number of its sector-specific rules, such as the 1981 Community rules for aid to the steel industry,[10] the fifth shipbuilding directive of the same year,[11] the 1984 Communication on the holdings by public authorities in company capital,[12] the 1993 Communication concerning public undertakings in the manufacturing sector, and the 1994[13] Guidelines on the application of State aid rules to the aviation sector. It also

---

[8] C 303/88 *Italy v Commission* [1991] ECR 1470.

[9] C-305/89 *Italy v Commission* [1991] ECR 1635.

[10] Commission Decision No 2320/1981/ECSC establishing Community rules for aids to the steel industry, Official Journal 1981/C L 228/14.

[11] Council Directive 1981/363/EEC on aid to shipbuilding, Official Journal 1981/ L 137/39.

[12] Commission communication to the Member States—Application of Articles 92 and 93 of the EEC Treaty and of Article 5 of Commission Directive 1980/723/EEC to public undertakings in the manufacturing sector, Official Journal 1980/C 307/3.

[13] Communication on the application of Articles 92 and 93 of the EC Treaty and Article 61 of the EEA Agreement to State aids in the aviation sector, Official Journal 1994/C 350/07.

features in the Commission's letter of 1989 to Member States on the rules regarding State guarantees[14] and the Commission's Communication on State aid elements in public land sales.[15]

## V. THE 1994 GUIDELINES ON THE APPLICATION OF THE STATE AID RULES TO THE AVIATION SECTOR

In order to obtain an overview of the state of play regarding State aid in the airline sector the Commission conducted a survey over 1992 and 1993 in order to compile an inventory of State aid then in force. The Commission concluded that State aid rules was prevalent in the sector and that existing transparency requirements were not being satisfactorily implemented. In the summer of 1993 the Commission set up a *Comité des Sages* of experts in the transport sector to make recommendations for future policy initiatives. The *Comité* urged the Commission to apply more strictly the Treaty rules regarding State aid. That said, the *Comité* did consider that for a limited period of time State aid to airlines could be considered as being in the Community interest as long as they were part of a general programme of restructuring in order to put airlines on a viable commercial footing and thus increase the overall competitiveness of the aviation sector. It recommended a number of conditions for such approval:

i.   that such aids would be granted on a clear and genuine 'one time, last time' basis;
ii.  the submission of a restructuring plan leading to economic and commercial viability within a specified time frame and capable of drawing significant private sector investment. The *Comité* proposed that this restructuring plan ought eventually lead to privatization;
iii. an undertaking given on behalf of the government of the relevant Member State to refrain from interfering in the commercial and financial decisions of the carrier concerned;
iv.  a prohibition of the use by the airline in question of public funds to increase capacity unless warranted by the evolution of the market; and
v.   acceptable proof that the aid did not compromise the competitive interests of other airlines.

It is interesting to note that while the vast bulk of the *Comité*'s recommendations are given voice in the Guidelines the Commission chose not to demand that all restructuring plans lead eventually to privatization. Such a statement of policy would have seemed at odds with the Treaty's express neutrality regarding the choice between public and private ownership. Yet the Commission's expression of neutrality in the Guidelines is far from unequivocal: 'As the EC Treaty is

---

[14] Commission's Letter to Member States of 5 April 1989 SG(89) D/4328.
[15] Commission communication concerning aid elements in land sales by public authorities, Official Journal 1997/C 209/3.

neutral on public or private ownership of companies, Member States are at liberty to sell their stakes in public companies'.[16]

One might have thought that the Treaty's neutrality would equally imply that Member States were free to maintain their holdings in public companies or indeed even increase their shareholdings so long as a market economy investor would do likewise under similar circumstances. However the Commission chose not to emphasize this point. While there is no obligation on restructuring plans to lead to privatization, as Ben Van Houtte a head of unit in DG Transport has noted when writing in a private capacity, such restructuring plans do enjoy heightened credibility.[17]

Furthermore while the Commission did not go as far as the *Comité* and insist on an absolute 'one time, last rule' rule, the Communication leaves no doubt that a second injection of State aid will only be considered in the most exceptional of circumstances and in the light of unforeseeable events external to the company.

Not surprisingly the market economy principle features heavily in the Guidelines. It is noted that the principle will normally be satisfied when the structure and future prospects for the company are such that a normal return, by way of dividend payments or capital appreciation by reference to a comparable enterprise, can be expected within a reasonable period.[18] The Commission took note of the Court of Justice rulings mentioned above and emphasized that the private investor with whose behaviour the Member State's conduct is to be compared is not necessarily one motivated by short-term profitability but rather that of a private company pursuing a structural policy in the longer term according to its sector of operations.[19] This principle has been seen in action in the Commission's 1996 decision regarding an investment by the Spanish government in Iberia. Here the Commission decided in the light of the high returns that could be expected from the investment that the injection was such that a private investor would have done likewise and that therefore there was no State aid involved. It is worth noting that the market economy principle applies not only to capital injections but also to loan financing and guarantees.

The Court of First Instance has been called upon on a number of occasions to rule on challenges against Commission decisions approving the grant of State aid in the context of restructuring plans.[20] The Court has generally endorsed the Commission's analysis. As Van Houtte notes, the Commission's priority has been to balance the need to give the traditional flag-ship air carriers the opportunity to set their house in order with the need to avoid distortions of competition in what is a newly liberalized industry.[21]

---

[16] Guidelines para. 43.

[17] Damien Geradin (ed.) *The Liberalisation of State Monopolies in the European Union and Beyond*, Kluwer European Monographs, 2000, p. 67.

[18] Paragraph 26 of the 1994 Guidelines.

[19] Paragraph 28 of the 1994 Guidelines.

[20] For an example of the Court's approach see Case T-140/95 *Ryanair v Commission* [1998] ECR II 3327.

[21] Note 9 above, p. 88.

What perhaps poses the most significant challenge to the Commission's policy regarding the difficulties currently facing many of Europe's flagship carriers is the fact that many of them, such as Sabena and Aer Lingus, have already received State aid on the back of restructuring plans that were intended to restore them to commercial viability once and for all. As regards the approval recently given to the bridging loan granted by the Belgian government to Sabena, it is important to emphasize that this was classified as *rescue* aid rather than *restructuring* aid. The interaction between this distinction and the 'one time, last time rule' is most interesting and may well have significant consequences for the future survival of the airline.

## VI. RESCUE AID AND THE SABENA DECISION

The Commission's original Guidelines on State aid for Rescuing and Restructuring Firms in Difficulty date back to 1994 and were altered in 1999. These Guidelines are said to apply to all sectors without prejudice to specific rules applying to firms in difficulty in specific sectors, such as the 1994 Guidelines for the aviation sector.[22]

For the purposes of these Guidelines, the Commission defines a firm as being in difficulty where it is: 'unable, whether through its own resources or with the funds it is able to obtain from its owner/shareholders or creditors, to stem losses which, without outside intervention by the public authorities, will almost certainly condemn it to go out of business in the short or medium term'.[23]

Rescue aid, we are told, is by nature temporary assistance. It is intended to keep the ailing company afloat for as long as is needed to develop a restructuring or liquidation plan and for the Commission to reach a decision on the plan.[24] In order to be approved by the Commission the rescue aid must:

i.   Consist of liquidity support in the form of loan guarantees or loans;
ii.  be provided at an interest rate no more advantageous than that which would be offered to a healthy firm;
iii. be granted for a period not longer than six months;
iv.  be justified by serious social difficulties; and
v.   not entail spill over effects in other Member States.

It is worth noting that the Commission, when granting approval to the recent payment to Sabena, drew attention to the fact that the measure amounted to rescue aid under the terms of the 1999 Guidelines.[25] As such the Commission's

---

[22] Section 2.4 of the 1999 Guidelines.
[23] 1999 Guidelines section 2.2.
[24] ibid.
[25] Commission Press Release IP/01/1432 of 17 October 2001. In the following months almost all Member States notified such schemes and all were treated by the Commission on the basis of the same criteria as were employed in relation to the UK's notification.

press release points out that rescue aid, unlike restructuring aid, is not subject to the 'one time, last time principle'. However, the press statement goes on to say that, since Sabena had already benefited from restructuring aid in 1991, any further restructuring plan to come at the end of the period facilitated by the rescue aid cannot involve State aid of any kind.

## VII. POST-SEPTEMBER 11: THE ROLE OF EMERGENCY AID IN THE EU'S RESPONSE

Clearly, the appalling events of 11 September 2001 have badly affected a sector that was already facing an extremely grave financial crisis. While the terror attacks have certainly created new problems for the airline industry they have also significantly exacerbated existing ones. The challenge for the European Commission is to address the immediate crisis in the sector while trying to maintain the coherence of a strict policy on State aid which it had been developing since the early 1990s at the time of the first Gulf War, the last seismic shock to affect the European aviation industry to such a pronounced extent.

The immediate problems for many of the European carriers appear to be so grave as almost to defy exaggeration.[26] In the days immediately following September 11 demand fell on transatlantic routes by somewhere in the region of 75 per cent. All US airspace was closed for four days. On the basis of a sample of some thirteen carriers the Association of European Airlines is estimating losses of three and half to four billion euros by the end of the year. 17,000 jobs are directly threatened by this crisis.

Furthermore the reliance of the airline industry on its insurers has been exposed. In the days following the events in the US, insurers announced the withdrawal or severe reduction of liability cover for risks related to war and terrorism. Many companies were left without cover sufficient to function as commercial carriers. For the forms of cover the insurance were still willing to provide they announced enormous premium hikes. In the wake of this all Member States introduced temporary measures to provide liability insurance for airlines for a period of thirty days pending the restoration of an acceptable level of cover by the commercial insurers. The Commission has requested that such measures be notified to it for consideration under the State aid rules.

On 22 September 2001 the Council of Finance Ministers discussed emergency measures that Member States could take to assist airlines in meeting the increased cost of insurance. The Council concluded that:

i.  such support must be limited to addressing a failure in the commercial insurance market in order to ensure third-party cover for risks related to war and terrorism remains available;

---

[26] See the Communication from the Commission to the European Parliament and the Council on the repercussions of the terrorist attacks in the United States on the air transport industry.

ii. governments must charge a reasonable premium which as far as is possible must reflect the risks to be covered although this obligation may be waived in the short term;

iii. the duration of the schemes shall be limited to one month while work will continue on finding a more permanent solution to the problem and to encourage the insurance industry to return to the airline market.

On 23 October 2001 the Commission authorized emergency aid granted by the authorities in the United Kingdom to carriers left without adequate insurance.[27] The Commission found the aid to meet its criteria for the grant of emergency aid, in that;

i. it addressed only the withdrawal of terrorist-related risk policies by the commercial insurance market;

ii. it was limited to thirty days (any extension must be notified and authorized once more);

iii. it re-established insurance cover to levels similar to those contracted by airlines before the attacks in the United States;

iv. it did not put beneficiary companies in a better position than they were before the attacks and must apply without discrimination to all airlines in the United Kingdom.

This last point cited above regarding the granting of benefits to all competitors in the market is emphasized in the Commission's Communication to the European Parliament and the Council on the repercussions of the terrorist attacks in the United States on the air transport industry. The Commission points out that in examining State aid measures it gives priority to those measures that are least likely to distort competition between European carriers, ie those that are applicable to all undertakings in a uniform manner. The Commission considers the events of September 11 and the days immediately following it to have been of such an extraordinary nature and magnitude as to justify the grant of State aid on a temporary basis under Article 87(2)(b) of the EC Treaty, which renders compatible with the common market '[ . . . ] aid to make good the damage caused by natural disasters or exceptional occurrences'.

However, such aid will be required to satisfy a number of conditions:

i. it must be paid in a non-discriminatory fashion to all airlines in a given Member State;

ii. it must concern only the losses incurred during the days from 11 September to 14 September 2001 following the decision by the US authorities to ground air traffic;

iii. the amount of compensation is to be calculated accurately and objectively by comparing the traffic recorded by each airline during the four days in question with that recorded by the same airline in the preceding week. The

---

[27] Commission press release IP/01/1473 23 October 2001.

amount of compensation must be less than four-365ths of the airline's turnover.

Naturally the consequences of the approach taken in Europe did not occur in a vacuum. The larger European carriers engage in fierce competition with their American rivals, most obviously on the transatlantic routes. The United States federal government has been quick to respond to the needs of American carriers who are also suffering the dual effects of the cyclical downturn and the aftermath of the terrorist attacks. On 21 September 2001 the US Congress approved an emergency package with a total value to the airline industry in the region of US$18 billion, consisting of direct payments of US$5 billion to the carriers to compensate them for the losses that have been and would be experienced from 11 September right up to the end of that year (2001) as well as in excess of US$10 billion dollars in the form of subsidized treasury loans or loan guarantees. Many in the European airline sector fear that these grants will be used to subsidize cheaper air fares to revive interest among the American public, which would inevitably undercut the fares being offered by European carriers.

The 1994 Guidelines contain an acknowledgement of the effect that State aid granted by third countries can have on the conditions of competition for European carriers. However, the Commission argue that that cannot justify a non-application of the Treaty rules within the European Community, although it does note that were such State aid to result in extremely low fares being offered by third-country carriers, then such 'tariff dumping' would need to be addressed in the context of the Community's external policy. In the Commission's most recent communication regarding the repercussions of the 2001 terrorist attacks in the United States there is a marked reluctance to contemplate unilateral action in response to aids granted by the American authorities. Equally, the Commission puts the issue in the context of its continuing concerns regarding bilateral agreements in operation between the various Member States and the United States: 'The possible distortions of competition caused by direct aid to the American airlines cannot be addressed in the absence of a contractual framework for relations between the Community and the United States. Member States have opted for a framework of bilateral agreements which deprives them of any capacity to react.'

The Commission clearly feels that the issue can only be satisfactorily resolved in the context of an EU–US agreement and have said that it will propose a joint code of conduct to the American authorities.

## VIII. TOWARDS THE FUTURE

The Commission emphasizes in its recent Communication that the events of 11 September 2001 should not be used by Member States or indeed the airlines themselves as a 'pretext for bypassing the existing framework for aid [for] restructuring'.

That existing framework remains best encapsulated by the 1994 Guidelines. While we have already noted that the Commission chose not to follow the guidance offered by the *Comité des Sages* and wed itself irreparably to the 'one time, last time principle', the strong endorsement of the principle by the Commission following its grant of approval for rescue aid to Sabena seems to suggest that any bail-out by the State could only be in the short term. For those airlines that have already supped at the altar of State aid, a full application of the principle amounts to a choice between a restructuring plan focused on redundancies, capacity reduction, a scaling down of services of such extent as to render the company attractive to private capital, or, alternatively, liquidation. While the challenge for Europe's air carriers of returning to viability is an enormous one, the challenge for the Commission to stick to its tough line in the face of pressure from the Member States may be just as stiff.

# 12

# *State Guarantees as State Aid: Some Practical Difficulties*

MARK FRIEND

## I. Overview

This chapter provides an overview of the evolution of the Commission's policy on State guarantees and seeks to highlight a number of practical difficulties to which the Commission's current policy on State guarantees gives rise. These difficulties are most acutely faced by lenders to recipients of State guarantees who, in the worst case scenario, may find not only that the guarantee on which they have purported to rely is unenforceable as a matter of national law, but also that they themselves are regarded as recipients of aid, under an obligation to repay the 'benefit' to the Member State concerned.

The ideological objection to a State guarantee is that it enhances the borrower's credit position, enabling it to borrow more cheaply, thereby distorting competition with other firms operating on the market who have to pay a commercial borrowing rate. Indeed, the saving in borrowing costs to which the State guarantee gives rise may well be substantial if, in the absence of State support, the borrower would have only a 'speculative' or 'junk status' credit rating. Unless the borrower has paid an arm's length fee to the State, it follows that the guarantee will normally confer an aid on the borrower. This can be regarded as an application of the market economy investor principle, because it can reasonably be assumed that a private sector guarantor would not be willing to issue a guarantee without being paid a fee commensurate with the risk involved. Thus, where the borrower has paid an arm's length fee, the State is acting no differently from a private sector guarantor. Moreover, the Commission (rightly) takes the view that the distortion of competition caused by a State guarantee occurs at the time when the guarantee is issued, even if it is never called. The current position of the Commission, as set out in the November 1999 Notice,[1] is that the aid element inherent in a State guarantee is normally the net difference in borrowing costs between what the borrower would have to pay without the guarantee and what it pays with the benefit of the guarantee. However, the Commission considers that the aid element may equal the entire amount of the loan if the borrower would be unable to obtain a loan without a

---

[1] Commission Notice on the application of Articles 87 and 88 of the EC Treaty to State aid in the form of guarantees ([2000] OJ C71/14) (hereinafter 'November 1999 Notice').

guarantee: 'Where at the time the loan is granted, there is a strong probability that the borrower will default, e.g. because he is in financial difficulty, the value of the guarantee may be as high as the amount effectively covered by that guarantee'.[2]

This approach is somewhat arbitrary, because it assumes that the lender will not be repaid at all (which may not be the case). Thus, it is not obvious why one should regard the principal amount of the loan as an aid to the borrower. In addition, there is an ambiguity in the expression 'the amount effectively covered by the guarantee': does it include interest on the loan, as well as principal? The answer to this question is unclear, although in a number of cases where the Commission has ordered recovery of the whole amount of the loan, it appears that only the principal amount of the loan has been treated as an aid.[3]

More worryingly for lenders, the Commission also takes the view that, in certain circumstances, a State guarantee may confer aid not just on the borrower, but also on the lender.[4] Normally this will not be the case, because the lender will be lending on arm's length commercial terms, one of which requires the provision of a guarantee, so the lender is not receiving any non-commercial benefit. A similar analysis applies to investors who buy a State guaranteed bond: they are simply getting what they pay for (a low-risk investment which will typically produce a low return). The circumstances in which a State guarantee may be treated as conferring aid on the lender are considered below.

## II. What sorts of guarantees are covered by the State aid rules and why does it matter?

As the November 1999 Notice makes clear,[5] the State aid rules apply to 'all forms of guarantees, irrespective of their legal basis and the transaction covered'. The clearest example of such a guarantee is an express contractual guarantee, for example covering a bank loan or a bond issue: in this situation the lender (or the trustee for the investors in a bond issue) will have a direct contractual claim against the State.

However, the State aid rules also apply to guarantees arising by operation of law. A number of examples may be given of such guarantees:

---

[2] November 1999 Notice (note 1 above), at paragraph 3.2.

[3] See eg *JAKO Jadekost* [1996] OJ L246/43, where the Commission appears to have calculated the 'net subsidy equivalent' by reference to the principal amount of the loan. Similarly, in *Bremer Vulkan* [1993] OJ L185/43 the Commission seems to have calculated the value of the aid as the principal amount covered by the guarantee: 'The Commission therefore identifies the following aids: BV received DM126 million aid from Hibeg. This aid operation was made possible by a guarantee on DM 126 million plus credit costs and interest . . .' But note that when the Commission orders recovery of an aid, it is required also to order payment of interest from the date of receipt until the date of recovery: Article 14(2) of Council Regulation (EC) No. 659/1999 (hereinafter 'Procedural Regulation') ([1999] OJ L83/1).

[4] November 1999 Notice (note 1 above), at paragraphs 2.2.1–2.2.2.

[5] November 1999 Notice (note 1 above), at paragraph 1.1.

(i) *Anstaltslast* This is an unwritten rule of German administrative law which provides that the owner of a public law institution or corporation (the classic example being the German *Landesbanken*) is required to maintain its solvency to enable it to fulfil its purposes (for example, by the provision of capital). It does not provide creditors with any direct rights.

(ii) *Gewährträgerhaftung* A provision contained in the statutes creating certain public law institutions (notably, the German *Landesbanken*) which provides that the owner of that public law institution is directly liable to creditors for all liabilities of the institution.[6]

(iii) Implicit guarantees arising by operation of law, such as Article 2362 of the Italian Civil Code, providing that a sole shareholder of a company is liable for all the debts of that company. The theory here is that if the State becomes the sole shareholder of a company in circumstances where a market economy investor would not make such an investment, the State may be conferring an aid on the company. This was the reasoning behind the Commission's decision in *IOR*,[7] where the Commission objected to a loan provided to the chronically loss-making IOR by Sofin (a State owned entity) and the subsequent waiver by Sofin of its right to repayment:

[T]he Italian Government claimed that Sofin had acted as any investor in a similar position would have done by covering IOR's losses, because it was the one and only shareholder of IOR until 15 October 1986 and therefore liable under Italian law for all its debts. The liquidation of IOR would consequently have entailed higher costs for Sofin.

The Commission cannot subscribe to this point of view. A private investor will normally be reluctant to become the one and only shareholder of a company, if as a consequence he must assume unlimited liability for it; he will make sure that this additional risk is outweighed by additional gains.

On the facts of the case, the Commission concluded that, as IOR had never made a profit during the years covered by its investigation, Sofin had, by becoming the sole shareholder of IOR, accepted a risk which a private investor would have refused.

In the *EFIM*[8] case, which concerned the liquidation of the Italian State owned holding company EFIM, the Commission again objected to the operation of Article 2362 of the Italian Civil Code. This time the objection related to the

---

[6] On 1 March 2002, the Commission announced (see Press Release IP/02/343) that final agreement had been reached with the German Government on the steps to be taken to make the guarantee system of *Anstaltslast* and *Gewährträgerhaftung* compatible with the EC State aid rules. The compromise entails the following elements: (i) the abolition of *Anstaltslast*; (ii) a commitment by Germany to repeal the law preventing the *Landesbanken* from becoming insolvent; (iii) a limited grandfathering of *Gewährträgerhaftung* so that (a) in respect of liabilities incurred before 18 July 2001, *Gewährträgerhaftung* would continue to apply without limit of time; and (b) in respect of liabilities incurred up to 18 July 2005, *Gewährträgerhaftung* would continue to apply provided the maturity of the obligation does not extend beyond 31 December 2015.

[7] *IOR* [1992] OJ L 183/30, at page 31.

[8] *EFIM* [1993] OJ C 349/2.

lower credit risk inherent in the fact that creditors proving in a liquidation of a State owned company would have access to the 'effectively infinite financial resources' of the State:[9]

Therefore, the creditor of a 100% State owned company will have higher security to receive full repayment in the event of a liquidation. This allows a public undertaking, notwithstanding its increasing debts, to continue trading long after a comparable private undertaking would have been placed in liquidation. When a company wholly owned by a market economy investor goes into liquidation, the creditors' repayment is limited to the amount that can be raised by the sale of the company's and the shareholder's assets. As these are not infinite, the whole of the company's indebtedness will normally not be repaid.

It is therefore clear that cases may arise under Article 2362 of the Civil Code, which constitute such discrimination between public and private companies. Moreover, aid is involved even if the company is in liquidation, as in the present case, as the payment enables an operating company to continue in business by the elimination of intra-group indebtedness. The fact that it is the creditors and not the company which receive payment is irrelevant as these operating companies are the final beneficiaries of such aid payments.

Although the cases under Article 2362 are now largely of historical significance, given the commitment by the Italian Government gradually to reduce the impact of 100 per cent State shareholdings,[10] two remarks may be made at this point. First, the Commission's analysis of the so-called advantage enjoyed by a company that is wholly owned by the State marks a significant step beyond the thinking in *IOR*. In *IOR* the concern was with the circumstances in which the State had assumed sole ownership; in *EFIM* the Commission seems to be articulating a wider concern about State ownership. It is submitted that this comes dangerously close to disregarding the fundamental principle enshrined in Article 295 of the EC Treaty (Treaty of Rome, as amended) regarding neutrality as between public and private ownership.

Secondly, it is significant that the Commission does *not* regard creditors of EFIM as recipients of aid. This is undoubtedly correct, as creditors are simply getting what they bargained for when agreeing to lend in the first place (ie a low-risk loan carrying (one assumes) a correspondingly low rate of interest).

(iv)    A further category of guarantee is what is sometimes known as a 'soft' guarantee, or a 'comfort letter' provided by the State. To the extent to which this enables the beneficiary firm to reduce its cost of borrowing, or to continue trading even when it is loss-making, it is clear that this should be regarded as aid in exactly the same way as an express contractual guarantee.

---

[9]  *EFIM* [1993] OJ C 349/2, at page 3, paragraph 5.
[10]  The so-called Andreatta/Van Miert accord (see Annex 3 of the *EFIM* decision, note 8 above) records the commitment of the Italian Government to effect a gradual reduction in such holdings to 'normal levels', with exceptions for companies providing public services and those in the defence sector.

(v)  It is an open question whether aid may also be deemed to be given to those companies whose legal status precludes bankruptcy.[11] It is certainly arguable that the lower cost of borrowing which such companies enjoy should be regarded as an aid, but once again there is the difficulty that Article 295 of the Treaty provides for neutrality as between public and private ownership.

Notwithstanding the Commission's assertion in the November 1999 Notice that it applies to 'all forms of guarantees, irrespective of their legal basis',[12] it is submitted that it is too sweeping to say that all obligations in the nature of guarantees accepted by the State should be treated as aid. Indeed, as the Commission itself acknowledges in the November 1999 Notice, only if trade between Member States is affected can there be aid within the meaning of Article 87(1) of the Treaty.[13] Similarly, if a market premium is paid, that ought logically to be sufficient to prevent the guarantee being regarded as aid within the meaning of Article 87(1) of the Treaty. It is submitted that if a guarantee does not affect trade between Member States (for example, because the borrower is engaged in an activity where there is no possibility of such trade occurring) there can be no obligation to notify the measure pursuant to Article 88(3) of the Treaty.[14] In addition, it is submitted that there is no aid where, for example, the State is selling an asset and gives the buyer a warranty or similar commitment to underwrite the performance of that asset: the natural conclusion in this situation is that (assuming such a warranty is the kind of commitment which a private seller would have been willing to undertake) the warranty is effectively priced into the transaction, so that the buyer is simply getting what he has paid for.

As to the question of why it matters if a guarantee is State aid, the answer is that, unless it has been notified pursuant to Article 88(3) of the Treaty before being put into effect, it will be unlawful as a matter of Community law,[15] and

[11] The Commission's view is that aid is involved in this situation: see paragraph 2.1.3 of the November 1999 Notice (note 1 above). This is also one of the grounds at issue in the Commission's investigation into EdF (see Press Release IP/02/1485, 16 October 2002): as an *établissement public à caractère industriel et commerciel (EPIC)*, EdF benefits from an unlimited State guarantee on all its liabilities under the legal status of EPIC, '. . . a status which grants exemption from insolvency law'. The Commission states, however, that it '. . . is in no way questioning the ownership by the State of EdF's capital, nor is it contesting its EPIC statute. The Commission is only questioning advantages that EdF draws from certain features of the EPIC status, namely the exemption from insolvency and bankruptcy proceedings and the role played by the State as ultimate guarantor for the company's debts.'

[12] November 1999 Notice (note 1 above), at paragraph 1.1.

[13] *ibid*, at paragraph 2.1.1; the same point is acknowledged at paragraphs 2.2.2 and 4.1.

[14] This is implicit in Article 1(a) of the Procedural Regulation where 'aid' is defined as 'any measure fulfilling all the criteria laid down in Article [87(1)] of the Treaty'. But the threshold for a finding of 'effect on trade' is low. For example, the mere fact that an undertaking provides only local or regional transport services in a single Member State will not be sufficient to rule out an 'effect on trade' if undertakings established in other Member States also compete in that market (Case C-280/00 *Altmark*, judgment of 24 July 2003 (not yet reported), at paragraphs 77–82.

[15] 'Unlawful aid' is defined in Article 1(a) of the Procedural Regulation as 'new aid put into effect in contravention of Article [88(3)] of the Treaty'.

may be unenforceable as a matter of national law. The curiosity here is that, if sued on a guarantee in a national court, it seems that the State would be allowed to plead its own wrongful act as a defence and thereby resist payment: this appears to follow from the direct effect of Article 88(3) of the Treaty and to be supported by the decision of the Court of Justice in *Alcan (No. 2)*: '[U]ndertakings to which aid has been granted may not, in principle, entertain a legitimate expectation that the aid is lawful unless it has been granted in compliance with the procedure laid down in [Article 88(3)]. A diligent businessman should normally be able to determine whether that procedure has been followed.'[16]

Yet this does not sit easily with the case law on repayment of aid, where the rationale for refusing to allow a State to rely on the legitimate expectations of the beneficiary to justify failure to seek repayment is said by the Court of Justice to be to prevent Member States from relying on their unlawful conduct so as to deprive Commission decisions of their effectiveness.[17] Whilst, in policy terms, it might be justifiable to seek to prevent Member States from disbursing aid, it seems unfair to penalize a lender (who in the normal course will not be a recipient of aid) from enforcing a guarantee against the State. Moreover, it seems anomalous to allow the State to do precisely what the Court of Justice has sought to prevent in relation to orders for repayment: namely, to rely on its own wrongful act as a defence.

The difficulty in this situation stems from the fact that, although the lender will not typically be regarded as an aid recipient at the time when the guarantee is issued (the beneficiary of the aid is normally the borrower), it can be argued that if the State makes a payment under an unlawful guarantee (ie one that has not been notified pursuant to Article 88(3)), it is by definition making a voluntary payment, which is itself an aid to the lender.[18] This point has yet to be resolved by the Court of Justice, but given that the lender is not normally regarded as an aid recipient at the time when the guarantee is issued, it is submitted that there is a case for allowing the lender to recover in this situation; to hold otherwise is effectively to treat the lender as if it were an aid recipient from the moment when the guarantee is given, even though, assuming that the loan carries a commercial rate of interest, the lender derives no non-commercial benefit from entering into the transaction.[19]

[16] Case C-24/95 *Land Rheinland-Pfalz v Alcan Deutschland (Alcan No. 2)* [1997] ECR I-1591 at paragraph 28; see generally Bellamy and Child, *European Community Law of Competition*, (5th edn, 2001), at paragraphs 19-080, 19-081.

[17] See the cases cited in Bellamy and Child (note 16 above), at paragraph 19-080, note 26.

[18] See Jeremy Lever QC, *Discussion Paper: State Guarantees as State Aid: The effect of European Community Law, a special supplement to Butterworths Journal of International Banking and Financial Law* (January 2002), at paragraph 2.5(b). See Lever below.

[19] But see Lever (note 18 above), at paragraph 2.5(a), who points out that where the borrower could not have obtained the loan at all without a State guarantee, the State has 'created' business for the lender, and the lender who enters into such a transaction gets an advantage over competitors who are unwilling to participate in the giving of unlawful State aid. Lever acknowledges that this analysis has never yet been advanced by the Commission.

## III. DEVELOPMENT OF THE COMMISSION'S POLICY ON
## STATE GUARANTEES

The proposition that a State guarantee of a loan or similar obligation will normally be regarded as State aid seems relatively uncontroversial. Yet it was not until 1989 that this proposition was clearly articulated by the Commission, in a letter to Member States:[20]

The Commission has the honour to inform you of its decision to examine in future State guarantees under the following conditions.

It regards all guarantees given by the State directly or given by the State's delegation through financial institutions as falling within the scope of Article [87(1)] of the [EC] Treaty.

Each case of the granting of State guarantees has to be notified under Article [88(3)] of the [EC] Treaty whether the granting is done in application of an existing general guarantee scheme or in application of a specific measure.

The Commission will accept the guarantees only if their mobilisation is contractually linked to specific conditions which may go as far as the compulsory declaration of bankruptcy of the benefiting undertaking or any similar procedure.

This text raises a number of questions. First, it is far from clear what the word 'accept' is intended to mean, but presumably this refers to the Commission deeming the aid to be compatible with the common market. Secondly, the term mobilization is unclear, although one assumes that it refers to the act of honouring the guarantee. Thirdly, the reference to mobilization being linked to conditions which 'may' go as far as bankruptcy, seems to suggest that the guarantee may only be honoured after the borrower has been placed in liquidation.

The position of individual guarantees given pursuant to a notified aid scheme was clarified in a Commission letter to Member States in October 1989.[21] This confirmed that such guarantees were not required to be notified.

A significant advance in the Commission's thinking in this area came with the Commission's communication to Member States of 1993.[22] This document contained a useful explanation of the case law concerning the market economy investor principle and a summary of the Commission's position on loan guarantees which appeared relatively favourable to lenders:[23]

The position currently adopted by the Commission in relation to loan guarantees has recently been communicated to Member States. It regards all guarantees given by the State directly or by way of delegation through financial institutions as falling within the scope of

[20] Commission letter to Member States SG(89) D/4328 of 5 April 1989.
[21] Commission letter to Member States SG(89) D/12772 of 12 October 1989.
[22] Commission communication to the Member States: Application of Articles [87] and [88] of the [EC] Treaty and of Article 5 of Commission Directive 80/723/EEC to public undertakings in the manufacturing sector ([1993] OJ C307/3).
[23] ibid, at paragraph 38.

Article [87(1)] of the [EC] Treaty. It is only if guarantees are assessed at the granting stage that all the distortions or potential distortions of competition can be detected. The fact that a firm receives a guarantee even if it is never called in may enable it to continue trading, perhaps forcing competitors who do not enjoy such facilities to go out of business. The firm in question has therefore received support which has disadvantaged its competitors ie it has been aided and this has had an effect on competition. An assessment of the aid element of guarantees will involve an analysis of the borrower's financial situation (see paragraph 37 above). The aid element of these guarantees would be the difference between the rate which the borrower would pay in a free market and that actually obtained with the benefit of the guarantee, net of any premium paid for the guarantee. Creditors can only safely claim against a government guarantee where this is made and given explicitly to either a public or a private undertaking. If this guarantee is deemed incompatible with the common market following evaluation with respect to the derogations under the Treaty, reimbursement of the value of any aid will be made by the undertaking to the government even if this means a declaration of bankruptcy but creditors' claims will be honoured.[23]

Although this passage is not without its difficulties, particularly, the reference to a guarantee 'given explicitly' could be taken to suggest that it covers only express contractual guarantees, and not guarantees arising by operation of law, the phrase 'but creditors' claims will be honoured' was widely taken to mean that lenders would not suffer as a result of challenges to unnotified guarantees. In particular, paragraph 38 appeared to suggest that failure to notify a State guarantee would not, of itself, affect the enforceability of the guarantee in national courts, and that it was only if the guarantee was found to be incompatible with the common market that the aid would be recovered from the borrower; but even this would not prejudice the position of lenders, who would (presumably) have an enforceable claim under the guarantee against the State.

   However, it seems likely that this degree of optimism was to some extent misplaced, because even before the adoption of the 1993 communication there were examples of the Commission requiring the withdrawal or abolition of unnotified guarantees.[24] Moreover, the Commission continued to intervene in this way following the adoption of the 1993 communication.[25] Indeed, in the *EPAC* case, the Commission required the interim suspension of an unnotified guarantee; in other words, this decision was not dependent on a prior finding of incompatibility.

   During the mid-1990s the Commission embarked on several attempts to restate its policy in relation to State guarantees. A number of drafts appeared, not all of which were formally published; one version suggested a move to a much more hard-line position under which lenders would effectively become the policemen of the State aid rules. This particular draft also highlighted the risk of lenders being regarded as recipients of unnotified aid.

---

[24] *Magefesa* [1991] OJ L 5/18; *Schiffswerft Germersheim* [1991] OJ L 158/71; *Bremer Vulkan* [1993] OJ L 185/43.
[25] *JAKO Jadekost* [1996] OJ L 246/43; *EPAC* [1997] OJ L 186/25 and L 311/25.

By the time of the circulation of the March 1995 draft notice[26] the Commission appeared to have retreated from this extreme position, although the position of lenders was considerably less favourable than in the 1993 communication, as there was no reference to the comforting words 'but creditors' claims will be honoured':[27]

The Commission would also remind the Member States of the risks which they and recipients of State guarantees run when they infringe the procedures of Article [88(3)]. A State guarantee which is considered incompatible with the common market following an assessment with respect to derogations under the Treaty may have to be repaid. The Member State will have to recover the value of the aid from the recipient(s), even if this means a declaration of bankruptcy.

The March 1995 draft notice was novel for its recognition that not all State guarantees necessarily constituted aid. It attempted to define the conditions which would mean that the guarantee satisfied the market economy investor principle and which therefore would not require notification. Failure to comply with some of those conditions did not necessarily mean that the guarantee was to be regarded as aid, but it would constitute 'a sufficient presumption of aid to justify compulsory notification'.[28]

Although numerous further iterations of the Commission's position appeared in the years which followed, it was not until November 1999 that the Commission formally adopted the current Notice.[29] The November 1999 Notice expressly replaces the two 1989 letters to Member States and paragraph 38 of the 1993 communication. It is stated to apply to 'all forms of guarantees, irrespective of their legal basis and the transaction covered',[30] which would presumably cover (in addition to loans) swaps, bonds, and similar instruments. It makes clear that Article 87(1) applies to guarantees given by undertakings that are under the dominant influence of public authorities,[31] and therefore leaves open the possibility that one such undertaking could confer aid on another. An example of such a situation would be a majority-State owned bank guaranteeing a loan in favour of a majority-State owned widget manufacturer: one would need to examine the degree of control exercised by the State over the bank and how the decision to issue the guarantee was arrived at to see whether, on the facts, the bank was acting on the direction of the State and therefore whether its decision was imputable to the State.[32]

The November 1999 Notice represents a hardening of the Commission's position, at least compared to the 1993 communication, since it suggests that

---

[26] Draft Commission notice on the application of Articles [87] and [88] of the EC Treaty to State aid in the form of guarantees (IV/1135/94-EN Rev 3, 7 March 1995).

[27] *ibid*, at paragraph 4.3.

[28] *ibid*, at paragraph 2.7.

[29] November 1999 Notice (note 1 above).

[30] *ibid*, at paragraph 1.1.

[31] *ibid*, at paragraph 2.1.4.

[32] For the requirement of 'imputability' see Case C-482/99 *France v Commission* [2002] OJ C169/3, due to be reported in [2002] ECR I-4397.

lenders may be on risk if they accept unnotified guarantees, albeit that questions of enforceability are acknowledged to be a matter for national law.[33] However, the November 1999 Notice is not all bad news for lenders: it contains a recognition that not all guarantees (even those which fail the market economy investor test) are notifiable: for example, if there is no effect on trade between Member States.[34] By implication, the Commission seems to acknowledge that Member States are entitled to form their own judgement on this issue.[35] The November 1999 Notice identifies a list of conditions, fulfilment of which will ensure that an individual State guarantee does not constitute aid:

(a)   the borrower is not in financial difficulty;
(b)   the borrower would, in principle, be able to obtain a loan on market conditions from the financial markets without any intervention by the State;
(c)   the guarantee is linked to a specific financial transaction, is for a fixed maximum amount, does not cover more than 80 per cent of the outstanding loan or other financial obligations (except for bonds and similar instruments) and is not open-ended; and
(d)   the market price for the guarantee is paid (which reflects, amongst others, the amount and duration of the guarantee, the security given by the borrower, the borrower's financial position, the sector of activity and the prospects, the rates of default, and other economic conditions).[36]

Interestingly, the November 1999 Notice displays a more moderate approach than the March 1995 draft to the question of whether non-compliance with any of the four conditions creates an obligation to notify. Whereas the March 1995 draft stated that non-compliance would create a 'sufficient presumption of aid to justify compulsory notification',[37] the Commission's current position is that: 'Failure to comply with any one of the above conditions [...] does not mean that such guarantee or guarantee scheme is automatically regarded as State aid. If there is any doubt as to whether a planned guarantee or scheme does constitute State aid, it should be notified.'[38]

   Whilst this could be interpreted as a recommendation to Member States to notify in cases of doubt, it does not clearly oblige them to do so. Indeed, as a matter of law, it is difficult to see how a non-binding Commission notice could create obligations for Member States (as the March 1995 draft purported to do). As an instrument of soft law, the value of the November 1999 Notice is principally in the Commission's articulation of the factors which, in the Commission's

---

[33] Draft Commission notice on the application of Articles [87] and [88] of the EC Treaty to State aid in the form of guarantees (IV/1135/94-EN Rev 3, 7 March 1995), at paragraphs 6.4–6.5.

[34] *ibid*, at paragraph 4.1. But see the discussion at note 14 above.

[35] This also appears consistent with the Procedural Regulation, which only requires notification of aid fulfilling all the criteria of Article 87(1) of the Treaty (note 13 above).

[36] Note 1 above, at paragraph 4.2.

[37] Note 26 above, at paragraph 2.7.

[38] Note 1 above, at paragraph 4.4.

view, will enable one to conclude that the market economy investor principle is satisfied. However, the market economy investor principle itself has been endorsed by the Court of Justice,[39] and it therefore follows that the important question in determining whether a State guarantee constitutes State aid is whether, in all the circumstances of the case, the Member State can be said to be acting in the same way as a market economy investor would act.

The November 1999 Notice notes that the usual beneficiary of a State guarantee will be the borrower,[40] but does not rule out that the lender may also benefit from the aid:

In particular, for example, if a State guarantee is given *ex post* in respect of a loan or other financial obligation already entered into without the terms of this loan or financial obligation being adjusted, or if one guaranteed loan is used to pay back another, non-guaranteed loan to the same credit institution, then there may also be an aid to the lender, in so far as the security of the loans is increased. Such aid is capable of favouring the lender and distorting competition, and generally falls within the scope of Article 87(1), if trade between Member States is affected.[41]

In the examples cited by the Commission, the lender's credit position is improved, without the lender having provided any consideration. It is plain that the lender in that situation can be said to derive an 'advantage', which can be treated as aid. Conversely, as indicated above, there will be no aid to the investors in a State guaranteed bond issue merely by reason of the guarantee, as they are simply getting what they are paying for.

## IV. PRACTICAL DIFFICULTIES

In practice, there are serious difficulties in applying the four conditions in the November 1999 Notice, which create uncertainty for lenders and their advisers.

The first requirement, that the borrower should not be in financial difficulty, suffers from a lack of definition of the phrase 'not in financial difficulty'. It would, however, seem reasonable to apply the definition used in the Guidelines for Rescuing and Restructuring Firms in Difficulty, where it is stated that:

There is no Community definition of what constitutes 'a firm in difficulty'. However, for the purposes of these Guidelines, the Commission regards a firm as being in difficulty where it is unable, whether through its own resources or with the funds it is able to obtain from its owner/shareholders or creditors, to stem losses which, without outside intervention by the public authorities, will almost certainly condemn it to go out of business in the short or medium term.

---

[39] See Case 40/85 *Belgium v Commission (Boch No. 2)* [1986] ECR 2321; Case C-301/87 *France v Commission (Bousssac)* [1990] ECR I-307; Case C-303/88 *Italy v Commission (ENI-Lanerossi)* [1991] ECR I-1433; Case C-305/89 *Italy v Commission (Alfa Romeo No. 1)* [1991] ECR I-1603.

[40] Note 1 above, at paragraph 2.1.1.

[41] *ibid*, at paragraphs 2.2.1–2.2.2.

In particular, a firm is, in any event and irrespective of its size, regarded as being in difficulty for the purposes of these Guidelines:

(a)  in the case of a limited company, where more than half of its registered capital has disappeared and more than one quarter of that capital has been lost over the preceding 12 months; or

(b)  in the case of an unlimited company, where more than half of its capital as shown in the company accounts has disappeared and more than one quarter of that capital has been lost over the preceding 12 months; or

(c)  whatever the type of company concerned, where it fulfils the criteria under its domestic law for being the subject of collective insolvency proceedings.[42]

The second area of uncertainty arises from the requirement that the borrower would be able to obtain a loan without a guarantee. This is clearly a question of fact, where a legal adviser, in giving an opinion, would need to make certain assumptions. In practice, it might be thought that the easiest way to resolve the uncertainty would be to ascertain whether the borrower has ever done so in the past. However, where the borrower is a newly created entity there will be no track record on which to rely, in which case the lender will need to be satisfied that the borrower would be able to obtain a non-guaranteed loan from the private sector.

The third requirement in the November 1999 Notice is that the guarantee must be limited to 80 per cent of the outstanding loan. The theory behind this is that, by giving the lender some exposure to the risk of borrower default, the lender will be incentivized to assess the creditworthiness of the borrower. Accordingly, the November 1999 Notice states that the Commission will generally examine critically any guarantee covering the entirety (or nearly the entirety) of the transaction.[43] It must be emphasized, however, that the 80 per cent test is an arbitrary limit invented by the Commission, which has no firm legal basis. Rather, it may be thought of as an expression of the market economy investor test in one particular situation.

Lenders and their advisers will no doubt be relieved that the 80 per cent limit does not apply to issues of bonds or other similar debt securities. However, it is unclear whether it applies to swaps (ie transactions designed to provide a hedge against a fluctuating amount, such as interest rates or exchange rates) or, if it does, how one is supposed to calculate the maximum potential liability arising under the swap which, by its very nature, is likely to be open ended. In the case of the *Channel Tunnel Rail Link*,[44] the Commission concluded that a guarantee covering 100 per cent of the exposure under a swap amounted to State aid but was compatible with the common market, even though it breached the

---

[42]  Community Guidelines on State Aid for Rescuing and Restructuring Firms in Difficulty ([1999] OJ C 288/2), at paragraph 2.1 (footnotes omitted).

[43]  Note 1 above, at paragraphs 3.3–3.4.

[44]  Commission Decision C (2002) 1446 fin of 24 April 2002 (State aid No. 706/2001—United Kingdom, the Channel Tunnel Rail Link), available on the Commission's web site.

80 per cent limit in the 1999 Notice. It was not necessary, in this particular case, to consider whether a guarantee covering 100 per cent of the exposure under a swap, given in return for an arm's length fee, could satisfy the market economy investor principle. Logically, however, there seems no reason why it could not do so.

In this case, the Commission recognized the difficulties in trying to quantify the potential exposure under a swap. Its analysis focused on the methodology for valuing the guarantee. The UK argued that the value of the guarantee was the theoretical cost of purchasing a similar guarantee from a private sector institution. This approach was confirmed by the Commission:

[T]he UK Government has calculated the value of the hedging guarantees at the theoretical cost of purchasing similar guarantees from a private sector institution to £13 million and will guarantee 100% of LCR's potential exposure under the interest swaps it has entered into.

The Commission acknowledges that, for this particular form of financial transactions, it is not possible to calculate in advance the final amount that will be effectively covered by the guarantees and considers, in this particular case, that the method used by the UK Government to value the guarantees, ie based on a hypothetical purchase price, is justified and represents the most accurate estimation of the value of the guarantees.

Moreover, the Commission takes note of the fact that LCR's counterpart banks under the hedging arrangements, acting commercially, are not prepared to take any risk on the credit of LCR and require collateral for the full amount exposed at any particular time. Therefore, if the guarantees were to cover less than 100%, LCR would still have to provide collateral for the difference, using funds already raised with the result that less financial resources would ultimately be available to fund LCR's cash flow requirements for construction purposes. Under such circumstances, the Commission finds that it can accept that the State guarantees in question covers [sic] the underlying transactions in full.[45]

The fourth condition for the application of the November 1999 Notice is that the market price is paid for the guarantee. Again, this is a question of fact, which will in practice have to be verified by the lender. Presumably, the question on which the lender will have to be satisfied is that the premium charged by the State is the same as that which a private sector bank would charge for giving an equivalent guarantee. But here one runs into a further complication: the fact that a guarantee from a State arguably has greater value to a lender than a guarantee provided by a private sector bank, as the former will provide the lender with zero-risk weighting on its balance sheet. Nevertheless, given that the premium for a guarantee will reflect the borrower's credit position, rather than the implications for the lender's balance sheet, it seems wrong in principle to draw a distinction between a State guarantee and a private sector guarantee. Although they may have different accounting consequences from a lender's point of view, they have the same effect from a borrower's perspective.

---

[45] *ibid*, at paragraphs 78–80.

Finally, it is worth highlighting one potentially important practical difference between the text of the November 1999 Notice and the March 1995 draft. The March 1995 draft suggested that it was necessary to monitor the financial health of the borrower throughout the duration of the guarantee, implying that a State guarantee which was not considered to be aid when issued could at some point in the future be regarded as aid if, for example, the borrower ceased to be in a financially sound position. Fortunately for the lending community, this condition was not included in the November 1999 Notice. Indeed, to have done so would have been strangely illogical, since it is implicit in the November 1999 Notice that the time for assessing whether a guarantee constitutes aid is when it is issued, irrespective of whether it is ever called.[46] Against this, it might be objected that the definition of 'existing aid' in the Procedural Regulation appears to cover measures which are not aid when put into effect but which subsequently become aid 'due to the evolution of the common market'.[47] However, it is submitted that there is an important distinction between (a) the assessment of a guarantee to support a loan in favour of (for example) a State owned monopoly utility at the time is is issued and following the introduction of competition; and (b) a guarantee satisfying all four conditions of the November 1999 Notice at the time it is issued where the borrower subsequently gets into financial difficulty. In the former case there is a legitimate policy objective in ensuring that one firm operating in a competitive market does not enjoy advantages, as a result of its historic position as a State owned monopolist, which are denied to its competitors in a newly liberalized market. In the second case, however, the interests of legal certainty dictate that the position of lenders in large financial transactions is not suddenly called into question by subsequent events over which they have no control.

[46] Note 1 above, at paragraph 2.1.2.        [47] [1999] OJ L83/1, Article 1(a).

# 13

# *State Aid and Environmental Protection*

GERRY FACENNA

In 1986 the Single European Act added a new Title on environment to the EC Treaty, which was the basis of what is now included in Articles 174–176 EC. The provisions gave the Community express powers to act to protect the environment for the first time and signalled a significant change in the whole context of the Community's environmental policies. Following further amendments of the Treaty, environmental protection is now among the highest of Community priorities: Article 2 EC provides that the Community's task includes the promotion of 'a high level of protection and improvement of the quality of the environment'; Article 3(l) EC expressly provides that the Community shall have 'a policy in the sphere of the environment'; and Article 6 EC states: 'Environmental protection requirements must be integrated into the definition and implementation [of all Community policies and activities], in particular with a view to promoting sustainable development'.

In line with this 'integration principle' in Article 6 EC, the Community has increasingly sought to use market-related instruments to promote environmental protection: the Sixth Environment Action Programme (2001) refers to policies 'encouraging the market to work for the environment'.[1] The rules on State aid are obvious contenders for integration: they can be easily manipulated and applied to favour environmentally friendly activities. As the Sixth Environment Action Programme recognizes, although certain types of subsidies might have unintended environmental impact, 'subsidies can also be used in a beneficial way when they are used to pump-prime the development of environmentally friendly production processes and products . . . '[2]

The 2001 Community Guidelines on State aid for environmental protection[3] seek to maximize the potential of State subsidies to promote environmental protection, with the minimum possible impact on competition in the internal market. As a general rule this application of the objectives of the Community's environmental policy within the confines of competition policy means that State

---

[1] COM(2001)31 final, 15 (available at http://europa.eu.int/comm/environment, last visited on 2 July 2003).
[2] ibid 19.
[3] [2001] OJ C37/03.

aid for environmental protection will only be justified where any adverse effects on competition are clearly outweighed by benefits for the natural environment.

## I. Background to EC policy on environmental State aid

### A. The 'polluter pays' principle

More than a decade before the Single European Act amended the EC Treaty, the Commission and the Member States adopted the 'polluter pays' principle as a key aspect of the Community's burgeoning environmental policy.[4] The principle provides that the costs of measures required to deal with pollution should be borne by those responsible for the pollution. As a result, environmental costs should be 'internalized' as part of the production costs of firms responsible for creating environmental dangers. This internalization of costs provides such firms with an incentive to reduce pollution and to find more environmentally friendly production methods and technologies, while at the same time reducing the financial burden on the Community and Member States.

State aid that favours environmental objectives generally works against the 'polluter pays' principle because recipients of such aid can rely on it as a means to avoid internalizing the costs of pollution caused by them. As early as 1975, in what is still regarded as the principal Community statement on the 'polluter pays' principle, the European Council recommended: 'environmental protection should not in principle depend on policies which rely on grants of aid and place the burden of combating pollution on the Community'.[5]

According to that Council Recommendation, exceptions to the 'polluter pays' principle are justified in certain limited cases: (a) where the immediate application of very stringent standards or substantial charges is likely to lead to serious economic disruption; and (b) where, in the framework of other policies such as agricultural, regional, or social policy, environmental investment is designed to resolve certain structural problems of a regional or sectoral nature. Specifically, the following are not considered to be contrary to the 'polluter pays' principle:

(a) financial contributions which might be granted to local authorities for the construction and operation of public installations for the protection of the environment, the cost of which could not be wholly covered in the short term from the charges paid by polluters using them;

(b) financing designed to compensate for the particularly heavy costs which some polluters would be obliged to meet in order to achieve an exceptional degree of environmental cleanliness;

---

[4] Declaration of the Council of the European Communities and of the representatives of the Governments of the Member States of 22 November 1973 on the programme of action of the European Communities on the environment, Part I, Title II, para 5 [1973] OJ C112/1.

[5] Council Recommendation 75/436 of 3 March 1975 regarding cost allocation and action by public authorities on environmental matters [1975] OJ L194/1, para 2.

(c) contributions granted to foster activities concerning research and development with a view to implementing techniques, manufacturing processes and products causing less pollution.[6]

The role of the 'polluter pays' principle in State aid practice was succinctly put in a recent Opinion of Advocate General Jacobs:

In its State aid practice the Commission uses the polluter-pays principle for two distinct purposes, namely (a) to determine whether a measure constitutes State aid within the meaning of Article 87(1) EC and (b) to decide whether a given aid may be declared compatible with the Treaty under Article 87(3) EC.

In the first context, that of Article 87(1) EC, the principle is used as an analytical tool to allocate responsibility according to economic criteria for the costs entailed by the pollution in question. A given measure will constitute State aid where it relieves those liable under the polluter-pays principle from their primary responsibility to bear the costs.

In the second context, that of Article 87(3) EC, the polluter-pays principle is used by contrast in a prescriptive way as a policy criterion. It is relied on to argue that the costs of environmental protection *should* as a matter of sound environmental and State aid policy ultimately be borne by the polluters themselves rather than by States.[7]

## B. Development of Commission policy on environmental State aid

An increasing number of State subsidies allegedly aimed at protecting the environment were referred to the Commission in the mid-1970s, at a time of growth in State aid generally. In response, in November 1974 the Commission produced its first policy statement on the role of environmental issues in the rules on State aid, which attempted to lay down conditions under which aid might be granted to assist industries to adapt to new environmental standards.[8]

The initial view of the Commission at that time was that the use of State aid for environmental protection was essentially a transitional measure helping to lay the foundations for full implementation of the 'polluter pays' principle as part of a long-term Community environmental policy. A period of six years until 31 December 1980 was thought to be a sufficient period for firms subject to an extraordinary financial burden in adapting to Community and national environmental standards to be supported. Such aid was said to qualify under Article 87(3)(b) EC as aid necessary for the execution of 'important projects of common European interest'.[9]

---

[6] ibid, para 7.

[7] Case C-126/01 *Ministre de l'économie, des finances et de l'industrie v GEMO SA* (30 April 2002), paras 68–70.

[8] Commission's Memorandum of 6 November 1974 on State aid in environmental matters, annexed to a letter to the Member States (S/74/30807) of 7 November 1974; Fourth Report on Competition Policy (1974) 101–106.

[9] ibid. For a fuller analysis of the historical development of Commission policy in this area see G Van Calster, 'Greening the EC's State Aid and Tax Regimes' [2000] ECLR 294 and P Renaudiere, 'Environnement, concurrence et transports: vers l'integration?' [1994] 7–10 Journal des Tribunaux-Droit Europeen 8.

This initial transition period proved optimistic and the Commission's framework guidance was extended for a further six years to 1986,[10] when the new Treaty provisions contained in the Single European Act confirmed the 'polluter pays' principle and called for the integration of environmental protection into other Community policies. The Community's Fourth Programme on the Environment in 1987 acknowledged that economic instruments such as taxes, levies, State aid, and rebates had a role to play in environmental protection that should be developed further,[11] but the Fifth Environmental Action Programme in 1993, *Towards Sustainability*, went much further. It recognized the need to reconcile on a long-term basis the development of the European economy with protection of the environment, and encouraged the Commission to update its guidance on environmental State aids to take into consideration the growing importance of subsidies for particular types of environmental expenditure and the effectiveness of fiscal incentives in speeding up the transition towards sustainability.[12]

The Commission's existing guidance was subsequently extended a number of further times while a re-examination of the approach to State aids and environmental protection took place, before new guidelines were finally published in 1994.[13] These were much more comprehensive and precise than earlier guidance and for the first time included the Commission's views on operating aid as well as investment aid. The Guidelines have since been updated to reflect new environmental concerns and more sophisticated forms of environmental State aid, resulting in the publication of the new Community Guidelines on State aid for Environmental Protection in February 2001.[14]

## II. The 2001 Guidelines

The 2001 Guidelines ('the Guidelines') define 'environmental protection' as 'any action designed to remedy or prevent damage to our physical surrounding or natural resources, or to encourage the efficient use of these resources'.[15] This includes energy-saving measures and the use of renewable sources of energy. The Guidelines provide a guide to the circumstances in which State aid will be justified because it ensures environmental protection and sustainable development without disproportionate effects on competition and economic growth.

---

[10] *Tenth Report on Competition Policy* (1980) at para 224.

[11] Resolution of the Council of the European Communities and the representatives of the Governments of the Member States, meeting within the Council of October 19, 1987 on the continuation and implementation of a European Community policy and action programme on the environment (1987–1992) [1987] OJ C328/1, at 's'.

[12] [1993] OJ C138/1.

[13] Community Guidelines on State Aid for Environmental Protection [1994] OJ C72/3.

[14] [2001] OJ C37/3.       [15] 2001 Guidelines, point 6.

The Guidelines apply to all sectors governed by the EC Treaty except the agricultural sector.[16]

The Guidelines are not meant to encourage Member States to grant aid for environmental protection; rather they are intended to promote transparency and consistency in the Commission's approach to assessing this type of aid. The fact that certain types of aid may run counter to the 'polluter pays' principle and may conflict with the principle of 'internalisation of costs', is stated at the outset.[17] The Commission is keen to point out that taking long-term environmental requirements into account does not mean that all environmental aid should be authorized. On the contrary, the Commission's view is: '[i]f environmental requirements are to be taken into account in the long term, prices must accurately reflect costs and environmental protection costs must be fully internalised'.[18]

The Guidelines are divided into rules on investment aid and rules on operating aid. It is essential that any proposed State aid be classified as one or the other in order to determine whether it may be authorized under the Guidelines: failure to do so by the Commission may render its decision defective because the Member State concerned (and any interested party) will not be able fully to defend its rights.[19]

*Legal base for authorization of State aid*

Prior to 1994, the Commission's method of dealing with State aid for environmental protection relied on Article 87(3)(b) EC, namely 'aid to promote the execution of an important project of common European interest'. However, the 2001 Guidelines, like the 1994 Guidelines before them, assume Article 87(3)(c) as the main exemption provision ('aid to facilitate the development of certain economic activities or of certain economic areas').[20] The conditions for the application of Article 87(3)(c) are less restrictive than those attached to Article 87(3)(b), and Article 87(3)(c) appears to be more appropriate for the kind of aid concerned.

The Guidelines do provide that certain types of aid with an environmental priority may continue to be approved at higher rates under Article 87(3)(b), but only where the aid is necessary for a project that is 'specific, well defined and qualitatively important' and makes 'an exemplary and clearly identifiable contribution to the common European interest'.[21] In its decision on the UK's scheme for emission trading in greenhouse gas allowances[22] the Commission did not exclude the possibility that emission trading systems could be considered as

---

[16] ibid, point 7: the Community Guidelines for State aid in the agriculture sector [2000] OJ C28/2 apply. State aid for research and development in the environmental field is subject to the rules set out in the Community framework for State aid for research and development [1996] OJ C45/5.

[17] 2001 Guidelines, point 4.

[18] ibid, points 4, 20.

[19] C-351/98 *Spain v Commission* [2002] ECR I-8031, at paras 83–85.

[20] 2001 Guidelines, point 72.     [21] ibid, point 73.     [22] N 416/2001 [2002] OJ C88/16.

projects of common European interest. However, in the absence of an EU-wide scheme, and since certain aspects of the UK scheme differed significantly from a similar Commission proposal and might limit the extent to which experiences could be transferred to other Member States, the Commission assessed (and authorized) the scheme under Article 87(3)(c).

## A. Investment aid

The Guidelines limit the authorization of aid for investments to: investments in land that are strictly necessary in order to meet environmental objectives; investments in buildings, plant, and equipment intended to reduce or eliminate pollution and nuisances; and investments to adapt production methods with a view to protecting the environment. Spending on technology transfer through the acquisition of operating licences or of patented and non-patented know-how may also qualify, subject to certain conditions.[23]

The 'eligible costs' of an investment determine the 'intensity' of investment aid that may be authorized under the Guidelines. These costs are strictly limited to the extra investment costs necessary to meet the environmental objectives.[24] Where such costs cannot be easily identified, objective methods of calculation may be used, such as the difference between the total cost of the investment and the cost of a technically comparable investment that does not provide the same degree of environmental protection. Determining the eligible costs is particularly important in those cases where investment results in increased production as well as improved environmental protection: in all cases, eligible costs must be calculated net of any benefits accruing from any increase in capacity and any cost savings or additional ancillary production engendered during the first five years of the life of the investment.

### 1 Transitional investment aid for SMEs adapting to new Community standards

The 1994 Guidelines allowed temporary aid to be granted to help existing firms adapt to meet new environmental standards. However, the Commission has hardened its view and now considers that the full internalization of environmental costs by polluters remains a critical process and aid should not be used to make up for the absence of such cost internalization.[25] Consequently, State aid is not permitted under the 2001 Guidelines for investments that do no more than assist to bring companies into line with new or existing Community standards. According to the Commission, new or existing Community environmental standards 'constitute the ordinary law with which firms must comply, and it is not necessary to provide them with aid in order to encourage them to obey the law'.[26]

---

[23] 2001 Guidelines, point 36.      [24] ibid, point 37.      [25] ibid, points 4, 20.
[26] ibid, point 21.

The Guidelines make special allowance for small and medium-sized enterprises ('SMEs')[27] however, and investment aid to assist SMEs to reach new Community environmental standards may be authorized for a period of up to three years from the adoption of new compulsory standards, up to a maximum of 15 per cent of eligible costs.[28] The Commission's view is that this exception is necessary in order to address the 'special difficulties' faced by SMEs.[29] A recent study by the Commission identified these difficulties as including lack of time/ staff resources, lack of financial resources and expertise, and lack of understanding of environmental problems and risks.[30] The study indicated that, although relatively little is known about the contribution of SMEs to pollution and waste in the EU, it is clear that they make a very considerable collective contribution, probably around 50 per cent overall.[31]

The 1994 Guidelines contained detailed provisions on horizontal aid measures including those to increase general environmental awareness or awareness of specific environmental goals, which do not appear from the 2001 Guidelines.[32] However, the new Guidelines recognize that advisory and consultancy services play an important part in helping SMEs to make progress in environmental protection, and so aid may be granted for such services under the Regulation on State aid for SMEs.[33]

## 2 Investment aid to firms improving on Community standards

The Guidelines note that, by comparison with aid that merely helps firms to meet existing Community standards, there is some usefulness to aid that provides an incentive to achieve levels of environmental protection higher than those required by Community standards.[34] This arises where a Member State adopts more stringent standards than the Community so as to achieve a higher level of environmental protection, where a firm invests in environmental protection

[27] As defined in Commission Recommendation 96/280/EC of 3 April 1996 concerning the definition of small and medium-sized enterprises [1996] OJL 107/4.

[28] 2001 Guidelines, point 28. The reference to the date of adoption of new standards may be problematic because the majority of Community environmental standards are laid down in the form of directives whose date of adoption is invariably earlier than the date of publication, the date of entry into force, and the deadline for implementation: see H Vedder, 'The New Community Guidelines on State Aid for Environmental Protection: Integrating Environment and Competition' [2001] ECLR 365, 368.

[29] 2001 Guidelines, point 20.

[30] Report on SMEs and the Environment, 17 February 2000, 61 (available at http://europa.eu.int/comm/environment/sme, last visited on 2 July 2003).

[31] ibid, 60.

[32] The 1994 Guidelines acknowledged that such aid is often so general in scope and distant from the working of market forces that it does not confer an identifiable financial benefit on specific firms.

[33] 2001 Guidelines, point 41, referring to Commission Regulation (EC) No. 70/2001 of 12 January 2001 on the application of Articles 87 and 88 of the EC Treaty to State aid for small and medium-sized enterprises [2001] OJL 10/33.

[34] 2001 Guidelines, point 20. Aid for investment to improve on Community standards, or undertaken where no Community standards exist, may not be granted where such improvements merely bring companies into line with Community standards that have already been adopted but are not yet in force.

beyond that required by Community standards, or where no Community standards exist at all. In such cases, investment aid enabling firms to improve on applicable Community standards may be authorized at a level of up to 30 per cent of the eligible investment costs.[35]

Where a firm is adapting to national standards more stringent than Community standards or undertaking a voluntary improvement on Community standards, the eligible costs comprise the additional investment costs necessary to achieve the higher level of environmental protection; the cost of investment necessary to achieve the level required by Community standards is not eligible.[36] Where no Community standards exist, the eligible costs comprise the investment costs necessary to achieve a higher level of environmental protection than that which the firm or firms in question would achieve in the absence of any environmental aid.[37]

### Bonus for SMEs and firms located in assisted regions

Where investments improving on Community standards are carried out by SMEs, aid may be increased by 10–40 per cent of the eligible investment costs.[38] SMEs also qualify for a bonus of 10 per cent when investing in energy as described below.

Under Articles 87(3)(a) and 87(3)(c) EC, certain geographical areas are eligible for State aid to promote regional development. To encourage firms in those assisted regions to invest in environmental protection, such firms are eligible under the Guidelines to an increase of either 5 per cent on the basic rate for regions covered by Article 87(3)(c) and 10 per cent in the regions covered by Article 87(3)(a) or, if higher, to the prevailing regional aid rate plus 10 per cent.[39] The bonuses for assisted regions and SMEs may be combined, so long as the maximum rate of environmental aid never exceeds 100 per cent gross of the eligible costs.

### 3 Investment in energy

#### (i) Energy-saving measures

Investments that enable companies to reduce the amount of energy used in their production cycles are seen as promoting environmental protection: according to the Commission such investments play a major role in achieving economically the Community objectives for the environment.[40] Under the 2001 Guidelines

---

[35] 2001 Guidelines, point 20. Aid for investment to improve on Community standards, or undertaken where no Community standards exist, may not be granted where such improvements merely bring companies into line with Community standards that have already been adopted but are not yet in force, point 36.

[36] A firm may be given aid to enable it to comply with national standards that are more stringent than Community standards only if the firm complies with those national standards by the final date laid down in the relevant national measures: investments carried out after that date do not qualify (ibid, point 40).

[37] ibid, point 37.

[38] ibid, point 35.

[39] ibid, point 34.

[40] Commission's Action Plan to Improve Energy Efficiency in the European Community COM(2000) 247 final, 26.4.2000.

such investments may therefore receive aid at the basic rate of 40 per cent of eligible costs.[41] The Commission is alive to the fact that almost all new investments in technological developments have an indirect positive effect on the environment and that there is a temptation to present normal productive investments as being determined by environmental factors in order to attract State aid.[42] Aid ostensibly intended for environmental protection measures that is in fact for general investment is not covered by the Guidelines.[43]

### (ii) Cogeneration of electricity and heat

Increased energy use from the combined production of heat and power is also a Community priority for the environment.[44] Investments in the combined production of electric power and heat qualify for aid at the basic rate of 40 per cent of eligible cost if the measures are shown to benefit the environment because of the efficiency of the process in question, because the measures will allow energy consumption to be reduced, or because the production process will be less damaging to the environment.[45]

### (iii) Renewable sources of energy

The Commission has a very favourable attitude towards renewable energy sources, pointing out in the Guidelines that measures in support of renewable sources of energy are one of the Community's environmental priorities and one of the long-term objectives that should be encouraged most.[46] The basic rate of aid for investment in support of these forms of energy is 40 per cent of eligible costs. Where renewable energy installations serve all the needs of an entire community, such as an island or a residential area, they may additionally qualify for a bonus of 10 per cent on top of the basic rate.

Eligible costs for investments in renewable energy are extra investment costs beyond those required for a conventional power plant with the same energy production capacity.[47] In view of the importance and overwhelming environmental benefits offered by renewable sources of energy, where it can be shown to be necessary, Member States will be able to grant investment aid to support renewable energy installations of up to 100 per cent of eligible costs, on condition that the installations do not receive any further support.[48]

---

[41] 2001 Guidelines, point 30.

[42] eg Commission Decision (C34/2000) of 28 March 2001 on proposed State aid from Germany for the steel firm BRE.M.A Warmwalzwerk GmbH & Co. KG [2002] OJ L35/15.

[43] C-351/98 *Spain v Commission* [2002] ECR I-8031, para 78.

[44] Council Resolution of 18 December 1997 on a Community strategy to promote combined heat and power [1998] OJ C4/1. See also the Proposal for a Directive of the European Parliament and of the Council on the promotion of cogeneration based on a useful heat demand in the internal energy market (COM(2002) 415 final).

[45] 2001 Guidelines, point 31.

[46] ibid, point 32. See also Council Resolution of 8 June 1998 on renewable sources of energy [1998] OJ C198/1 and case C-379/98 *PreussenElektra AG v Schleswag AG* [2001] ECR I-2099, at para 73 of the judgment, and para 110 of the AG's Opinion.

[47] 2001 Guidelines, point 37.     [48] ibid, point 32.

## 4 Rehabilitation of polluted industrial sites

State aid for the rehabilitation of polluted land only falls within the scope of Article 87(1) where a gratuitous financial benefit is conferred on particular firms or industries. Rehabilitation work carried out by public authorities is not caught by Article 87 of the Treaty, although the Guidelines caution that problems of State aid may arise if land is sold after rehabilitation at a price below its market value.[49]

In line with the 'polluter pays' principle, where the person responsible for pollution is clearly identified,[50] that person should finance rehabilitation of the land and no State aid may be provided. Where the person responsible for the pollution is not identified or cannot be made to bear the cost, State aid may be given to the person responsible for the rehabilitation work. Such aid may cover up to 100 per cent of the eligible costs (being the cost of the work less any increase in the value of the land), plus 15 per cent of the cost of the work. The total amount of aid may never exceed the actual expenditure incurred by the firm.

The environmental damage in question may be damage to the quality of the soil or surface water or groundwater, and all expenditure incurred by a firm in rehabilitating its site ranks as eligible investment costs, whether or not such expenditure can be shown as a fixed asset on its balance sheet.

## 5 Relocation of firms

There is no general entitlement under the Guidelines to aid for the relocation of firms to new sites: the Commission's view is that, as a rule, relocation does not constitute environmental protection. Relocation aid may be granted in very limited circumstances where pollution from firms established in urban areas or sensitive environmental areas gives rise to major problems. When a firm established in an urban area or in a *Natura 2000* designated area[51] lawfully carries on an activity that creates major pollution and is ordered by administrative or judicial decision to move to a more suitable area on environmental protection grounds, aid for relocation may be authorized in accordance with the general conditions applying to aid for firms improving on Community standards (ie up to 30 per cent of the eligible investment costs).[52] This is subject to the firm complying with the strictest environmental standards applicable in the new location.

In determining eligible costs, the Commission will take into account a number of factors, including the yield from the sale or renting of the plant or land abandoned, and any compensation paid in the event of expropriation, along with the costs connected with the purchase of land or the construction or purchase of new plant of the same capacity as the plant abandoned. Investments resulting in an increase in capacity will not be taken into consideration.[53]

---

[49] 2001 Guidelines, point 38, fn 34.

[50] ie the person liable under the national law of the Member State concerned, without prejudice to the adoption of Community rules on the matter.

[51] A special area of conservation designated under Council Directive 92/43/EEC of 21 May 1992 on the conservation of natural habitats and of wild fauna and flora [1992] OJ L206/7.

[52] 2001 Guidelines, point 39.        [53] ibid.

## B. Operating aid

Operating aid that relieves firms of the costs associated with the environmental harm they cause is in general prohibited: such aid obviously undermines the 'polluter pays' principle. However, the Guidelines do permit certain types of operating aid: aid for waste management and energy conservation; aid in the form of tax reductions or exemptions; aid for renewable energy sources; and aid for the combined production of electricity and heat.

### 1 Operating aid to promote waste management and energy saving

Operating aid for the management of waste or for energy conservation is allowed only where it is shown to be absolutely necessary.[54] It is limited to the difference between the production cost (including a normal level of profit) and the market price of the products or services. The aid must be temporary and, in general, 'degressive' ('wound down over time') so as to provide an incentive for prices to reflect costs reasonably rapidly.[55]

The Commission's view is that firms should normally bear the costs of treating industrial waste in accordance with the 'polluter pays' principle. Operating aid for the management of waste will only be granted where national standards have been introduced that are more stringent than Community standards or where national standards are introduced in the absence of Community standards. Where that is the case, operating aid is considered justified because firms are likely temporarily to lose competitiveness at an international level.

Where it is allowed, operating aid to promote waste management and energy-saving may only be granted for up to five years. In the case of 'degressive' aid, the intensity must fall in a linear fashion from 100 per cent to zero by the end of the fifth year; 'non-degressive' aid is limited to an intensity of 50 per cent throughout the five-year period.

The Guidelines do not provide detailed guidance on operating aid for energy-saving activities. Many energy-saving measures will result in more efficient production methods with lower operating costs: the circumstances under which it is 'absolutely necessary' for such energy-saving measures to receive operating aid are likely to arise much less frequently than the circumstances under which such measures would be eligible for investment aid.[56]

---

[54] The waste management concerned must also be in line with the Community Strategy for Waste Management (COM(1996) 399 final).

[55] 2001 Guidelines, point 43.

[56] See H Vedder, 'The New Community Guidelines on State Aid for Environmental Protection: Integrating Environment and Competition' [2001] ECLR 365, 369–70, who suggests that the Commission should have provided more guidance on operating aid in the energy-saving field, in particular as to whether the environmental impact of any increase in the use of raw materials or personnel that results in higher operating costs should be taken into account in determining the net environmental benefit of any such measures.

## 2 *Operating aid in the form of tax reductions or exemptions*

A number of Member States have taken steps to promote environmental protection through the use of 'eco-taxes'. In some cases, exemptions from or reductions in these taxes may constitute State aid within the meaning of Article 87 EC.[57] However, in the Commission's view the positive effects of adopting environmental taxes may outweigh any adverse effect of the aid and the Guidelines therefore set out conditions under which such tax reductions or exemptions may be granted.

Temporary exemptions from taxes levied for reasons of environmental protection are considered justified in particular because of the absence of harmonization of eco-taxation at a European level and the resulting risk of a temporary loss of international competitiveness for firms in Member States where such taxes have been adopted. In general, any exemption or reduction from these taxes should make a significant contribution to protecting the environment, and the Guidelines caution that care should be taken to ensure that exemptions do not, by their very nature, undermine the general objectives pursued.[58]

Three types of exemption (or reduction) from taxation schemes may be authorized: (i) temporary exemption from or reduction in a tax imposed independently by a Member State, enabling firms to adapt to a new situation;[59] (ii) temporary reduction in a tax levied as a result of a Community directive where the rate of taxation imposed by a Member State is higher than the level in the directive and the reduction results in firms paying less than the higher domestic rate but not less than the minimum rate laid down in the directive;[60] and (iii) an exemption from or reduction in a minimum rate of taxation laid down in a Community directive insofar as it is permitted by the directive and is necessary and not disproportionate in the light of Community objectives (in particular, it should be strictly limited in time).[61]

The Guidelines lay down a number of specific conditions that must be met before any exemption from or reduction in a taxation scheme will be authorized.

For *new* taxation schemes where there is no Community tax harmonization or where the level of taxation envisaged exceeds that laid down by Community legislation, 'non-degressive' exemptions/reductions lasting for up to ten years may be allowed:

(i)  where the Member State concerned concludes agreements with recipient firms (or voluntary agreements with the same effect are entered into) under which the firms undertake to achieve environmental protection objectives during the period of the exemption;[62] or

---

[57] 2001 Guidelines, point 23.    [58] ibid, point 50.    [59] ibid, point 48.
[60] ibid, point 49(a).    [61] ibid, point 49(b).
[62] ibid, point 51.1(a). Such agreements or undertakings may relate, among other things, to a reduction in energy consumption, a reduction in emissions, or any other environmental measure. The substance of the agreements will be assessed by the Commission when the aid projects are notified to it and Member States must ensure strict monitoring of the commitments entered into by the firms. The agreements must stipulate any penalties that are applicable if the commitments are not met.

(ii)  (for taxes originating in Community legislation) where the tax level effectively paid by firms after any reduction remains higher than the Community minimum;[63] or

(iii)  (for domestic taxation schemes imposed in the absence of Community harmonisation) the firms eligible for the reduced tax level nevertheless pay a 'significant proportion of the national tax'.[64]

The rules relating to operating aid in the form of tax reductions or exemptions were applied for the first time by the Commission in its consideration of the UK climate change levy on the non-domestic use of energy.[65] A total tax exemption from that levy was subsequently authorized for natural gas in Northern Ireland in the light of the special circumstances of the infant natural gas market there and in the interests of developing a gas infrastructure there.[66]

A reduction or exemption from an *existing* taxation scheme may be authorized, subject to the same conditions, if the tax in question has an appreciable positive impact in terms of environmental protection and the exemption or reduction was decided on when the tax was adopted, or has become necessary as a result of 'a significant change in economic conditions that places firms in a particularly difficult competitive situation'.[67] An exemption or reduction may also be authorized where an existing domestic tax is significantly increased and the Member State takes the view that derogations are needed for certain firms.[68] Where a reduction or exemption is adopted in response to a significant change in economic conditions, it may not exceed the actual increase in costs resulting from the change and must be disapplied 'once there is no longer any increase in costs'.[69]

Where there has been harmonization of taxation at Community level and the level of domestic tax is equal to or lower than the Community minimum (where permitted by the directive), any exemptions or reductions must be covered by an express authorization in the Community legislation to derogate from the Community minimum level. Such measures are also subject to the conditions set out in points 45 and 46 of the Guidelines, ie limited to five years and (for 'degressive' aid) falling in a linear fashion from 100 per cent to zero by the end of the fifth year or (for 'non-degressive' aid) limited to an

---

[63]  ibid, point 51.1(b).      [64]  ibid.

[65]  Invitation to submit comments [2001] OJ C185/22, 23, 38–40. (Subsequent decision [2002] OJ L229/15). See also the XXXIst Report on Competition Policy (2001), at 382.

[66]  N 660a/2000, 18 July 2001 [2001] OJ C236/10.

[67]  2001 Guidelines, point 51.2.

[68]  ibid, point 52.

[69]  This presumably refers to a time when the increased costs brought about by the 'significant change in economic conditions' cease to exist and the production cost returns to its level prior to the increase, rather than when the costs are no longer increasing: cf H Vedder, 'The New Community Guidelines on State Aid for Environmental Protection: Integrating Environment and Competition' [2001] ECLR 365, fn 41. In any event the reduction or exemption may only be authorized for up to 10 years.

intensity of 50 per cent throughout the five-year period. Long-term exemptions will not be justified.[70]

A five-year 'non-degressive' exemption may also be granted to encourage the development of processes for producing electric power from efficient conventional energy sources, such as gas, that have a 'very much higher energy efficiency than that obtained with conventional production processes'.[71] A ten-year derogation is also possible, subject to the conditions applying to new taxes.

### 3 Operating aid for renewable energy sources

Operating aid for renewable energy sources merits special treatment 'because of the difficulties these sources of energy have sometimes encountered in competing effectively with conventional sources'.[72] The development of renewable sources of energy is a Community priority and operating aid for the production of such energy is available to cover the difference between the cost of producing energy from renewable sources and the (generally lower) market price of that energy. The Guidelines provide that Member States may grant aid for renewable energy sources in the following four ways.

### (i) Aid compensating for high investment costs

Energy production from renewable sources often involves high unit investment costs that must be factored into firms' production costs which may present a significant barrier to competitive market entry. To counter this Member States can grant aid to compensate for the difference between the production cost of renewable energy and the market price of energy produced. Such aid may last only for the period required for full depreciation of the plant. The aid may cover a fair return on capital where this can be shown to be indispensable given the poor competitiveness of the type of energy source involved, but once the costs of the plant have been amortized no further aid can be granted. The length of the depreciation period is left to the discretion of the Member States, although account must be taken of any investment aid granted in respect of the plant.

Biomass[73] installations generally require less investment, but have higher running costs than other renewable energy installations. They can therefore be granted, for an indefinite period, operating aid exceeding any investment costs, provided that the total costs after plant depreciation are still higher than the market price of the energy produced.

---

[70] ibid, point 53. The English language version of the Guidelines incorrectly refers to a situation where *no* harmonization at Community level is present, cf the other language versions.

[71] ibid, point 51.3.

[72] ibid, point 55.

[73] Products from agriculture and forestry, vegetable waste from agriculture, forestry, and the food production industry, and untreated wood waste and cork waste: 2001 Guidelines, point 6, referring to the Commission proposal for a Parliament and Council Directive on the promotion of electricity from renewable sources in the internal electricity market [2000] OJ C311/320.

*(ii) Green certificates and other market mechanisms*

Member States are permitted to use market mechanisms such as 'green certificates', which help to ensure a guaranteed demand for energy from renewable sources. Many such schemes will not in fact constitute State aid.[74] In *Preusse-nElektra AG v Schleswag AG*[75] the European Court of Justice examined a German law that required regional electricity distributors to purchase electricity from renewable energy sources at fixed minimum prices above the market price of electricity, and obliged upstream suppliers of electricity from conventional sources partially to compensate the distributors for the additional costs brought about by that requirement. Although the law in question clearly gave an economic advantage to producers of electricity from renewable sources and had the potential to distort competition, the Court held that the purchase obligation imposed on distributors did not involve any direct or indirect transfer of State resources to undertakings and was therefore not within the definition of State aid under Article 87(1) EC.[76]

By comparison, in its decision on the UK's Renewables Obligation and Capital Grants for Renewable Technologies, which obliges all licensed electricity suppliers in Scotland, England, and Wales to ensure that a proportion of electricity supplied to customers in Great Britain comes from renewable sources of energy, the Commission found that one aspect of the scheme (a redistribution fund) did constitute State aid, but was compatible with the environmental guidelines.[77]

Where measures do fall within the definition of State aid, they may be authorized where they are shown to be essential to ensure the viability of the renewable energy sources concerned. Member States must ensure that the granting of the aid does not result in overcompensation or dissuade renewable energy producers from becoming more competitive. This type of aid may be granted for a period of ten years, after which the Commission will assess whether the support measure needs to be continued.[78]

*(iii) Aid calculated on the basis of external costs avoided*

Member States may also grant operating aid to renewable energy installations on the basis of 'external costs avoided', ie the environmental costs society would otherwise have to bear if the same quantity of energy were produced by a conventional production plant.

The Commission funded the 'ExternE' (External Costs of Energy) study, which was published in 2001 after ten years of work involving researchers from all EU Member States and the US.[79] That study concluded, among other things, that the cost of producing electricity from conventional sources such as coal or oil would

---

[74] See, for example, the Commission's decisions on green certificates in Sweden (N789/2002, 5.2.2003) and on a regional system of green certificates in Belgium (N 415/A/01) [2002] OJ C30/14.
[75] [2001] ECR I-2099.
[76] ibid, at paras 57–62 of the judgment. See also the Advocate General's Opinion at paras 160ff.
[77] N 504/2000, 28 November 2001 [2002] OJ C30/15.
[78] 2001 Guidelines, point 62.
[79] Full results may be accessed at http://externe.jrc.es/, last visited on 2 July 2003.

double, and the cost of electricity production from gas would increase by 30 per cent, if external costs such as damage to the environment and to health were taken into account. The study proposed two possible ways forward: accounting for socio-environmental costs by applying taxation penalties to the most damaging fuels,[80] or granting subsidies to encourage greater use of cleaner technologies that do not carry the same environmental and health costs. Since taxation at Community level is difficult to achieve and likely to result in higher energy bills for consumers, the Commission has opted for the second solution.

The results of the ExternE study varied among each Member State, but the external costs produced by renewable energy sources such as wind were invariably calculated to be much lower than the related socio-environmental costs of electricity produced by conventional fossil fuel-burning power stations. A national implementation programme was launched after the publication of the study and the European Commission is now funding further studies to refine the methodology used for assessing these 'hidden energy costs'. The Guidelines simply provide that a Member State granting operating aid on the basis of external costs avoided must use an internationally recognized method of calculation that has been communicated to the Commission and that provides a reasoned and quantified comparative cost analysis, together with an assessment of competing energy producers' external costs, so as to demonstrate that the aid genuinely compensates for external costs avoided. In any event, the amount of aid granted must not exceed €0.05 per kWh, and any aid granted under this option that exceeds the amount that might be granted under option (i) (aid compensating for the high investment costs of renewable energy sources) must be reinvested by the firms in the production of renewable energy.

Further conditions also apply to ensure that aid results 'in an actual overall increase in the use of renewable energy sources at the expense of conventional energy sources, and not in a simple transfer of market shares between renewable energy sources'. The fear appears to be that producers may be encouraged to switch from one form of renewable energy production, for example solar or tidal energy, to another, such as wind energy, which is at present a cheaper and more economically attractive method of producing renewable energy. Any aid granted under this option must therefore form part of a scheme that treats firms in the renewable energy sector on an equal footing; the scheme must provide for aid to be granted without discrimination as between firms producing the same renewable energy and must be re-examined by the Commission every five years.[81]

### (iv) Aid in accordance with the rules applicable to energy saving

Finally, the Guidelines provide that Member States may grant operating aid to renewable energy installations in accordance with the standard rules on

---

[80] According to the study, if the external cost of producing electricity from coal were to be factored into electricity bills, between 2 and 8 €cents per kWh would have to be added to the current price in the majority of EU Member States.

[81] 2001 Guidelines, point 64.

operating aid for waste management and energy saving contained in points 45 and 46 of the Guidelines, ie limited to five years and either falling in a linear fashion from 100 per cent to zero by the end of the fifth year or limited to an intensity of 50 per cent throughout the five-year period.

In line with the priority of encouraging renewable energy sources and the favourable approach set out in the Guidelines, the Commission is likely to allow Member States a certain amount of flexibility in applying the options set out in the Guidelines. A case by case basis is generally adopted: no objection was raised, for example, to a scheme for operating aid for renewable electricity in Belgium under which producers could relinquish green certificates in exchange for direct subsidies.[82]

### 4 *Operating aid for the combined production of electric power and heat*

Operating aid for the cogeneration of electric power and heat may be justified under the same conditions that apply to investment aid for such installations, namely where the measures are shown to benefit the environment because of the efficiency of the process in question, because the measures will allow energy consumption to be reduced, or because the production process will be less environmentally damaging.[83] Operating aid can be granted to firms distributing electric power and heat to the public (ie for *civilian* use) where the costs of producing the electric power or heat exceed its market price. Aid may also be granted in accordance with the four options set out above relating to renewable energy sources.

Operating aid for the combined production of electric power and heat intended for *industrial* use may be granted only where it can be shown that the production cost of one unit of the energy produced exceeds the market price of one unit of conventional energy. The production cost may include a normal return on capital, but gains resulting from the production of heat must be deducted.[84]

### III. THE FUTURE DIRECTION OF COMMUNITY POLICY

#### A. The Kyoto Protocol

In 1998 the EU Member States and the Community signed the Kyoto Protocol to the United Nations Framework Convention on Climate Change.[85] Under that

---

[82] [2002] OJ C292/6, [2002] Bulletin EU 9, 1.3.64.

[83] 2001 Guidelines, point 66, referring to point 31.

[84] It is not clear why only the benefit resulting from the production of heat must be deducted from the production cost and not any benefit resulting from use of the electrical energy produced; cf H Vedder, 'The New Community Guidelines on State Aid for Environmental Protection: Integrating Environment and Competition' [2001] ECLR 365, 372.

[85] The Convention and associated documents are available at http://unfccc.int, last visited on 2 July 2003.

Protocol the parties undertook to limit or reduce greenhouse gas emissions during the period 2008–2012: for the Community as a whole, the target is to reduce greenhouse gas emissions by 8 per cent of their 1990 level. The Protocol and the Community's commitments under it clearly influenced the drafting of the 2001 Guidelines, as illustrated by the favourable approach the Commission has adopted towards energy saving investments.[86]

The Guidelines also acknowledge that the Member States and the Community will have to achieve greenhouse gas reductions by means of co-ordinated policies, including economic measures, some of which might constitute State aid. As the Commission noted in the Thirty-first Report on Competition Policy (2001), a number of Member States have introduced taxes on environmentally unfriendly energy as a means of reducing greenhouse gas emissions. Moreover, the Court of Justice's decision in the *PreussenElektra* case recognizes the link between the international commitments of the European Community aimed at reducing greenhouse gases and national measures aimed at the promotion of renewable sources of energy.[87] The energy sector is therefore likely to remain at the centre of the interaction between State aid and environmental policy.

The 2001 Guidelines provide that, in the absence of any Community provisions on the Kyoto commitments, and without prejudice to the Commission's right of initiative in proposing such provisions, it is for each Member State to formulate the measures it wishes to adopt in order to comply with the Protocol's targets.[88] Although the Guidelines do not lay down specific conditions for authorizing such aid, it is clear that a significant number of the measures likely to be notified to the Commission in the coming years will be concerned with climate change and will be assessed with the Community and the Member States' international obligations in mind.

## B. Continued requirement for environmental State aid

The 2001 Guidelines maintain the combined principles of 'polluter pays' and 'internalization of costs' as the basis of the Commission's policy in this area: the principles are referred to directly or implicitly a number of times throughout the Guidelines. Indeed, one of the most significant developments since the 1994 Guidelines is the hardening of the Commission's position on State aid that simply assists firms to comply with new or existing standards: such aid will now rarely be justified in the absence of some degree of internalization and other special factors.

The 2001 Guidelines also begin and end with references to Article 6 EC and the 'integration' principle, according to which environmental protection

---

[86] See also the Commission's communication *Preparing for Implementation of the Kyoto Protocol* COM(1999) 230, 7, available at http://europa.eu.int/comm/environment, last visited on 2 July 2003.

[87] *PreussenElektra AG v Schleswag AG* [2001] ECR I-2099, at paras 73 ff. Cf M Bronckers and R Van der Vlies 'The European Court's PreussenElektra judgment: Tensions between EU principles and national renewable energy initiatives' [2001] ECLR 458.

[88] 2001 Guidelines, point 70.

requirements must be integrated into all Community policies and activities, in particular with a view to promoting sustainable development. By quoting Article 6 EC in full the Commission emphasizes its intention to consider how the requirements of the Article can best be taken into account in other Community guidelines or frameworks on State aid. At the time of publication of the 2001 Guidelines the EU Competition Commissioner, Mario Monti, stated that competition policy and environmental policy are not at variance with one another, and this is reflected in the Guidelines. They provide a perfect working example of integration of environmental policy into another area of Community competence: a sustainable environmental policy that emphasizes the internalization of environmental costs sits quite comfortably with a competition policy that generally discourages State aid. Although environmental State aid may be justified where it provides a useful incentive or a temporary solution, the Guidelines recognize the fact that, ultimately, the best guarantee of effective environmental protection is the accurate reflection of environmental costs in market prices.[89]

Calculating the true environmental and social costs of economic activities is therefore likely to become increasingly important. In particular, by permitting aid to be granted by reference to 'external costs avoided', the Guidelines lay the foundation for an approach that takes into account the 'hidden' costs to society of traditional fossil fuels. Until such time as these costs can be properly factored into prices, renewable energy sources whose production costs exceed the market price of energy from conventional sources are likely to continue to require State support, whether or not that support is technically classified as State aid within the meaning of Article 87 EC.

Targeted State aid will, it seems, continue to be used to promote environmentally friendly and sustainable economic activity in the EU, particularly among SMEs. The enlargement of the Union is also likely to result in an increased need for environmental State aid in a number of the new Member States: there is a relevant precedent in Article 87(2)(c) EC, which authorizes State aid for parts of Eastern Germany following German reunification, insofar as it is required to compensate for economic disadvantages caused by the division of that country.[90]

In addition, although the harmonization of eco-taxes in the Community is, in the Commission's view, a priority, such harmonization seems some way off. Member States that have developed their own system of eco-taxes therefore find themselves bound to grant reductions or exemptions from such taxes to firms that would otherwise be placed at a competitive disadvantage compared to their competitors in Member States without such taxes. In the light of the Guidelines' provision for derogations lasting up to ten years, the use of State aid by means of fiscal manipulation is likely to remain at the forefront of national environmental policies for some time to come.[91]

---

[89] ibid, point 20.
[90] See G Van Calster, 'Greening the EC's State Aid and Tax Regimes' [2000] ECLR 294, 300–301.
[91] ibid.

There will continue to be a need for some degree of environmental State aid simply because of the growing and unforeseen challenges that the Community's environmental policy must adapt to meet. This is illustrated by the inclusion in the 2001 Guidelines of a number of measures aimed at reduction of greenhouse gas emissions in accordance with the Kyoto Protocol, concerns that did not figure to the same extent in earlier guidance. As new environmental issues emerge and existing best practice develops, circumstances that prevent the full internalization of environmental costs and inhibit investment in improved environmental practices will continue to arise, and State aid will have some role to play in ensuring a continued transition towards real sustainability.

# 14

# *The Financing of Public Service Broadcasting*

SANDRA COPPIETERS

## I. Introduction

Since the deregulation of the broadcasting sector, due to a large extent to the European Television Without Frontiers Directive, the calls for a 'level playing-field' have been growing louder from the commercial broadcasting sector. The sector claims that the mixed funding of the public service broadcasters by public funds and advertizing fees creates a distortion of competition. Ever since the early 1990s the European Commission was landed with a series of complaints over alleged cases of unlawful funding in public service broadcasting.

The relationship and compatibility of the funding of public service broadcasting with the State aid rules has turned out to be a difficult test case for the European Commission, especially because of the politically sensitive nature of the issue. Public service broadcasting is an important part of public policy in most—if not all—Member States. As soon as the first signs of European intervention through the State aid rules became apparent, Member States have, not unsurprisingly, reacted by adding a specific protocol to the EC Treaty. This Amsterdam Protocol acknowledges the important role of the public broadcasting remit and emphasizes the competence of the Member States to define and organize public broadcasting services, and subsequently to provide the public service broadcaster with the necessary funds for the fulfilment of its remit. However, the European Commission has continued its search for practical guidelines to implement the principles of the Protocol. In November 2001 this resulted in the publication of a Communication on the application of the State aid rules to public service broadcasting[1] (hereafter referred to as the Communication). The Commission's plan to resolve the ongoing complaints in a relatively short time has, however, turned out to be a bit too ambitious. The intrinsic complexity of these cases, together with new case law on the very premiss of the Communication, i.e. that funding of a service of general economic interest constitutes aid, seems to have complicated the work of the Commission, and has thus forced it to continue its investigations or to postpone its final decision.

[1] [2001] OJ C 320/4.

This Chapter outlines the origin and significance of the Amsterdam Protocol, and the content and impact of the Communication.


## II. THE ORIGIN AND SIGNIFICANCE OF THE AMSTERDAM PROTOCOL

The Amsterdam Protocol recognizes that public service broadcasting fulfils certain social, cultural, and democratic needs of society and plays an important role in maintaining pluralism in the media. Furthermore, the Protocol deals with the competence of the Member States to define, organize, and finance their public service remits. The text of the Protocol provides as follows:

The provisions of the Treaty establishing the European Community shall be without prejudice to the competence of the Member States to provide for the financing of public service broadcasting insofar as such funding is granted to broadcasting organisations for the fulfilment of the public service remit as conferred, defined and organised by each Member State, and insofar as such funding does not affect trading conditions and competition in the Community to an extent which would be contrary to the common interest, while the realisation of the remit of that public service shall be taken into account.

The Protocol, which is binding as a component of the EC Treaty, essentially confirms the prevailing view of the time that the public financing of public service broadcasting does not qualify as State aid in the sense of the Treaty where such financing is granted to enable broadcasters to realize the public service remit conferred upon them by the Member States.[2]

However, the Protocol did not bring to an end complaints about the financing of public service broadcasting. Questions arose as to the extent to which the provision of entertainment programmes could be regarded as a public service mission and thereby qualify for public funding. Public service broadcasters that generated revenues from public service activities and advertizing were accused of trading under an unfair competitive advantage. With the exception of a few relatively simple cases the European Commission's handling of these complaints has also appeared problematic.[3] In moves to simplify the assessment procedure the European Commission has made several attempts to prescribe how competition law can be applied to the mechanisms of financing public

---

[2] See Working text of the European Commission, DG IV 'Vers la société de l'information: Lignes directrices pour les aides d'Etat en faveur des arts et de la culture, concernant plus particulièrement le secteur audiovisuel' as discussed by the Member States at the hearing of 4 July 1995; State aid NN141/95 'State aid to fund public service television in Portugal'[1997] OJ C 67/7.

[3] The Commission has indeed processed the complaints relating to the British and German broadcasters (See State aid measures NN70/98 'State aid to public broadcasting channels 'Kinderkanal and Phoenix', [1999] OJ C238/3; State aid measures NN 88/98, 'Financing of a 24 hour advertising free news with licence fee by BBC', [2000] OJ C78/6), but has not yet completed its investigation into the funding of Portuguese French, Italian, Spanish, Greek and Irish public service broadcasting. The Commission has already made a decision in this case (see State aid measures NN141/95 'Stade aid to the Portugese public broadcaster', [1997] OJ C 67/7), but it was annulled by the Court of First Instance (see Case T-46/97, *SIC v Commission* [2000] ECR II-2125)).

service broadcasters. Not until November 2001, however, did it make any real progress in this political minefield.

Meanwhile public service broadcasting did not disappear from the European political agenda. In a resolution of 25 January 1999 the Council stated that 'the fact that public service broadcasting, in view of its cultural, social and democratic functions which it discharges for the common good, has a vital significance for ensuring democracy, pluralism, social cohesion, cultural and linguistic diversity' and recalled 'the affirmation of competence of the Member States concerning remit and funding'.

## III. THE COMMUNICATION

In the light of the views of the Member States, the case law of the Court of Justice, and the continuing complaints from private broadcasters, the European Commission, as announced at the Lille Colloquy in 2000,[5] finally issued a Communication on 'The application of State aid rules to public service broadcasting'[6] on 15 November 2001. After a general introduction and description of its scope, this Communication goes on to describe the role of public service broadcasting, the legal context, and the applicability of Article 87(1) EC on the prohibition of State aid, and the exemption from this prohibition under the EC Treaty (Articles 87(2–3) and 86(2) EC).

### A. The role of the public service broadcasters

In essence this section of the Communication lists the legal and policy instruments that deal with the role of public service broadcasting, such as the communications on services of general economic interest in Europe, the findings of the Oreja working group, Article 16 of the EC Treaty, the Amsterdam Protocol on public service broadcasting in the Member States, and the Council's Resolution of 25 January 1999.[7] Obviously, the Amsterdam Protocol occupies a prominent place in the analysis.

It is notable that the Commission views the Protocol merely as an interpretation of the principles of Articles 16 and 86(2) EC, as applied to the broadcasting sector. However, the Protocol was written with Article 87 EC in mind, albeit to stress that the financing of public service broadcasting does not qualify as State aid.[8] The informal Council meetings on cultural and audiovisual affairs in

---

[4] [1999] OJ C 30/1

[5] Speech Mrs Viviane Reding 'What prospects for public television in Europe?' at the Conference on European public television in times of economic and technological change, Lille, 20 July 2000.

[6] [2001] OJ C 320/4.

[7] Council Resolution on public service broadcasting, [1999] OJ C30/1.

[8] See speech by M. A. Wagner, 'Competition, regulation, state aid and the impact of liberalization' at the Seminar on Liberalization and Public Service Broadcasting, London, 15 October 1999 (text available online at www.ebu.ch/home_5html).

Galway (September 1996) and Maastricht (April 1997) emphasized that the financing of public service broadcasting did not qualify as State aid.[9] The ground-breaking judgment of the Court of First Instance in the *FFSA* case,[10] in which benefits to cover the costs of a public service mandate (in this case, tax benefits) were regarded as State aid for the first time, was arrived at after the Member States had reached political consensus on the point that the financing of public service broadcasting should not be viewed as State aid. The Court's decision did not affect the wording of the Amsterdam Protocol (which the European Council approved in June 1997). The final phrase of the Protocol, which clearly states that financing should not alter the development of trade conditions and competition to an extent that would be contrary to the interests of the Community, is in no way an implicit reference to the text of Article 86(2) EC, but a straightforward confirmation of the rule of 'Community loyalty' as laid down in article 5 TEC.[11] In its document on the draft Protocol (May 1997) the Commission itself still held to the idea that the financing of the public service remit did not qualify as State aid insofar as it was awarded to cover the net costs of public service obligations. Only later was there an about turn in the Commission's policy, whereby virtually every form of State funding was automatically regarded as State aid in the sense of Article 87 EC.[12] The exemption clause of Article 86(2) EC has been used on several occasions to justify (illegally granted) new aid measures, and the Commission has also sought support in this provision to justify the financing of the public service broadcasting remit.[13] At the same time the Protocol has unfolded as an interpretation of Article 86(2) EC, with all the (procedural) implications that this carries.

Although the section on the role of public service broadcasting confines itself to a descriptive summary of the documents available on this subject, the recognition of these basic elements represents a change in Commission policy. It recognizes the competence of the Member States to give a detailed definition of the public service remit, so that a broadcaster can offer a wide choice of programmes with the aim of attracting a given percentage of the audience. It also emphasizes that public broadcasters should be able to keep pace with technological developments so as to afford the public the benefit of new audio-visual and information services and new technologies. Prior to that, the Commission had confined its interpretation of public service broadcasting to cultural,

---

[9] Hence the decision of the Member States not to make use of the possibility afforded under Art. 89 TEC (ex Art. 94 TEC) to establish an regulation on the application of Art. 87 TEC (ex Art. 92 TEC), but rather to append a protocol to the new Treaty.

[10] Case T-106/95 *FFSA and Others v Commission* [1997] ECR II-229.

[11] K.-H. Klar, 'Das EU-Protokoll zum öffentlich-rechtlichen Rundfunk', EPD MEDIEN no. 52, 11–13.

[12] The qualification as 'new' aid assumes prior reporting to the Commission and the obligation not to execute the aid before the final approval of the Commission.

[13] State aid Measures NN70/98 'State aid to public broadcasting channels "Kinderkanal and Phoenix", [1999] OJ C238/3; State aid Measures NN 88/98, 'Financing of a 24 hour advertising free news channel with licence fee by BBC', [2000] OJ C78/6.

educational, and news programmes. Sports and entertainment programmes were expressly excluded and were not therefore eligible for public funding.

In the Communication the Commission somewhat surprisingly turns its attention to the role of the commercial broadcasters. Point 14 of the Communication states: 'It should be noted that commercial broadcasters, of which a number are subject to public service requirements, also play a role in fulfilling the objectives of the Protocol [of Amsterdam], to the extent that they contribute to ensure pluralism, enrich the cultural and political debate and widen the choice of programmes.'

The preparatory working document already included a paragraph on private broadcasters in which the Commission joined the debate as to who should shoulder the public service obligation. This interference in the issue of competence, being inconsistent with the Amsterdam Protocol, met with fierce criticism, and rightly so.[14] The wording has been altered, but it is not altogether certain what the Commission seeks to achieve with the above paragraph. It seems likely that it aims to recognize the dual broadcasting system, in which public and commercial broadcasters operate alongside each other. The link with the Amsterdam Protocol is entirely inappropriate. The Commission views the Protocol merely as an interpretation of the principles laid down in Article 86(2) EC as applied to the public service broadcasting sector. Therefore it cannot recognize commercial broadcasting in any way. Although there can be no doubt that the dual broadcasting system contributes to pluralism, enriches cultural and political debate, and widens the choice of programmes, it is questionable whether a statement of this type is apposite in a Communication on the financing of public service broadcasting.

## B. The State aid character of State financing

Public service broadcasting is financed in many different ways in the European Union.[15] In most cases public service broadcasters are partially or largely financed out of the State budget or through a levy on television and radio owners. Some Member States have capital holdings in the public service broadcaster and finance the broadcasting by means of fresh injections of capital. As is well known, under Article 87(1) EC the concept of State aid assumes the presence of four components:

(i)   aid provided by the State or in any way funded through State resources;
(ii)  aid favouring certain undertakings or products;
(iii) aid distorting or threatening to distort competition; and
(iv)  aid adversely affecting trade between the Member States.

[14] Point 13 of the working document reads: 'In the light of the Protocol of Amsterdam the very same goals of public service in broadcasting require that a role also recognised to commercial broadcasters, to the extent that they contribute to ensure of pluralism, enrich the cultural and political debate and widen the choice of programmes'.

[15] For a detailed study of this matter see the EBU report, 'The funding of public service broadcasting' of 9 November 2000 (www.ebu.ch/home_5html).

Although the Commission accepts that as a rule the financing of public service broadcasting must be viewed as State aid, it emphasizes that the existence of State aid should be assessed on a case-by-case basis. No doubt this declaration arises from the public broadcasters' comments on the impact of the *PreussenElektra* judgment.[16] In this case the Court of Justice ruled that a German regulation, under which private electricity companies were forced to purchase electricity generated from renewable sources within their distribution area at minimum prices in excess of the actual economic value, did not constitute aid because it did not involve a direct or indirect transfer of State resources. This judgment may be relevant to the situation facing the German public service broadcasters, which are financed through 'licence fees' paid directly to a private authority by television set owners, with no government intervention. The Communication makes no specific reference to the *PreussenElektra*[17] judgment, probably because the Commission is not convinced that it will set a precedent for the broadcasting sector.[18]

The Commission does, however, refer to a precedent indicating that State resources covering the costs of public service obligations must also be regarded as State aid.[19] On 22 November 2001, however, the Court of Justice delivered an important judgment[20] in the case of *Ferring*, which raised a question mark over this 'established' jurisprudence. The judgment came about after a dispute between pharmaceutical laboratories and the French government over a tax on direct sales of medicines. This tax measure, which was designed to finance the social security system, did not apply to the medicine wholesalers. The 'exemption' was intended to offset the costs of the latter's obligation to keep certain quantities of medicine in stock. The competing pharmaceutical laboratories that were required to pay the tax argued that this tax measure did, in fact, constitute aid. The Court, analogous with the *ADBHU* judgment,[21] came to the conclusion that

> provided that the tax on direct sales imposed on pharmaceutical laboratories corresponds to the additional costs actually incurred by wholesale distributors in discharging their public service obligations, not assessing wholesale distributors to the tax may be regarded as compensation for the services they provide and hence not State aid within the meaning of Article 92 of the Treaty [now Article 87 EC]. Moreover, provided there is the necessary equivalence between the exemption and the additional costs incurred, wholesale distributors will not be enjoying any real advantage for the purposes of Article 92(1) of the Treaty [now article 87(1) EC] because the only effect of the tax will be to put distributors and laboratories on an equal competitive footing.[22]

---

[16] Case C-379/98, *PreussenElektra AG v Schleswag AG* [2001] ECR I-2099.

[17] Again the Commission refers to this judgment in its Communication on certain legal aspects relating to cinematographic and audio-visual works, COM (2001) 534, p. 9.

[18] Written question Rapkay, [2002] OJ C40E/37.

[19] Case T-106/95, *FFSA and Others v Commission* [1997] ECR II-229; Case T-46/97, *SIC v Commission* [2000] ECR II-2125; Case C-332/98, *France v Commission* [2000] ECR I-4833.

[20] Case C-53/00, *Ferring SA v ACOSS* [2001] I-9067.

[21] Case 240/83, *ADBHU* [1985] ECR 531, point 18.

[22] Case C-53/00 *Ferring SA v ACOSS* [2001] ECR 9067, para 27.

With this judgment the Court confirmed the detailed recommendations of Advocate General Tizzano.[23] This issue was discussed in the *GEMO* and *Altmark* cases which are still pending before the Court of Justice. The Advocates General in these cases seem to be in disagreement on the issue. While Advocate General Léger[24] has pleaded for a resolute rejection of the *Ferring* precedent, Advocate General Jacobs[25] is in favour of a more pragmatic, *quid pro quo* approach.[26] The European Commission has already announced that it will await the outcome of these proceedings before taking a Community position.[27] However, it also emphasizes that the concept of State aid will remain relevant, irrespective of the developments in the case law of the court, in cases of excess public service compensation[28] and that, even if *Ferring* is upheld, a text explaining in particular the methods for calculations of compensation would help to increase legal certainty.[29]

In the Communication the Commission also looks at the distinction between 'new' and 'existing' aid.[30] It is essential that the Commission makes this distinction because its powers of supervision differ for each type. New aid must be notified to the Commission in advance and may not be executed by the Member State before receiving the Commission's approval. Existing aid, on the other hand, is subject to constant review, whereby the Commission can only propose measures relating to aid as yet unrealized. The Commission recognizes the complexity of the distinction and suggests a case-by-case approach in this area, too.

## C. Applicability of the derogations in Article 87(2–3) EC

Prohibited State aid may be declared compatible with the common market on the grounds of the derogations in Article 87(2–3) EC. This is an exhaustive list of exemptions under which the Commission can or must declare aid compatible with the common market. To clarify its policy the Commission has issued a series of interpretative texts on the application of these derogations.

---

[23] Opinion of Advocate General Tizzano of 8 May 2001 in Case C-53/00 *Ferring SA v ACOSS* paras 50–63.

[24] Opinion AG Léger of 19 March 2002 and 14 January 2003 in Case C-280/00 *Altmark Trans GmbH Regierungspräsidium Magdeburg v Nahverkehrsgesellschaft Altmark GmbH*, nyr.

[25] Opinion AG Jacobs of 30 April 2002 in Case C-126/01 *Ministre de l'économie des finances et de l'industrie v GEMO SA*, nyr.

[26] For an extensive analysis of this case law see the contribution by Rizza above.

[27] Commission Report to the Seville European Council 'on the status of work on the guidelines for State aid and services of general economic interest', D (2002), point 10.

[28] European Commission 'Non-paper on Services of general economic interest and State aid' of 12 November 2002, point 23.

[29] Commission Report to the Seville European Council 'on the status of work on the guidelines for state aid and services of general economic interest', D(2002) point 14; European Commission 'Non-paper on Services of general economic interest and state aid' of 12 November 2002, point 6.

[30] Both concepts are defined in Article 1, sub b, of Council Regulation 659/1999 establishing more detailed provisions on the application of Article 93 EC Treaty [now Art. 88 TEC] [1999] OJ L 83/3.

In the Communication the Commission only deals with the applicability of the derogations in Article 87(3)(d) EC (aid to promote culture). This provision of the Treaty is of particular relevance to the broadcasting sector. The Commission indicates that the notion of culture should be interpreted restrictively. The Commission also explicitly states that the educational and democratic needs of a Member State have to be regarded as distinct from the promotion of culture, although education may have a cultural aspect. A restrictive interpretation of the exemption clause means that a Member State that wishes to entrust a public service broadcaster with a cultural mission must define this explicitly in the remit, and that when financial aid is provided precise details must be given of the amount set aside to cover the cultural component of the public service requirement.

## D. Applicability of the derogations in Article 86(2) EC

In the Communication the Commission describes the actual conditions for applying the derogations in Article 86(2) EC, as clarified by Community jurisprudence. At the same time the Commission points out that its task is to see that these conditions are met, but that where the broadcasting sector is concerned it must also take account of the Amsterdam Protocol.

The Commission's analysis of Article 86(2) EC revolves around three core concepts: the definition of the public service remit, entrustment and supervision, and the proportionality test.

### 1 Definition of the public service remit

First, the application of Article 86(2) EC requires a clear and precise definition of the public service mandate formally entrusted to the public service broadcaster. In each case the Member State is required to describe the public service remit so that the Commission can assess, 'with sufficient legal certainty', whether the derogation under Article 86(2) is applicable.[31] Further, if the Commission is not given as precise a definition as possible it will not be able to carry out its tasks and so will be unable to grant an exemption.

The Commission also expressly recognizes that, in conformity with the Amsterdam Protocol, the definition of the public service mandate falls within the competence of the Member States. A 'wide' definition may, in view of the interpretative provisions of the Protocol, be considered legitimate under Article 86(2) EC.[32] However, this is not an unbridled freedom. Under existing case law the Commission has the authority to supervize the public service remit.

The basis is the sovereignty of the Member State in defining the public service mandate. In this context the Member State can decide which services (including the 'new' services, such as online information services) it wishes to entrust to the public service broadcaster. The Commission stresses that it would exercise only

---

[31] Para 32 of the Communication.        [32] Para 34 of the Communication.

marginal control over this definition of the public service remit, dealing solely with activities that 'evidently' do not belong to the public service mission. The definition of the public service remit would be in manifest error 'if the latter included activities that could not, reasonably, be considered to meet—in the wording of the Protocol—the "democratic, social and cultural needs of each society"'[33]. The Commission postulates that electronic commerce cannot be viewed as a part of the public service remit since it does not fulfil the cultural, social, and democratic needs of a society. Moreover, it stresses that commercial activities too, even when their revenues are used to finance the public service remit, cannot be regarded as part of the public service broadcasting remit.

During the public hearing with the broadcasters the Commission stressed that the device used to carry out the public service obligation was of little significance. Thus, public service broadcasters are entitled to propagate their 'programmes' via terrestrial transmitters, cable, satellite, internet, etc. Ensuring that the public service broadcaster remains a 'substantial player' in the broadcasting landscape is recognized as a legitimate concern of the Member States. The Communication implicitly enshrines these principles in its sections dealing with the role of public service broadcasting and the definition of the public service remit. In these sections it refers to the need for public service broadcasters to give the public the benefit of technological developments, and the evolutionary nature of the services provided under the public service remit.

The Commission also notes the importance of a clear definition of the activities included in the public service broadcasting remit, because this will enable the commercial broadcasters to plan their activities. The relevance of this comment is questionable. Moreover, it gives the impression that private and public service broadcasters should develop different activities. This is difficult to explain since the Commission backs the idea that public service broadcasters—like commercial broadcasters—can offer a wide and varied choice of programmes if this is specified in their remit.

## 2 Entrustment and supervision

In addition to a formal entrustment of the public service broadcasting remit, the Commission attaches importance to the actual performance of this task. A precise definition of the public service broadcasting remit should enable the national governments to monitor its application. Whereas the preparatory working document called for a compulsory supervisory mechanism, the Commission confirms that a mechanism of this type would be recommendable. It falls within the competence of the Member States to organize appropriate supervision. In any case, the Commission should receive sufficient and reliable indications that the public service is actually supplied as mandated. In the absence of such indications the Commission would not be able to carry out its tasks and could not therefore grant any exemption under that provision.

---

[33] Para 37 of the Communication.

## 3 Proportionality

As regards the financing of public service broadcasting, the Commission assumes that public service duties, whether quantitative or qualitative, justify compensation 'as long as they entail supplementary costs that the broadcaster would not normally have incurred'.[34] It has been customary to use the theory of 'net surplus cost' in applying Article 86(2) EC. These surplus costs are easily calculated in traditional utility sectors, such as telecommunications, water, electricity and gas, post, etc. When, for example, a gas provider is duty bound to lay gas pipes in remote areas, these infrastructural works are easily costed. In the area of public service broadcasting most of the Member States do not employ the term public service 'tasks', but refer to an overall broadcasting mandate on which a number of quantitative and qualitative demands are made. As the Member States and broadcasters have repeatedly argued, net surplus costs cannot be applied to public service broadcasting. The Communication rejects the reference to the 'net surplus cost' theory in Article 86(2) EC by making explicit reference to the 'net costs' of public service tasks when assessing the proportionality of the aid.[35]

In choosing a financing mechanism the Member States are free to make use of single funding (solely public funds) or dual financing (combining public funds with advertizing revenues) provided that they respect the proportionality principle in Article 86(2) EC.

In view of the broad definition of the public service broadcasting remit, which in some Member States can even include the generation of sales revenues from programmes and advertizing time as a means of financing the public service mandate, doubts have arisen as to the proper interpretation and application of the Transparency Directive.[36] As explained above, the Commission has expressly indicated that advertizing, even where its revenues are used to finance public service broadcasting, cannot be regarded as a part of public service duty in the broadcasting sector. This implies that public service broadcasters too—save in certain exceptional cases under the Transparency Directive—are required to separate their accounts, booking all expenses and revenues against their public service duties or against their commercial activities. However, the Commission is aware that not all costs for public service duties and commercial activities can be broken down objectively. By way of illustration, it refers to the costs of producing a programme for broadcasting, which is then sold on to another broadcaster, and to investments in attractive programming that have an indirect influence on sales of advertizing space. In both examples the costs are entirely attributable to the public service, but also benefit the broadcaster's commercial activities. There is no objective means of breaking these costs down over both activities, and there is little sense in splitting them for the sake of the Transparency Directive. That does not, however, preclude an assessment of the broadcaster's pricing policy.

---

[34] Para 45 of the Communication.     [35] Para 58 of the Communication.
[36] Commission Directive 2000/52 amending Directive 80/723 on transparency in the financial relations between Member States and State enterprises, [2000] OJ L193/75.

In applying the proportionality test the Commission assumes that the funding is proportional to the net costs of the public service duty,[37] but adds that 'it is necessary that the State aid does not exceed the net costs of the public service mission, taking also into account other direct or indirect revenues derived from the public service mission. For this reason, the net benefit that non public service activities derive from the public service activity will be taken into account in assessing the proportionality of the aid.'[38] There is no real clarity as to when the non-public service activities derive 'net benefits' from the public service activities. In this author's opinion, one should refer back to the above analysis in connection with the Transparency Directive, which indicates that there is no objective means of splitting some of the public service mission costs and the non-public service activity costs between both activities in the accounts. Logically, the revenues from this type of non-public service activity should be taken into account when applying the proportionality test. In real terms, we are dealing with revenues from the sale of programmes and advertizing time. For other non-public service activities from which no direct financial benefit can be derived for the public service mission, the revenues should not be taken into account when assessing the proportionality of the aid. The revenues that an inventive broadcaster generates through the commercial use of its name (by applying its brand or logo to all kinds of merchandise) are purely commercial. Combining these purely commercial revenues with public funds to cover the public service mission would imply indirect interference in the commercial opportunities open to public service broadcasters. The Commission does not have the authority to do this. It is not clear how an intervention of this kind would serve to promote fair competition between the public service and commercial broadcasting organizations.

In addition, the Commission is particularly watchful for market distortions that are not necessary for the fulfilment of the public service mission. The Commission will ensure that State funding is not used to (co-)finance other activities or is not misused for strategies to undermine competition, such as the sale of goods or services below the market price.[39] These may include, for example, depressing the price of advertizing with the aim of reducing the revenue of competitors. Here, too, the Commission indicates that it will need to look at the actual structure of the competition.

Finally, the Commission points out that in its assessment it may consider whether 'the system as a whole might also have the positive effect of maintaining

---

[37] Moreover, it should be stressed that public service broadcasters, like any other enterprise, must be capable of laying aside financial reserves for investments in short and (mid to) long-term projects.

[38] Point 58 of the Communication.

[39] By market price is understood 'the level necessary to recover the stand-alone costs that an efficient commercial operator in a similar situation would normally have to recover'. The term 'stand-alone cost' is not a current accounting term. On the assumption that this term is being used to refer to immediately demonstrable costs, i.e. without association with indirect costs and the addition of overheads, only the production costs, for example, would be accounted for in the sale of advertizing time.

an alternative source of supply in some relevant markets'.[40] State aid cannot be used to create artificial competition: 'state aid which allows an operator to stay in the market in spite of its recurrent losses causes a major distortion of competition, as it leads in the long run to higher inefficiency, smaller supply and higher prices for consumers'.[41] In each case the positive effects of the system will need to be weighed against the potential negative effects of the aid. The Commission will also take into account the specific problems that smaller Member States may have in collecting the funds needed to finance broadcasting 'if the costs per inhabitant of the public service are, *ceteris paribus*, higher'.[42]

## IV. Conclusion: impact and future of the Communication

The Communication undoubtedly signifies a breakthrough in Commission policy. It recognizes a number of principles that the Member States and the Commission were unable, and seemed unlikely ever, to agree to a few years ago. The Commission now recognizes the specific character of public service duty in the broadcasting sector. Moreover, the competence of the Member States to define the public service broadcasting remit has been explicitly confirmed, and it was expressly recognized on two occasions that this can be a 'wide definition' through which the broadcaster can offer 'a wide choice of programmes' with a view to 'preserving a certain level of audience'. This means that the Commission no longer confines the public service remit to cultural, educational, and news programmes which appeal to only a small segment of the population, but now includes sports and entertainment programmes too. It also stresses that public service broadcasting should benefit from technological developments, and must therefore be capable of providing the population with new, online services.

From its inception the Communication had two important goals. First, it was intended to provide public service broadcasters with a 'safe area'. This has been a general concern in the field of public service compensation. In its report 'on services of general interest' to the Laeken European Council of December 2001[43] the Commission announced a two-step approach to improve legal certainty in the field of public service compensation. As a first step the Commission would set up a Community framework which would indicate the conditions under which State aid granted for the imposition of public service obligations can be authorized by the Commission. On the basis of the experience gained with the application of this framework, the Commission would then, if appropriate, adopt a regulation exempting certain aids in the area of services of general interest from the obligation of prior notification. The adoption of the Communication should therefore be considered as a first step towards providing legal certainty in the

---

[40] Para 62 of the Communication.    [41] Footnote 20 of the Communication.
[42] Para 62 of the Communication.
[43] Commission Report to the Laeken European Council, COM(2001) 598 final, point 27–29.

public service broadcasting sector. It should be noted, though, that in the Communication the Commission recognizes the need for a 'case-by-case' approach. This may to some extent undermine the legal certainty that the Communication is designed to provide, but at the same time it offers the kind of flexibility that this sector needs. At the same time it must be said that the section dealing with the proportionality test is unclear on a number of points.

Secondly, the Communication was designed to be a practical, and politically acceptable, tool to allow the Commission to deal with outstanding complaints in the not too distant future. After the adoption of the Communication, the Commission decided to open a formal investigation procedure under Article 88(2) EC in a number of ongoing cases.[44] The Commission also reached a final decision in the cases notified to it by the Belgian[45] and British[46] governments (see below). The Commission has also been faced with a new complaint about the way in which the Dutch public broadcaster is funded. It is also worth mentioning that, in its ongoing efforts to ensure that the rules of the Directive governing the transparency of financial relations between the Member States and their public service undertakings are implemented into national laws,[47] the Commission has sent reasoned opinions under Article 226 EC to Belgium and Luxembourg and has decided to bring Finland, France, Ireland, Italy, Portugal, and Sweden before the Court of Justice for failure to implement the aforementioned Directive.[48]

So far the Commission has implemented the guidelines of its Communication on two occasions. First, the Commission has assessed the funding scheme installed by the francophone community in Belgium intended to compensate local television stations for the fulfilment of their public service remit. In short, this remit encompassed a duty to provide informative, entertaining, cultural, and educational programmes to the population of their particular region. In a second case the Commission reviewed a decision of the British authorities extending the public service remit of the BBC to a number of digital services. Both cases were quite straightforward and presented no real challenge to the practical applicability of the guidelines set out in the Communication. However, there are a number of points worth looking into.

The first point of interest is the analysis of the State aid character of the measures notified to the Commission. Both cases were resolved after the ruling in the *Ferring* case. However, in the Belgian case this precedent seems to have had no impact at all. The Commission conducted its traditional State aid analysis and

---

[44] State aid NN 133/A/01, NN 85/A/01 en NN 94/A/99 'Compensation payments to the public broadcaster RTP', [2002] OJ C 098/2. On 21 January 2003 the Commission decided to launch a probe into the financing by Denmark of its public broadcaster TV2. According to the Commission there are reasons to believe that the broadcaster has been overcompensated for its services and has possibly used these excess public funds to cross-subsidize its advertising business. The Commission is also investigating whether TV2 is undercutting advertizing prices (IP/03/913).

[45] State aid N548/2001 'Belgian aid to the local television stations in the French Community', C(2002)446 fin.

[46] State aid N631/2001 'UK BBC licence fee', C(2002)1886 fin.

[47] Member States had until the end of July 2001 to implement the Transparency Directive.

[48] IP/03/19.

concluded that the measure did constitute State aid. Especially the assessment of the effect of the measure on trade between the Member states can be questioned. On one hand the Commission admitted that the effect on the market for the acquisition of broadcasting rights is negligible and that local broadcasters operate on a different advertizing market. However, as the revenues from television advertizing are partly influenced by the actual audience of the broadcaster and the local television stations are in a position to attract audiences away from their competitors, there is—according to the Commission—at least an indirect effect on the commercial revenues of the other broadcasters and hence a potential effect on intra-Community trade. Such reasoning seems far-fetched and almost rules out the possibility that a measure benefiting public service broadcasters could not have a negative effect on intra-Ccommunity trade.

The Commission did take the *Ferring* case into consideration in its decision in the BBC digital services case, even if the decision shows a level of ambiguity on the matter. The Commission first conducted its traditional State aid analysis, after which the new case law of *Ferring* was explained and implemented. However, in the final part of the decision the Commission shortly demonstrated that even if the measure were to be considered as State aid, it would be compatible with the Treaty on the basis of Article 86(2) EC.[49] The precarious nature of the *Ferring* precedent undoubtedly incited the Commission to be cautious, hence the ambiguity of the decision.

It is also no surprise that the definition of the remit and the formal entrustment of this remit to the public service broadcaster are important elements of both decisions. As for the definition of the remit, the decisions only confirm the principles set out in the Communication, making it clear that discussions on whether entertainment programmes and new services can be part of the public service remit definitely belong to the past. Moreover, the analysis by the Commission in the BBC case shows that even a public service broadcaster may create of a number of specialized channels which do not all cover the whole spectrum of programmes indicated in the public service remit. As for the entrustment of the remit, the Commission stated in the BBC case that it 'regrets' that the extension of the remit was only effected by letter and was not formalized in the relevant legal documents. According to the decision, 'the Commission considers that a clear and precise identification of the activities covered by the public service remit, and the conditions under which such activities have to be performed, is important for non-public service operators, so that they can plan their activities'. This concern for transparency was already formulated in the Communication. However, the wording used by the Commission in the decision shows that such a formalization of the entrustment cannot be legally imposed upon the Member States.

Finally, the proportionality of the measures notified to the Commission was assessed. In line with its Communication, the Commission emphasized that the

---

[49] See para 55 of the decision.

measure should be necessary for the fulfilment of the net cost of the public service remit and that there should be no over-compensation, cross-subsidization, or any other behaviour by the broadcaster which could distort competition. The Commission rightly determined that in an *ex ante* analysis it cannot determine any distortions of competition, but that adequate supervisory mechanisms should be put in place to prevent any such undue distortion of competition. According to the Commission, both the Belgian and British authorities had complied with this requirement.

The BBC case shows that the *Ferring* ruling has placed the Commission in a dilemma. On one hand the Commission has no choice but to implement the case law of the Courts, but on the other hand it is uncertain whether this case law will be confirmed by the Court in the *GEMO* and *Altmark* cases. It seems that the Commission is, for the time being, unwilling to take a Community position on public service compensation. In fact this has even obliged the Commission to delay its regulatory work in the field of services of general economic interest.[50] This may also imply that the Commission will postpone the adoption of any final decision in a number of outstanding complaints in the broadcasting sector.

The question remains, though, what impact a possible confirmation of the *Ferring* case will have on the content of the Communication. The Commission has already explained that, even if *Ferring* is upheld, an explanatory text indicating for instance the methods for the calculation of the cost of public service would be advisable to increase legal certainty. In this author's opinion the confirmation of the *Ferring* precedent will require that the Commission reconsider the premiss of the Communication. The substantive part of the Communication on the application of Article 86(2) EC will remain unchanged. The impact of the *Ferring* doctrine will in practice be felt mainly at the procedural level, an aspect which is not addressed in the Communication at all.

[50] Commission Report to the Seville European Council 'On the status of work on the guidelines for state aid and services of general economic interest', D(2002) para 10.

# REMEDIES AND ENFORCEMENT

# 15

# Remedies in the European Courts

## LEO FLYNN[1]

## I. INTRODUCTION

The Court of Justice (hereafter the 'Court') and the Court of First Instance are faced with actions involving state aids on a regular basis. Although this litigation can arrive through several channels, the Court of First Instance deals with most cases in this field. That court's primacy, in numerical terms, is likely to be consolidated in the future. While the Court plays a secondary part in terms of the quantity of actions, it still has a steady flow of cases in this field, giving it the opportunity to confirm or clarify existing jurisprudence and to develop the principles governing the law on state aids. This chapter starts, therefore, by noting that the Court of First Instance is, from a practical standpoint, the most important forum for the determination of questions relating to state aid.

A second initial observation is that the adoption of Regulation 659/99, the legislative framework for the procedures under which state aid issues are to be investigated and assessed, will obviously generate new issues relating to remedies.[2] However, according to its second recital, that Regulation is intended to codify and reinforce the Commission's consistent practice for the application of Article 89 EC, in the form of certain procedural rules and principles adopted in accordance with the case law of the Court. As a result, although the case law discussed in this paper deals with the pre-Regulation period, that jurisprudence remains broadly applicable.

## II. CONTROL OF LEGALITY OF STATE AID DECISIONS BY THE COMMUNITY COURTS

### A. Article 230 EC

At present the Court has a general supervisory role as regards the legality of all measures adopted by the Community institutions. This jurisdiction is conferred

---

[1] Thanks are due to Friedrich Erlbacher for his comments on an earlier draft. All views expressed remain personal to the author.

[2] Council Regulation (EC) No 659/1999 of 22 March 1999 laying down detailed rules for the application of Article 93 of the EC Treaty, OJ 1999 L 83/1. See generally, Keppenne, '(R)évolution dans le système communautaire de contrôle des aides d'États', [1998] RMUE 125 and Sinnaeve and Slot, 'The new Regulation on State Aid Procedures', (1999) 36 CMLRev. 1153.

by Article 230 EC and is equivalent to both judicial review and constitutional review. This role is shared with the Court of First Instance. At present the demarcation between their respective spheres of jurisdiction is determined by the identity of the plaintiff who challenges the Community measure. Where an action is brought by a private party, that is, a natural or legal person (including a sub-national government entity),[3] the Court of First Instance has jurisdiction; the Court has jurisdiction where the action is brought by a Member State or by another Community institution.

In the field of State aid this concurrent jurisdiction means that a Commission decision can be challenged simultaneously before both courts. For example, when the Commission declares an aid unlawful, the Member State that has granted that aid would therefore bring its challenge before the Court while the aid's beneficiaries would go to the Court of First Instance. The Court might also be faced with a challenge by another Member State against a decision to declare a state aid compatible with the common market while the competitors of beneficiaries of such an authorized aid could seize the Court of First Instance.

Shared jurisdiction over substantive issues creates practical problems, particularly given the volume of actions seeking annulment of state aid decisions.[4] In order to avoid duplication of judicial effort and, more importantly, the risk of conflicting simultaneous judgments, one of the two Courts will suspend the procedures in the actions pending before it, leaving it to the other Court to issue judgment in the case(s) before it. Normally it is the Court that suspends its procedures.[5] This course of action is dictated in part by a practical consideration; when a Member State challenges the Commission decision before the Court it is also invariably a party before the Court of First Instance in any parallel proceedings. There is therefore little risk that the Court of First Instance will not know of the Member State's arguments.[6] A second concern that underlies this practice is

---

[3] See Case T-214/95 *Vlaams Gewest* v *Commission* [1998] ECR II-717, para. 28: '[T]he term Member State, for the purposes of the institutional provisions and, in particular, those relating to proceedings before the courts, refers only to government authorities of the Member States of the European Communities and cannot include governments of regions or autonomous communities, irrespective of the powers which they may have. [ . . . ] By contrast, since it has legal personality under Belgian national law [the Flemish Region] must, on that basis, be treated as a legal person within the meaning of the [fourth] paragraph of Article [230 EC].'

[4] Of the 449 actions for annulment brought by Member States up to March 2001, 20% concerned state aid. See P. van Nuffel, 'What's in a Member State? Central and Decentralized Authorities before the Community Courts', (2001) 38 CMLRev. 871.

[5] However, it is possible for the Court of First Instance to surrender jurisdiction over an action brought by a private person, allowing the case to be transferred to the Court and to be joined to parallel proceedings commenced by a Member State; see e.g. Joined Cases C-15/98 and C-105/99 *Italy and Sardegna Lines* v *Commission* [2000] ECR I-8855.

[6] Note that observations of an intervening party are limited to supporting the form of order sought by the party in whose support they have intervened. See Article 37, EC Statute of the Court, and Article 93(1) and (5) ECJ Rules of Procedure. However, since the form of order will be that of an annulment of the decision under attack, this limitation is not of major significance in this field.

As to the rights of interveners at first instance in a subsequent appeal, see Case C-390/95 P *Antillean Rice Mills* v *Commission* [1999] ECR I-769, paras. 17–24; such interveners are not restricted by the original principal parties to the action at first instance as to the form of order they can seek.

one of principle, namely that private parties are entitled to a double degree of judicial protection in judicial review actions.[7] If the Court proceeded while the Court of First Instance suspended, the risk would arise that the Court's judgment would in effect bind the Court of First Instance (or create the risk of conflicting findings of fact by the two courts); this prospect might diminish the level of protection offered to the individuals bringing an action before the latter court.

The Court's practice of suspending the proceedings before it is now well established. In recent years, this course of action has been followed, for example, in relation to aids to Volkswagen,[8] to Italian road hauliers,[9] and to West-deutsches Landesbank.[10] However, it significantly lengthens the time taken by the Court to give judgment on the validity of the impugned Commission decision. Suspension necessarily defers a final ruling by the Court. Further delay flows from the fact that the judgment of the Court of First Instance is, almost invariably, appealed in such parallel state aid cases, and both the appeal and the action for annulment are dealt with in tandem.

Whether the proposals to change the balance of jurisdiction between the Court and the Court of First Instance comes to fruit is an open question at the present time.

## B. Article 234 EC

As regards Article 234 proceedings, the Court has exclusive competence to rule on questions of interpretation of EC law and of the validity of EC law measures that are posed by national courts arising out of litigation before them. Questions relating to the state aid rules may arise before national courts in several ways. Because the prohibition in Article 88(3) EC on new aid being granted prior to notification to, and approval by, the Commission is of direct effect,[11] interpretation of the state aid rules may be posed in litigation commenced by competitors or other third parties objecting to the alleged aid. The requirement to recover aids illegally granted using the mechanisms established under national law also

---

[7] See Council Decision 88/591 of 24 October 1988 establishing a Court of First Instance of the European Communities, OJ 1988 L 319/1, fourth recital: 'Whereas, in respect of actions requiring close examination of complex facts, the establishment of a second court will improve the judicial protection of individual interests'.

[8] Case C-301/96 *Germany* v *Commission (Mosel and Chemnitz)*, pending, which was suspended while the Court of First Instance dealt with challenges to the same decision in Joined Cases T-132/96 and T-143/96 *Freistaat Sachsen* v *Commission* [1999] ECR II-3663.

[9] Case C-372/97 *Italy* v *Commission (Italian road hauliers)*, pending, which was suspended while the Court of First Instance dealt with challenges to the same decision in Case T-288/97 *Regione autonoma Friuli-Venezia Giulia* v *Commission* [2001] ECR II-1871, judgment of 4 April 2001 and in Joined Cases T-298/97, T-312/97, T-313/97, T-315/97, T-600–607/97, T-1/9, T-3–6/98, and T-23/98 *Alzetta* v *Commission* [2000] ECR II-2319.

[10] Case C-376/99 *Germany* v *Commission (Westdeutsche Landesbank)*, pending, which was suspended until the Court of First Instance dealt with Joined Cases T-228/99 and T-233/99 *Westdeutsche Landesbank Girozentrale* v *Commission* [2003 ECR II-0000, judgment of 3 March 2003].

[11] Case C-354/90 *FNCEPA* v *Commission* [1991] ECR I-5505, para. 14.

creates a possibility of state aid decisions being challenged in a national court by the beneficiary of the aid. These situations create distinct problems.

Where a national court is called on to apply the state aid rules, it may make use of the Notice on co-operation between national courts and the Commission in the state aid field.[12] If the national court has doubts about the interpretation of the state aid rules, it is free to make a reference to the Court.[13]

Because a national court has the competence to determine whether new state aid, subject to the obligation of notification, exists,[14] the possibility arises that the Commission may take a decision as to whether there is state aid, which is challenged before the Court or the Court of First Instance, while the same issue is litigated before a national court. *Masterfoods* deals with the management of such overlapping jurisdiction in the field of competition law and offers some guidance as to the general principles that are applicable to such situations.[15] The Court held that a national court must not reach a conclusion that is contrary to a decision of the Commission. In order to fulfil the role assigned to it by the Treaty, the Commission cannot be bound by a decision given by a national court in application of Articles 81(1) and 82 EC. The Commission is therefore entitled to adopt at any time individual decisions under Articles 81 and 82 EC, even where an agreement or practice has already been the subject of a judgment by a national court and the decision contemplated by the Commission conflicts with that judgment. On foot of the obligation of loyal co-operation under Article 10 EC, national courts must, in order to avoid reaching a decision that runs counter to that of the Commission, stay proceedings pending final judgment in the action for annulment by the Community Courts. An exception is contemplated by the Court: a national court need not stay proceedings if it considers that, in the circumstances of the case, a reference for a preliminary ruling on the decision's validity is warranted.

This analysis seems transposable to Articles 87(1) and 88(3) EC. It must be noted that the addressee of a State aid decision is the Member State and that this extends to all organs of the State, including the national court itself. That factor implies that, in most cases where a potential overlap of assessment arises, there are even stronger reasons than in *Masterfoods* for a suspension by the national court pending the determination of the validity of the Commission's decision. Even in exceptional cases, where the national court examines a state aid decision relating to another Member State, the *Masterfoods* logic remains applicable.[16]

---

[12] OJ 1995 C 312/8.

[13] See e.g. Case C-379/98 *PreussenElektra* [2001] ECR I-2099, paras. 48–51.

[14] See Joined Cases C-72/91 and C-73/91 *Sloman Neptun* [1993] ECR I-887, paras. 11 and 12.

[15] Case C-344/98 *Masterfoods Ltd* v *HB Ice Cream* [2000] ECR I-11369.

[16] The perils of not following the *Masterfoods* can be seen in litigation relating to a Commission decision refusing an exemption from Article 81 EC to the Trans-Atlantic Liner Conference. The Court of First Instance was seized with an annulment action against the decision (Case T-395/94 *Atlantic Container Line AB*) that was suspended when a reference on the same decision was received from the High Court of England and Wales in 1995 (Case C-339/95 *Compagnia di Navigazione Marittima*). However, that reference was withdrawn in 1998, on the day before the Advocate General was to deliver his Opinion. The final judgment of the Court of First Instance in Case T-395/94 was delivered on 28 February 2002, over seven years after it was lodged.

Where the national court is faced with a challenge to the validity of a Community measure, as a general rule it must, where it has doubts about that measure's validity, refer this issue to the Court.[17] However, in *TWD* the Court ruled that a party who could have challenged the validity of a decision on state aid but failed to do so within the time-limits cannot sidestep those limits by means of proceedings in the national courts.[18] This limitation applies beyond the domain of state aid decisions, and resolves a potential conflict between the twin avenues of judicial control under Articles 230 and 234 EC in favour of the legal certainty provided for in the strict conditions governing the admissibility of annulment actions.

*TWD* is a significant practical obstacle to the invocation of Article 234 EC, especially given what is, for many legal advisers, the arcane nature of rules on standing under Article 230 EC.[19] It is also worth noting what is, from a practical perspective, the other major disadvantage of proceeding before a national court, namely that the ambit of any later examination of the decision's validity by the Court is determined by that request for a preliminary ruling. As a result, it is possible that not all the grounds of invalidity invoked before the national court by the parties will be raised before the Court; in essence, the parties lose control in this procedure, which is based on dialogue between the respective courts.

However, even if the parties fail to raise a point relating to the existence of an illegal state aid, it was suggested by Advocate General Geelhoed in *ARAP* that the Community judge is bound to deal with this point of his own motion.[20] Certain difficult issues arise if this premise is accepted. For example, does this obligation cover only respect for essential procedural requirements or does it also extend to, as the Advocate General suggests, the substantive respect of the state aid rules?[21] Moreover, does it make a difference to this obligation if the parties have not raised this issue because they are unable to do so, under *TWD* for example, as opposed to being unwilling to make that case or being unaware of it? In any event, the Court did not follow him on this point, nor indeed did it allude to his suggestion.

## C. Other forms of action

Article 232 EC provides a remedy where an institution has been called on to act and has failed to do so within two months contrary to Community law. Member

---

[17] Case 314/85 *Foto-Frost v Hauptzollamt Lübeck-Ost* [1987] ECR 4199.

[18] Case C-188/92 *TWD Textilwerke Deggendork v Germany* [1994] ECR I-833. This ruling was confirmed in Case C-178/95 *Wiljo v Belgian State* [1997] ECR I-585.

[19] This issue is raised in Joined Cases C-261/01 and C-262/01 *Van Calster*, pending, in which the Hof van Beroep Antwerpen asks if persons required to pay contributions under a Member State scheme which was authorized under the state rules are directly and individually concerned by the relevant Commission decision and whether they can raise the issue of lack of competence with regard to that measure.

[20] Case C-321/99 P *ARAP* [2002] ECR I-4287, Opinion of Advocate General Geelhoed, paras. 97–99, 189.

[21] Ibid, paras. 97–99

States may bring such an action, as may private persons who can show that the failure to act concerns a decision that would have been addressed to them. The Commission is under no obligation to commence Article 226 EC proceedings against Member States so a failure to take enforcement actions under this provision cannot be the subject of an Article 232 action. In respect of a complaint that initiates Article 88(2) EC proceedings, the Commission is under an obligation of good administration which requires it to adopt a decision.[22]

The Community institutions may be sued for causing non-contractual losses before the Court under Article 288(2) EC. Community law determined on the basis of principles common to the Member States governs such liability, and the applicant must show that an unlawful act or omission caused the loss.[23] The Commission could be liable if it knowingly approved unlawful state aid or if it ignored illegal implementation of aid. However, it would be very difficult to satisfy the causation requirement. For example, in *Société des Produits Bertrand* the applicants were unable to show that there was a causal link between aid given to its competitors in Italy and a decline in its own sales in France.[24] Similarly, in *BAI II* the applicant failed to show a causal link between the wrong allegedly committed by the Commission (delay in informing BAI of a decision to permit aid to its competitor such that it was unable to challenge the validity of that decision) and the claimed losses from that competitor's presence on the ferry rules it served.[25]

The Commission may decide to take infringement proceedings against a Member State for granting a state aid or failing to recover that aid. It has a choice of forms of action; it can proceed under Article 88(2) EC or under Article 226 EC;[26] the former derogates from the general infringement procedure and is adapted to the special nature of the state aid field.[27] Where a Member State fails to comply with a Court judgment finding that it has infringed its obligations under the Treaty, the Commission may, under Article 228(2) EC, bring a further action against that Member State requesting fines and penalty payments for this non-compliance. As yet, this facility has not been used in respect of state aids.

Finally, the Court or the Court of First Instance under Article 242 EC may also grant interim measures. This possibility is of little significance for state aid disputes. Of the seven such actions brought in the past four years[28] only one

---

[22] See Case T-95/96 *Gestevisión Telecinco* v *Commission* [1998] ECR II-3407.

[23] Case C-352/98 P *Bergaderm et Goupil* v *Commission* [2000] ECR I-5291, paras. 39–42; Case T-155/99 *Dieckmann & Hansen GmbH* v *Commission* [2001] ECR II-3143, paras. 40–46.

[24] Case 40/75 [1976] ECR 1.

[25] Case T-230/95 *BAI* v *Commission* [1999] ECR II-123, points 29–40.

[26] Indeed, where a national measure violates both the state aid rules and another Treaty provision, the Commission is free to bring actions using both procedures in respect of these distinct violations: see Case 73/79 *Commission* v *Italy* [1980] ECR 1533.

[27] Case C-35/88 *Commission* v *Greece* [1990] ECR I-3125.

[28] Case C-278/00 R *Greece* v *Commission (ANGO)* [2000] ECR I-8787; Case T-237/99 R *BP Nederland* v *Commission (Dutch Service Stations)* [2000] ECR II-3849; and Case T-111/01 R *Saxonia Edelmetalle* v *Commission* [2002] ECR II-2335; Joined Cases T-195/01 R and T-207/01 R *Government of Gibraltar* v *Commission* [2001] ECR II-3915; Case T-198/01 R *Technische Glaswerke Imenau* v *Commission* [2002] ECR II-2153; Case T-91/02 R *Klausner Nordic Timber* v *Commission* [2003] ECR II-0000, Order of 8 April 2003; and Case T-181/02 R *Neue Erba Lautex* v *Commission* [2002] ECR II-5081.

has been successful at first instance.[28a] In such cases the applicant can usually demonstrate that a *fumus boni juris* is present, but they are likely to fail on the urgency criterion. As to the latter, one obstacle is that damage caused to beneficiaries by removal of an aid, commonly invoked to show grave and irreparable harm, is of no effect in itself; the Court has stated in this context that the recovery of the aid is an inherent part of any decision stating the existence of an aid which is incompatible with the common market.[29] It is only where recovery would probably led, of itself, to the beneficiary's irreversible disappearance from the relevant market that grave and irreparable damage will be found.

## III. ANNULMENT PROCEEDINGS: WHAT CAN BE CHALLENGED

The admissibility of a direct action is dependent on the challengeable quality of the impugned measure and on the applicant having the requisite standing to challenge that measure. The first requirement has been less than straightforward to establish, given the wide variety of means by which the Commission may proceed in relation to state aids. The bright line in this area is offered by the rule that only a measure whose legal effects are binding on the applicant and are capable of affecting its interests is an act or decision that may be the subject of an action for annulment under Article 230 EC.[30] As a result, purely confirmatory decisions are not, in themselves, challengeable acts.

In respect of Regulation 659/99, the following are attackable acts:

- an Article 4(2) decision (measure is not an aid);[31]
- an Article 4(3) decision (measure is a compatible aid; decision not to raise objections);[32]
- an Article 4(4) decision (opening formal investigation procedure);[33]
- an Article 7(2) decision (after formal investigation procedure, measure is not an aid);[34]
- an Article 7(3) decision (after formal investigation procedure, measure is a compatible aid);
- an Article 7(4) decision (after formal investigation procedure, aid given conditional approval);

---

[28a] The Commission unsuccessfully appealed in Case C-232/02 P(R) *Commission* v *Technische Glaswenke Imenau* [2002] ECR I-8977.

[29] Case C-278/00 R *Greece* v *Commission (ANGO)* [2000] ECR I-8787, para. 21.

[30] See Case C-308/95 *Netherlands* v *Commission* [1999] ECR I-6547, para. 26.

[31] By analogy with the case law dealing with a decision that an aid does not require notification under Article 88(3) EC; Case C-313/90 *CIRFS* v *Commission* [1993] ECR I-1125.

[32] By analogy with the case law on decisions not to open the formal investigation procedure under Article 88(2) EC; Case C-225/91 *Matra* v *Commission* [1993] ECR I-3203.

[33] By analogy with case law dealing with a decision to open the formal investigation procedure under Article 88(2) EC; see Case C-312/90 *Spain* v *Commission (Cenemesa)* [1992] ECR I-4117, paras. 13 and 19 to 22 [a decision to open the formal investigation procedure depends on a categorization of the aid as 'new', as opposed to 'existing' (which is subject to Article 88(1) EC) aid, which has definite legal consequences; it is not merely a preparatory measure]; Case C-47/91 *Italy* v *Commission* [1992] ECR I-4145; and Case C-400/99 *Italy* v *Commission (Tirrenia)* [2001] ECR I-7303, paras. 56, 62.

[34] By analogy with case law on decisions terminating the formal investigation procedure under Article 88(2) EC; Case 169/84 *COFAZ* v *Commission* [1986] ECR 391.

- an Article 7(5) decision (after formal investigation procedure, negative decision);[35]
- an Article 9 decision (decision to withdraw previous decision);
- an Article 11(2) decision (provisional injunction to recover illegal aid);[36] and
- an Article 14 decision (decision not to order recovery of an illegal aid [note that there is an obligation to recover if an aid is illegal] )

A decision to extend the validity of a Community framework for State aid is also an attackable act.[37]

The following are probably not attackable measures:

- an Article 10(3) decision (injunction against Member State to provide further information during investigation into an illegal aid);
- a refusal to propose useful measures in relation to existing aids;[38]
- an Article 18 measure (proposal of useful measures in relation to existing aids);[39] and
- an Article 20(2) decision (decision not to pronounce in a case following a complaint).[40]

Thus it is possible to attack Commission decisions that approve or refuse to approve state aid, irrespective of the stage of the procedural cycle at which they are adopted, or which reject a complaint regarding alleged aid. However, it is important to recall that it is not sufficient that an act be attackable for an annulment action to admissible. It is therefore necessary to turn to the issue of standing.

## IV. ANNULMENT PROCEEDINGS: STANDING OF PRIVATE PARTIES

Private parties must, as has already been explained, bring their challenge to a Commission decision before the Court of First Instance. In order for a private party to have standing they must be either the addressee of a Commission decision or directly and individually concerned by a Commission decision. All decisions adopted by the Commission relating to State aids, including those not to open a formal examination procedure following a complaint, have as their sole addressees the Member States concerned.[41] Thus, a private party will necessarily have to demonstrate its direct and individual concern.

---

[35] By analogy with case law on decisions that an aid is not compatible with the common market; Case 730/79 *Philip Morris* v *Commission* [1980] ECR 2671.

[36] By analogy with case law dealing with decisions requiring repayment of an aid; Case C-303/88 *Italy* v *Commission (ENI-Lanerossi)* [1991] ECR I-1433.

[37] Case C-135/93 *Spain* v *Commission (Motor vehicle framework)* [1995] ECR I-1651.

[38] See Case T-330/94 *Salt Union* v *Commission* [1996] ECR II-1475, paras. 33–37.

[39] See Case T-330/94 *Salt Union* v *Commission* [1996] ECR II-1475, para. 35.

[40] Case T-182/96 *UPS Europe* v *Commission* [1999] ECR II-2857; the applicant must use Article 232 EC instead. Compare with Case C-400/99 *Italy* v *Commission (Tirrenia)* [2001] ECR I-0000, judgment of 9 October 2001.

[41] See Case C-367/97 P *Commission* v *Sytraval* [1998] ECR I-1719, para. 45. See Article 25, Regulation 659/1999.

## A. Beneficiaries

Where, in respect of a decision adopted by the Commission, national authorities do not have any discretion and the measures which they adopt merely constitute, as regards affected private parties, the implementation of that decision, those persons will be directly concerned within the meaning of Article 230(4) EC.[42] It is undisputed that beneficiaries and potential beneficiaries of aid will be directly concerned by the Commission decision requiring that an aid be recovered that is the consequence of a statement of its incompatibility with the common market.[43]

Direct concern is therefore not a major hurdle for the recipients of an aid who seek to demonstrate their *locus standi* before the Court of First Instance. However, establishing individual concern is more problematic for aid beneficiaries. There is no doubt that a decision that declares *individual State aids* to be incompatible with the common market constitutes a decision individually concerning the enterprise or enterprises that are specifically identified in that decision.[44] However, the situation is more complex where the decision under attack declares a *State aid regime* to be incompatible with the common market and requires the recovery of aid disbursed in application of that regime. The difficult issue here is whether such a decision individually concerns the firms that could have benefited or did benefit from such a regime.

Several judgments of the Court support a restrictive view of standing in these circumstances. In *DEFI* it was underlined that a system of aids does not identify the undertakings in whose favour the aid will be distributed and that as a result every enterprise which could quality for an aid under this scheme is concerned by the Commission's decision in the same way as all other undertakings within the given sector.[45] Subsequently, in *Van der Kooy*, the Court pointed out that the decision attacked concerned the applicants by reason of their objective status as horticultural firms established in the Netherlands who were entitled to obtain preferential tariffs for gas on the same basis as all other horticultural firms in the same situation.[46] The decision under attack was therefore, in respect of them, a measure of general scope applying to situations determined objectively and

---

[42] See, *inter alia*, Joined Cases 106 and 107/63 *Toepfer* [1965] ECR 405; Joined Cases 41 to 44/70 *International Fruit Company* v *Commission* [1971] ECR 411, paras. 23–28.

[43] See Case 730/79 *Philip Morris* v *Commission* [1980] ECR 2671, para. 5; Joined Cases 296 and 318/82 *Netherlands and Leeuwarder Papierwarenfabriek* v *Commission* [1985] ECR 809, para. 13. As regards the situation of competitors see also Case T-435/93 *ASPEC* v *Commission* [1995] ECR II-1281, paras. 60 and 61; and Case T-442/93 *AAC* v *Commission* [1995] ECR II-1329, paras. 45 and 46.

[44] See Case C-730/79 *Philip Morris* v *Commission* [1980] ECR 2671, para. 5; Joined Cases C-296/82 and C-318/82 *Netherlands and Leeuwarder Papierwarenfabriek* [1985] ECR 809, para. 13. See also Case C-188/92 *TWD Textilwerke Deggendorf* [1994] ECR I-833, para. 14; Case C-241/95 *Accrington Beef* [1996] ECR I-6699, para. 16; and Case C-408/95 *Eurotunnel* [1994] ECR I-6315, para. 28. See also Joined Cases T-131/95 and T-413/96 *Freistaat Sachsen* v *Commission* [1999] ECR II-3663 and Case T-72/98 *Astilleros Zamacona* v *Commission* [2000] ECR II-1683.

[45] Case 282/85 *DEFI* v *Commission* [1986] ECR 2475, para. 16.

[46] Joined Cases 67, 68, and 70/85 *Van der Kooy* v *Commission* [1988] ECR 219, paras. 14 to 16.

involving legal effects with regard to a category of persons outlined in a general and abstract manner.[47] In *Federmineraria* the Court ruled that the impugned decision, relating to transport aid, affected not only the applicant's interests but also those of railways whose competitive position with regard to other modes of transport was favoured by the existence of a reduced tariff.[48] This decision also affected transport firms, as well as their clients who might have to support all or part of the transport costs. One could not therefore consider that it affected operators whose numbers were limited or determinable at the moment when that decision was adopted.[49]

A similar analytical framework is evident in judgments given by the Court of First Instance. In *Kahn Scheepvaart* it noted that the challenged decision had, as regards the potential beneficiaries of the aid, the character of a measure of general interests applying to situations determined objectively and having legal effects with regard to a category of persons envisaged in an abstract and general manner.[50] *Arbeitsgemeinschaft Deutscher Luftfahrt-Unternehmen*, where the impugned decision dealt with fiscal provisions of a general scope, shows that such a decision may be considered, as regards the potential beneficiaries of that regime, as a general measure applying to objectively determined situations.[51] As a result an undertaking benefiting from such measures could not claim that the advantage of which it is deprived by the decision is of an individual character. Most recently, *Mitteldeutsche Erdoel-Raffinerie* seems to start from the same premise,[52] although in that case it was held that the beneficiary of the aid was individually concerned by the decision because it could show that it was in a situation that differentiated it from all other operators.[53]

A significantly more liberal approach to standing can be seen in *CETM*,[54] a judgment of the Court of First Instance, and in *Sardegna Lines*, a Court judgment.[55] In both cases, an action by a private party was found to be admissible because they, or their members, were actual beneficiaries of individual aid granted under the impugned aid scheme, the recovery of which had been ordered

---

[47] Joined Cases 67, 68, and 70/85 *Van der Kooy v Commission* [1988] ECR 219, para. 15.

[48] Case C-6/92 *Federmineraria v Commission* [1993] ECR I-6357, paras. 11 to 16.

[49] See also Case C-106/98 P *Comité d'entreprise de la Société française de productions v Commission* [2000] ECR I-3659.

[50] Case T-398/94 *Kahn Scheepvaart v Commission* [1996] ECR II-477, paras. 39 and 43.

[51] Case T-86/96 *Arbeitsgemeinschaft Deutscher Luftfahrt-Unternehmen v Commission* [1999] ECR II-179, paras. 42 to 54.

[52] Case T-9/98 *Mitteldeutsche Erdoel-Raffinerie GmbH v Commission* [2001] ECR I-3367, paras. 73–77.

[53] Ibid, paras. 78–85. These factors were that a) the applicant definitely qualified for the aid available under the scheme; b) the scheme was adopted with the applicant's situation specifically in mind; c) that situation was expressly brought to the attention of the Commission during negotiation; and d) the German government proposed to apply the scheme to the applicant alone.

[54] Case T-55/99 *Confederación Española de Transporte de Mercancías v Commission* [2000] ECR II-3207, paras. 22 to 25.

[55] Joined Cases C-15/98 and C-105/99 *Italy and Sardegna Lines v Commission* [2000] ECR I-8855, paras. 31 to 35.

by the Commission. The Court of First Instance in *Alzetta* used a similarly generous analysis of the standing of aid scheme beneficiaries.[56]

Finally, it should be noted that the consequence of finding that the beneficiary of an aid has standing to challenge the Commission's decision before the Court of First Instance can be disadvantageous to that applicant because of the *TWD* doctrine.[57] Where an applicant had the opportunity to challenge a Commission decision and failed to do so within the time-limits set out in Article 230 EC, it is not free to impugn that decision's validity in subsequent proceedings before national courts in the hope of obtaining an Article 234 reference.[58] As a result it may be that an absence of standing before the Court of First Instance is, on balance, advantageous.[59]

## B. Competitors

As already stated, it is difficult for third parties to bring an admissible challenge against a Commission decision that authorizes a state aid.[60] As a result, competitors are unlikely to satisfy the criterion of individual concern. However, a distinction must be drawn between the preliminary stage of the procedure for reviewing aid under Article 88(3) EC, which is intended merely to allow the Commission to form a *prima facie* opinion on the partial or complete compatibility of the aid in question, and the formal investigation procedure under Article 88(2) EC. The Commission is obliged under the latter examination, which is designed to enable the Commission to be fully informed of all the facts of the case, to give concerned parties notice to submit their comments.[61] The Court ruled in *Cook*[62] and in *Matra*[63] that because the persons intended to enjoy the procedural guarantees set out in Article 88(2) EC would lose the benefit of those guarantees where the Commission adopts a decision of compatibility under Article 88(3) EC without initiating the formal investigation procedure, those persons must be able to challenge such a decision of the Commission before the Court. Therefore, an action for the annulment of a decision taken on the basis of Article 88(3) EC, brought by a party concerned within the meaning of Article 88(2) EC, will be admissible where that action seeks to safeguard those procedural rights under Article 88(2) EC.

---

[56] Joined Cases T-298/97, T-312/97, T-313/97, T-315/97, T-600 to T-607/97, T-1/98, T-3/98 to T-6/98, and T-23/98 *Alzetta* v *Commission* [2000] ECR II-2319.

[57] Case C-188/92 *TWD Textilwerke Deggendork* v *Germany* [1994] ECR I-833.

[58] See also Case C-178/95 *Wiljo* v *Belgian State* [1997] ECR I-585.

[59] Note Cases C-262/01 *Van Calster* and C-262/01 *NV Openbaar Slachthuis*, both pending, in which the Hof van Beroep Antwerpen raises the issue of whether persons who were required to pay charges under a national law which was approved by the Commission are directly and individually concerned.

[60] See Case 169/84 *Cofaz and Others* v *Commission* [1986] ECR 391, para. 22; Case T-11/95 *BP Chemicals* v *Commission* [1998] ECR II-3235, para. 71; and Joined Cases T-132/96 and T-143/96 *Freistaat Sachsen and Others* v *Commission* [1999] ECR II-3663, para. 83.

[61] Case T-188/95 *Waterleiding Maatschappij* v *Commission* [1998] ECR II-3713, para. 52.

[62] Case C-198/91 *Cook* v *Commission* [1993] ECR I-2487, para. 23.

[63] Case C-225/91 *Matra* v *Commission* [1993] ECR I-3203, para. 17.

   This possibility leads to the question of who is a 'party concerned' within the meaning of Article 88(2) EC. The case law establishes that this group covers not merely the beneficiaries of the aid but also those persons, undertakings, or associations whose interests might be affected by the grant of the aid, in particular competing undertakings and trade associations.[64] However, in order for its action to be admissible, a competitor of the recipient of the aid must demonstrate that its competitive position in the market is affected by the grant of the aid.[65] Direct competitors of the aid's recipients overcome this test relatively easily; however, the mere fact that an applicant's business is or would be affected by the aid does not suffice to overcome this hurdle.[66]

   As regards associations of competitors, their position as regards standing is neither better nor worse than that of their constituent members.[67] It is not possible, therefore, to claim individual concern by demonstrating that all persons affected by the decision are grouped together in an association.

   Finally, it is worth observing that where a competitor seeks to attack an existing aid, rather than a new aid, its options are extremely limited. Unless it can show that the conditions under which the aid has been given do not respect the conditions imposed by the Commission (so that the aid is, in effect, new)[68] it is faced with several obstacles. If the Commission informs it that the aid respects the conditions of the authorization, the true source of the competitor's problems is the original authorization decision which will no longer be attackable. Moreover, while the Commission has an obligation to monitor existing aids, it is not obliged to adopt decisions in respect of them. Given that most aids granted in the Community are covered by existing schemes, in practical terms this hurdle can create severe difficulties for competitors.

## C. Other third parties

Given the difficulties faced by competitors, it is not surprising that parties other than competitors rarely have standing to challenge a Commission decision relating to state aid. The Court confirmed that position in *Landbouwschap* in relation to annulment proceedings brought by a group of undertakings not in competition with the recipients of an environmental aid approved by the Commission who sought to obtain the same aid for themselves.[69] The Court ruled their application inadmissible on the basis that they had no interest in acting

---

[64] Case 323/82 *Intermills* v *Commission* [1984] ECR 3809, para. 16, and Case C-367/95 P *Commission* v *Sytraval and Brink's France* [1998] ECR I-1719, para. 41. See Article 1(h) Regulation 659/1999.

[65] Case T-69/96 *Hamburger Hafen und Lagerhaus Aktiengesellschaft* v *Commission* [2001] ECR II-1037, para. 41.

[66] Ibid, paras. 42–48.

[67] Joined Cases 19/62 to 22/62 *Fédération nationale de la boucherie en gros et du commerce en gros des viandes and Others* v *Council* [1962] ECR 491; Case C-321/95 P *Greenpeace Council and Others* v *Commission* [1998] ECR I-1651, paras. 14 and 29.

[68] Case C-47/91 *Italy* v *Commission (Italgrani)* [1994] ECR I-4635.

[69] Case C-295/92 *Landbouwschap* v *Commission* [1991] ECR I-5003.

against the decision (raising, in effect, a prior obstacle to their action), adding that they produced no evidence of being directly or individually concerned.[70]

## D. Complainants

There is a body of case law that provides for a more lenient approach to standing where an applicant shows that it was involved in the procedure leading to the adoption of the challenged decision. This exception arises principally where the applicant can show that it participated in the formal investigation procedure under Article 88(2) EC as a complainant.[71] Where a Commission decision refuses to open the formal investigation procedure set out in Article 88(2) EC, the complainant cannot obtain respect of that provision's procedural guarantees except by contesting such a decision before the Community judge.[72] On the other hand, where the Commission adopts its decision at the end of the formal investigation procedure, interested third parties have in effect benefited from their procedural guarantees; they can therefore no longer be considered by reason of that sole quality as being individually concerned by the final decision.[73]

## E. Absence of remedies at national level

The restrictive rules on standing mean that a party may consider itself to be left without legal remedy, before either the Community or the national courts, in order to challenge the aid. The Court of First Instance has held that the absence of an effective remedy before the national courts cannot constitute a ground for expanding *locus standi*.[74] The Court has also taken this view, in the past.[75] The Court emphatically confirmed that position in *Unión de Pequeños Agricultures*.[75a]

## F. Intervening parties

Finally, the situation of intervening parties in admissible actions should also be mentioned. Member States and institutions have an unrestricted right of intervention while other persons are permitted to intervene in cases that involve private parties where they establish an interest in the case.[76] This requirement

[70] Ibid, paras. 12 and 13.
[71] See Case 169/84 *Cofaz* [1986] ECR 391; Case C-313/90 *CIRFS v Commission* [1993] ECR I-1125.
[72] Case T-86/96 *Arbeitsgemeinschaft Deutscher Luftfahrt-Unternehmen v Commission* [1999] ECR II-179, paras. 42 to 54.
[73] Ibid, para. 49.
[74] See Case T-398/94 *Kahn Scheepvaart v Commission* [1996] ECR II-477, para. 50; Case T-86/96 *Arbeitsgemeinschaft Deutscher Luftfahrt-Unternehmen and Hapag-Lloyd* [1999] ECR II-179, para. 52.
[75] Case C-300/00 P *Federación de Cofradías de Pescadores de Guipúzcoa* [2000] ECR I-8797, para. 37. Contrast Case C-321/95 *Greenpeace Stichting* [1998] ECR I-1651, paras. 32 and 33.
[75a] Case C-500/00 P *Unión de Pequeños Agricultores v Council* [2002] ECR I-6677.
[76] Article 37 EC Statute of the Court of Justice.

sets the bar for participation in a case at a far lower level than that to be surmounted in demonstrating direct and individual concern. However, the intervener is restricted in the scope of their submissions: these must be limited to supporting the submissions of the party on whose behalf they have intervened.[77] One consequence of this restriction is that the absence of any limitation on the right of a Member State to bring an action for annulment does not render admissible an action brought by a private party in which that Member State intervenes.[78]

## V. TIME-LIMITS

Any action for annulment is subject to the two-month limit laid down in Article 230 EC. This period runs from the date on which the party had knowledge of the decision in question; the Court of First Instance has held that this requires that the applicant have exact knowledge of the reasons for the contested act so as to permit them to exercise their right of challenge.[79] However, exact knowledge does not require that the applicant had knowledge of all elements of the decision, but merely the essential aspects of its contents.[80] Thus, for example, in *Dreyfus* the Court of First Instance held that a telex that contained two brief extracts from a Commission decision addressed to a third party could not cause the time-limits under Article 230 EC to begin to run.[81]

The starting point from which these time-limits are set in motion is not easy to identify in the cases of decisions adopted, without the opening of a formal investigation procedure, under Article 4(2) (no aid) and (3) (compatible aid) of Regulation 659/1999. Although a brief communication of the decision must be published in the Official Journal,[82] this does not set out the full text of the decision. On the other hand, the full text is made available on the Internet; that publication could be taken as the starting point for an annulment action.[83]

There is a second relevant time-limit, that concerning the period of grace under the Rules of Procedure. The prescribed time-limits are extended to take account of delay for distance by ten days; this grace period now applies to all parties.[84] These

---

[77] See Article 93(1) and (5) ECJ Rules of Procedure.

[78] See Case T-138/98 *ACAV* v *Commission* [2000] ECR II-341.

[79] Case C-102/92 *Ferriere Acciaierie Sarde* v *Commission* [1993] ECR I-801, para. 18.

[80] Case T-468/93 *Frinli* v *Commission* [1994] ECR II-33, para. 32.

[81] Joined Cases T-485/93, T-491/93, T-494/93, and T-61/98 *Dreyfus* [2000] ECR I-3569, paras. 50–52.

[82] Article 26, Regulation 659/1999.

[83] Keppenne, 'Une vue d'ensemble des règles de procédure de l'article 88 CE et commentaires sur leur application depuis l'entrée en vigueur du Règlement 659/1999', in *European Competition Law: A new role of the Member States* (Bruylant: Brussels, 2000), 224. On the time-limits generally, see Case C-122/95 *Germany* v *Council* [1998] ECR I-973, paras. 35–39. Applied in Case T-14/96 *BAI* v *Commission* [1999] ECR II-139, Case T-110/97 *Kneissle Dachtein Sportartikel* v *Commission* [1999] ECR II-2881, and Case T-123/97 *Salomon* v *Commission* [1999] ECR II-2925.

[84] Article 81(2) ECJ Rules of Procedure; Article 102(2) CFI Rules of Procedure.

time-limits are of strict application;[85] when dismissing an action brought by Ireland because its application had arrived after the time-limit under Article 230 EC had expired,[86] the Court, without ruling on that government's claim of *force majeure*, held that these rules were not to be waived where the application was delayed because of an unforeseen air transport strike.[87]

## VI. Annulment proceedings: Extent of review

The grounds of annulment under Article 230 EC are: lack of competence, infringement of an essential procedural requirement, infringement of the Treaty or of any rule of law relating to its application, or misuse of powers.

### A. Substantive control

A distinction must be made between the various substantive elements underlying a state aid decision. The existence of the factual components of a state aid, such as the transfer of state resources, is a question that is objective in nature and is subject to a strict control by the reviewing courts.[88] However, the extent of review of the substance of a decision on state aid is limited where a complex economic appraisal is involved. Where the reviewing court is asked to annul a decision relating to the existence of a state aid, it must confine itself to verifying whether the Commission complied with the relevant rules governing procedure and the statement of reasons, whether the facts on which the contested finding was based have been accurately stated, and whether there has been any manifest error of assessment or misuse of powers.[89] Similarly, in determining whether an aid should be permitted under Article 87(3) EC, the Commission must weigh the beneficial effects of the aid against its adverse effects on trading conditions and the maintenance of undistorted competition.[90] In so doing, it has a wide discretion to allow aid, following an examination that entails consideration and appreciation of complex economic facts and conditions; as a consequence, the level of review is relatively light.[91]

Where a manifest error of assessment of the facts is alleged, the burden of proof lies on the party who raises this plea.

---

[85] Case 276/85 *Cladakis* v *Commission* [1987] ECR 495.　　[86] Eleven days late.

[87] Case C-239/97 *Ireland* v *Commission* [1998] ECR I-2655.

[88] Similarly, verification of the existence of those facts which underlie a decision under Article 87(2) EC is an objective question, subject to strict control: see Joined Cases T-132/96 and T-146/96 *Freistaat Saschsen* v *Commission* [1999] ECR II-3663, point 148.

[89] See Case C-56/93 *Belgium* v *Commission* [1996] ECR I-723, para. 11.

[90] Joined Cases C-278/92 to C-280/92 *Spain* v *Commission* [1994] ECR I-4103, para. 51.

[91] See Case 730/79 *Philip Morris* [1980] ECR 2671, para. 17 and 24; Case C-142/87 *Belgium* v *Commission (Tubemeuse)* [1990] ECR I-959, para. 56; and Case C-303/88 *Italy* v *Commission* [1991] ECR I-1433, para. 34.

## B. Review of procedural requirements

While there is a relatively light level of scrutiny in relation to the substance of a state aid decision, stricter control is exercised as regards the Commission's obligation to respect the relevant procedural requirements. This higher level of judicial review is a direct consequence of the fact that these procedures offer the sole mechanism by which interested parties may participate in the decision-making process. However, it must be noted that the violation of these rules does not, by itself, suffice to ground a successful action for annulment; the applicant must show that in the absence of this breach, the procedure would have led to a different outcome.[92] The question also arises whether a party can raise a plea based on the failure to respect the procedural rights of another person.[93]

Procedural requirements that have been successfully invoked against Commission decisions include:

- failure to open formal investigation procedure under Article 88(2) EC where serious doubts as to the compatibility of the aid with other Treaty provisions are raised;[94]
- excessive length of time taken to open formal investigation procedure under Article 88(2) EC after the national authorities have provided enough information to allow the Commission to carry out its preliminary examination under Article 88(3) EC;[95]
- excessive length of time taken to conduct the formal investigation procedure under Article 88(2) EC;[96]
- violation of the right to be heard[97] or the rights of the defence;[98] and
- violation of the principle of collegiality through the adoption of a state aid decision involving complex factual and legal questions by means of the habilitation procedure.[99]

---

[92] Case 40/85 *Belgium* v *Commission (Boch II)* [1986] ECR 2321, paras. 30–31, and Case C-142/97 *Germany* v *Commission (Jadekost)* [2000] ECR I-8237, para. 99–106.

[93] Advocate General Lenz took the view in Cases 62 and 72/87 *Exécutif régional wallon and SA Glaverbel* v *Commission* [1988] ECR 1573, point 15, that they could not do so and advised the Court that a third party could not invoke the non-respect of a Member State's procedural rights. The Court, however, rejected this plea on its substance, stating that there was no violation of rights of the defence, (para. 37), and added that because the person raising the plea (the Walloon Regional Authority) was to be regarded as acting for the Belgian government which held information that the Region claimed had been withheld, it could not be regarded as unaware of this information (para. 38).

[94] Case C-204/97 *Portugal* v *Commission (French eau-de-vie)* [2001] ECR I-3175, paras. 41–49.

[95] Case C-99/98 *Austria* v *Commission (Villach)* [2001] ECR I-1101, paras. 73–76.

[96] Case C-223/85 *RSV* v *Commission* [1987] ECR 4617. See Article 7(6), Regulation 659/1999.

[97] The extent of the right to be heard varies depending on the nature of the person's involvement in the procedural leading to the contested decision: See Joined Cases T-371/94 and T-394/94 *British Airways* v *Commission* [1998] ECR II-2405, paras. 59–64, and Case T-613/97 *Ufex* v *Commission* [2000] ECR II-4055, para. 89. In general terms, these rights are not as extensive in the field of state aid as in that of competition law.

[98] Case 40/85 *Belgium* v *Commission (Boch II)* [1986] ECR 2321, paras. 28–30.

[99] Case T-435/93 *ASPEC* v *Commission* [1995] ECR II-1281, paras. 100–124.

## C. Adequacy of reasoning

When the statement of reasons underlying a decision is reviewed, the two strands of jurisprudence relating to substantive content and proper procedures come together. The Court carefully distinguishes the obligation to state reasons, which is an essential procedural requirement, from the question whether the reasons given are correct, which goes to the substantive legality of the contested measure. The statement of reasons required by Article 253 EC must be appropriate to the act at issue and must disclose in a clear and unequivocal fashion the reasoning followed by the institution which adopted the measure in question in such a way as to enable the persons concerned to ascertain the reasons for the measure and to enable the competent court to exercise its power of review.[100] The stringency of that requirement is dependent on the circumstances of each case, in particular the content of the measure in question, the nature of the reasons given, and the interest which the addressees of the measure, or other parties to whom it is of direct and individual concern, may have in obtaining explanations. It is not necessary for the reasoning to go into all the relevant facts and points of law, since the question whether the statement of reasons meets the requirements of Article 253 EC must be assessed with regard not only to its wording but also to its context and to all the legal rules governing the matter in question.[101]

The requirement to state reasons prevents the Commission from using a presumption that one of the material elements necessary to show the existence of a state aid is present. For example, the Court has held that, although in certain cases the very circumstances in which the aid has been granted may show that it is liable to affect trade between Member States and to distort or threaten to distort competition, the Commission must at least set out those circumstances in the statement of reasons for its decision.[102]

Where the preliminary examination of aid raises indications that the aid in question would violate other Treaty provisions, the Commission is obliged to give reasons supporting its decision not to open a formal investigation.[103]

## VII. Consequences of annulment

It is worth emphasizing that starting an action under Article 226 EC has no consequences in itself. All decisions adopted by the institutions are presumed to

---

[100] See Case C-17/99 *France v Commission (Nouvelle Filature Lainière de Roubaix)* [2001] ECR I-2481, para. 35.

[101] See Case C-367/95 P *Commission v Sytraval and Brink's France* [1998] ECR I-1719, para. 63.

[102] Joined Cases 296/82 and 318/82 *Netherlands and Leeuwarder Papierwarenfabriek v Commission* [1985] ECR 809, para. 24; Joined Cases C-329/93, C-62/95 and C-63/95 *Germany and Others v Commission* [1996] ECR I-5151, para. 52; and Joined Cases C-15/98 and C-105/99 *Italy and Sardegna Lines v Commission* [2000] ECR I-8855, paras. 66–70.

[103] Case C-204/97 *Portugal v Commission (French eau-de-vie)* [2001] ECR I-3175, para. 50.

be valid and must be treated as such until their invalidity has been declared.[104] Annulment proceedings do not therefore have any suspensory effect in relation to the impugned decision; it is necessary to bring a separate application for interim measures if such suspension is sought. Moreover, the addressee of a Commission decision requiring recovery of an illegal aid is under a duty to execute that obligation[105] (and the Commission is free to bring infringement proceedings for failure to do so[106]), notwithstanding the existence of an annulment action before the Community courts.

Where an annulment action is successful, the consequences of this judgment depend, in part, on the nature of the decision and the scope of the judgment. A decision concerning an individual aid will fall, in whole or in part, as the operative part of the judgment requires. The status of a decision concerning an aid scheme after such a judgment is less straightforward. In the first place, an annulment action brought by a private party is only admissible to the extent that the aid scheme concerns it directly and individually; therefore, those parts of the decision in respect of which it has no standing to challenge will not be covered by the eventual judgment.[107] Secondly, the status of a decision condemning aid to several undertakings that is annulled following an action by one of the beneficiaries is not clear. The Court has ruled in the fields of competition law and anti-dumping that an action for annulment against a decision is individual in nature and has no effect *erga omnes*;[108] as a result, other persons who could have challenged that decision but did not do so cannot free-ride on the successful outcome of the action undertaken by others, whether by bringing a direct action before the Court of First Instance or by seeking a preliminary ruling on the validity of the decision. However, in those areas the impugned decisions have several addressees, and those who do not act are unable to take the benefit of the challenge of those who do. A state aid decision is addressed only to the Member State and so, if successfully challenged as a whole, it should fall for all those affected by the parts annulled.

Even for persons who have successfully brought an annulment action, the consequences of a judgment in their favour is not always clear-cut. The Commission is required, under Article 233 EC, to take the necessary measures to comply with a judgment that is given.[109] Thus the reasoning of the judgment must be examined to determine the Commission's obligations. For example, if a decision not to open a formal investigation procedure is annulled on the basis

---

[104] Article 242 EC.

[105] See also Article 14(3), Regulation 659/99.

[106] See Case C-404/97 *Commission v Portugal* [2000] ECR I-4897.

[107] Case T-55/99 *Confederación Española de Transporte de Mercancías v Commission* [2000] ECR II-3207, paras. 24 and 25.

[108] Case C-310/97 P *Commission v AssiDomän Kraft Products* [1999] ECR I-5363, para. 53; Case C-239/99 *Nachi Europe* [2001] ECR I-1179, para. 27.

[109] It is not possible for the Court to make an order requiring that another Community institution or body adopts a particular course of action; see Case C-227/00 P *Goldstein v Commission*, Order of 9 November 2000, para. 28.

that the Commission was obliged to do so, the Commission should open a formal investigation procedure under Article 88(2) EC.[110] Similarly, a decision that an aid was not a new but an existing aid, if annulled on the basis of a substantive error, should be replaced by a decision finding that there is a new aid (and determining whether it is compatible with the common market). The consequences of an annulment of a decision to open a formal investigation procedure under Article 88(2) EC will depend on precise basis of the judgment. Where the decision resulting from the formal investigation procedure is annulled, the consequences once again depend on the basis for the judgment. For example, where the Commission committed a manifest error of appreciation in deciding that a new gas tariff system in the Netherlands did not constitute an aid[111] it had to recommence the procedures that culminated in the adoption of a new decision.[112] On the other hand, where the Court identified insufficient reasoning in a decision that Spain had given illegal aid to a textile firm[113] the Commission was able to adopt a fresh decision, in which it condemned the aid on the basis of the information originally used and without reopening the formal investigation procedure.[114]

[110] See Case C-198/91 *Cook v Commission* [1993] ECR I-2487 and Commission Decision of 14 March 1995 concerning investment aid granted by Spain to the company Piezas y Rodajes SA, a steel foundry located in Teruel province (Aragon), Spain: OJ 1995 L 257/45.

[111] Case C-169/84 *Chimie AZF v Commission* [1990] ECR I-3083.

[112] OJ 1992 C 10/3.

[113] Joined Cases C-278/92, C-279/92, and C-280/92 *Spain v Commission (Hytasa I)* [1994] ECR I-4103.

[114] Case C-415/96 *Spain v Commission (Hytasa II)* [1998] ECR I-6993, para. 34.

# 16

# *The EC State Aid Regime: The Need for Reform*

SIR JEREMY LEVER KCMG, QC*

## I. SUMMARY

This Chapter explains why the European Community's State aid regime is in urgent need of a complete overhaul. When State aid is unlawfully given, the breach of the Treaty is committed by the Member State which, or an organ of which, grants the aid and not by the recipient of the aid. Yet under the present regime the State is placed in a 'win-win' situation. If the unlawful grant is *not* detected, the grantor State simply achieves the object that led it to grant the aid, albeit at the pre-determined cost to the State. Alternatively, if the unlawful grant *is* detected, the State gets back the aid, with interest at a commercial rate (indeed, under the present practice, in certain cases of State aid through the giving of a State guarantee of a loan by a third party, the State gets the uncovenanted bonus of a sum equal to *the value of the guaranteed loan* plus interest). In many cases, the State *also* gets much, and sometimes all, of the benefit of activity that has been undertaken as a condition for the grant of the aid.

The substantive position of the recipient of unlawful aid, recovery of which is ordered by the European Communities Commission, is recognized by the fact that, for the purposes of applications to the EC Court of First Instance for annulment of the Commission's decision, the recipient, who is indeed the person primarily prejudiced by the recovery decision, has been held to be directly and individually concerned by that decision. Yet despite the matters referred to in the two preceding paragraphs, the recipient has only a very limited opportunity to participate in the Commission's administrative procedure that leads up to the recovery decision.

In so far as there is any philosophy underlying the Community's present policy and practice with regard to unlawfully granted State aid, the philosophy would seem to be:

(a)  to make it disadvantageous *for enterprises to receive* unlawfully granted State aid (and disadvantageous for financial institutions to lend money on the strength of State guarantees that give rise to unlawful State aid to the

* The writer is indebted to Julian Gregory of Monckton Chambers for his help in connection with one aspect of this paper. But any errors remain exclusively the responsibility of the writer.

borrower) rather than to make it disadvantageous *for Member States unlawfully to grant* the aid; yet, at the same time

(b)    to rely on a procedural fiction that the administrative procedure conducted by the Commission under Article 88(2) of the EC Treaty is a procedure between the Commission and the Member State in question, to which the recipient of the putatively unlawful aid is merely a third party, indeed a third party with less rights than those enjoyed by a complainant.

Such a philosophy is highly discreditable to the Community. The present legislative policy and administrative practice urgently require revision. In important respects the revision would require not only that the Commission take the initiative but also that the Council implement a revising measure. However, the Council is controlled by the governments of the Member States; and the national governments have a vested interest in maintaining the regime in, at least largely, its present form, i.e. favouring the Member States both procedurally and substantively. Certainly, in the absence of effective pressure from the European and national Parliaments, there is no obvious incentive for the national governments to instigate an end to the present system under which recipients of aid that the Member States have unlawfully granted are treated as whipping boys with minimal procedural opportunities to defend their interests in the crucially important administrative procedure.

Despite the likelihood of, at best, inertia and, at worst, entrenched opposition on the part of national governments to the needed measures of reform, this Chapter suggests that:

(i)    the alleged recipient of putatively unlawful State aid should be treated by the EC Commission as *a full party* to any Article 88(2) administrative procedure in respect of the aid;

(ii)    if that procedure culminates in a decision by the Commission that aid has been unlawfully granted, the amount ordered to be recovered from the recipient should be limited to *the amount by which the recipient's economic position has been improved* by reason of the grant of the aid, taking into account not only the face value of the aid but also the cost to the recipient of qualifying for the grant and the economic benefit to it of having done so;

(iii)    the recipient should then be ordered to pay that amount, plus interest, *to the Community* and not to the grantor Member State which, by definition in the circumstances under consideration, acted unlawfully in granting the aid and should not be enabled to benefit from its own unlawful conduct;

(iv)    any difference between the face value of the aid and the resulting economic benefit to the recipient (see (ii) above) should be ordered to be paid *by the Member State to the Community*;

(v)    a Community procedure should be established whereby competitors of recipients of unlawful State aid should be enabled to recover *from the Community* (up to the amount of the unlawful State aid recovered by the

Community: see (iii) and (iv) above) *compensation* for the loss that they have suffered as a result of the unlawful grant of the aid; in the absence of such a procedure, the 'level playing field' that the Community's State aid regime is supposed to secure is in fact only partly secured and the incentive for competitors to complain is less than it might be; and

(vi) when it is a *State guarantee* that is held to have given rise to unlawful State aid to the recipient of the guaranteed loan, and the guaranteed loan would not have been made at all but for the State guarantee, the Commission's present practice, which has not been struck down by the Community Courts, has been to order the Member State *to annul the guarantee and to recover from the borrower an amount equal to the amount of the guaranteed loan;* that practice is *unnecessary, disproportionate, and indefensible*; instead, in such cases, the Commission's decision should order that the loan must be *immediately repaid* to the lender, if necessary thereby bankrupting the borrower; according to the Commission itself, the enforceability of the guarantee is a matter for national law and, if only for that reason, should not be addressed by the Commission's decision.

Each of those proposals is addressed in turn in the following sections of this paper.

## The Article 88(2) procedure: The position of the recipient of the putatively unlawful aid

Article 88(2)1° of the EC Treaty provides that:

*If, after giving notice to the parties concerned to submit their comments, the Commission finds that aid granted by a State or through State resources is not compatible with the common market having regard to Article 87, or that such aid is being misused, it shall decide that the State concerned shall abolish or alter such aid within a period of time to be determined by the Commission.*

The importance of the Article 88(2) administrative procedure is evident when one recalls that in the Court of First Instance the Commission regularly relies on 'the well established case law' according to which an applicant who seeks annulment of a State aid decision by the Commission is not entitled to raise new matters of fact before the CFI that were not part of the Article 88(2) procedure.[1]

If that correctly represents Community law at its present stage of development, it is clear that an alleged recipient of putatively unlawful State aid has a very strong interest in participating fully in the relevant Article 88(2) procedure.

---

[1] Case T-110/97 *Kneissl Dachstein Sportartikel AG v Commission* [1999] ECR II-2881, paragraph 102: 'The *Court considers that it would not be admissible for the applicant to rely on factual arguments which were unknown to the Commission and which it had not notified to the latter during the examination procedure (see, to this effect, the judgment of the Court of Justice in Joined Cases C-278/92, C-279/92 and C-280/92* Spain v Commission *[1994] ECR I-4103, paragraph 31, and the judgment of the Court of First Instance in Case T-37/97* Forges de Clabecq v Commission *[1999] ECR II-859, paragraph 93).'*

It might be thought, on the basis of Commission publications, that such persons were well protected procedurally. Thus, in the Commission's *Explanation of the rules applicable to State aid (Competition law in the European Communities*, Volume IIB, 1997) one finds at paragraph 38e:

*Before considering the rights of third parties in Community State aid proceedings we must first make it clear what we mean by 'third parties'. The recipient firm is not an immediate party to the proceedings between the Commission and the Member State concerned, and strictly speaking this makes it a third party. But its position is different from that of other third parties, and in terms of the judicial protection of its rights it is in fact in the same position as the Member State, except that the court with jurisdiction is the Court of Justice in actions brought by a State and the Court of First Instance in actions brought by a firm. The recipient is entitled to take part throughout the Article 93(2) [now Article 88(2)] proceedings.*

Everything up to, but not including, the last sentence of that statement is technically correct in that it is well established that a person from whom a Member State is ordered by the Commission to recover unlawful State aid is a person to whom the Commission's decision is 'of direct and individual concern' and can therefore, by virtue of Article 230, 4° of the EC Treaty, no less than the Member State as addressee of the decision (see Article 230, 2°), *apply to the Community Courts*[2] for annulment of the decision.[3]

In considering the putative *interest* in the *administrative* procedure relating to allegedly unlawful State aid, the following considerations are clearly relevant:

(i)   The putative recipient is the party who will eventually pay, and the public purse of the Member State concerned will be replenished, as a result of any recovery order that the Commission may make. In those circumstances, it certainly cannot be presumed that the Member State will exercise the *diligentia* of a *bonus paterfamilias*[4] in procuring and placing before the Commission all the relevant facts and considerations that are favourable to the putative recipient. Thus for whatever reason the Member State may not bestir itself in the administrative procedure on behalf of the recipient.

(ii)  In any event, the Member State will generally have its own concerns and standpoint and they may not be the concerns and standpoint of the putative recipient.

(iii) The allegedly unlawful State aid may have been granted by an organ of the Member State, other than a department of central government, and may not have any first-hand knowledge of the matter.

---

[2]  As stated by the Commission in the citation quoted above, an application by the recipient of the aid is made to the Court of First Instance; an application by the Member State is made to the European Court of Justice.

[3]  See Case 730/79 *Philip Morris v Commission* [1980] ECR 2671, paragraph 5.

[4]  Justinian's Digest at paragraph 19.2.25.7.

(iv)   The Member State may give to the Commission inaccurate, incomplete, or otherwise misleading information, which the recipient could and might correct.

(v)   However diligent and comprehensive the Member State may seek to be, and may even sometimes in fact be, justice cannot be seen to be done if the putative beneficiary is dependent on the Member State, with its obvious conflict and divergence of interests, to represent the putative beneficiary in the administrative procedure.

Despite the foregoing and despite the fact that the Court of First Instance has ruled that a recipient of State aid has the right to be involved in the Article 88(2) administrative procedure to the extent appropriate in the light of the circumstances of the case,[5] the practice of the Commission, which is now based on Council Regulation No. 659/1999, leaves recipients woefully unprotected procedurally in the administrative procedure. Thus, Article 6(1) of Regulation No. 659/1999 allows the alleged recipient of putatively unlawful State aid, as an 'interested party', 'to submit comments *within a prescribed period which shall normally not exceed one month.* In duly justified cases, the Commission *may* extend the prescribed period' (emphases added).

Even where the Commission can be persuaded to extend the 'prescribed period' beyond its normal one month, the recipient of the aid is generally faced with a narrow window of opportunity such as to prevent it from participating fully in the administrative procedure, which in any event it could not do since the Commission does not, and the Member State may not and often does not, disclose to the recipient the Commission's questions to the Member State or the Member State's answers and documentary material annexed to those answers.

In considering the extent of the value to the recipient of the right to submit observations to the Commission during the 'window of opportunity', one must also bear in mind that:

(i)    the recipient may have had virtually no prior notice of the pendency of the Article 88(2) procedure when the 'window of opportunity' opens and the recipient's limited period to comment begins;

(ii)   the aid may be alleged to have been granted many years earlier: the limitation period provided by Article 15 of Regulation No. 659/1999 is ten years and that period starts to run afresh on the occurrence of any interrupting event (even if, according to the Commission, the interrupting event was unknown to the putative recipient of the aid), and

(iii)  although the outlines of the Commission's 'case' will be contained in the notice published by the Commission pursuant to Article 88(2)EC, the

---

[5] Case T-158/96 *Acciaierie di Bolzano v Commission* [1999] ECR II-3927, paragraph 45, judgment of 16 December 1999 and therefore given after the coming into operation of Council Regulation (EC) No. 659/1999 of 22 March 1999, to which further reference is made below.

administrative procedure may then progress in ways that the recipient may not foresee and in relation to which the Commission has no obligation to keep the recipient informed or to receive from the recipient any further communication, provided only that the 'case' does not change to such a degree as to necessitate publication of a further Article 88(2) notice.

In practice even when the putative recipient of unlawful aid has significant comments to make outside the 'window of opportunity', e.g. because the putative grantor Member State has shown the recipient questions raised by the Commission with the Member State, the Commission will refuse to accept material from the recipient, insisting that the procedure is between the Commission and the Member State and that, outside the 'window of opportunity', the recipient has no standing in the procedure.[6] Unless the Member State is willing to act as a channel of communication to the Commission of the material furnished by the recipient, the recipient's observations will fall outside the scope of the administrative procedure and will therefore, as Community law apparently now stands, be inadmissible in subsequent proceedings brought by the recipient in the Court of First Instance for annulment of a decision by the Commission ordering recovery of the aid from the recipient. Moreover, the recipient may have no means of knowing whether, and if so to what extent and in what terms, the Member State communicates to the Commission information or submissions provided or made to the Member State by the recipient in connection with the Article 88(2) procedure.

The thesis that an Article 88(2) procedure is between the Commission and the Member State and that the putative recipient of unlawful aid is merely an—interested—third party may be contrasted with the fact that if a potential recipient of State aid is to be able to rely on a legitimate expectation that the Community rules on State aid have been complied with, the *potential* recipient needs to verify *direct with the Commission* that any benefit or consideration that it is to receive from any organ of its Member State has been the subject of a positive decision by the Commission; in the absence of a direct assurance to that effect from the Commission, the recipient cannot have any such legitimate expectation, no matter what assurances to the contrary the recipient may have received from the Member State.[7] Thus, the potential recipient of State aid is at risk if it does not enter into direct contact with the Commission in advance of receiving from the organs of its Member State any benefit or consideration that might be held to constitute State aid to which the EC Treaty rules apply; but where the benefit or consideration is subsequently alleged to have given rise to

---

[6] The present position is particularly objectionable by reason of the fact that *in a few cases* (which may be 'politically sensitive') the Commission, in its discretion, allows the recipient 'to take part throughout the Article 88(2) proceedings', as misleadingly its *Explanation of the rules applicable to State aid*, cited above, claimed that the Commission allowed *generally*.

[7] For a recent statement of the need for a potential recipient of aid to verify its clearance direct with the Commission, failing which it cannot have any legitimate expectation that the Commission has taken a positive decision in respect of the matter, see Case T-55/99 *CETM v Commission* [2000] ECR II-3207 at paragraph 121.

such unlawful aid, the recipient is highly constrained as to the direct contact that it is permitted to have with the Commission in the Article 88(2) procedure.

The thesis that an Article 88(2) procedure is between the Commission and the Member State and that the putative recipient of unlawfully granted State aid is merely a third party with a strictly limited right to submit observations in the administrative procedure may also be contrasted with the extensive rights enjoyed by a *complainant* in the administrative procedure. Thus in Case T-95/94 *Sytraval and Brink's France v Commission*[8] the CFI held (at paragraph 78 of the judgment) that '*the Commission needs to ascertain what view the complainant takes of the information gathered by it in the course of its inquiry (see the Opinion of Advocate General Tesauro in Case C-198/91* **Cook v Commission** *[1993] ECR I-2487, at I-2502, paragraphs 17–19).*' One might have supposed that, by even stronger reasoning, a putative recipient of unlawfully granted aid should enjoy a corresponding right.

Lastly, even the 'judicial protection' enjoyed by the recipient of the aid which, in a passage from the Commission's *Explanation of the rules applicable to State aid*, cited above, is said to be the same as that of the Member State, is in fact greatly inferior to the judicial protection enjoyed by the Member State if the recipient's right to participate in the administrative procedure is strictly limited whilst the recipient apparently cannot raise in the judicial proceedings new matters of fact that were not part of the administrative procedure.

At least one alleged recipient of unlawful State aid from whom the Commission has ordered the Member State to recover the aid is currently contending before the CFI that the regime described above gives rise to:

(i)  a breach of essential procedural requirements;
(ii)  a breach of the European Convention on Human Rights; and
(iii)  in so far as the resulting recovery order required the Member State to act in a manner that was inconsistent with the 'equitable treatment' guaranteed by a bilateral Treaty to which the Member State was a party, a breach of public international law.

However, it is not the purpose of this Chapter to discuss whether, as a matter of *lex lata*, the regime operated by the Commission pursuant to Regulation No. 659/99/EC is unlawful; its purpose is to argue that, if it is not so, then as a matter of *lex ferenda*, it *ought* to be.

## II. The real value of State aid

Sometimes State aid is granted without strings, e.g. an unconditional grant of money to prop up a failing company. In such cases the value of the benefit to the grantee is indeed equal to the face value of the grant.

---

[8] [1995] ECR II-2651.

Sometimes, however, the aid is conditional upon the grantee doing something or takes the form of a payment for something that the grantee contracts to do. Where the aid consists of an overpayment for goods or services provided by the recipient, the 'value' of the goods or services should clearly be deducted from the amount of the payment in order to arrive at the amount of the aid—though the 'value' may be problematic: should it be a fair price as between a willing buyer (who almost certainly did not exist at such a price) and a willing seller? Or should it be only the variable costs incurred by the seller in producing and supplying the goods in question? The Commission would no doubt argue for the latter (and has been heard to argue that there should be no deduction at all).

More serious is the problem where the activity subsidized by the Member State would not be undertaken but for the grant of the aid because the market value of the result is less than the cost of realizing it. Thus, suppose that the cost of building a factory in a geographically unattractive location would be €10 million (the cost being increased because of the location) and the market value of the factory when completed would be €8 million (the value being reduced because of the location). Obviously, in the absence of State aid, no private operator would build the factory. However, if State aid of €3 million is available, a private operator may find it attractive to do so.

Although the gross cost[9] of the aid to the State is €3 million, the net value of the aid to the recipient is only €1 million because, in order to get the aid, the recipient has to spend €10 million on a project that will have a realizable value in the hands of the recipient of only €8 million.

Despite the foregoing, in such circumstances a recovery order for €3 million will almost certainly be made (assuming that the aid was capable of affecting, even slightly, trade between Member States, was granted unlawfully, and is found by the Commission to be 'incompatible with the common market').

The intellectually dubious foundations of the State aid regime are highlighted when one compares the circumstances just described with a situation in which the State itself builds the factory, at a cost of €10 million, and then sells it, by means of a well publicized, open, and unconditional auction at which the factory fetches €8 million. Here the Commission takes the view that there is *no* State aid. Yet the net economic advantage conferred by the aid on the recipient in the first case was only €1 million relative to the economic position of the successful bidder in the second case.

As has been shown above, the same is true where the Member State procures e.g. the construction of a factory (for which the Member State pays only a competitive price) and then disposes of the factory by way of sale or lease to the highest bidder under an open competitive bidding regime even though the State knew that pursuing that course would entail its making a loss: both the first

---

[9] The *net cost* to the State of the aid may be much less than €3 million (indeed there may be no net cost) because of the reduction in unemployment benefit, the increase in personal taxes paid, and the increase in property taxes resulting from the establishment of the factory.

and the second stage of the operation involve competitive prices; therefore there is no State aid.

However, it does not follow that a Member State can avoid the Community's State aid regime by limiting grants to undertakings to the amount required to induce them e.g. to build a factory for their own use or to make a certain goods for commercial sale.[10] Otherwise State aid could always be granted to undertakings provided that the aid was limited to the amount required to induce the undertakings to carry out the favoured activity within the Member State. But that fact highlights the point already made, namely that the amount of the aid may greatly exceed the benefit (if any) that the recipient gains from undertaking the activity in the State and at the place in question rather than elsewhere. In the result, an order that the Member State recover the amount of the aid from the recipient will leave the recipient worse off than if the recipient had not undertaken the activity with the benefit of the aid. In this sense, despite the Commission's averments to the contrary, recovery orders can have penal consequences.

This consideration makes all the more objectionable the treatment of the putative recipient of the aid as a third party in the investigation procedure, considered above, and leads one logically onto the objectionable nature of recovery orders, as currently made, considered in Section III below.

## III. A MORE APPROPRIATE FORM OF RECOVERY ORDER

Cases of the following kind illustrate how unsatisfactory are recovery orders of the kind presently made by the Commission.

A Member State desires to see established in a particular location a factory the operation of which will be labour-intensive. Without a substantial government grant or other subvention, it would not be worth anyone's while to establish such a factory at that location. The Member State therefore makes inquiries and ascertains that X (which may be a foreign-owned company; there is not necessarily any preference for a locally owned company) is willing to build and equip the desired factory at the desired location for a lower subvention than any other enterprise, namely €20 million. The gross cost to X of the land, building, and equipment is €40 million (i.e. €20 million net of the subvention of €20 million). Six years later the Commission makes a recovery order which, as a result of the inclusion of interest, amounts to €27 million. In order to satisfy the recovery order, the recipient sells the factory at an arm's length price of €20 million (reflecting an initial open market value of €24 million and depreciation on the building and the equipment totalling €4 million).

Thus, X has incurred initial costs, net of the State subvention, of €20 million; six years later it sustains a further net negative cash flow of €7 million

---

[10] See e.g. Case C-354/90 *Fédération Nationale du Commerce Extérieur des Produits Alimentaires v France* [1991] ECR I-5523.

(the €27 million that it is required to pay to the State, less the proceeds of sale of the factory of €20 million); it no longer has the factory but it enjoyed its use for some six years; but the value of that use is very unlikely to exceed twice the depreciation of €3 million incurred during the six-year period. At the end of the process it is worse off to an extent almost certainly in excess of €20 million than if it had not entered into the transaction in the first place.

In the hypothesized circumstances the Member State has achieved its objective of causing the factory in question to be established at the location in question; the factory remains in operation, albeit under new ownership, and the new owner acquires it for much less than its original cost with normal depreciation; the Member State continues to enjoy the stream of revenue from fiscal and parafiscal charges attributable directly and indirectly to the existence and operation of the factory; yet

(i)  as a result of the recovery order, the Member State recovers the original cost to it of the subvention and

(ii) it also makes a profit on the notional loan of the subvention since the rate of interest used in calculating the interest included in the amount ordered to be recovered is the rate payable by commercial operators and therefore exceeds the rate of interest payable by the Member State on 'risk-free State paper'.

It is not surprising that such a regime does not discourage, let alone deter, Member States from granting unlawful State aid where so doing serves, in the judgement of the grantor organ of the Member State, the public interest for which that organ is responsible.

The obviously needed reform is that not more than the economic benefit to the recipient of unlawfully granted aid (i.e. the difference between the recipient's overall economic position with and without the aid) should be recoverable (with interest) from the recipient and the balance should be recoverable (with interest) *by the Community from the errant Member State*.

## IV. IN WHOSE FAVOUR SHOULD RECOVERY ORDERS BE MADE IN GENERAL?

The foregoing raises the question whether even the aid that is ordered to be recovered from the recipient of unlawful State aid should be payable to the Member State that granted the aid or to the Community.

The prohibition of the grant of unlawful State aid imposed by the last sentence of Article 88(3) of the EC Treaty is of direct effect. The infringer of the prohibition is the Member State and not the recipient of the aid (who is often much less well placed than the Member State to appreciate the unlawfulness of the grant of the aid and the effect of such unlawfulness).

As the European Court of Justice observed in Case C-453/99 *Courage Ltd v Crehan*, judgment of 20 September 2001 at paragraph 31: 'Under a principle which is recognised in most of the legal systems of the Member States and which the court has applied in the past (see Case 39/72 *Commission v Italy* [1973] ECR 101 at paragraph 10), a litigant should not profit from his own unlawful conduct, where this is proven'.

Applying that principle whilst ensuring that the total amount of all unlawful State aid is recovered, the *whole* of the aid ought to be recovered *by* the Commission on behalf of the Community. Such a course would have the added advantage of providing an assurance of actual recovery which, so long as the effectuation of the recovery is left to the Member State, cannot be taken for granted.

## V. THE NEED FOR USE OF RECOVERY MONIES TO COMPENSATE DISADVANTAGED ENTERPRISES

A person, typically a competitor of the recipient of unlawful aid, almost certainly cannot recover from the recipient compensation for any loss that it has suffered as a result of the unlawful subvention of the recipient's activities: the recipient of the aid has not committed any breach of the EC Treaty so that there does not even arise the question whether a provision of the Treaty infringed by the recipient was intended to confer a subjective right (to compensation) from the recipient.[10a]

It is true that the grantor Member State, in unlawfully granting the State aid, *has* infringed the obligation imposed by the last sentence of Article 88(3) of the Treaty. That obligation is of direct effect and can therefore be relied on by any person with a sufficient interest, typically a competitor of the recipient of the unlawfully granted aid, in the national courts. If, then, the breach by the grantor Member State of the obligation imposed by the last sentence of Article 88(3) is to be sufficiently characterized as a breach of the Treaty,[11] i.e. sufficiently obvious to a knowledgeable practitioner, a person with a sufficient interest should be able to recover from the grantor Member State compensation for any damage directly caused to the claimants by the breach of the Treaty.[12]

Notwithstanding the foregoing, the writer is unaware of any case in which a person who has suffered loss as a result of the unlawful grant of State aid to another person has sued and recovered damages from the grantor Member State. The explanation is probably that it requires a well resourced claimant which is willing to take on its national government in its national courts in a claim for compensation in circumstances where the national government may have a

---

[10a] But see Case C-39/94 *SFEI v La Poste* [1996] ECR I-3547 at paragraph 75 of the judgment.

[11] Wrongly rendered in the English language texts as 'a sufficiently serious breach': see, in each case where the phrase is used by the ECJ, the French language version.

[12] See Joined Cases C-46/93 and C-48/93 *Brasserie du Pêcheur and Factortame III* [1996] ECR I-1029.

number of arguable defences,[13] unless the claim is so clear that the national government will almost certainly have to settle it.

However, as is indisputable, the object of the State aid regime is to restore a 'level playing field' in circumstances in which competition has been distorted at the Community level by the unlawful grant of State aid; that being so, and following the suggestions made earlier in this Chapter, once the Community has recovered, from the recipient and from the grantor of unlawfully granted aid, the amount of the aid, it is obvious that the recovered sums should be available as a fund to compensate those who, at least as a direct result of the unlawful grant of the aid, have suffered loss.

Under the State aid regime, subject to the reforms suggested in this Chapter, the recipient of such aid would forgo the benefit that it had actually enjoyed as a result of the aid (a condition not fulfilled by the present regime) and those to whom the unlawful grant of the aid had directly caused loss would recover compensation (at least in part, if not wholly) for the loss (again a condition, not *necessarily* satisfied, and not *in practice* satisfied, under the present regime).[14]

## VI. THE CURRENTLY ANOMALOUS TREATMENT OF STATE GUARANTEES THAT GIVE RISE TO STATE AID

The current generally unsatisfactory effect of EC law on State aid as a result of the giving of State guarantees is considered in *Application of the European Community Rules on State aid to State Guarantees*[15] (hereafter 'JIFBL Supplement'). A State guarantee of a loan given by a State organ otherwise than in conformity with the 'market investor principle' and not in consideration of a commercially realistic commission will generally give rise to State aid *to the borrower*. If the conditions for the application of Article 87 EC are satisfied, the

---

[13] Obviously, if the aid was properly pre-notified by the Member State to the Commission and was the subject of a positive decision, or even if only an implied positive decision by reason of the Commission's failure to take a negative decision, there will not be a sufficiently characterized breach of the Treaty by the Member State, notwithstanding that the Commission's decision is subsequently annulled by the Community Courts; but even in cases where there was no positive decision by the Commission, express or by default, there is considerable scope for argument by the Member State that it was not sufficiently clear that the State's conduct gave rise to aid that satisfied the conditions enumerated by Article 87(1) EC for the application of the Treaty ('any aid granted by a Member State or through State resources in any form whatsoever which distorts or threatens to distort competition by favouring certain undertakings or the production of certain goods in so far as it affects trade between Member States').

[14] Clearly, claimants who recovered any compensation should not be allowed to recover it twice over: once from the Community and once again in the national courts from the delinquent grantor Member State.

[15] Supplement to Butterworth Journal of International Banking and Financial Law, January 2002, based on a Clifford Chance/All Souls College Seminar held at All Souls College, Oxford in January 2001. Pages 3–38 contain a discussion paper by the present writer, on which the text above draws freely. See also Friend above.

aid will be deemed to have been granted unlawfully unless the aid was pre-notified to the Commission and, before the guarantee became legally binding, was the subject of a positive decision by it, express or by default. In relatively rare circumstances that have been identified by the Commission[16] the aid, whether or not an aid to the borrower, may constitute aid *to the lender*, in particular, for example, if a State guarantee is given *ex post* in respect of a loan or other financial obligation already entered into, without the terms of the loan or financial obligation being adjusted; or if one guaranteed loan is used to repay another, non-guaranteed, loan to the same credit institution, then there may be an aid to the lender, in so far as the security of the loan is increased. Such aid is capable of favouring the lender and distorting competition, and generally falls within the scope of Article 87(1) if trade between Member States is affected.

Again, a State guarantee will give rise to State aid to the lender, whether or not also to the borrower, where it is given to enable a particular lender or lenders to undercut competitors, in whose favour the State guarantee is not available, for a particular piece or class of business.[17]

The present Chapter considers only State guarantees given contractually[18] after 11 March 2000. The position before then is complicated by reason of the existence of a Commission Communication of 18 October 1991 (republished in 1993) which indicated that, even if a State guarantee gave rise to unlawful State aid *to the borrower*, creditors would not be affected. The Commission Communications of 1991 and 1993 may therefore be relied on by persons who extended credit on the faith of a State guarantee before 11 March 2000 when the Commission published the Notice.[19]

Where a loan would have been made by a lender to a borrower even in the absence of a State guarantee, but as a result of a State guarantee the loan is made on more favourable terms than those on which it would have been made but for the State guarantee, the State guarantee gives rise to State aid to the borrower. If the transaction that gives rise to the State aid is not duly pre-notified by the State to the Commission and is not then, before the guarantee becomes binding, the subject of a positive decision, express or by default, by the Commission, the State

---

[16] Commission Notice on the application of Articles 87 and 88 of the EC Treaty to State aid in the form of guarantees [2000] OJ C71/14 of 11 March 2000, at paragraph 2.2.2.

[17] JIFBL Supplement at page 8, paragraph 2.4(a). As to the risk that State guarantees may give rise to State aid to lenders more commonly, see ibid., pages 8–9, paragraph 2.5.

[18] In other words, this Chapter does not consider guarantees that arise through operation of some general law, such as statutory liability imposed in some jurisdictions on 100 per cent owners of companies for debts incurred by the latter.

[19] See fn. 16 above. See also the Commission Communication of 18.10.91 [1991] OJ C273/2, republished on 13 November 1993 [1993] OJ C307/3, as amended—in respects not material hereto—following on the judgment of the European Court of Justice in Case C-325/91 *France v Commission* [1993] ECR I-3283, relating to other parts of the 1991 Communication. Although the first sentence of paragraph 38 of the Communication, as published in both 1991 and 1993, refers to a Commission Communication dated 5 April 1989 as amended by letter of 12 October 1989, that earlier Communication, unlike paragraph 38 of the 1991 and 1993 Communications, did not refer to the position of creditors.

aid will have been granted unlawfully; and if the aid is subsequently found by the Commission to have been 'incompatible with the common market', the Commission will order the State to recover from the borrower an amount equal to the benefit enjoyed by the borrower as a result of the State guarantee: generally, what the borrower would have had to pay by way of commission for a rock-solid guarantee of the loan, plus interest.[20] Such an order correctly reflects the principle that the recipient of unlawfully granted aid that is incompatible with the common market should be deprived of the benefit derived by it as a result of the grant of the aid.

The problem with which this section of this Chapter is concerned is where the loan simply would not have been made by the lender to the borrower in the absence of the State guarantee. In such cases, the Commission's practice is to order the Member State (i) to 'recover' from the borrower a sum equal to the value of the loan and (ii) to cancel the guarantee.

An Opinion of Mr Advocate General Cosmas in Joined Cases C-329/93, C-62/95, and C-63/95 *Germany v Commission (Bremer Vulkan)*[21] and the judgment of the Court of First Instance in Joined Cases T-204/97 and T-270/97 *EPAC v Commission*[22] approve the Commission's practice described above. The relevant considerations do not appear to have been drawn to the attention of the Community Courts in those cases. One of those considerations is relevant only when the State guarantee in question was given before 11 March 2000 (see the text to footnote 19 above); and the Commission's present view that the enforceability of a State guarantee in the circumstances under consideration is a matter of national law to be determined by the national courts, almost certainly emerged after close of the written procedures not only in the *Bremer Vulkan* case but also in *EPAC*, though the fact that the Commission has now formally adopted that position will clearly be relevant if in the future the Commission includes in a recovery decision an order that the Member State annul the State guarantee that gave rise to unlawful State aid, a provision that is clearly incompatible with the Commission's position that the enforceability of the guarantee is a matter of national law to be determined by the national courts.

However, this Chapter is concerned with what the law *should be* rather than with what it *is*; and the fact that the considerations that show that the Commission's present practice is irrational, unnecessary, and disproportionate appear never to have been argued before the Community Courts is relevant to this Chapter only in that it means that the position is capable of being remedied by the Community Courts rather than necessarily requiring legislative action.

---

[20] The text of paragraph 3.7 at page 12 of JIBFL Supplement, which refers to such a case, is corrupt in that the reference (in the penultimate line of the paragraph) to the position in which the borrower would have been if the loan had been made *with* the benefit of a State guarantee should refer to the position in which the borrower would have been if the loan had been made *without* the benefit of the State guarantee.

[21] [1996] ECR I-5151 at pages 5194–5196.

[22] [2000] ECR II-2267, especially at paragraph 144.

The proper object of a decision by the Commission where State aid has been granted unlawfully and is found by the Commission to be incompatible with the common market is to deprive the recipient of the aid of the benefit that has been conferred on it. The Commission vigorously denies that its decisions where State aid has been granted unlawfully are penal in nature; and although, as has been shown earlier in this Chapter, such decisions as presently formulated may have incidental penal effects, the whole system becomes even more objectionable to the extent that it overtly seeks to penalize persons who have not themselves been guilty of any breach of Community law.

One can take an extreme hypothetical case to illustrate the objectionable consequences of the Commission's present practice:

(i)   A Member State establishes a company X for a particular purpose; X is given a negligible equity share capital.

(ii)  X borrows from a consortium of financial institutions €100 million that it requires to achieve its intended purpose; the Member State guarantees the loan without which X could not borrow any significant sum.

(iii) None of the foregoing is notified by the Member State to the Commission.

(iv)  Before X has begun to spend the €100 million, the Commission learns of what has happened and, following on an administrative procedure under Article 88(2) EC, the Commission condemns the transaction as giving rise to State aid to X, granted unlawfully and incompatible with the common market.

(v)   The Commission orders the Member State to 'recover' €100 million, plus interest, from X and to cancel the guarantee given by it to the lenders.

The result, in such circumstances, is to transfer to the Member State money advanced by the lending institutions although the Member State has itself incurred no expenditure (other than trivial legal and administrative costs associated with drawing up the guarantee). The lenders' position will be ameliorated, but not remedied, if before the Member State has recovered from X the €100 million plus interest, X is put into insolvent liquidation and its funds are divided equally between the Member State and the lenders; but even then the (delinquent) Member State, which has incurred no significant expenditure nor, with the annulment of the guarantee, any relevant liability, is enabled to pocket some €50 million of what is in effect the lenders' money.

Consider now an alternative order. The Commission could order the Member State to require the borrower forthwith to repay the loan in its entirety and could make an appropriate order to deprive the borrower of the benefit of having, in the interval, borrowed the money at a rate of interest that was unlawfully lowered by reason of the State guarantee (under the present practice, by ordering the Member State to 'recover' from the borrower a sum equal to the underpaid interest *or*, under the practice suggested earlier in this paper, by a requirement that the sum in question *be paid to the Commission*). Subject to a largely theoretical qualification, such an order would deprive the borrower of the benefit of the aid, which so far as aid to the borrower is concerned, is the purpose, or at least the only legitimate purpose, of the procedure.

The theoretical qualification to the foregoing is that, by definition, if no lender would have been prepared to make the loan, at no matter how high a rate of interest, without the State guarantee, it is impossible to say at what rate of interest the loan would have been made but for the State guarantee.

However, that problem exists in any event in cases of this kind, and if the Commission orders the Member State to require immediate repayment of the loan and quantifies the shortfall of interest paid by reference to the interest payable on 'junk bonds':

(i)   the order will be the best that it is practicable to make in the circumstances, and

(ii)  if the borrower is actually able, in accordance with such an order and without being put into liquidation as insolvent, to repay the loan and to pay the shortfall of interest paid relative to that paid on junk bonds, considerable doubt must be thrown on the initial hypothesis that the borrower could not without the State guarantee have borrowed the sum in question at no matter how high a rate of interest, whereas

(iii) if the order results in the liquidation of the borrower as insolvent, the position for the future will have been regularized at least to the greatest practicable extent.

What of the position of the *lender* where the Commission finds that, but for the State guarantee, the loan would not have been made at all? The position under the Commission's present practice is that the Commission orders the Member State to annul the guarantee and at the same time to require the borrower to pay it a sum equal to the loan. Yet the transaction will then not only have cost the State *nothing* (either in terms of a payment by the State treasury or in terms of incurring a potential liability under the guarantee) but will also have greatly enriched the State and gravely prejudiced the lender, not only by depriving the lender of the benefit of the guarantee but also by making it almost certain that the borrower, now burdened with a new liability to the State, will default on the loan agreement even if it could otherwise have repaid the loan. Thus the EC State aid regime is used, in the circumstances under discussion, as an engine for the unjust enrichment of the Member State, which is the one body that has committed a breach of the Treaty.

One can now contrast that disreputable outcome with the form of order that will perform the function that such an order is intended to perform, namely deprive undertakings of benefits unlawfully conferred on them by State measures, without any unjust oppression or any unjust enrichment. In the circumstances under consideration, the State guarantee will have created for the lender the benefit of business that would not otherwise have been available to it (because, by definition, it would not have made the loan at all but for the guarantee). It is therefore arguable[23] that an incidental effect of the giving of the State guarantee was to give State aid to the lender: one can quantify the value of that aid by comparing the cost of funds to the lender with the interest on the loan charged by the lender; to the amount thus calculated there may need to be added something for the value to the lender of being able, because the loan was covered by a State guarantee, to take on the business in question without there being any effect on the lender's capital adequacy ratio. In this way, in conformity with the fundamental EC law principle of proportionality, the lender can be deprived of the value to it of the guarantee, i.e. the amount by which the lender's economic position was improved as a result of *entering into the transaction.* By contrast, under the present practice, the Commission looks exclusively at the 'gross' value of the guarantee without reference to the consideration given by the lender, namely the making of the loan, in consequence of receiving the guarantee. The fallacy is the same as that which would be involved if, goods worth €1 million having been sold to the State for €3 million with the intent of conferring on the seller State aid of €2 million, the State were then to be ordered to recover from the seller €3 million, ignoring the fact that the seller delivered to the State goods worth €1 million.

If the foregoing analysis is accepted, not only is there no need, or basis, for the Commission to order annulment of the State guarantee; there is equally no need, or basis, for the national courts to refuse to enforce the guarantee.

One may here recall that, as noted above, where a State-guaranteed loan *would have been* made even in the absence of a State guarantee, but *at a higher rate of interest*, the Commission's practice is to order the State to recover from the borrower a commercial commission for the guarantee, which will be of the order of the saving to the borrower of borrowing the money with the benefit of the guarantee compared with what it would have cost the borrower to borrow the money without the benefit of the guarantee. Where, in such a case, the State aid to the borrower, resulting from the absence of an appropriate commission at a commercial rate, was given unlawfully, the EC Commission has never, so far as the writer is aware, suggested either that the guarantee should be ordered to be annulled or that the guarantee might be liable to be treated as unenforceable in the national courts because of the Member State's breach of Article 88(3) EC. The position can be completely remedied, so far as the EC State aid regime is concerned, by depriving the borrower of the benefit of the unlawfully granted aid. There is no reason to adopt a wholly different approach where the loan would not have been made at all but for the State guarantee and to impose, uniquely in that situation, a 'remedy' intended to operate *in terrorem* to deter lenders from becoming involved in transactions in which a State guarantee gives rise to State aid.

Thus, the present treatment by the Commission, with the approval of the Community Courts, of State guarantees of loans that would not otherwise

---

[23] JIFBL Supplement at page 8, paragraph 2.4 (a). As to the risk that State guarantees may give rise to State aid to lenders more commonly, see ibid., pages 8–9, paragraph 2.5.

have been made at all and that gave rise to unlawful State aid is indefensible. However, the problem to which such State guarantees give rise is a real one. The giving of a State guarantee is often the easiest way in which a Member State can give State aid, for the following reasons:

(i)   it does not, at least in the first instance, increase the Public Sector Borrowing Requirement;

(ii)  it may not be readily detectable;

(iii) State-guaranteed loans are a particularly attractive class of business for banks since making such loans has no effect on a bank's capital adequacy ratio, i.e. such loans can be made without any need for the bank to increase its capital base at all since the loan is regarded as risk-free (a potentially explosive fallacy depending on the treatment of the transaction under the EC State aid rules);

(iv)  if lenders, on the faith of State guarantees that give rise to unlawful State aid, are liable to be subjected to draconian penalties, they may be induced to act as unpaid policeman for the Commission and may ensure a respect for the EC State aid rules that the Commission is (or believes itself to be) unable to ensure.

The Commission's 'soft law' solution to the problem (under its Notice of 11 March 2000,[24] as opposed to its contrary decisional practice referred to above) is to shift the problem to the national courts to deal with as a matter of national law, working in combination with Community law. That is no solution. Thus the national law treatment of the 'tainting' of contracts by illegality, a notoriously difficult topic, may vary from Member State to Member State; and if any national law combines with Community law to render unenforceable a State guarantee which did not itself give rise to State aid to the lender, it will have the paradoxical effect of converting the transaction into State aid if and when the guarantee is honoured, since such a payment of money by the State to an undertaking in the absence of an enforceable legal obligation to make the payment constitutes a grant of State aid. In consequence, lenders to whom payments have been made by a State organ pursuant to a State guarantee that gave rise to unlawful State aid to the borrower *but not to the lender*[25] would be at risk of the Commission, at any time within ten years of the State guarantee being honoured,[26] ordering recovery, with interest, *from the lender* of the *whole amount paid to the lender* under the State guarantee.

---

[24] Commission Notice on the application of Articles 87 and 88 of the EC Treaty to State aid in the form of guarantees [2000] OJ C71/14 of 11 March 2000, at paragraph 2.2.2.

[25] If (as has been mooted above) when the State guarantee is given to the lender, it gives rise to State aid to the lender simply because it creates a profitable opportunity for the lender which would not have existed under 'normal market conditions', such aid to the lender is to be quantified by reference to the profit gained by the lender and its amount falls far short of the total amount of the guaranteed loan.

[26] Article 15 of Council Regulation 659/1999 creates a limitation period of ten years, which moreover may be extended by 'interrupting events'.

Moreover, there seems to be no logical reason to single out State guarantees for invalidation under national law. Thus, suppose that a Member State, after going through a proper public procurement procedure, engages a builder to construct a factory for a normal market price of €20 million, on terms that on completion of the construction the builder shall transfer the factory to X. The builder may or may not know the terms of the agreement between the Member State and X as a result of which the transfer will be effected and the builder may well not verify with the Commission in advance that the agreement between the Member State and X has been the subject of a positive decision by the Commission under the EC State aid rules. In those respects the builder will be in a position very similar to that of a financial institution that lends money on the faith of a State guarantee. If the transaction between the Member State and X does give rise to unlawful State aid, because X is to pay the Member State less than the market value of the factory, can it be right that national law and Community law combine to render unenforceable the builder's right to be paid for the construction of the factory (and to convert payment by the State to the builder for that work into State aid) because the builder had no right to be paid?

The Commission's desire to harness national law to produce such a result in the case of (some but not all) State guarantees that give rise to unlawful State aid, even though the lender receives no State aid when it makes the guaranteed loan, is simply a result of the weakness of the State aid rules *vis-à-vis* the Member State that unlawfully grants State aid to the borrower by means of giving a guarantee of the loan and is, by reason of so doing, the one party that commits a breach of the Treaty. Once Member States became subject to effective sanctions if they unlawfully grant State aid, rather than remaining in their present 'win-win' situation, the need to penalize third parties, such as lenders to whom State guarantees are given, would disappear. All the more reason, therefore, for undertaking fundamental reforms of the present regime along the lines foreshadowed in this Chapter.

# 17

# The Role of National Courts

JAMES FLYNN QC

The purpose of this chapter, in complement to that of Leo Flynn on the role of the Community courts in Luxembourg, is to consider the circumstances in which national courts can intervene in state aid issues and their powers to grant relief. This chapter contains no detailed review or critical assessment of individual judgments in particular cases.[1] The question it addresses is 'how much use can national courts be in dealing with state aids?' The focus is on actions brought by competitors or others who consider themselves adversely affected by the grant of aid to someone else. Roughly the order that will be followed in this chapter is like that in *Time's Arrow*: against the chronology of what should happen in the procedural history of a state aid. For reasons which this chapter endeavours to set out, the writer's view is that, for such claimants, national courts are at their least useful when the measure has been duly notified to the Commission for examination under the procedures set out in Article 88 EC[2] and the Procedural Regulation,[3] not much use when a non-notified measure produces its effects abroad, and at their most useful when what is at issue is a non-notified measure benefiting competitors in the same jurisdiction. National courts also have a central role, for which they are perfectly equipped, in actions brought by defaulting member states to recover aid that they should never have paid out.

## I. RECOVERY ORDERS

That is the first stopping point: the situation where the Commission has taken a decision finding that a particular grant is a state aid which is incompatible with the common market and ordering that it be recovered. Here the national court will have a role if the beneficiary resists recovery. The national authorities, if they are doing their job, should bring proceedings in the courts to extract the money

---

[1] See Bacon below for a critical assessment of some of the English cases.

[2] The latest treaty numbering is used throughout (in square brackets in quotations in which the old numbering was used). This chore is resented. The text refers throughout to the EC Treaty and the relevant provisions. However, it should not be overlooked that there is still some life in the state aid (and competition) provisions of the European Coal and Steel Community Treaty: see *Banks v Coal Authority*, concerning the state aid provisions of the ECSC Treaty, which led to the reference in Case C-390/98 [2001] ECR I-6117, which led the Court of Appeal to dismiss Banks's appeal: see [2002] EuLR 483 ([2002] EWCA Civ 841).

[3] Regulation 653/99, 1999 OJ L 83/1.

from the recipient. Such proceedings, often grudgingly and tardily brought, have led to an extensive case-law (by way of Article 234 reference to the ECJ) on the extent to which national law principles such as legitimate expectations, the principle of security of administrative payments and so on may be used to defeat such claims. It was in such a case also that the important *TWD*[4] principle arose, namely that a party who would have been admissible to challenge the Commission's decision in a direct action under Article 230 EC cannot sit on his hands and wait until national proceedings are brought before he alleges that the decision is illegal. If he is out of time to bring an annulment action, he cannot object to the decision in the national proceedings.

The position is now also affected by the separate obligation imposed on national authorities by Article 14(3) of the Procedural Regulation, which provides:

> Without prejudice to any order of the Court of Justice of the European Communities pursuant to Article [242] of the Treaty,[5] recovery shall be effected without delay and in accordance with the procedures under the national law of the Member State concerned, provided that they allow the immediate and effective execution of the Commission's decision. To this effect and in the event of a procedure before national courts, the Member States concerned shall take all necessary steps which are available in their respective legal systems, including provisional measures, without prejudice to Community law.

While that provision may to some extent cut down the excuses which a domestic authority can advance for not taking proceedings, it does not purport to prevent the beneficiary from raising any possible defence. The issues are untested in the English courts, but the national authority concerned has to tread a fine line between relying solely on the Commission decision as grounding the claim for recovery and relying on its own illegal act in putting an un-notified aid into effect, especially if the aid was granted pursuant to a contract. English law takes a robust approach to the consequences of illegality, barring any recovery by a person who has to plead his own illegal act. It seems since *Courage v Crehan*[6] that this approach, and notably the concept of *in pari delicto*, may need to be moderated where the case concerns breach of a directly effective Treaty prohibition, but the factual circumstances referred to by the Court in *Crehan* are not easy to transpose to state aid cases. It is inconceivable that the state, on whom the obligation to notify rests, could be equated with the brewery tenant as the party who had a markedly weaker bargaining position such as to reduce or eliminate his freedom to negotiate the terms of the contract, or as bearing no significant responsibility for the distortion of competition concerned.

For example, it would be hard to characterize the Department of Trade and Industry, in its role of disposing owner of the Rover Group back in 1988, in those terms. When the Commission found that undisclosed terms of the sale agreement

---

[4] Case C-188/92 *TWD Textilwerke Deggendorf GmbH v Germany* [1994] ECR I-833.
[5] i.e. requiring interim suspension of a Community measure.
[6] Case C-453/99 *Courage Ltd v Crehan* [2001] ECR I-6297.

amounted to further aid to Rover which was in breach of the conditional approval it had given to the principal terms of the transaction, the DTI duly began recovery proceedings. British Aerospace ('BAe') had already brought annulment proceedings before the ECJ[7] and applied to the High Court for a stay of the recovery proceedings. That stay was granted[8] and while the judgment has been criticized,[9] it seems, at least to one who was advising BAe, a perfectly permissible exercise of the court's discretion, given that the alternative would have been to make a reference on the validity of the decision.

Consider the analogy of *Masterfoods*[10] which concerned actual and potential conflicts between Commission decisions and national court rulings on the application of Article 81. The Court there held that: 'where the addressee of a Commission decision has [ . . . ] brought an action for annulment of that decision [ . . . ] it is for the national court to decide whether to stay proceedings until a definitive decision has been given in the action for annulment or in order to refer a question to the Court for a preliminary ruling'; but that 'where the outcome of the dispute before the national court *depends* on the validity of the Commission decision, it follows from the obligation of sincere cooperation that the national court *should*, in order to avoid reaching a decision that runs counter to that of the Commission, stay its proceedings pending final judgment on the action for annulment by the Community Courts, unless it considers that, in the circumstances of the case, a reference to the Court of Justice for a preliminary ruling on the validity of the Commission decision is warranted.'[11]

On that basis, it would have been wholly wrong of the national court in *BAe* to order recovery before the Court had ruled, and indeed if it had done so its action would have been shown to be wrong by the subsequent annulment of the Commission's decision.

There is one significant difference between the situation contemplated in a case such as *Masterfoods* and that in *BAe* which goes to the legal nature of a decision under Article 249 EC (a 'decision shall be binding in its entirety on those to whom it is addressed'). Whereas, in the antitrust context, the Commission's decision is addressed to one or more undertakings, in the case of a decision ordering recovery of a state aid it is addressed to the granting member state and is therefore directly binding on the national court. That suggests that the freedom of action of the national court should if anything be wider in an antitrust case. The Court has come down in the *Masterfoods* judgment in favour of a considerable limitation of the national court's freedom (holding notably that, whereas the national court must in effect never reach a decision which is inconsistent with one taken or to be taken by the Commission, the Commission is

---

[7] In which it was ultimately successful: Case C-294/90 *British Aerospace and Rover v Commission* [1992] ECR I-493.

[8] *Department of Trade v British Aerospace and Rover* [1991] 1 CMLR 165.

[9] e.g. by Sharpe in *State Aid: Community Law and Policy* ed Harden (1993) p 95.

[10] Case C-344/98 *Masterfoods v HB Ice-Cream* [2000] ECR I-11369

[11] In paras 55 and 57; emphasis added.

quite free to take a decision which is inconsistent with a prior decision of a national court). It follows that the freedom of a national court which is the addressee of the Commission decision can be no wider in the state aids context.

## II. Compatibility decisions

There are two routes by which the Commission may give clearance to a notified state aid. By analogy with Merger Regulation procedure, these might conveniently be called Phase I and Phase II clearances. More correctly, they are respectively a decision either not to object to aid after review under Article 88(3),[12] or to give it a declaration of compatibility under Article 88(2).[13]

It is conceivable but in practice highly unlikely that, faced with either such decision, a competitor would take action in a national court, for example to secure a stay of disbursement of the aid. In such circumstances the clearance decision is evidently a serious obstacle to be overcome. By reason of the *Foto-Frost*[14] rule, the national court would be obliged to make an Article 234 reference even if it could be persuaded that the decision is vitiated by illegality of one sort or another. It might be possible in an extreme case to have the operation of the exemption decision (or national measures putting the aid into effect) suspended under the *Atlanta*[15] doctrine.

There is also the possibility that in such proceedings the *TWD* rule may be turned against the competitor. On its facts *TWD* was confined to the beneficiary of a prohibited aid who had received a copy of the decision and a letter informing him that he could bring Article 230 proceedings. However, the standing of competitors to bring Article 230 proceedings is fairly clear in certain circumstances. These include the *Cook*[16]/*Matra*[17] situation, where the Commission has given clearance in Phase I, thus denying 'interested parties' the benefit of being able to submit their comments that is accorded by the Phase II procedure, and the *Cofaz*[18] situation where the competitor in question has played an active role in the Phase II procedure, especially if it was his complaint which originally tipped off the Commission. A claimant in national proceedings who falls into either of those categories but has not applied to the CFI under Article 230 in time might well find himself 'TWD'd'.[19]

---

[12] In the clumsy nomenclature of the Procedural Regulation, a 'decision not to raise objections': see Article 4(3) thereof.

[13] A 'positive decision' as it is called in Article 7(3) of the Procedural Regulation.

[14] Case 314/85 *Foto-Frost v HZA Lübeck-Ost* [1987] ECR 4199.

[15] Case C-456/93 *Atlanta Fruchthandelsgesellschaft mbH v Bundesamt für Ernährung und Forstwirtschaft* [1995] ECR I-3761; cf. also Joined Cases C-143/88 and 92/89 *Zuckerfabrik Süderdithmarschen AG v HZA Itzehoe* [1991] ECR 1415.

[16] Case C-198/91 *William Cook v Commission* [1993] ECR I-2487.

[17] Case C-225/91 *Matra v Commission* [1993] ECR I-3203.

[18] Case 169/84 *Compagnie française de l'azote v Commission* [1986] ECR 391.

[19] See now Case C-239/99 *Nachi Europe GmbH v HZA Krefeld* [2001] ECR I-1197.

Admissibility to bring Article 230 proceedings is much more restricted in respect of, for example, Phase II clearances where the would-be challenger has not played a clearly defined role in the administrative proceedings.[20] In such circumstances *TWD* is not an obstacle. However, it is evident that a national court is likely to require forceful persuasion to entertain proceedings in respect of a cleared state aid. In practical terms, to take an example from the writer's experience, it is most unlikely that BP Chemicals would have got very far in trying to persuade the Italian courts that the terms of two state capital injections into Enichem were unlawful when they had been cleared by the Commission after a Phase II review. Since the CFI reached the conclusion that that part of BP's challenge to the Commission's decision was inadmissible,[21] the likelihood is that there is no viable forum for relief in such cases. Likewise, even leaving aside *TWD*, it is most unlikely that BP Chemicals would have been able to persuade a French court that the tax exemption for fuel blenders using fuel oxygenates of agricultural origin should be suspended on the grounds that the Commission Phase I clearance was invalid and that the validity of that decision should be referred to the ECJ under Article 234. It is conceptually a valid route to achieve the objective, but a direct action in the CFI was plainly the preferable option.[22]

Once again, if at the time when national proceedings are brought the Commission decision is being challenged in the Community courts, the national court is likely to stay the proceedings. It plainly has the option itself to make an Article 234 reference concerning the validity of the decision, which it might be persuaded to do especially if different issues were raised by the parties before it from those already before the Community courts in the annulment action. If the annulment action had been brought by a member state, it would be heard by the ECJ, which would give rise to the possibility of hearing and deciding that action and the reference in parallel, as was done in the tobacco advertizing litigation.[23] However, if the annulment action were brought by a private party, it would be heard by the CFI and then a reference from the national court (which would have to go to the ECJ as matters stand) could be awkward.

## III. BLOCK EXEMPTIONS

A new role for national courts so far untested is the interpretation of block exemptions for state aids. Maria Rehbinder has referred in her Chapter above to the three block exemptions so far adopted: training aid, *de minimis*, aid and aid

---

[20] e.g. Case T-11/95 *BP Chemicals v Commission* [1998] ECR II-3235.

[21] ibid.

[22] Case T-184/97 *BP Chemicals v Commission* [2000] ECR II-3145. The Commission appealed against the judgment but withdrew its appeal before a hearing (Case C-448/00 P).

[23] Case C-74/99 *R v SoS for Health ex p Imperial Tobacco* [2000] ECR I-8599; the hearing was held on the same day as that in Case C-376/98 *Germany v Parliament and Council* [2000] ECR I-8419 and Advocate General Fennelly delivered a single opinion.

to SMEs. The structure of them, in short, is that the categories of aid they cover need not be specifically notified and are deemed to be exempt provided the specified ceilings are respected. Member states are supposed to give the Commission periodic reports on the levels of aid made available of the types covered by the block exemptions. Although it is the Commission that drafts and promulgates the block exemptions, it is the courts (that is, national courts and ultimately the Community courts) that have the task of interpreting them. It is possible for the national courts and the Commission to disagree on how a block exemption should be interpreted, as has happened in England in respect of the exclusive purchasing block exemption for beer supply agreements (see the Court of Appeal case law summarized by Lawrence Collins J in *Whitbread v Falla*[24]).

## IV. NON-NOTIFIED AID

So much for state aid which has been considered by the Commission. Where a member state has jumped the gun and put aid into effect either without notifying it, or, more rarely, after notification but before the Commission's decision, the situation starts to become more exciting.

The situation of non-notified aid is that to which the Commission's Notice[25] is primarily addressed. This reflects the logic of the Court's case-law, and especially *FNCEPA*.[26] That case was the corollary to *Boussac*[27] in which the Court held[28] that the Commission could not declare aid illegal merely because the notification requirement in Article 88(3) had not been complied with: it had to go on and appraise the aid's compatibility with the common market. The facts in *FNCEPA* were that notified aid had been implemented before the Commission had approved it; it seems that what was subsequently approved was a variant of the original scheme. The issue was whether *Boussac* implicitly also limited the national court's powers to give relief in respect of the illegal introduction of the aid.

The Court, making a clear distinction between the respective roles of the Commission and national courts, held that it did not.[29] The relevant passages merit extensive quotation as they explain with some clarity how national courts fit into the scheme of Articles 87 and 88.

9. As far as the role of the Commission is concerned, the Court pointed out in its judgment in Case 78/76 *Steinike und Weinlig v Germany* [1977] ECR 595, at paragraph

---

[24] [2001] EuLR 150 (paras 16–20). But now see *Crehan v Inntrepreneur* ([2003] EWHC 1510 Ch).

[25] Notice on co-operation between national courts and the Commission in the field of state aids (1995 OJ C 312/7).

[26] Case C-354/90 *Fédération nationale du commerce extérieur des produits alimentaires et Syndicat national des négociants et transformateurs de saumon v France* [1991] ECR I-5505.

[27] Case C-301/87 *France v Commission* [1990] ECR I-307.

[28] Against the view of Advocate General Jacobs, which the writer respectfully prefers (having earlier taken a similar line in Flynn, *State aid and self-help* [1983] ELRev 297).

[29] On this occasion, in line with the opinion of Mr Jacobs.

9, that the intention of the Treaty, in providing through Article [88] for aid to be kept under constant review and supervised by the Commission, is that the finding that aid may be incompatible with the common market is to be arrived at, subject to review by the Court, by means of an appropriate procedure which it is the Commission's responsibility to set in motion.

10.   As far as the role of national courts is concerned, the Court held in the same judgment that proceedings may be commenced before national courts, requiring those courts to interpret and apply the concept of aid contained in Article [87] in order to determine whether state aid introduced without observance of the preliminary examination procedure provided for in Article [88(3)] ought to have been subject to this procedure.

11.   The involvement of national courts is the result of the direct effect which the last sentence of Article [88(3)] has been held to have. In this respect, the Court stated in its judgment in Case 120/73 *Lorenz v Germany* [1973] ECR 1471 that the immediate enforceability of the prohibition on implementation referred to in that article extends to all aid which has been implemented without being notified and, in the event of notification, operates during the preliminary period, and if the Commission sets in motion the contentious procedure,[30] until the final decision.

12.   In view of the foregoing considerations, it must be held that the *validity of measures giving effect to aid* is affected if national authorities act in breach of the last sentence of Article [88(3)] of the Treaty. National courts must offer to individuals in a position to rely on such breach the *certain prospect* that all the necessary inferences will be drawn, in accordance with their national law, as regards the validity of measures giving effect to the aid, the recovery of financial support granted in disregard of that provision and possible interim measures.

13.   [distinguishes *Boussac*]

14.   [...] the principal and exclusive role conferred on the Commission by Articles [87 and 88] of the Treaty, which is to hold aid to be incompatible with the common market where this is appropriate, is fundamentally different from the role of national courts in safeguarding rights which individuals enjoy as a result of the direct effect of the prohibition laid down in the last sentence of Article [88(3)]. Whilst the Commission must examine the compatibility of the proposed aid with the common market, even where the member state has acted in breach of the prohibition on giving effect to aid, national courts do no more than preserve, until the final decision of the Commission, the rights of individuals faced with a possible breach by State authorities of the prohibition laid down by the last sentence of Article [88(3)]. Where those courts make a ruling in such a matter, they do not thereby decide on the compatibility of the aid with the common market, the final determination on that matter being the exclusive responsibility of the Commission, subject to the supervision of the Court of Justice.

16.   [...] the Commission's final decision does not have the effect of regularising *ex post facto* the implementing measures which were invalid because they had been taken in breach of the prohibition laid down by the last sentence of Article [88(3)], since otherwise the direct effect of that prohibition would be impaired and the interests of individuals, which as stated above, are to be protected by the national courts, would be disregarded. Any other outcome would have the effect of according a favourable outcome to the

---

[30] i.e. that in Article 88(2). 'Contentious' was never the best word (or rather, translation) for this procedure; the author prefers 'consultative'. The Procedural Regulation characteristically calls it the 'formal investigation procedure': see Articles 4(4) and 6 thereof.

non-observance by the Member State concerned of the last sentence of Article [88(3)] and would deprive that provision of its effectiveness.

It will be appreciated that, from the third party litigant's perspective, when he considers himself affected by a non-notified aid, the choice is between starting proceedings in the national courts and making a complaint to the Commission (perhaps via his national authorities) in the hope that the Commission will take action.

In the Notice the Commission stresses the powers of the national courts and contrasts that with what it goes so far as to characterize as its 'limited powers'. It notes that a national court may need or be obliged to make an Article 234 reference on the interpretation of the concept of 'aid' within Article 87,[31] but cannot determine whether or not it is compatible with the common market. It rightly draws attention[32] to the relevant ECJ case-law laying down the obligations of national courts when faced with a breach of a directly effective Treaty provision, such as the obligation to set aside inconsistent provisions of national law,[33] to grant interim relief, and to award damages[34].

In relation to the limits on its own powers, it observes[35] that it cannot award damages or costs, nor deal with claims under national law. It also suggests that national courts may be able to adopt interim measures and order the termination of infringements more quickly than the Commission.[36]

In order to assess the extent to which there had been recourse to the national courts in the state aid context, the Commission obtained a survey, conducted by the Association of European Lawyers and available on the Commission's website.[37] It makes very interesting reading. Over the period surveyed (that is, from the accession of each member state up to 1998) the national reporters found a total of only 116 cases in which reliance had been placed on the state aid provisions, and only three in which a competitor had successfully challenged a grant of state aid (one of which was *Lunn Poly*[38]). There was no successful damages action against a member state. Given the volumes of aid granted by the member states and the persistent problem of failure to notify, these numbers are plainly very low indeed.

The report concludes[39] that

---

[31] See Plender's wide-ranging Chapter, above.     [32] In points 10–12 of the Notice.

[33] Citing Case 106/77 *Simmenthal* [1978] ECR 629.

[34] Referring to Joined Cases C-6/90 and C-9/90 *Francovich v Italy* [1991] ECR I-5357 and what were then the pending cases of *Brasserie du Pêcheur* and *Factortame* (Cases C-46/93 and C-48/93, [1994] ECR I-3829), *Peterbroeck* (Case C-312/93, [1995] ECR I-4599) and *Van Schijndel* (Cases C-430/93 and C-431/93, [1995] ECR I-4705).

[35] In point 13 of the Notice.

[36] ibid. and point 3 ('. . . the Commission is not always in a position to act promptly to safeguard the interests of third parties . . .')

[37] http://europa.eu.int/comm/competition/state_aid/legislation/app_by_member_states, last visited on 5 July 2003.

[38] *R v HM Customs & Excise ex parte Lunn Poly* [1999] EuLR 653 (CA). See Bacon below for a discussion.

[39] ibid, note 35, para 4.3.4.

the lack of successful actions by competitors is due probably not to deficiencies of the national legal systems, but rather to the limited knowledge of national judges and lawyers, and the traditional intransparency of the rules of EC state aid law. National judges normally will be reluctant to apply complex EC rules to a national set of facts in a manner which may have far-reaching consequences for private companies.

It recommends a continuation of efforts to make the rules more transparent and better known, especially so as to improve the application of the rules in interlocutory proceedings. However, the report saw no need to propose any general harmonization of national court procedures, which were thought to work satisfactorily.

The Commission has welcomed the report and broadly endorsed its conclusions. In a foreword to the report, the then Commissioner, Mr Van Miert, writes: 'I believe that part of the explanation for the current situation is probably the lack of knowledge of the State aid rules by the people concerned (administrations, enterprises, lawyers etc.)'

It is possible to be sceptical about these conclusions. It is undoubtedly true that the state aid rules are complex, and there are perhaps not many practitioners who would claim to be fully familiar with them (to say nothing of judges). It is also fair to point out that, since the report was issued, there have been (in this country) at least the same number of cases again as were available to the writers of the report, which suggests that there may now be greater familiarity with the rules. However, it is certainly untrue to say, if one considers the careful and detailed consideration given by the courts to the arguments in English cases such as *Lunn Poly*,[40] *PCG*,[41] and *BT3G*,[42] that the judges are unwilling or unable to engage with the issues when they are brought to their attention.

There may be other, more deep-seated reasons for the low number of proceedings brought. One reason in this country is that for several years there has not been a culture of generosity in the giving of aid by government and regional agencies. The cases here have largely concerned a category which one might call 'inadvertent' aid: competitive distortions perpetrated through discriminatory taxation which was adopted, not so much to subsidize particular firms or categories of business, but to deal with a perceived problem. Privatization and government auctions have also given rise to allegations of state aid in domestic proceedings,[43] but again the pace here has slackened off from the heady days of the 1980s and '90s.[44] It is therefore perhaps unsurprising that there has been no flood of actions from aggrieved competitors from other member states,

[40] *R v HM Customs & Excise ex parte Lunn Poly* [1999] EuLR 653 (CA).

[41] *R v Commissioners of Inland Revenue ex parte Professional Contractors Group* [2001] EuLR 514 (High Court, Burton J); [2002] EuLR 329, [2002] 1 CMLR 1332, CA (EWCA Civ 1945).

[42] *R v Secretary of State for Trade and Industry ex parte BT3G and Others* [2001] EuLR 325 (High Court, Silber J); [2001] EuLR 822, CA ([2001] EWCA Civ 1448).

[43] See *Banks v Coal Authority* (note 1 above); *BT3G* (note 42 above).

[44] Given recent developments in connection with rail infrastructure in the United Kingdom, it may be that renationalization aid will fall for consideration under the state aid rules.

equivalent to those that have been seen in the area of breaches of the free movement provisions.[45]

However, given the huge volumes of state aid still granted within the EC,[46] there must, it may be thought, be considerable scope and incentive for competitors to take action. The paucity of cases in fact suggests that national courts are not an appropriate forum, or that there are real difficulties in bringing proceedings.

There are of course cultural and tactical factors which discourage the taking of proceedings in jurisdictions with which a company is not familiar: language, court procedure, differences in administrative structures; concerns about taking on the administration in a country in which the potential litigant may do business and pay taxes and so on. These are concerns which apply generally to cross-border litigation, but have perhaps a particular resonance in the state aid field where by definition it is necessary to take on the authorities in the country concerned to make any headway.

More fundamentally, the real difficulty is likely to be one of evidence and disclosure, particularly in the case of covert subsidies and discretionary treatment by the administration. A company may believe that its competitor in another member state is exonerated from social security charges or has a sweetheart deal for electricity supply. The trade press may be alive with such reports. However, making it stand up in court is quite another matter. Likewise, where aid is effected through the tax system, what is the locus of an overseas competitor who does not pay tax in that jurisdiction?

It may be suggested that here the Commission has understated its own advantages in its Notice, and that the position is starker following the adoption of the Procedural Regulation: the Commission has the ability to act on suspicions and stray indications and to compel member states to produce the necessary information. Article 10 provides:

1.  Where the Commission has in its possession information from whatever source regarding alleged unlawful aid, it shall examine that information without delay.
2.  If necessary, it shall request information from the Member State concerned. [There is reference to other provisions in the Regulation requiring member states to provide full information and entitling the Commission to ask for further information.]
3.  Where, despite a reminder [ . . . ] the Member State concerned does not provide the information requested within the period prescribed by the Commission, or where it provides incomplete information, the Commission shall by decision require the information to be provided [ . . . ]

No court would or perhaps even could act in such a way on the strength of the sort of indications that may well found a valid complaint to the Commission. At

---

[45] Most spectacularly, the litigation culminating in *R v Secretary of State for Transport ex parte Factortame* [2000] EuLR 40 (HL); cf also *Bourgoin SA v MAFF* [1986] QB 716.

[46] An annual average of 90 billion euros in the years 1997–1999 according to the Commission's 2001 survey of state aid (COM (2001) 403 final, available at http://europa.eu.int/ eur-lex/en/com/cnc/ 2001/ com2001_0403en01.pdf (last visited on 5 July 2003).

the level of evidence, the Commission is in a far better position than third party competitors.

However, where the aggrieved competitor does have access to the courts in respect of non-notified aid, undoubtedly reliance on the state aid rules is a powerful weapon in the armoury. The effects of success are dramatic: the national measures (even Acts of Parliament) are illegal because of the failure to notify; unlike the position in antitrust litigation, a 'deathbed' notification (i.e. once the proceedings have begun or as a device to obtain a stay) will not cure the initial defect for the period in which the aid was put into effect; and the national court is wholly unconcerned with the issue of whether the aid may ultimately be declared compatible with the common market by the Commission. Furthermore, the wording of the relevant paragraphs of *FNCEPA* (quoted above) is rather stern, referring to an *obligation* on national courts to offer the *certain* prospect that *all* the necessary inferences will be drawn as regards the illegality of the national measures.

What remedies should national courts therefore be affording? They obviously include injunctions and declarations. It is not surprising that most of the English cases have arisen in the context of judicial review and that the primary remedy sought is a declaration of illegality.

However, the focus is now turning to financial remedies, namely restitution or damages. In principle it is plainly right, as the Commission's Notice suggests, that *Francovich/Factortame* damages should be available for breach of the state aid rules. The difficulties associated with causation and quantum in the field of competitive harm are well known. Indeed, the AEA report states that they 'do not think that this category of cases should deserve special attention because the problem of causation which is common to all legal systems makes successful actions virtually impossible'.[47] While this seems unnecessarily defeatist, this chapter is not the place to explore the issue in depth.

It is understood that damages are currently being sought by various companies adversely affected by differential rates on insurance premium tax in cases which follow on from *Lunn Poly*. However, those proceedings are awaiting rulings by the VAT Tribunal on whether those taxes amount to state aid and the scope of the remedies available if so. Those issues have been raised in the recent *GIL* reference to the ECJ.[48] *GIL* concerns differential rates of IPT relating to insurance linked to sales of domestic appliances. The Tribunal is seeking guidance from the ECJ on whether there must be an appreciable effect on inter-state trade for an aid to be caught by Article 87 and how that effect may be shown. It is also seeking guidance on the appropriate remedy in the case of a differential tax amounting to a state aid. The taxpayer argues that it is entitled to a refund of the tax overpaid (which may be the whole amount, or the difference between what

---

[47] Note 37 above, para 4.2.3.

[48] *GIL Insurance v Commissioners of Customs & Excise* [2001] EuLR 401 (VAT Tribunal): Article 234 reference to ECJ from VAT Tribunal pending as Case C-308/01 (see 2001 OJ C 303/8). See further Bacon below.

was paid and what would have been paid if tax had been levied at the lower rate). The Commissioners argue that the illegality resides in the preferential rate and that the right remedy is for the lower rate taxpayers to be charged at the higher rate.

One final issue deserves mention in the context of the search for the appropriate remedy. The Court of Appeal in *BT3G* framed a conundrum. The alleged state aid in that case was the payment holiday given to Vodafone and Orange for their third generation licences, working to the disadvantage of two competitors, BT and One 2 One. A remedy canvassed was that the Secretary of State should, as a matter of discretion, give the same payment holiday to them. The Court of Appeal thought that, if the payment holiday to Vodafone and Orange was a state aid, then so would be any payment holiday given to BT and One 2 One. 'There would simply have been four beneficiaries of state aid distorting competition within the market rather than two.'[49] This proposition reinforced the Court of Appeal in its view that the payment holiday was not state aid. However, while the conundrum does suggest that an important component of the normal remedy should be recovery of a positive benefit from the recipient, that corrective will not always be in the power of the court. Furthermore, the correction of a disadvantage constituted by an underpayment by some operators may require a different solution. It is a nice conceptual question whether and to what extent damages from a court may themselves constitute state aid.[50] It is submitted that, in principle, a remedy granted by a court to a claimant in order to provide relief in respect of a state aid to another does not itself constitute state aid.

## V. WHERE NO AID HAS BEEN GRANTED

Last of all in this counter-chronological survey is the situation where no aid has been granted. Can there be judicial review of a decision not to grant aid at all? Articles 87 and 88 start from the presumption that all aid is incompatible with the common market unless the special considerations which they set out apply. The Treaty state aid provisions can be categorized according to the classical Dutch schema as instruments of negative integration: they do not require or even encourage the granting of national aid in any circumstances whatsoever.[51] There is therefore no scope for a company to say that the state has erred in not granting it assistance. The situation may be different where a member state has put into

---

[49] Note 42 above, para 101.

[50] Compare the judgment of the Court in Joined Cases 106–120/87 *Asteris v Hellenic Republic* [1988] ECR 5515, which says that damages awarded by national courts are not state aid, with the Opinion of Sir Gordon Slynn in that case which was that they might be if they represented compensation for an unlawful promise to pay state aid.

[51] It is submitted that that consideration exposes the policy misconception vitiating the Court's *Boussac* ruling: it is a matter of indifference to the common market whether or not a state grants aid that is compatible with it. The Commission should therefore be entitled to strike down a national measure simply on the ground of a failure to notify it.

effect a national scheme which allows grants to be made if certain conditions are satisfied. A firm wishing to contend that it meets those conditions and has wrongly been denied its support may allege that it is the victim of discrimination but is unlikely to find much support from the EC state aid rules themselves.[52]

[52] A slightly different case is where the member state has failed to apply for Community aid from one of the structural funds. Such a decision was unsuccessfully judicially reviewed in *R v Secretary of State for Trade and Industry and others ex parte Isle of Wight Council* (High Court, Newman J, 7 April 2000, unreported).

# 18

# State Aids in the English Courts: Definition and Other Problems

## KELYN BACON*

After a much earlier exploratory foray into the area in the *ICI* case,[1] the landmark judgments of the Divisional Court and Court of Appeal in *Lunn Poly*[2] appeared to herald a new era in the use of EC state aid rules in the English courts. The case marked a willingness by the courts not only to grapple with the application of Articles 87 and 88 EC, but also to enforce their requirements rigorously as against national fiscal legislation (in that case differential rates of Insurance Premium Tax) which discriminated between two classes of undertakings.

Since *Lunn Poly*, state aid arguments have been put forward in a series of cases. All turned, in essence, on allegedly discriminatory state measures, which had not been notified to the Commission. In every case it was argued that the measures were state aid within the meaning of Article 87(1) which were unlawful under Article 88(3) for lack of notification.[3] However these assertions of state aid infringements have met with a somewhat less enthusiastic reception. In four cases the courts held that the measures under challenge did not constitute state aid.[4] In one case on very similar facts to those in *Lunn Poly*, the VAT and Duties Tribunal held most of the elements of state aid to be present, but referred the issues of effect on inter-state trade and remedies to the Court of Justice for a preliminary ruling.[5] Finally, in a parallel case on facts identical to *Lunn Poly*, the VAT and Duties Tribunal applied *Lunn Poly* as binding upon it, but found against the Appellants on other grounds.[6] These subsequent cases expose the

---

* The author is very grateful for the helpful comments of Gerald Barling QC and Aidan Robertson of Brick Court Chambers. All errors remain, however, her own.

[1] *R v AG ex p ICI* [1985] 1 CMLR 588, Div Ct; [1987] 1 CMLR 72, CA.

[2] *R v Commrs of Customs & Excise ex p Lunn Poly* [1998] EuLR 438, Div Ct; [1999] EuLR 653, CA.

[3] See the Chapter by James Flynn above, dealing with non-notified aids.

[4] *BT v Director General of Telecommunications* (Moses J, 4.8.00); *R v Secretary of State for Trade and Industry ex p BT3G and One2One* [2001] EuLR 325, Silber J; [2001] EuLR 822, CA; *R v Commrs of Inland Revenue ex p Professional Contractors' Group* [2001] EuLR 514, Burton J; [2002] EuLR 329, [2002] 1 CMLR 1332, CA (EWCA Civ 1945); *R (British Aggregates Association) v HM Treasury* [2002] EWHC 926 (Admin), [2002] EuLR 394, Moses J.

[5] *GIL Insurance et al v Commrs of Customs & Excise* [2001] EuLR 401, currently pending before ECJ as Case C-308/01.

[6] *CGNU, Airtours et al v Commrs of Customs & Excise*, Decision 8.10.01, currently on appeal to the High Court.

real difficulties which the courts have found in resolving issues of the definition
of aid and remedies.

## I. THE *LUNN POLY* CASE

In *Lunn Poly*[7] the applicants sought judicial review of the introduction of
differential rates of Insurance Premium Tax (IPT) on insurance contracts. Until
1997 IPT had been charged at a uniform rate of 2.5 per cent. From 1 April 1997
IPT was charged at a 'standard' rate of 4 per cent, and a higher rate of 17.5 per
cent which applied to, among others, travel insurance contracts concluded with
tour operators and travel agents. The purported justification was an alleged
practice of tax avoidance by 'value shifting' in the travel trade, by setting low
margins on the VAT-able holiday package, but high margins on travel insurance,
which was not subject to VAT but rather subject to IPT at a much lower rate.

In the Divisional Court, Maurice Kay J and Kennedy LJ found the differential
rates of IPT in respect of the travel trade to constitute state aid, contrary to
Article 87 of the EC Treaty. The judgment was upheld by the Court of Appeal in
February 1999. Significantly, the Court of Appeal rejected the argument of
Customs and Excise that the measure could not be classified as aid, since the
lower rate of IPT was the 'standard' rate; thus the higher rate (it was argued) did
not involve a transfer of state resources or a forgoing of tax revenue. Clarke LJ
stated trenchantly that it was no more than a 'matter of form' whether the tax
was expressed to be a 4 per cent standard rate with a higher rate of 17.5 per cent,
or a 17.5 standard rate with a lower rate of 4 per cent.[8]

The Court also rejected the other principal argument put forward by Customs
and Excise, that the measure was objectively justified. On the facts of the case,
the evidence was that 'value shifting' did not and indeed could not occur.
Nevertheless, Lord Woolf MR thought that objective justification might in
other circumstances be relevant.

To take an example relevant to the present case: if a higher rate of tax were imposed to
rectify an actual loss of tax due to a tax avoidance scheme initiated by certain members of
a group of taxpayers, that would not mean that the remainder of the relevant group of
taxpayers were receiving an aid because of the higher discriminatory rate of tax imposed
specifically on the tax avoiders. Nor should it make any difference if, instead of the rate of
tax being increased for those who are involved in the tax avoidance, it is reduced for those
not so involved. In both situations what is being achieved is a level playing field. *Where an
explanation of this nature is put forward, if the court is satisfied that what had happened is
justifiable, the result would be that there would be no discrimination which could
constitute an aid.*[9]

---

[7] *R v Commrs of Customs & Excise ex p Lunn Poly* [1998] EuLR 438 (Div Ct); [1999] EuLR 653
(CA). For a more detailed commentary on this case see Bacon, 'Differential Taxes, State Aids and the
Lunn Poly case' [1999] ECLR 384.
[8] ibid, 667–668.     [9] ibid, 663–664, emphasis added.

Clarke LJ agreed, but for slightly different reasons, characterising the cited case-law of the court as evidence of what he termed a 'pragmatic approach', namely that 'the court should have regard principally to the effect of the measure concerned, but should also give some consideration to its aim or purpose in answering the broad question whether it provides state aid'.[10]

Even before the judgment in *Lunn Poly*, the differential rates of IPT were removed and replaced by a uniform rate of 17.5 per cent on all insurance transactions. More significantly, however, the judgments in *Lunn Poly* have been relied upon heavily in the six subsequent state aid cases in which the High Court, Court of Appeal, and VAT and Duties Tribunal have delivered judgment. The facts and judgments in these cases are set out below, followed by more detailed analysis of the decisions and reasoning of the various courts and tribunals.

## II. Subsequent case-law

### A. *BT v DGT*

A year and a half after the Court of Appeal judgment in *Lunn Poly*, the High Court gave judgment in *British Telecommunications v Director General of Telecommunications ('BT v DGT')*.[11] The case was a statutory appeal[12] against a determination of the DGT that BT should pay 50 per cent of the total costs of providing 'interim carrier pre-selection' or 'ICPS' on their networks. ICPS was a system allowing consumers to select in advance to have all, or certain types of call services provided, not by BT, but by another telecommunications operator. The system required the provision to consumers of 'autodiallers': boxes installed at the customer's premises to route calls through the pre-selected operator. This system was not, however, new: prior to the introduction of ICPS, some operators already provided autodiallers to their customers, at their own expense. OFTEL in its evidence had admitted that the BT contribution was imposed in order to allow ICPS to be offered at a lower price than the existing service with autodiallers.

BT claimed, *inter alia*, that it was in effect being required to subsidize the cost of other operators, creating a distortion of competition amounting to state aid. Moses J accepted that the determination relieved the other operators of 50 per cent of the costs which they previously had to bear. However, he rejected the suggestion that this constituted state aid, on the basis that the determination represented 'merely a division of the burden of the costs which result from the new system'.[13]

It was therefore not necessary, in the judge's view, to resolve the further difficult question of whether, if the determination constituted 'aid' in principle,

---

[10] ibid, 672.　　[11] *BT v Director General of Telecommunications* (Moses J, 4.8.00).
[12] Under s. 46B of the Telecommunications Act 1984.　　[13] Above n. 11, para 131.

the advantage was granted directly or indirectly through state resources. However he observed that the issue was far from clear, and he would have referred it to the European Court had it been necessary to do so.[14]

## B. *BT3G and One2One*

Hot on the heels of *BT v DGT* came the judgment of Silber J in *BT3G and One2One*,[15] arising from the much publicized auction by the UK government of licences for third-generation mobile phones. The successful bidders, announced on 27 April 2000, were the four established mobile telephone providers, Vodafone, BT3G, One2One, and Orange, and a new entrant TIW, raising a total sum of £22 billion. Vodafone's licence alone went for £5.964 billion.

During the auction, however, a problem had arisen in relation to the acquisition by Vodafone of Mannesmann AG, which owned Orange. Under the Auction Rules, this led to an association between Vodafone and Orange which, *prima facie*, precluded either from bidding in the auction. Foreshadowing this possibility, the Rules included a power in the Secretary of State to disregard certain associations between bidders. The Secretary of State duly exercised this power for the purposes of the auction bidding procedure, on the condition that Vodafone divested itself of Orange by 30 September 2000. Vodafone and Orange thus continued to participate, and were ultimately successful bidders in the auction.

The association between Vodafone and Orange had, however, an important consequence. The Auction Rules provided for bidders to obtain, and pay for, their licences following the auction. However, following the rules for grant of and payment for the licences, Vodafone and Orange could not receive (and thus would not pay for) their licences until Vodafone had sold Orange, up to five months after the auction. Given the vast sums involved, delay in payment for the licences would save Vodafone and Orange considerable sums. BT3G and One2One therefore requested that the Secretary of State (pursuant to various powers) ensure that all successful bidders should pay for their licences at the same time, thus removing the advantage to Vodafone and Orange. The Secretary of State refused.

In judicial review proceedings[16] BT3G and One2One claimed, *inter alia*, that the payment advantage afforded to Vodafone and Orange was state aid. Silber J, at first instance, rejected this contention. He did accept that the benefit to Vodafone and Orange was 'capable' of being state aid on the basis that Article 87(1) was wide enough to cover the failure by the government to exercise its

---

[14] Above n. 11, paras 132–137.

[15] *R v Secretary of State for Trade and Industry ex p BT3G and One2One* [2001] EuLR 325. For the judge's reflections on this case, see the Chapter by Silber below.

[16] BT3G and One2One also brought statutory appeals under s. 1F of the Wireless Telegraphy Act 1949. However it was common ground that these raised identical issues to the judicial review proceedings, so were not dealt with separately.

powers to accelerate the liability of Vodafone and Orange to pay a debt, or defer the obligations of the other applicants.[17]

However, he ultimately found that the measure was not 'aid granted by the British Government or through state resources' on the basis of six criteria, which he considered to be relevant: (i) a normal market conditions test; (ii) an analogy with the Commission's guidelines on state aid in the context of privatization; (iii) the general scheme of the Auction Rules; (iv) objective justification and discrimination; (v) a pragmatic test; and finally (vi) a status quo test.[18] Paradoxically, however, the judge went on to find that the advantages to Vodafone and Orange did distort competition and affect inter-state trade, since 'the advantages to Vodafone of being able to defer payment from May until 1 September, of the balance of the licence fee of £5.9 billion, would, it seems, have an effect on the market'.[19]

The Court of Appeal endorsed the reasoning of Silber J on points (i), (ii), (iv), and (v), and dismissed the appeal of BT3G and One2One on those grounds. Regarding (iii) it considered that the 'general scheme' principle was not relevant in the present case; on (vi) the court noted that the judge's reasoning on 'status quo' contradicted his conclusions on distortion of competition and effect on trade.[20]

## C. Professional contractors' group

The hearings in the High Court and Court of Appeal in the *Professional Contractors' Group* case[21] took place a few months after those in *BT3G and One2One*. The facts were, however, very different, concerning this time a new method of taxing small contracting companies which came into force on 1 April 2001 and was known, after the Inland Revenue press release in which it had been announced, as 'IR35'. The stated aim of IR35 was to eliminate the avoidance of tax and national insurance contributions by contractors who were, in fact, equivalent to employees. However, the result was more broad: many legitimate contracting companies were caught by the legislation and, where caught, were required to pay more tax than they had hitherto been paying under the normal rules of company taxation. More significantly, many such contractors—particularly in the IT industry—competed with larger contracting companies which continued to be taxed under the normal company taxation rules, and escaped the application of IR35. In consequence, IR35 companies paid a greater proportion of tax than their competitors.

---

[17] Above n. 15, para 64.

[18] ibid, paras 77–142.

[19] ibid, paras 143–159.

[20] *R v Secretary of State for Trade and Industry ex p BT3G and One2One* [2001] EuLR 822.

[21] *R v Commrs of Inland Revenue ex p Professional Contractors' Group* [2001] EuLR 514, Burton J; [2002] EuLR 329, [2002] 1 CMLR 1332, CA (EWCA Civ 1945).

The Professional Contractors' Group, an organization with some 11,000 members (primarily small contracting companies in the IT, engineering, telecommunications, and management and business consulting industries) challenged IR35 on various grounds, including infringement of the EC state aid rules. Both in the High Court before Burton J, and in the Court of Appeal, the state aid arguments were rejected on the ground that IR35 was a general tax avoidance measure, and thus did not 'favour' any specific individuals or sectors within the meaning of Article 87(1).

## D. The *GIL* and *Airtours* cases

The hearings in the VAT and Duties Tribunal in *GIL*[22] and *Airtours*[23] arose directly from the *Lunn Poly* judgment. The groups of appellants in both cases had been subject to IPT at the higher rate. They claimed repayment of the difference between the tax paid at the higher rate, and the tax which would have been payable at the lower rate, during the period in which the differential rate was in force, on the ground (*inter alia*) that the differential rate had been found in *Lunn Poly* to constitute state aid.

However, there were two material differences between the appellants in the two cases. First, in *Airtours* the appellants were travel agents, tour operators, and their insurers: the case was therefore on all fours with the *Lunn Poly* case. In *GIL* the appellants were suppliers of insurance relating to domestic appliances (mainly televisions and video recorders). They had also been subject to the higher rate of IPT; but the *Lunn Poly* case had concerned the differential rate for travel trade insurance alone. The second material difference was that in *GIL* the appellants had both provided the insurance and sold the insurance at a retail level. In *Airtours*, by contrast, the insurance trade was split between the 'wholesale' provision of insurance by the insurer, and the 'retail' sale of that insurance by the travel agent or tour operator. Of the six appellants in the case, only the first, CGNU, was an insurer; the remainder were travel agents or tour operators in the Airtours Group.

In *GIL* the Tribunal found, on the basis of *Lunn Poly* and the jurisprudence of the European Court, that the differential rate of IPT in respect of domestic appliances constituted aid granted through state resources, which distorted competition, which favoured certain undertakings over others, and which was not objectively justified. However, it made a reference to the Court of Justice on the questions of whether the higher rate affected trade between Member States, and whether repayment (as sought by the appellants) was the appropriate remedy. The judgment of the European Court is not expected before the end of 2003.

[22] *GIL Insurance* et al *v Commrs of Customs & Excise* [2001] EuLR 401, currently pending before ECJ as Case C-308/2001.
[23] *CGNU, Airtours* et al *v Commrs of Customs & Excise*, Decision 8.10.01, currently on appeal to the High Court.

The Tribunal came to a different conclusion in *Airtours*. On the issue of state aid it considered itself bound by the decision in *Lunn Poly* (notwithstanding the contrary arguments of Customs and Excise) and held accordingly that the differential rate of IPT did satisfy all the criteria in Article 87(1). However the problem, in its view, was one of entitlement to initiate a claim before the Tribunal for a repayment. The only insurer among the appellants, CGNU, had paid the IPT but had been reimbursed by the 'retail' sellers of the travel insurance (including the second and fourth appellants in the case). The Tribunal therefore held that CGNU would be unjustly enriched by any repayment of the tax differential. However, neither were the remaining appellants, in the view of the Tribunal, entitled to a repayment. The Tribunal found that their role was merely to collect the insurance premiums and IPT from their customers to pass on to the insurers, and that they were not therefore affected by the increase in IPT. The separation of insurer and retailer in the travel industry thus resulted in a situation where neither could claim repayment.

### E. *British Aggregates Association*

The final and most recent case was that of the *British Aggregates Association*.[24] Of all the post-*Lunn Poly* cases, this came closest to a paradigm example of state aid. As in many of the cases, this involved a challenge by way of judicial review to fiscal legislation: this time the imposition of a levy on aggregates. By contrast with the *Professional Contractors' Group* case, it was not suggested that the imposition of the levy itself amounted to state aid. Rather, the claimants challenged a number of exemptions contained within the levy. In particular the legislation exempted exports, and certain specific aggregates such as those consisting of slate and shale. It also exempted aggregates consisting of the spoil (and in some cases other by-products and waste) from the separation of certain specified minerals from the rock in which they are found, including china clay, fluorspar, gypsum, potash, pumice, and talc.

The British Aggregates Association claimed that these exemptions amounted to state aid to the undertakings producing the exempted products. The exempt aggregates produced from slate, or from the spoil from separation of the specified minerals, competed with other, non-exempt aggregates. Many of the exempted products resulted from exactly the same harmful process (namely quarrying) as formed the basis for the introduction of the levy. The levy would thus simply lead to the substitution of the exempted aggregates in construction, in place of the non-exempted aggregates currently used.

Moses J in the High Court rejected the claims. He found that the export exemption was not aid, on the basis that it was the repayment of an internal,

---

[24] *R (on the application of British Aggregates Association) v HM Treasury* [2002] EWHC 926 (Admin), [2002] EuLR 394, Moses J.

indirect tax, which was permitted under Articles 90–92 EC.[25] Regarding the exemptions for specific products he observed that, unlike other cases such as *Professional Contractors' Group*, where it had been claimed that the legislation was aimed at putting undertakings on an equal footing, the essence of the aggregates levy *was* to make distinctions between certain products so as to shift demand from one to the other.[26] However, he considered that these distinctions were justified by the nature or general scheme of the system of the aggregates levy, and thus did not satisfy the state aid requirement of favouring or selectivity. The legislation, he thought, stemmed from the objective of discouraging the extraction of primary or virgin aggregates from natural rock, while encouraging the use of secondary aggregates or recycled material such as the waste from the production of clay or fluorspar. The judge held that the distinctions in the legislation were consistent with that objective.[27]

### III. The definition of an aid[28]

As is clear from the above, the most thorny issue facing the courts, both in *Lunn Poly* and in the subsequent cases, has been the question of whether, applying the law to the facts of the cases, the contested measures constitute state aid: in other words, whether the measures fall within the definition of aid as set out in Article 87(1). The centrality of this issue is not surprising: it is the basic question which a national court has to ask, in order to determine whether the measure should have been notified to the Commission, and if not notified, whether it is accordingly unlawful under the 'standstill' provision of Article 88(3).[29]

### A. The elements of state aid

The first and obvious difficulty is the elliptical wording of Article 87(1). On its face, it prohibits 'any aid granted by a Member State or through State resources in any form whatsoever which distorts or threatens to distort competition by favouring certain undertakings or the production of certain goods [ . . . ] in so far as it affects trade between Member States'.

---

[25] *R (on the application of British Aggregates Association) v HM Treasury* [2002] EWHC 926 (Admin), [2002] EuLR 394, Moses J., paras 90–96.

[26] ibid, para 107.

[27] ibid, paras 108–115. The judgment is currently under appeal to the Court of Appeal. The matter is also currently pending before the Court of First Instance as Case T-210/02 *British Aggregates Association v Commission*, an application for the annulment of the Commission decision of 24 April 2002 declaring the levy to be compatible with the common market. The decision followed the notification by the UK government of a specific, temporary exemption in the levy for Northern Ireland (not in issue before Moses J). The Commission has approved the exemption for Northern Ireland under Article 92(3) (press release IP/02/607).

[28] See more generally on the definition of an aid the Chapter by Plender above.

[29] See the seminal judgment of the Court in Case C-354/90 *Fédération nationale du commerce extérieur des produits alimentaires v France ('FNCEPA')* [1991] ECR I-5505, §§ 9–16, cited in the Chapter James Flynn above.

This raises several questions. Is a measure 'state aid' simply when it is 'aid granted by a Member State or through State resources in any form whatsoever', or does the definition of state aid encompass the further requirements of a distortion of competition, favouring certain undertakings, and effect on inter-State trade? Is the issue of favouring certain undertakings or certain goods part of the question of whether the aid distorts competition, part of the analysis of whether there is 'an aid', or a wholly separate matter? Is it necessary to show an *actual* distortion of competition and effect on trade? The confusion in the interpretation of Article 87(1) is highlighted, in particular, in the judgments in *BT3G and One2One*.

Burton J in *Professional Contractors' Group* clarified these questions. His interpretation,[30] followed in subsequent judgments,[31] is that the national court must consider six ingredients, namely whether there is:

(i) an aid in the sense of a benefit or advantage;
(ii) which is granted by the state or through state resources;
(iii) which favours certain undertakings over others (the 'selectivity' principle);
(iv) which distorts or threatens to distort competition;
(v) which is capable of affecting trade between Member States; and
(vi) which has not been notified to the Commission.

This interpretation corresponds closely to the approach adopted in the recent case-law of the European Court.[32]

In all the cases discussed above, the measures challenged had not been notified to the Commission.[33] The last state aid criterion was therefore unproblematic. The difficulties arose with the other five criteria, which are considered in turn below.

## B. 'Aid' in the sense of a benefit or advantage

While some English courts have conflated this question with the third state aid criterion of favouring,[34] the two are distinct criteria and should not be confused. The criterion of an 'aid', in the sense of a benefit or an advantage, does not engage questions of selectivity, or general measures, which are considered under the third state aid criterion of favouring. Rather, it addresses four issues.

First, the criterion emphasizes that 'aid' within the meaning of Article 87(1) need not be granted by a direct cash grant, but may take many other forms. As

---

[30] *Professional Contractors' Group* [2001] EuLR 514, para 55.

[31] Court of Appeal in *Professional Contractors' Group* [2002] 1 CMLR 1332, para 28; Moses J in *British Aggregates Association* [2002] EWHC 926 (Admin), [2002] EuLR 394 para 81. Cf also Robertson, 'Challenging state aid in the courts' [2002] Judicial Review 91, 92–93.

[32] See e.g. AG Jacobs in Case C-342/96 *Déménagements-Manutention Transport ('DMT')* [1999] ECR I-3913; AG Tizzano in Case C-53/00 *Ferring v ACOSS* [2001] ECR I-9067; AG Léger in Case C-280/00 *Altmark*, opinion 19.3.02, para 55.

[33] Although regarding *British Aggregates Association* see n. 27 above.

[34] See Burton J and the CA in *Professional Contractors' Group* [2001] EuLR 514 and [2002] 1 CMLR 1332; and Moses J in *British Aggregates Association* [2002] EWHC 926 (Admin), [2002] EuLR 394.

Moses J noted in *BT v DGT*, according to the European Court's oft-cited definition, the concept of aid is more general than that of a subsidy, and includes not only positive benefits but also measures 'which, in various forms, mitigate the charges which are normally included in the budget of an undertaking'.[35]

Secondly, as the European Court has stated in many recent cases, the test of an 'aid' is whether the recipient undertaking 'receives an economic advantage which it would not have obtained under normal market conditions'.[36] This test, also known as the 'market investor' or 'market creditor' test, is used to determine whether a benefit or advantage has been conferred in circumstances in which the State has acted as a participant in the market. In such cases, the question is whether the apparent advantage is one which would or could have been obtained from an private operator acting with a view to obtaining a return.

The classic example is that of a capital injection. A state (or state-financed) capital injection cannot be regarded as state aid where a 'private investor operating under normal market conditions' would have made the investment.[37] Similarly, where the state offers to undertakings loans and other financial facilities on preferential terms, the Court compares the terms offered by the State with the likely terms of a 'private creditor' or 'private operator',[38] asking whether such private operator 'would have entered into the transaction in question on the same terms and, if not, on which conditions he could have entered into the transaction'.[39]

Thus, as the Court of Appeal in *BT3G and One2One* correctly stated, '[t]he normal market conditions test involves comparing the position of the State with that of a commercial entity'.[40] This means that this criterion is not relevant where the state is acting, not as a market participant, but in the exercise of its sovereign or public functions, for example in the adoption of fiscal legislation or social policy. In such cases, by definition, there can be no 'normal market' comparator, and the focus is rather on whether the apparent advantage to certain undertakings 'favours' them within the meaning of the third criterion of favouring/selectivity.[41] But, as *BT3G and One2One* itself shows, it may be difficult to determine whether the state in a given case is acting as a regulator, or as a market participant. The Court of Appeal held there that the Secretary of State was performing regulatory functions, but also acted in a commercial capacity as the vendor of a valuable commodity, namely the licences. It was in

---

[35] Case 30/59 *Steenkolenmijnen* [1961] ECR 1, 19.

[36] Case C-342/96 *DMT* [1999] ECR I-3913, para 22.

[37] See e.g. Case C-303/88 *Italy v Commission ('ENI/Lanerossi')* [1991] ECR I-1433, paras 20–24; Case T-358/94 *Air France v Commission* [1996] ECR II-2109, para 70.

[38] Case C-342/96 *Spain v Commission* [1999] ECR I-2459, paras 41 et seq; *DMT*, above n. 36, paras 23–25; Joined Cases T-204/97 and T-270/97 *EPAC v Commission* [2000] ECR II-2267, paras 66–71.

[39] Case T-16/96 *Cityflyer Express v Commission* [1998] ECR II-757, para 51.

[40] [2001] EuLR 822, para 71.

[41] See AG Fennelly in Case C-390/98 *Banks v Coal Authority* [2001] ECR I-6117, opinion paras 18–20.

the latter respect that the normal market conditions test could, according to the court, legitimately be applied.[42]

Thirdly, the requirement of a benefit or an advantage has often been used to exclude from the concept of aid a benefit, granted by the state, which is used to compensate an undertaking for the costs of public service obligations. The situation is analogous to the provision by the state of consideration for services rendered by the undertaking. In the case of *Ferring*, the Court of Justice reaffirmed that, where the benefit corresponds to the costs incurred by the undertaking in discharging its public service obligations, it may be regarded as compensation for the services provided and not state aid. In such a case the undertaking does not enjoy 'any real advantage' for the purposes of Article 87(1).[43] This approach has been confirmed (although the conditions refined) in the Court's recent judgment in *Altmark*.[43a]

Finally, by contrast with the provisions of Article 4(c) of the ECSC Treaty, Article 87(1) applies only to 'aids' and not to 'special charges' imposed on undertakings. It is therefore not sufficient to complain simply of the selective imposition of a tax or charge. Rather, the state aid (if it exists) consists of the *non-imposition* of that charge on comparable competitors. This point was made by the Court of Appeal in *Professional Contractors' Group*: 'For the state to confer a benefit on an identifiable group of undertakings is at first sight state aid. For the state to impose a detriment (for instance, a "windfall" tax on privatised utilities) can be state aid only if it can be seen as occasioning a corresponding advantage to identifiable business competitors of those who have to bear the detriment'.[44]

## C. Granted by the state or through state resources

The issue of state resources has not generally caused problems in the English courts. While in *Lunn Poly* Customs and Excise did put forward the argument that, because the lower rate of IPT was the 'standard' rate, this criterion was not satisfied, the argument was roundly rejected by the courts, as discussed above. The correctness of the approach of the Court of Appeal in *Lunn Poly* has subsequently been confirmed by the Court of Justice in *Ferring*, which concerned the imposition of a tax on one group of undertakings and not on another competing group. The Court held that the non-imposition of the tax on the second group equated to a tax exemption, which was an economic advantage granted through state resources.[45]

The one situation where the state resources criterion is likely to cause problems is where a state measure requires one undertaking to subsidize another.

---

[42] Above n. 40, paras 47–53 and 65–77.

[43] Case C-53/00 *Ferring v ACOSS* [2001] ECR I-9067, paras 23–27.

[43a] Case C-280/00, judgment of 24.7.03. See further opinion of AG Jacobs in Case C-126/01 *GEMO*, opinion of 30.4.02, and the Chapter by Rizza above.

[44] [2002] 1 CMLR 1332, para 34.

[45] Above n. 43, para 20; also AG Tizzano's opinion in that case, paras 43–45.

This was the case in *BT v DGT*, where the contested determination of the DGT effectively required BT to subsidize, to the extent of 50 per cent, certain costs of other telecommunications operators. At the time the position of the European Court on the state resources criterion was not entirely clear, as Moses J noted.[46] Since then, however, the Court of Justice has clarified its position in the case of *PreussenElektra*. Following the opinion of AG Jacobs, the Court held that a German law, requiring electricity suppliers to purchase electricity from renewable energy sources at minimum prices, did not involve any direct or indirect transfer of state resources to the producers of that type of electricity; and that the fact that the purchase obligation was imposed by statute, and conferred an undeniable advantage on certain undertakings, did not give it the character of aid within Article 87(1).[47]

## D. Favouring or selectivity

This principle of favouring or selectivity is of fundamental importance to the definition of aid, as it is the primary means of differentiating between objectionable state aid, and general legislative measures applying to all undertakings without distinction.[48] Unfortunately, this criterion has been the most commonly misunderstood and misapplied state aid criterion in the case-law of the English courts.

Put simply, in order to constitute an aid it is not sufficient merely to identify a benefit or advantage to one or more undertakings (the first state aid criterion). Rather, in addition, the measure must favour 'certain' undertakings or the production of 'certain' goods. If an aid is a 'general measure' it is not selective and does not 'favour' certain undertakings; conversely, if a measure is selective it is not a general measure.[49] However, the English courts have had great difficulties in applying the concepts of selectivity and general measures. Too often the buzzwords of 'general system' and 'general measures' have been used as a cloak for judicial reticence in areas of fiscal and social policy. Some clarity is needed which, sadly, is conspicuously lacking, not only in the English courts but also in the jurisprudence of the European Court.

In this author's view, the test of favouring/selectivity and general measures is most conveniently divided into two cumulative questions.

*(1) Does the measure de facto favour certain undertakings or the production of certain goods?* It is necessary to identify a specific undertaking, or class of undertakings, to whom the benefit or advantage has been granted. This does not

---

[46] Judgment 4.8.00, paras 132–137.

[47] Case C-379/98 *PreussenElektra v Schleswag AG* [2001] ECR I-2099, paras 59–61. For a critique of this 'narrow' approach to the state resources criterion, see Bronckers and van der Vlies, 'The European Court's *PreussenElektra* Judgment: Tensions Between EU Principles and National Renewable Energy Initiatives' [2001] ECLR 458.

[48] Court of Appeal in *Professional Contractors' Group* [2002]1 CMLR 1332, para 30.

[49] For a detailed examination of the definition of a general measure, see Bacon, 'State Aids and General Measures' (1997) 17 YEL 269.

mean that the measure must only apply to individual undertakings, or that the particular recipients of the aid must be individually or exhaustively identified. As the Court of First Instance has held:

The fact that the aid is not aimed at one or more specific recipients defined in advance, but that it is subject to a series of objective criteria pursuant to which it may be granted, within the framework of a predetermined overall budget allocation, to an indefinite number of beneficiaries who are not initially individually identified, cannot suffice to call into question the selective nature of the measure and, accordingly, its classification as State aid within the meaning of Article [87(1)] of the Treaty. At the very most, that circumstance means that the measure is not an individual aid. It does not, however, preclude that public measure from having to be regarded as a system of aid constituting a selective, and therefore specific, measure if, owing to the criteria governing its application, it procures an advantage for certain undertakings or the production of certain goods, to the exclusion of others.[50]

Accordingly, the only relevant question (at this stage) is whether there is an advantage to some undertakings over others. In the context of tax measures this test was concisely summarized by Lord Woolf MR in *Lunn Poly*: 'You can have a State aid in relation to a group of taxpayers where you have the position [ ... ] of one body of taxpayers receiving a benefit which another body of taxpayers does not receive'.[51]

The case-law of the European Court provides numerous examples of selective measures. These include not only measures which favour a particular industry, such as the textile industry,[52] but also those which favour an entire macro-economic sector, such as the manufacturing sector.[53] Equally, a measure may be selective where it distinguishes according to the size of the undertaking, for example the favouring of smaller undertakings over larger undertakings in respect of the purchase of commercial vehicles,[54] or measures which favour large insolvent companies over smaller insolvent companies.[55]

In the English cases discussed here, it has not usually been difficult to conclude that the measures in question were *de facto* selective in this sense. However, the identification of a measure as being *de facto* selective is not the end of the story. A second question must also be asked.

*(2) Is the measure a general measure?* This aspect of the favouring or selectivity principle has produced most problems, principally because there is no precise definition of a general measure either in the case-law of the European Court, or in the decisional practice of the Commission.[56] The existing authorities seem,

---

[50] Case T-55/99 *CETM v Commission* [2000] ECR II-3207, para 40.
[51] [1999] EuLR 653, 665.
[52] Case 173/73 *Italy v Commission* [1974] ECR 709.
[53] Case C-143/99 *Adria-Wien Pipeline* [2001] ECR I-8365.
[54] Case T-55/99 *CETM v Commission* [2000] ECR II-3207, paras 33–55.
[55] Case C-200/97 *Ecotrade* [1998] ECR I-7907.
[56] Although the Commission has provide some guidance in its Notice on the application of the State aid rules to measures relating to direct business taxation, OJ 1998 C 384/3 ('Commission tax notice'), and its Notice on cooperation between national courts and the Commission in the State aid

however, to indicate two kinds of measures which may be considered to be 'general measures' and therefore not state aids.[57]

The first is a general measure of social or economic policy which applies 'to persons in accordance with objective criteria without regard to the location, sector or undertaking in which the beneficiary may be employed'.[58] The typical example is a measure which applies uniformly to *all* companies, for example the uniform reduction of corporation tax. The fact that such a uniform measure may, incidentally, affect certain undertakings more than others does not make the measure selective. A general measure reducing a tax on labour will produce a greater advantage for labour-intensive undertakings than capital-intensive undertakings, but will not be state aid.[59]

Secondly, a measure may be categorized as a general measure even if it applies differently to various undertakings, where the differential effects are 'inherent in the system' or where there is a 'justification [...] on the basis of the nature or general scheme' of the system, or whether 'the difference in treatment is justified by reasons relating to the logic of the system'.[60] This involves determining the 'general system' applicable, and then asking whether the differential effects of the measure derive 'directly from the basic or guiding principles' of that system.[61]

None of the English cases discussed here (and, indeed, few if any cases in the European Court) have involved measures in the former category. Rather, the English cases have all involved measures which explicitly (and intentionally) applied differentially. The courts have therefore had to confront the issue of whether such differential treatment was justified by, or inherent in the logic of, the 'general system'. This has given rise to several common errors.

The first common error is to regard the 'general system' as *the aid measure itself*, and to state that because that measure is objectively justified, or based on sound policy reasons, the measure is not aid. This is incorrect, for the following simple reason: if an aid measure could be regarded as a 'general system', then almost every aid measure would justify itself. Rather, if the concept of a 'general system' is to make sense at all, it must require reference to a broader benchmark applying to the generality of undertakings, against which the particular provisions alleged to be aid may be measured.

---

field, OJ 1995 C 312/7 ('Commission cooperation notice'), which were relied upon in many of the English cases surveyed here.

[57] Both are subject to the proviso that, if in fact the advantage flows not from the uniform application of the general measure, but rather from the exercise of a discretion, the measure will be regarded as selective: Case C-241/94 *France v Commission ('Kimberly Clark')* [1996] ECR I-4551, paras 23–24; *Ecotrade*, above n. 55, para 40.

[58] Commission cooperation notice, para 7.

[59] Commission tax notice, para 14.

[60] Joined Cases C-72/91 and C-73/91 *Sloman Neptun v Bodo Ziesemer* [1993] ECR I-887, para 21; Case 173/73 *Commission v Italy* [1974] ECR 709, para 15; Case C-53/00 *Ferring v ACOSS* [2001] ECR I-9067, para 17; Commission tax notice, para 12.

[61] Commission tax notice, para 16.

An example of this problem is the *Professional Contractors' Group* case. Prior to the introduction of the infamous IR35 rules, all contracting companies (large and small) were subject to corporation tax under the normal rules, and their employees were likewise subject to income tax on their salaries. IR35 introduced, for certain small contracting companies (as defined in the legislation) a different method of calculation of tax. The Professional Contractors' Group claimed that this represented a derogation from the general scheme; in fact, that it was entirely antithetical to the logic of the corporation tax and income tax system. The Court of Appeal evidently regarded the 'general system' as IR35 itself, emphasizing the aims and objectives of IR35.[62] However, this falls into the fallacy of justifying an aid measure by reference to itself. In fact, the only possible general or benchmark system was the general system of income and corporation tax which had applied to all undertakings without exception prior to IR35.

The second common error is to import into the concept of aid the possibility of an 'objective justification' analogous to that employed in the field of free movement.[63] In the definition of aid under Article 87(1), 'justification' is relevant in two contexts: (i) when applying the test of 'normal market conditions' to actions of the State as a market participant, it is legitimate and indeed necessary to inquire whether the benefit was justified on objective *commercial or economic* grounds;[64] and (ii) when applying the general measure test to a measure which has differential effects (i.e. the second kind of general measure) it is necessary to inquire whether the differential treatment is justified by the logic of the general system. However, it is clear that neither of these tests allows a general justification of state aid on the basis that the measure pursues a legitimate *policy* objective, such as the prevention of tax avoidance, or the encouragement of competition. The only body with authority to invoke such a policy objective is the Commission, in the exercise of its discretion under Article 87(2) or (3) to approve a notified aid on policy grounds.

This problem was recently identified by Moses J in *British Aggregates Association*. While (as set out above) he ultimately found the measures not to constitute state aid, the judge emphasized that it is 'not sufficient for the public authorities to invoke the legitimacy of the objectives the impugned measure seeks to achieve',[65] and that it was not enough merely to establish 'objective criteria' unless the criteria were justified by the nature or general scheme of the system.[66] Accordingly, he rejected the government's argument that the differential treatment in the impugned legislation simply reflected policy choices, and the implementation of those policies:

---

[62] [2002] 1 CMLR 1332, in particular at paras 49–51.
[63] See notably the judgments of both courts in *BT3G and One2One*, [2001] EuLR 325, Silber J; [2001] EuLR 822, CA.
[64] See Cases 67, 68, and 70/85 *Van der Kooy v Commission* [1988] ECR 219, para 30.
[65] [2002] EWHC 926 (Admin), [2002] EuLR 394, para 86(3).
[66] ibid, para 114.

Elegant though the propositions are, I believe there to be grave dangers in that approach. Many distinctions giving rise to state aid will be the result of a Member State's policy decisions and their implementation. No doubt the same could be said of the exemption for manufacturers from Austrian energy tax [in the *Adria-Wien* case[67]]. What is required is analysis of the scheme and of the justification for the exemptions on the basis of the nature of the scheme [ ... ] The Government cannot escape merely by asserting that the exemption reflects its own policy decision.[68]

## E. Distortion of competition

A basic question is whether it must be shown that the measure 'actually' distorts competition. This question, which was raised before Silber J in *BT3G and One2One*,[69] is answered in part by the explicit wording of Article 87(1), which requires merely that the aid 'distorts *or threatens to distort* competition'. No actual effect is required.

Moreover, this is the case both where an aid measure is notified to the Commission before its implementation (in which case, *ex hypothesi*, no actual distortion can exist since the aid has not yet been granted) and where, as in the present case, the aid has been implemented without notification. As the European Court has observed, if it were necessary to show a real distortion for an unnotified aid which had already been implemented, then this would put a Member State which unlawfully failed to notify aid in a better position than one which did notify its aid measure prior to implementation.[70]

## F. Effect on trade

Finally, the national court must consider the effect of the measure on inter-State trade. The same considerations apply to this criterion as to the criterion of distortion of competition: no actual effect on trade is required. If an actual effect were required, in respect of an unnotified aid, the non-notifying Member State would benefit by its failure to notify.[71] The test is therefore not whether the measure actually does affect inter-State trade, but rather whether it is *capable* of affecting inter-State trade.[72] This is the interpretation adopted in recent judgments in the English courts.[73]

---

[67] Case C-143/99 *Adria-Wien Pipeline* [2001] ECR I-8365.

[68] [2002] EWHC 926 (Admin), [2002] EuLR 394, para 106.

[69] [2001] EuLR 325, paras 143–159.

[70] C-301/87 *France v Commission* [1990] ECR I-307, para 33; Case T-214/95 *Vlaams Gewest* [1998] ECR II-717, para 67; Joined Cases T-204/97 and T-270/97 *EPAC v Commission* [2000] ECR II-2267, para 85.

[71] ibid.

[72] Case C-387/92 *Banco Exterior de España* [1994] ECR I-877, para 15; Case T-105/95 *FFSA v Commission* [1997] ECR II-229, para 169; Cases T-296/97 etc *Alzetta Mauro and Others v Commission* [2000] ECR II-2319, paras 79–80; *R v Secretary of State for National Heritage, ex p Getty Trust* [1997] EuLR 407, 417 (Neill LJ).

[73] *Professional Contractors' Group* [2001] EuLR 514, Burton J, para 55; *British Aggregates Association* [2002] EWHC 926 (Admin), [2002] EuLR 394, Moses J, para 81. The contrary view of Silber J in *BT3G and One2One* [2001] EuLR 325, paras 143–159, has not been followed.

There may be a question, however, of the extent and nature of the evidence required to establish that the aid is capable of affecting inter-State trade. The VAT and Duties Tribunal referred this question to the Court of Justice in *GIL*. In its judgment it set out the relevant case-law, which can be summarized as follows:

(i)   the basic requirement is that the aid strengthen the position of an under-taking compared with other undertakings competing in intra-Community trade;[74]

(ii)  it is not necessary to show that the beneficiary undertaking itself engages in cross-border activity. When aid is granted, this may maintain or increase domestic production of a product, thus reducing the opportunities for undertakings established in other Member States to export to the market of that Member State;[75] and

(iii) it is not necessary to show that inter-State trade exists in relation to the specific *products* affected by the aid. The relevant question is whether the recipient *undertaking* as a whole is strengthened, with the result that it could for example offer, in a market where there is inter-State trade, products not affected by the subsidy at more favourable prices than its competitors.[76]

## IV. REMEDIES IN THE NATIONAL COURTS[77]

The remaining question is that of the remedies which may be offered by the national court. In other words, beyond a declaration of unlawfulness, what is the obligation of the national court under Article 88(3)? The underlying principles are clear: where an aid has been implemented in breach of Article 88(3), the obligation of the national court has been variously described as 'a duty to provide protection in the final judgment it gives in [ ... ] a case against the consequences of unlawful implementation of aid';[78] an obligation to provide 'permanent remedies for the effect of the unlawful implementation';[79] and an obligation to take the steps necessary to 'nullify the effects of the breach'.[80] What do these principles mean in practice?

In most cases, a finding that aid has been granted contrary to the last sentence of Article 88(3) will entail the recovery of aid from the undertaking which has

[74] Case 730/79 *Philip Morris v Commission* [1980] ECR 2671, para 11.

[75] Case T-55/99 *CETM v Commission* [2001] ECR II-3207, para 86; Case 102/87 *France v Commission* [1988] ECR 4067, para 19.

[76] Joined Cases 62 and 72/87 *Exécutif régional wallon and SA Glaverbel v Commission* ('Flat Glass') [1988] ECR 1573, AG Lenz, opinion para 20; an approach apparently adopted by the Court at para 15 of the judgment.

[77] See further specifically on the role of the national courts in the chapter by James Flynn's above.

[78] Case C-39/94 *SFEI v La Poste* [1996] ECR I-3547, para 67.

[79] ibid, AG Jacobs para 70.

[80] Case C-354/90 *FNCEPA* [1991] ECR I-5505, AG Jacobs para 27.

received a benefit. This is consistent with the Commission's practice of requiring repayment when it finds that aid is unlawful.[81]

In some cases, however, repayment of aid already granted will not be an appropriate and/or adequate remedy. For this reason, recovery of aid is not the only means available to the national court to guarantee the effectiveness of the Article 88(3) prohibition.[82] Thus, for example, where aid has been financed by charges imposed on undertakings (for example parafiscal charges) the national courts, in order to nullify the effects of the aid, may have to order restitution of those charges.[83] The state may also be subject to claims for damages brought in the national courts by competitors who have incurred loss or damage as a result of the unlawfully implemented aid.[84] It has even been suggested that the recipient of aid may be subject to a claim under principles of non-contractual liability for damage to other economic operators by the grant of aid.[85]

An unresolved issue is the appropriate remedy in a case such as *Lunn Poly* (or the subsequent *GIL* and *Airtours* cases) where the complaint is of the imposition of a higher charge on a minority of taxpayers, by contrast with a lower rate applicable to the majority of taxpayers. If the tax differential is declared to be unlawful state aid, does the state come under an obligation to recover the 'aid' granted to the majority of taxpayers by the imposition on them, *ex post facto*, of the higher rate? Or may the competitive balance be restored by the repayment of the tax differential to the minority subject to the higher rate?

The latter question was referred to the Court of Justice by the VAT and Duties Tribunal in *GIL*. Since the reference, however, the Court has delivered judgment in two relevant cases, reaching contradictory conclusions. In *Banks* the Court considered the situation of royalties which had been charged to Banks but not to others. Although the differential charge was (to a certain extent) held to be state aid, in the circumstances of the case it was likely to be impossible to recover the aid from the benefiting undertakings. Banks therefore claimed that the government should repay the royalties to which it had been subject. The Court rejected this argument, on the basis that: 'Persons liable to pay an obligatory contribution cannot rely on the argument that the exemption enjoyed by other persons constitutes State aid in order to avoid payment of that contribution'.[86]

A different result is suggested by the more recent judgment in *Ferring*.[87] In that case, equally, the claimants in the national court sought repayment of a tax imposed, rather than a retrospective imposition of tax on their competitors. The French government argued that the reference was inadmissible, since the remedy sought could not, in any event, be granted by the national court.[88] AG Tizzano explicitly rejected the argument, on the basis that, in his view, the reimbursement

---

[81] *SFEI*, above n. 78, AG Jacobs para 72.     [82] *SFEI*, above n. 78, AG Jacobs para 77.
[83] *FNCEPA*, above n. 80, AG Jacobs para 27.
[84] *SFEI*, above n. 78, AG Jacobs para 77; also Case C-390/98 *Banks* [2001] ECR I-6117, para 80.
[85] *SFEI*, above n. 78, para 79.
[86] *Banks*, above n. 84, para 80.
[87] Case C-53/00 *Ferring v ACOSS* [2001] ECR I-9067.
[88] ibid, AG Tizzano para 20.

of the tax would represent an efficient means of restoring the status quo, and eliminating the distortions of competition which had resulted from the differential imposition of the tax. The Court implicitly concurred with its Advocate General, as it did not address the issue of admissibility but proceeded immediately to its analysis of whether state aid existed.[89]

The conflict between *Ferring* and *Banks* was discussed by AG Jacobs in his opinion in the *GEMO* case. Supporting the approach of AG Tizzano in *Ferring*, AG Jacobs expressed a forceful view that

one of several consequences of the violation of the last sentence of Article 88(3) EC is the invalidity of the measures giving effect to the aid and that the sanction of invalidity is as important as for example the sanction of the recovery of the aid.

Under the principle of procedural autonomy it is then in my view for the national legal order to determine precisely which national measures are affected by that invalidity and what consequences that invalidity has for example for the refund of charges collected on the basis of the measures concerned. The only limitations on that autonomy are the principle of equivalence and the principle of effectiveness.

It seems to me that a national court which wishes under its national law to order the refund of charges collected on the basis of a law adopted in violation of Article 88(3) EC does not violate any of those principles but furthers the effectiveness of Community law.[90]

It is hoped that this difficult issue will be resolved by the Court in its judgments in *GEMO* and *GIL*.

## V. CONCLUSION

The readiness of the English courts to address the complex issues involved in state aid analysis is encouraging. However, the reasoning of the courts highlights the difficulties in this area of the law, and the paucity of clear guidance from either the European Court or the Commission. In addition, though, the evolution of the case-law has raised several important issues which should be considered by both practitioners and courts alike when analysing state aid issues.

At the outset, the analytical framework is crucial. The wording of Article 87(1) is ambiguous, and has given rise to persistent problems. The above discussion has attempted to set out the correct framework. A second issue is the danger of over-reliance on previous English case-law. In particular, dicta from *Lunn Poly* have been widely used, and widely misunderstood, in the cases which have followed it. This could have been avoided by returning to the primary source: the case-law of the European Court. Finally, the case-law too often betrays a judicial reluctance to intervene in matters of legislative policy. This caution is misplaced. The interpretation of Article 87(1), by both the European Court and the Commission, reflects a careful balancing of the Community interest in undistorted competition with the national interests in legislative autonomy, particularly in

---

[89] AG Jacobs in Case C-126/01 *GEMO*, opinion 30.4.02, para 47.  [90] ibid, paras 43–45.

areas of fiscal and social policy. General legislative measures are not state aids. But, equally, policy choices are not—and cannot be—immune to scrutiny under the state aid rules. If a measure is a state aid under Article 87(1) it should be notified to the Commission: legitimate justification is not an escape route from this obligation.

# EPILOGUE

# 19

# *The Experience of an English Judge in Handling State Aid Cases*

THE HON MR JUSTICE SILBER

## INTRODUCTION

I first encountered the concept of state aid when I started preparing to hear the applications of BT and One-2-One for permission[1] to judicially review the decisions of the Secretary of State for Trade and Industry made during the course of the auction of the third-generation licences for mobile telephones. The purpose of this note is to set out the difficulties and surprises that I encountered during that application, but I must first explain the nature of the case.

Both those companies, together with companies in the Vodafone and Orange Group of companies, had been successful in obtaining four of the five licences that had been granted on the auction. The allegation that formed the basis of the application for judicial review was that the Secretary of State had given state aid to Orange and Vodafone as they had been allowed by the Secretary of State to pay for their licences four months later than BT and One-2-One. At first, it might seem surprising that interest for such a short period would justify commencing complex legal proceedings, but the cost of each of the licences was over £4 billion; so One-2-One contended that its loss was the interest that would have been saved by them if they could have paid their licence fee at the same time as Orange and Vodafone and this loss amounted to just under £86 million. It is likely that BT's claim would have been for an approximately similar amount.

The application before me raised three interesting issues on Article 87(1) (formerly 92(1)). The first was whether the Secretary of State by permitting Vodafone and Orange to pay for their licence fees later than BT and One-2-One was giving them assistance which was *capable of constituting state aid*, while the second was whether in fact state aid was actually granted in this case by the UK Government through state resources to Vodafone and Orange. The third issue was whether, if the answers to both the previous two questions were in the affirmative, the aid given by the Government to Vodafone and Orange actually distorted or threatened to distort competition by favouring certain undertakings and affected trade between member states.

---

[1] *R (on the application of BT3G Ltd) v. Secretary of State for Trade and Industry* [2001] EuLR 325 upheld on appeal [2001] EuLR 822

PROBLEM 1: UNCERTAINTY OF PRINCIPLES IN IDENTIFYING
STATE AID

When I read the allegations on the judicial review application, I assumed that, as control of state aid has always been an important aspect of European Community Law, the principles for determining whether it had been granted would have been clearly defined, especially as it was imperative that Governments should know the basis on which they could act and parties adversely affected should realize when they could challenge the decision.

This seemed especially important as, in determining the state aid issues raised on this judicial review application, I became very conscious of the tension between a number of conflicting principles. First, there is the right of an elected Government to regulate the affairs of its citizens, but second, there are requirements of the EC Treaty to ensure that a Government does not act in a way which distorts or threatens to distort competition by favouring certain undertakings. Not surprisingly, a leading textbook[2] describes the task of resolving this tension as 'perhaps the most sensitive activity' of the Commission which has to decide different aspects of the same issue, but this description is also apt to describe the task that a national court judge, like me, is required to perform.

The only pointers that emerged from the EC Treaty on the meaning of state aid were a number of general principles, such as that the Member State should adopt economic policies which will be 'conducted in accordance with the principles of an open market economy with free competition'.[3] Unfortunately, this principle is of little assistance in determining whether state aid has been granted in any particular case. Of course, various guidelines have been issued, such as the 23rd Report on Competition Policy of the Commission which sets out some of the rules which the Commission applies for privatization and which have been built up over the years on the basis of the scrutiny of individual cases.

Apart from those guidelines and much to my surprise, five different criteria have been suggested by the courts over the years as being determinative of whether state aid is given in a particular case. There was no authority which said which of those tests was overriding or what happened if different criteria produced conflicting decisions in respect of a particular factual situation.

The possibility of discrepancies between them results from the different thresholds in the different tests. First, there is the 'normal market conditions' test which means that 'it is necessary to establish whether the recipient undertaking receives an economic advantage which it would not have obtained under normal market conditions'.[4] The second test is the 'general scheme' test which relies on the principle that state aid does not arise unless there is a justification

---

[2] See Vaughan (ed.), *Law of the European Communities*, paragraph 23.01 (by James Flynn & Leo Flynn).
[3] Article 4 EC.
[4] See Case C-256/97 *Démenagements-Manutention Transport SA* [1999] ECR 3913, paragraph 24.

for this particular benefit on the basis of the nature or general scheme of the system.[5]

The third test requires the existence of an objective justification for the assistance and the absence of discrimination,[6] while a fourth test is 'a pragmatic one which depends on all the circumstances of the case'[7] and is to be applied 'in the light of the policy underlying the treaty'.[8] The final test is that 'the point of departure [for determining whether something was state aid] must necessarily be the competitive position existing within the common market before the adoption of the measure in issue'.[9] It does not require much imagination to realize that these tests would not necessarily produce the same result. This uncertainty on the appropriate applicable principles must cause uncertainty and lead to unnecessary claims being pursued. In addition, the preparation for and the actual hearing of those claims are likely to be prolonged because of the uncertainty of the law and the need to adduce evidence and arguments based on the different alternative tests for identifying state aid. It is to be hoped that the European Court of Justice will adopt a single comprehensive principle for identifying state aid, perhaps incorporating more than one of the tests to which I have referred.

None of the parties suggested that I should refer this case to the European Court of Justice. On the facts of this case, the same result would have been achieved by the application of each of the tests to which I have referred. In those circumstances, it would not have been appropriate to refer it.

## PROBLEM 2: OVERRULING OLD EUROPEAN COURT CASES

The uncertainty of the law on the criterion for identifying state aid might be a consequence of the failure of the European Court to state when some of its own decisions were no longer valid. An English lawyer is used to the practice that if a case has been overruled, that will be specifically stated. The position of the European Court seems rather different: there is a surprising coyness in stating that a decision of the European Court is no longer good law. The following passage from an Opinion of Advocate General Jacobs is of interest: 'The Court has consistently recognised its power to depart from previous decisions [ ... ] That the Court should in an appropriate case expressly overrule an earlier decision is I think an inescapable duty, even if the Court has never before expressly done so.'[10]

I respectfully agree because it is of vital importance that litigants know what their rights are and States know what they cannot do. There does not appear to

---

[5] Case 173/73 *Italy v. Commission* [1974] ECR 709, paragraph 15.
[6] See generally *R v. Commissioners of Customs and Excise ex parte Lunn Poly Limited* [1999] EuLR 653 at 622G.
[7] *Lunn Poly per* Clarke LJ at 674C.
[8] ibid at 675F.
[9] *Italy v. Commission* (note 5 above) at paragraph 17.
[10] Case C-10/89 *HAG GF* [1990] ECR I-3711 at 3749–50.

be a cogent reason why the European Court does not help the parties by saying what in some cases they must have agreed, namely that a previous decision of the Court is no longer good law.

## Problem 3: Understanding the economic factors

At the outset of the BT case, I was concerned about how I would be able to resolve the economic issues that had to be determined in the light of the requirement in Article 87(1) of deciding whether the alleged aid 'distorted or threatened to distort competition by favouring certain undertakings'.

Although I found that there was no state aid, I considered this requirement in respect of which there was a conflict of evidence and submissions. I confess I did not find the task more difficult than resolving many other areas in which there is conflicting expert evidence. In many ways, disputes on very complex medical issues are more difficult to understand and resolve than the economic issues raised in this case where the terminology and the calculations were easily comprehensible. Perhaps it was because the solution to this problem was not difficult on the facts of this case, but I do not consider that I would have benefited from or required assistance from the EC Commission on this aspect.

In conclusion, I greatly enjoyed considering the admirable submissions of counsel in this case and coming to my conclusions. The issues raised were interesting and intellectually challenging. I now look forward to hearing my next state aid case.

# Index